Disability and Human Rights

Disability and Human Rights

Global Perspectives

Edurne García Iriarte

Roy McConkey

Robbie Gilligan

macmillan education   palgrave

First published 2016 by
PALGRAVE

Palgrave in the UK is an imprint of Macmillan Publishers Limited,
registered in England, company number 785998, of 4 Crinan Street,
London, N1 9XW.

Palgrave Macmillan in the US is a division of St Martin's Press LLC,
175 Fifth Avenue, New York, NY 10010.

Palgrave is a global imprint of the above companies and is represented
throughout the world.

Palgrave® and Macmillan® are registered trademarks in the United States,
the United Kingdom, Europe and other countries.

ISBN 978–1–137–39065–3

This book is printed on paper suitable for recycling and made from fully
managed and sustained forest sources. Logging, pulping and manufacturing
processes are expected to conform to the environmental regulations of the
country of origin.

A catalogue record for this book is available from the British Library.

A catalog record for this book is available from the Library of Congress.

Printed in China

Contents

List of Illustrations

Figures

Tables

Boxes

Foreword

The United Nations Convention on the Rights of Persons with Disabilities (CRPD) articulates the principles of equality and non-discrimination in the rights of all persons with disabilities. Although it represents a significant development in the field of human rights, it poses multiple challenges to states, to society as a whole and to persons with disabilities themselves.

The CRPD generates a substantial leap in the legal sphere. It requires rethinking human rights and fundamental freedoms. It also requires developing analogous legal instruments so that the principle *pro omini* (for all) does indeed guarantee dignity, individual autonomy, freedom to make one's own choices and independence to all persons with disabilities.

The CRPD crystallizes the human rights-based approach to disability. It provides an advanced angle to look at the 'subject of right'. With a multi-level perspective, disability results from the interaction between persons with impairments and various barriers which limit their full and effective participation in society.

The implementation of the CRPD requires simultaneous action: the removal of barriers and promotion of accessible environments for persons with disabilities. Both generate a reciprocal impact on the participation of individuals with disabilities in society. In this context, the enjoyment of human rights and fundamental freedoms becomes the indicator of accomplishment.

Persons with disabilities do not conform to a homogeneous group. There is indeed a wide diversity of impairments, which result in disability becoming a unique experience for each person, in addition to personal characteristics such as gender, age, racial or ethnic origin, urban or rural background, the risks people with disabilities face from humanitarian emergencies, natural disasters, armed conflict, displacement or migration, among others.

The book *Disability and Human Rights: Global Perspectives* explores these different dimensions of disability from legal and interdisciplinary perspectives, providing a comprehensive account of themes that are examined in depth in each chapter, but which are interconnected and which the reader can approach in combination.

This body of work is also useful for the current analysis of sustainable, inclusive and accessible social development. This analysis is key in the Post-Millennium Development Goals 2015 Agenda, in which disability must be integrated.

The 21st century has been fortunate enough to witness this great socio-legal and political process. In all, the CRPD aims to make determined progress toward true inclusion of 15 per cent of the world population, which throughout history has faced oppression in different forms, from invisibility to discrimination.

The timing of this publication is crucial. The CRPD is rapidly approaching universal ratification, which means that nearly all the states in different regions of the world will incorporate this international standard in their normative standards and sociocultural policies. The work of this book's authors significantly contributes to raising awareness in order to catalyse and advance this global process.

Prof. María Soledad Cisternas Reyes
Lawyer–Political Scientist
Chairperson Experts Committee on UN Convention
of the Rights of Persons with Disabilities

Acknowledgements

The collection of works presented in this volume has been essentially made possible by the work of more than 30 researchers, academics and professionals – the authors of the book chapters – over the last two years. Their scholarship, international experience and collaboration with disabled people in the five world continents have truly enabled a genuine global perspective. It is to them that we are hugely indebted. In particular we want to pay tribute to Professor Peter Mittler for his advocacy on the rights of persons with disabilities for the past 50 years and more. This book is the fruit of the seeds that he and others have planted.

We are grateful to the commissioning editors of Palgrave: Lloyd Langman, who first encouraged us to embark on this project, and Helen Caunce and Peter Hooper, who worked alongside its development, for their editorial guidance and advice. We also wish to acknowledge the external reviewers who usefully helped us shape the volume as it has been published. Graduate students from the MSc in Disability Studies at Trinity College Dublin, inspired the idea of the book approach and contributed with their discussions and critical standpoints to the ideas presented herein. Support from one of them, Tabitha Carlson, was invaluable in sorting and formatting the references and in producing the index. Daniel Billingham painstakingly proofread some of the chapters and provided useful editorial feedback. Finally, we acknowledge and thank all those people whose stories have inspired the multiple case examples about disability presented in each of the book chapters.

The author and publisher would like to thank John Wiley & Sons for their kind permission to reproduce Chapter 3 by Peter Mittler, which is largely drawn from Peter Mittler 'The UN Convention on the Rights of Persons with Disabilities: Implementing a Paradigm Shift (pages 79–89)', *Journal of Policy and Practice in Intellectual Disability*, volume 12, 2015, Edited by Libby Gordon Cohen, Roy I. Brown, and Keith R. McVilly.

List of Abbreviations

AAIDD	American Association on Intellectual and Developmental Disabilities
AATE	Advancement of Assistive Technology in Europe
ABCD	asset-based community development
ADHD	attention deficit hyperactivity disorder
AFRO	World Health Organization Regional Office for Africa
AIDS	acquired immune deficiency syndrome
AISA	Africa Institute of South Africa
AMDD	Averting Maternal Death and Disability Program
ANC	Africa National Congress
ANED	Academic Network of Experts in Disability
AOPD	Arab Organization of Persons with Disabilities
APA	American Psychological Association
ASN	alternative support needs
AT	assistive technology
CAFOD	Catholic Agency for Overseas Development
CAPS	curriculum and assessment policy statements
CBA	computer-based applications
CBR	community-based rehabilitation
CDPF	China Disabled Persons' Federation
CEE	Central and Eastern Europe
CEECIS	Central and Eastern Europe and the Commonwealth of Independent States
CIL	Centre for Independent Living
CIS	Commonwealth of Independent States and the Baltic
CODESA	Convention for a Democratic South Africa
CRPD	Convention on the Rights of Persons with Disabilities
DAISY	digital accessible information system
DBST	District-Based Support Team
DFID	Department for International Development
DLTJ	Duskin Leadership Training Program in Japan
DPI	Disabled People's International
DPO	disabled people's organisations
DPSA	Disabled People South Africa
DRC	Democratic Republic of Congo
DRM	Disability Rights Movement
DRS	Disability Rights Syria
DSI	Down Syndrome International
EACD	European Academy of Childhood Disabilities

EDF	European Disability Forum
EDWP	Education White Paper
EFA	Education for All
EMRO	World Health Organization Regional Office for the Eastern Mediterranean
ENGO	European non-governmental organization
EURO	World Health Organization Regional Office for Europe
FARC	Revolutionary Armed Forces of Colombia
FSS	The Full-Service School
GATE	Global Cooperation on Assistive Health Technology
GES	Ghana Education Service
GPcwd	Global Partnership on Children with Disabilities
GPS	Global Positioning System
HAAT	human activity assistive technology
HCR	High Commissioner for Refugees
HIV	human immunodeficiency virus
HRBA	human rights-based approach
HRH	human resources for health
ICF	International Classification of Functioning, Disability and Health
ICF-CY	International Classification of Functioning, Disability and Health for Children and Youth
ICT	information and communication technologies
IDA	International Disability Alliance
I/DD	intellectual and developmental disabilities
IDDC	International Disability and Development Consortium
IDS-TILDA	The Intellectual Disability Supplement to The Irish Longitudinal Study on Ageing
IFHOH	International Federation of Hard of Hearing People
II	Inclusion International
IL	Independent Living
ILO	International Labour Organization
ILST	Institution Level Support Team
ISO	International Organisation for Standardization
ITS	Intelligent Tutorial Systems
IYDP	International Year of Disabled Persons
JICA-RI	Japan International Cooperation Agency's Research Institute
JIL	Japan Council on Independent Living
JSRPD	Japanese Society for the Rehabilitation of Persons with Disabilities
LCMS	Learning Content Management Systems
LMS	Learning Management Systems
LPHU	Lebanese Physically Handicapped Union
LSE	Learning Support Educators
LSMHP	Lesotho Society for Mentally Handicapped Persons
MDGs	Millennium Development Goals

MICS	Multiple Indicator Cluster Surveys
MNAs	Member National Assemblies
NATRI	National Assistive Technology Research Institute
NCDPZ	National Council of Disabled Persons of Zimbabwe
NGO	non-governmental organisation
NHCR	High Commissioner for Refugees
NHRIs	national human rights institutions
OECD	Organisation for Economic Co-Operation and Development
OED	Oxford English Dictionary
OHCHR	Office of the High Commission on Human Rights
ONCE	National Organization for the Blind – Spain
PAHO	World Health Organization Regional Office for the Americas
PDAs	personal digital assistants
PDF	Pacific Disability Forum
PI	principal investigator
PISA	Programme for International Student Assessment
PLAR	Participatory Learning and Action Research
PTSD	post-traumatic stress disorder
QR	Quick Response code
RIADIS	Latin American Network of Non-Governmental Organizations of Persons with Disabilities and their Families
SAFOD	Southern African Federation for the Disabled
SCIE	Social Care Institute for Excellence
SDGs	sustainable development goals
SEARO	World Health Organization Regional Office for South-East Asia
SEN	special education needs
SIAS	Screening, Identification, Assessment and Support
SINTEF	Foundation for Scientific and Industrial Research
SRP	SAFOD Research Programme
SSRC	Special School as a Resource Centre
TBI	traumatic brain injury
UK	United Kingdom
UN	United Nations
UNESCO	United Nations Educational, Scientific and Cultural Organization
UNHCR	United Nations High Commissioner for Refugees
UNICEF	United Nations International Children's Emergency Fund
UPIAS	Union of the Physically Impaired Against Segregation
US/USA	United States of America
USAID	United States Agency for International Development
VTC	vocational training centre
WBU	World Blind Union
WFD	World Federation of the Deaf
WFDB	World Federation of the Deaf and Blind
WHO	World Health Organization

WIDE	World Inequalities Data Base on Education
WNUSP	World Network of Users and Survivors of Psychiatry
WPRO	World Health Organization Regional Office for the Western Pacific
WSIS	World Summit on the Information Society
WW	World War
ZAPDD	Zanzibar Association for People with Developmental Disability
ZOU	Zimbabwe Open University

Notes on the Contributors

Daniel Balcazar is currently a sociology student at Market University, with a strong interest in social justice issues.

Dr Fabricio E. Balcazar is professor and director of the Center on Capacity Building for Minorities with Disabilities Research, at the University of Illinois at Chicago. Dr Balcazar has published over 70 peer-reviewed journal articles and co-edited the book entitled *Race, Culture and Disability: Issues in Rehabilitation Research and Practice*. Dr Balcazar is a fellow of the American Psychological Association (APA) and president of the Society for Community Research and Action (Division 27 of the APA).

Dr Esther Baños García is a lecturer at the Engineering Graphics and Pedagogical Design of Multimedia Applications at Polytechnic School, University of Burgos, Spain. She has a degree in Industrial Engineering and a PhD in Humanities. Her research interests focus on the development of new methodologies for the improvement of learning abilities by using Multimedia Resources as well as on the design of Multimedia Applications and 2D-3D animations aimed at the development of these learning abilities and skills.

Rebecca Barton is a lecturer in occupational therapy at the Faculty of Health Sciences, University of Sydney. Her primary research interests are in the areas of disability, family, and social and cultural context. Her doctoral studies explored the negotiation of cultural frameworks in the daily lives of migrant families raising a child with a disability in Australia.

Peter Coleridge is an independent consultant specializing in disability. He has over 40 years' experience in the Middle East, Africa and Asia in education and development, including policy formulation, project management, planning, monitoring and evaluation with NGOs and the United Nations.

Huib Cornielje is trained as a physiotherapist, has an MSc in Community Health and an MPH as well as a Higher Diploma in Adult Education and is director of Enablement, which is active in the field of disability and development.

Sarah Dababnah, PhD, MPH, MSW is assistant professor, School of Social Work, University of Maryland at Baltimore. She earned her PhD in social work from the University of North Carolina at Chapel Hill.

Antoinette D'amant is lecturer in the School of Education, University of KwaZulu-Natal. Her research interests are in social justice education, inclusive education and educating for diversity.

Edurne García Iriarte is assistant professor and director of the MSc in Disability Studies at Trinity College Dublin (TCD), Ireland. Edurne obtained her PhD from the University of Illinois at Chicago where she also worked at the Centre for Capacity Building on Minorities with Disabilities Research. Her research has focused on disabled people's individualized supports, disabled people's human rights, and, for the last ten years, on inclusive approaches to research and evaluation.

Subharati Ghosh, PhD, MSW is assistant professor, Center for Health and Mental Health, School of Social Work, at the Tata Institute of Social Sciences in Mumbai, India. She earned her PhD from the University of Wisconsin at Madison and completed a postdoctoral research fellowship at the Lurie Institute for Disability Policy, Brandeis University.

Robbie Gilligan is professor of Social Work and Social Policy at Trinity College Dublin. He served as founding head of the School of Social Work and Social Policy from August 2005 to July 2011. He is currently Associate Director of the Children's Research Centre at TCD. He is also a research fellow (2013–2016) at SFI – The Danish National Centre for Social Research and Extraordinary Professor at the Optentia Research Programme at North Western University, South Africa.

Trynos Gumbo is a senior lecturer within the Department of Town and Regional Planning at the University of Johannesburg, South Africa. He is also a research specialist in the Africa Institute of South Africa (AISA) within the Human Sciences Research Council (HSRC) in South Africa. He holds a PhD from Stellenbosch University and masters and honours degrees in Rural and Urban Planning from the University of Zimbabwe. His research interests include contributing to discourses in urban management, poverty and social protection, human rights, informality, service delivery, pollution and climate change mitigation.

Leah Igdalsky, BA is a research associate at the Lurie Institute for Disability Policy, Brandeis University.

Kamal Lamichhane, PhD is currently a research fellow at the Japan International Cooperation Agency's Research Institute (JICA-RI) in Tokyo. He is the first person with disabilities to work at JICA-RI as a researcher, as well as the first person with visual impairments to have received a doctorate in his home country, Nepal. He obtained his doctorate in Advanced Interdisciplinary Studies with a focus on disability studies from the University of Tokyo, where he works as an affiliated researcher. His fields of research are disability studies, education, international cooperation and development studies.

Alexandra Lewis Gargett is a research associate and PhD candidate with the Centre for Disability Research and Policy, University of Sydney. Her research interests are in disability inclusive development, in particular the use of traditional health practices for people with disabilities and rehabilitation workforce development in low- and middle-income countries.

Gwynnyth Llewellyn is professor of Family and Disability Studies and director of the Centre for Disability Research and Policy, University of Sydney (http://sydney.edu.au/health-sciences/cdrp/). Her research interests include parenting by people with disabilities, disability inclusive development, and social and economic participation of people with disabilities.

Malcolm MacLachlan, PhD is director of the Centre for Global Health, Trinity College Dublin. He is Extraordinary Professor of Rehabilitation at the Centre for Rehabilitation Studies, University of Stellenbosch, South Africa.

Joshua Teke Malinga holds an MPhil Degree in Disability Studies and is currently studying for a PhD with the Zimbabwe Open University (ZOU). He has been involved in building up the worldwide movement of disabled people, among others the Disabled People's International (DPI). He is an accomplished businessman, politician and disability activist, and is very vocal in advocating for the rights, eradication of poverty, marginalization and exclusion of social groups such as people with disabilities.

Hasheem Mannan is senior research fellow, Nossal Institute for Global Health, and he started his career as a community-based rehabilitation worker in India. Currently, he is an associate editor of *BMC International Health and Human Rights*, an open access, peer-reviewed journal that publishes on the impact of health policies, programmes and practices on human rights. Hasheem completed his PhD on disability policy and family studies at the University of Kansas, United States, in 2005.

Prof. Philip McCallion, PhD is Distinguished Professor and co-director of the Center for Excellence in Aging & Community Wellness at the University at Albany, as well as Visiting Professor at the School of Nursing & Midwifery, Trinity College Dublin. Currently translating evidence-based health promotion programmes for use with people with intellectual disabilities, Professor McCallion is principal investigator (PI) for secondary analyses of health claims data to better understand contributors to health and ill health in older age for people with ID and is co-PI of the Intellectual Disability Supplement to The Irish Longitudinal Study on Aging.

Prof. Mary McCarron, PhD, RNID, RGN, BNS, FTCD is dean of the Faculty of Health Sciences; professor, School of Nursing and Midwifery Studies, Trinity College Dublin; a leader in multidisciplinary health sciences; and an international expert in the fields of intellectual disability, ageing, dementia and palliative care. Professor McCarron is the principal investigator and leads the large and multidisciplinary research team for the first ever Longitudinal Nationally Comparative Study on Ageing in Persons with Intellectual Disability (IDS-TILDA) to be conducted in Ireland or internationally.

Roy McConkey is Emeritus Professor of Developmental Disabilities at the University of Ulster in Northern Ireland and a visiting professor at Trinity College Dublin; the University of Cape Town; and the University of Sydney. His research interests include family support, early childhood intervention, community-based services and social inclusion. He has acted as consultant to various UN and international NGOs.

Joanne McVeigh is currently conducting PhD psychological research into positive psychology interventions and maritime health at the School of Psychology and Centre for Global Health, Trinity College Dublin. She holds degrees in both business studies and psychology from Trinity College Dublin.

Peter Mittler worked as a clinical psychologist for ten years but moved to the University of Manchester as the first director of the Hester Adrian Research Centre for the Study of Learning Processes in the Mentally Handicapped (1968–1982) and then as professor of Special Needs Education, head of the School of Education and dean of the faculty (1982–1995). He has undertaken a range of consultancies for United Nations agencies, most recently UNESCO and UNICEF, and is a former president of Inclusion International. His autobiography, *Thinking Globally Acting Locally: A Personal Journey*, is available from Author House, 2010.

Pholoho Morojele is an associate professor in the College of Humanities, School of Education, University of KwaZulu-Natal. His research interests and publications are in gender studies, children's geographies and social justice in education.

Nithi Muthukrishna is a professor in the School of Education, University of KwaZulu-Natal. Her research interests are in the areas of children's geographies, social justice education, inclusion/exclusion in education, disability studies and HIV and AIDS education.

Jaqueline Naidoo is a lecturer in the School of Education, University of KwaZulu-Natal. She received her PhD in Social Justice Education. Her research interests include HIV and AIDS education, teacher identities, teacher professional development, teacher emotionality and children's geographies.

Susan L. Parish, PhD, MSW is Nancy Lurie Marks Professor and Director, Lurie Institute for Disability Policy, and Associate Dean for Research at the Heller School for Social Policy at Brandeis University. Her research investigates the health and financial well-being of children and adults with disabilities, and their caregiving families.

Leslie Swartz is Distinguished Professor of Psychology at Stellenbosch University. He is editor-in-chief of the *African Journal of Disability* and has published widely on disability studies and mental health, with a focus on southern Africa. He has a particular interest in issues of capacity building.

Sainimili Tawake is a resource trainer with the Secretariat of the Pacific Community's Regional Rights Resource Team (SPC RRRT). Her research interest is the 'intersectional discrimination' of disability and gender in the Pacific.

Antoni Tsaputra works with an Indonesian DPO called Persatuan Penyandang Disabilitas Indonesia (Indonesian Association of Persons with Disabilities) which advocates for disability rights and implementation of the UN CRPD. He has a great interest in research about disability and social and public policies in Southeast Asia, such as disability and employment, and disability and civil service.

Daniel Tsengu is trained as a teacher and has an MSc in Community Disability Studies as well as an Advanced Diploma in Health and Social Services Management. He is currently doing a PhD study at the University of Jos, Nigeria. He is director, AVA-NA Inclusive Development Solutions Ltd, an organization that is active in programme development and general disability and development issues in Nigeria.

Sai Kyi Zin Soe is an activist from Myanmar working on human rights for persons with disability, as well as consumer rights and fair trades. He is also an entrepreneur in IT business and an Australia Award scholar doing a PhD on inclusive policy research at the Centre for Disability Research and Policy, University of Sydney. He is working with Action Aid Myanmar, Myanmar Consumers Union, Social Policy and Poverty Research Group and many other civil society networks in Myanmar. He co-authored an umbrella model of a vulnerability mapping tool which was presented at the 1st CBR World Congress in November 2012 in Agra.

Disability and Human Rights: Global Perspectives

1

Edurne García Iriarte
Roy McConkey
Robbie H. Gilligan

> *[A] comprehensive and integral international convention to promote and protect the rights and dignity of persons with disabilities will make a significant contribution to redressing the profound social disadvantage of persons with disabilities and promote their participation in the civil, political, economic, social and cultural spheres with equal opportunities, in both developing and developed countries.*

**UN Convention on the Rights of Persons with Disabilities
Preamble (y)**

Introduction

The first two decades of the 21st century are a critical period in the history of disability and human rights. The first human rights treaty of the current century – the Convention on the Rights of Persons with Disabilities (CRPD) – was adopted by the United Nations in 2006. The signing by 158 countries within eight years of the adoption of the CRPD demonstrates that the world community has embraced disability – at least at an aspirational level – as a human rights issue. Empirical data from the *World Report on Disability*, furthermore, illustrates that disability is a global phenomenon experienced by more than 1 billion people.

The majority of disabled people, about 80 per cent, concentrate on the developing world and they are among the poorest in developed countries. Disabled people the world over continue to experience poorer access to education, employment and health services, and their outcomes in those areas are significantly worse than the rest of the population. Despite this striking reality, we know little about the disability experience outside developed and Western countries. It is timely, therefore, that the goal of this book is to explore disability and human rights using a global approach.

This book aims more specifically at exploring a number of themes in relation to specific articles of the CRPD and doing it from various global perspectives: with a focus on disability experiences in a variety of countries and socio-economic contexts, reflecting the diversity of impairments, using the voices of disabled people, families and professionals, and providing the evidence for developing mainstream policies and services. The approach of the book is applied, building on empirical evidence and using individual experiences of disability. In this introductory chapter, we seek to provide a common background for understanding the approach and scope of the following chapters. We start the chapter by briefly presenting the CRPD, which is used as a common thread in all the chapters. We also present some of the challenges the CRPD faces in its implementation. We move on to outline the global dimensions that the book aims to convey. We then introduce three key strategies where different actors can collaborate on the implementation and monitoring of the CRPD: advocacy, research and evaluation. The chapter concludes with a brief note on terminology.

The Convention on the Rights of Persons with Disabilities (CRPD)

We have chosen the CRPD as the compass for the analysis of rights in this book because it builds on previous human rights instruments, it culminates decades of work by disabled people across the world and it is the result of ground-breaking collaboration between disabled people, their organizations and national governments. The UN General Assembly adopted the CRPD in December 2006. It is a human rights treaty including 50 articles referring to civil and political rights, as well as economic, social and cultural rights (Quinn, 2009; Schulze, 2010). Rights are basic standards that enable people to have dignified lives and be valued for their inherent worth as human beings. The CRPD does not create any new rights but refocuses on the existing rights within the realm of disability (Quinn, 2009). It effectively shifts the focus from treating disabled persons as objects of charity to seeing them as active holders of human rights. The quote from the CRPD below this chapter's title shows the scope of the treaty. It focuses on protecting the rights and dignity of disabled people, redressing the social disadvantage they experience and promoting their participation in all areas of life with equal opportunities, covering both developing and developed countries. Explicit in the CRPD is the view that disabled people should experience human rights on an equal basis to non-disabled people and the acknowledgement of their contribution to the overall well-being and diversity of their communities.

Challenges to the implementation of the CRPD. The CRPD provides a completely new framework within which to think and act in relation to disability issues. It addresses many actors. It supports and challenges those actors to embrace new ways of seeing, understanding and responding to disability. But treaties or words on paper do not guarantee actions. The words on the pages of the CRPD represent intentions, but the harsh reality is that intentions are not always honoured; they do not always translate into actions. Common challenges to the CRPD and other human rights instruments are difficulty in monitoring their implementation, too abstract or ambiguous terminology that can have different interpretations depending on culture, norms, laws and so on and dependence on state resources (Stein, 2007). Yet securing such state resources may become increasingly difficult. 'Austerity' has become a guide word in policy-making in many countries. This austerity may come as a response to tackling public debt, or it may represent a new hostility among many political elites to the very principle of public spending on social programmes in general. In such a climate, the role of civil society seeking reform and investment in CRPD inspired disability programmes becomes even more vital. There are many metaphors that can meaningfully be used to emphasize the significance of the CRPD: it serves as a *conscience* for the global community on disability issues; it serves as a *bridge* between disability and development issues, especially for developing countries; it serves as a *stimulus* to ensure that new policy instruments such as the Sustainable Development Goals (successors to the Millennium Development Goals) or national statutes can no longer be silent on issues of disability; it serves as a *monitor* of key budgetary and policy decisions as they impact on disability; it serves as a gathering point for civil society and other interested actors who wish to promote disability issues and awareness.

CRPD and this book. As noted in the CRPD preamble, rights are inalienable, universal, indivisible, interrelated and interdependent. So rather than reading this book as isolated chapters on specific rights, it should be read as one whole consisting of complementary chapters that together provide a unique resource on how disabled people can be enabled to fully enjoy their human rights. The first set of chapters (2–6) examines the main premises around which the CRPD is based. The next eight chapters (7–14) focus on specific articles in the CRPD that are integral to achieving full and equal participation of disabled people in human societies and across the life cycle. The final three chapters (15–17) examine the contribution that family carers, professionals and researchers can make to the realization of rights. In parallel to the analysis of rights, the book provides a broad exploration of underlying themes, which are examined in depth in dedicated chapters and elaborated upon in other chapters: poverty, support and culture.

A billion people experience disability and about 80 per cent of them live in developing countries in conditions of poverty. Ghosh, Dababnah, Parish and Igdalsky present a comprehensive picture of disabled people's experience of poverty and social exclusion in Chapter 6. This is closely interrelated with war and disability, which is explored by Balcazar and Balcazar in relation to a number of armed conflicts around the world (Chapter 7), and with livelihoods, the focus of Coleridge's discussion in Chapter 12.

The theme of support in its multiple forms is pivotal in a number of chapters. Gilligan in Chapter 8 offers a thorough review of disabled children's rights and the support to them and their families in their varied and unique experiences of childhoods; MacLachlan, Mannan and McVeigh discuss health care support through the concept of inclusive health in Chapter 10; Baños provides a broad account of assistive technology as a source of support in

Chapter 11; McCallion and McCarron focus on support in relation to ageing disabled people in Chapter 14; McConkey explores support to family carers in Chapter 15 and Cornielje and Tsengu analyse the role of professionals as supporters of disabled people in Chapter 16.

Through the different chapters, authors analyse and contest the global rights discourse when applied to specific local contexts. Lewis Gargett and colleagues provide a thorough discussion of the cultural dimensions of disability in Chapter 5, a theme later applied by Muthukrishna and colleagues to their critical review of international inclusive education policies as they are implemented in the Global South (Chapter 9); Lamichhane analyses the Japanese independent living model in the Asian region in light of local cultural realities (Chapter 13) and Swartz draws on organizational culture in his discussion of research training to disabled people's organisations (DPOs) in Africa (Chapter 17).

Although the CRPD is a springboard for the development and implementation of programmes, policies and legislation to ensure disabled people exercise their rights, these are mediated by the lived experience of disability in all its dimensions: the individual experience of impairment, the cultural understanding and culturally mediated responses to disability, the particular ontology of the human being according to various ideologies and its corresponding alignment with human rights and the contextual sociopolitical and economic realities of (un)democratic regimes, war, armed conflict and poverty. These factors play critical roles in deciding how a global disability rights discourse can be implemented or even whether it is desirable for it to be implemented within specific cultures (Ingstad and Reynolds Whyte, 2007).

The book nevertheless does not cover the full spread of articles and rights provided for in the CRPD. Due to limitations of space we had to be selective. We hope that our example will encourage others to undertake a similar review of the articles that we have not featured in this book. A full text of the CRPD can be viewed at United Nations Enable: the official website of the secretariat for the CRPD (http://www.un.org/disabilities/).

Global perspectives

The authors, drawn from all continents, provide readers with global perspectives on disability in four senses. Firstly, they aim to address core issues underlying the denial of disabled people's human rights and their continuing social exclusion (Barnes and Mercer, 2010; Goodley, Hughes and Davis, 2012; WHO and World Bank, 2011). On a more positive note, they identify practical ways to effect change locally, with examples from a variety of countries in Africa, the Americas, Australia and Oceania, Asia and Europe. Secondly, the chapters bring together examples of the myriad insights of disabled people, professionals, families and carers from across the world. Thirdly, a diversity of impairments is covered including those that require more intensive support – intellectual, physical, sensorial and psychosocial – and this is done within a life-course perspective from early childhood to old age. The similarities in terms of exercising human rights are striking across all these impairment groupings, yet traditionally they have pursued separate and often competing agendas (Barnes and Mercer, 2010). Fourthly, our focus is on providing the evidence to develop mainstream services and policies that are available to all citizens, in all countries, and that can better respond to the needs of disabled persons. Specialist disability services in the 21st century also need to be transformed globally if they too are to respect and promote the human rights of their consumers (WHO and World Bank, 2011).

Implementation

The purpose of the CRPD is 'to promote, protect and ensure the full and equal enjoyment of all human rights and fundamental freedoms by all persons with disabilities, and to promote respect for their inherent dignity' (UN, 2006). A core theme throughout the book is therefore the exploration of new ways of thinking about the implementation of the CRPD and how equality and participation in all life areas can become a reality for most, rather than for just a small percentage of, disabled people.

While the CRPD signposts the direction of travel, there are a myriad of starting points for the journey and countless means of travelling on what can be a difficult and bumpy road. The *World Report on Disability* (WHO and World Bank, 2011) marks a common path for change, both nationally and globally, to help accomplish the goals of the CRPD. One of its recommendations is the collaboration of different actors – governments, civil society organizations, professionals, the private sector and disabled people's families – around various areas as summarized in Table 1.1.

Following on this recommendation, the focus of this book is on change primarily at the micro level of interactions between disabled persons and those closest to them: family, carers, fellow citizens and professional workers. This is one of the levels where a significant impact can be made in enabling disabled people to live dignified lives. Thus the book provides both a conceptual and practical understanding of how empowered disabled persons, professionals, families and carers can contribute to the 'bottom-up' implementation of the CRPD within specific local contexts at differing stages of the life cycle and around key themes of poverty, civil conflict, education, health, assistive

Table 1.1.   Recommendations from the *World Report on Disability*

1. Enable access to all mainstream policies, systems and services
2. Invest in specific programmes and services for people with disabilities
3. Adopt a national disability strategy
4. Involve people with disabilities
5. Improve human resource capacity
6. Provide adequate funding and improve affordability
7. Increase public awareness and understanding of disability
8. Improve disability data collection
9. Strengthen and support research on disability

technology, livelihoods and independent living. Cooperation between these key players is an essential contributor to success (WHO and World Bank, 2011).

The chapters of this book articulate, in various ways, the collaboration between these key stakeholders – disabled people, professionals, carers and family members. Three strategies prove to be particularly significant at enhancing the interaction between these stakeholders so that they work together to achieve disabled people's goals and improve the life chances of those who experience disability: advocacy, research and evaluation. The brief introduction given to them here will be further developed in later chapters.

Advocacy

The role of advocacy cannot be overstated in the passage of disability anti-discrimination legislation, change of attitudes towards disability and equality of disabled people both nationally and internationally (Bickenbach et al., 1999). Advocacy is about using political participation to influence decisions about political, economic and social systems and organizations. Further reviewed by Malinga and Gumbo in Chapter 4, advocacy is perhaps the strategy most widely used worldwide by disabled people, and their families, to ensure they are active agents in change.

Disability movements across the world have been major drivers of change (Barnes and Mercer, 2010; Bickenbach, 2009; Goodley, 2011). Indeed, disabled people's activism has helped to shift international approaches to disability from individualized to social responses and put disability on the human rights agenda since the 1970s (Barnes and Mercer, 2010; Goodley, 2011; WHO and World Bank, 2011) – a theme developed further in Chapter 3. Chapters 3 and 4 explain how the CRPD emerged from the intense lobbying and engagement with disabled activists from around the world. The goals of the disability movement have therefore been embedded in the CRPD through the active participation of disabled people and international disabled people's organisations (DPOs) (Schulze, 2010). For example, the goal of independent living was incorporated into Article 19 of the CRPD, 'Living independently and being included in the community' (see Chapter 13). Moreover, a broad coalition of DPOs and allied non-governmental organisations (NGOs) formed the International Disability Caucus, which developed into the strongest civil society voice in the negotiations (Schulze, 2010). Thus, the process of negotiating and drafting the CRPD and the final document honour with each of its articles the disability maxim 'Nothing about us without us' (Charlton, 1998).

Advocacy, then, is a strategy led by disabled people, in which professionals and families/carers can offer support in various forms. In essence, this supportive function requires a radical reappraisal of professional and familial conceptions of their role in relation to disabled persons from 'doing things for them' to supporting them 'to be in charge of their own lives'. More profoundly, it entails a deepening appreciation of disabled persons as 'rights holders', of disability as a form of social oppression and of the multiple oppressions experienced by disabled people, especially in relation to poverty. Along these lines, professional advocacy aligned with disability rights is recommended in Chapter 16. The book provides examples of this spirit of empowerment which needs to be replicated at a local level with leadership coming from disabled persons, supported and empowered by families and professionals with the engagement of local and national politicians (WHO and World Bank, 2011).

Research and evaluation

Research and evaluation are two additional strategies that have the potential to enable the interaction among various stakeholders in order to promote the exercise of disabled people's rights. In recent years research endeavours have taken on a new dimension by involving disabled people in research and evaluation through participatory approaches. In this way the stakeholders involved contribute their knowledge and expertize, increase their awareness of the issues being tackled and learn technical aspects as they participate in the identification of the problem, data collection, data analysis, report writing and so on. This involvement aims to ensure that these processes are relevant to all; that findings can be applied to address disability issues; and that disabled persons can gain ownership over the resources, process and outcomes of research and, in turn, influence advocacy. A major focus of such research is to assess the extent to which disabled people's rights are respected and enforced as provided for in Article 31 of the CRPD ('Statistics and data collection').

Three main approaches to participation in research have been used with and by disabled people: *participatory action research* (MacDonald, 2012), involving disabled people in research that aims at taking action and producing change; *inclusive research*, in which people with the label of intellectual disability participate as co-researchers (Walmsley and Johnson, 2003); and *emancipatory research* (Barnes, 2006; Zarb, 1992), in which disabled people hold the power over the research process and this process is oriented towards social change (Walmsley, 2001).

Likewise, two main approaches have evolved in relation to evaluation: *participatory evaluation* (Cousins and Earl, 1992) and *empowerment evaluation* (Fetterman and Wandersman, 2005). Underlying both approaches is the involvement of programme participants who contribute valuable knowledge to the evaluation process as experts with the lived experience of the issue being researched – in this case, disability. Evaluation is not only about identifying which activity impacts on what outcome (for example, implementing a disability-awareness campaign to change public attitudes towards disabled people) but about how valid that assumption is (for example, how much evidence is there to suggest that an awareness campaign really produces a change in the public attitudes towards disabled people?). This involves thinking and developing theory about how individual and social change is produced (Lipsey and Cordray, 2000). The collaboration of disabled people, professionals and families/carers in evaluation of programmes, community initiatives and policies within local contexts can enable monitoring of the implementation of the CRPD by civil society as provided in Article 33 ('National implementation and monitoring').

Terminology

We appreciate that disability terminology is contested. 'People with disabilities', 'disabled people', 'people with impairments', 'Deaf people', 'people with intellectual disabilities' and 'visually impaired people' are all commonly used terms in disability research, legislation, policy, advocacy, testimonies and so on. In recent years they have come to be accepted as politically correct terms in international fora, replacing the stigmatizing and discriminatory language that can still be present in all societies around the world. The varying terms reflect, however, differing perspectives about disability. The CRPD offers the following description of disability and disabled persons (see Box 1.1).

The CRPD, similar to previous international UN documents, and the *World Report on Disability* use the terminology 'persons with disabilities', which emphasizes the human value of people (people-first language) and does not lead to an interpretation that the ability to function as a person has been disabled, as 'disabled persons' may imply (Schulze, 2010). Other scholars and activists, however, prefer to call people with impairments 'disabled people' to accentuate society's role in disabling individuals from their participation in various life areas (the disabling role of society is further explained in Chapter 2). Although the use of one or another term ('people with disabilities' or 'disabled people') often generates vivid debate within Anglophone contexts and among native English speakers, the differences underlying the terms – 'impairment' and 'disability' – do not necessarily translate into other languages, for example, Nordic languages (Traustadóttir, 2004) or in Zairean Songye terminology (Devlieger, 1995). Although some of these terminological differences are further explored in the book, authors were free to use the various terms above to reflect their own and others' understanding of disability. We concur with Albrecht, Seelman and Bury (2001) in that 'the discussion needs to continue, be respectful and aim at understanding' (p. 3). In the future, perhaps

---

Box 1.1.   CRPD description of disability

CRPD Preamble (e)

Recognizing that disability is an evolving concept and that disability results from the interaction between persons with impairments and attitudinal and environmental barriers that hinders their full and effective participation in society on an equal basis with others.

CRPD Article 1

Persons with disabilities include those who have long-term physical, mental, intellectual or sensory impairments, which in interaction with various barriers may hinder their full and effective participation in society on an equal basis with others.

Both these statements should be read in combination (Schulze, 2010).

the fundamental distinction between 'disabled and non-disabled' that we have inherited from previous generations will gradually lessen as the common rights of all human beings are more fully exercised internationally.

More central to the work presented in this book than the terminological debate is the fact that the CRPD has been officially published by the UN in just six different languages out of the few thousand languages in the world. Further, there is no official easy-to-read version or an official sign language version. The website of the CRPD secretariat makes available non-official translations of the document into spoken languages and sign languages (more than 25 in total) and easy-to-read versions (six in total). The following disclaimer, however, is made: 'These non-official versions of the Convention ... are for informational purposes only; they do not constitute endorsement of, or an approval by, the United Nations ... The United Nations bears no responsibility for the accuracy, legality or content ...' As key and basic as accessibility is for the exercise of disabled people's rights, the sacred text on this matter fails to provide minimal access to those with different language access needs and those speakers of other languages into which the CRPD is not translated. This is yet another example of the work that needs to be done at all levels if disabled people are to become active agents in the exercise of their rights. It is our hope that this volume is a start in bringing this about.

Book structure

The book has been carefully assembled so that readers gain a progressive understanding of disability and human rights. To facilitate readers' assimilation of ideas and generate critical thinking, each chapter includes a summary of key points followed by study questions. The summary of key points is a refresher of the main issues discussed in the chapter and provides a starting point to work on the study questions. Study questions can be used for individual self-reflection or in group discussions. It is our hope that both the key points and study questions generate vivid debate, further inquiries and multiple responses to local disability issues in all places where the book is read. Such discussions will be all the richer when disabled people invite their professional supporters and students in training to join in the dialogue.

Further reading and resources

United Nations. (2006). 'Convention on the Rights of Persons with Disabilities'. Available from http://www.un.org/disabilities/default.asp?navid=12&pid=150.
WHO and World Bank. (2011). *World Report on Disability*. Available from http:// www.who.int/disabilities/world_report/2011/en/.

Models of Disability

Edurne García Iriarte

[d]isability is an evolving concept and that disability results from the interaction between persons with impairments and attitudinal and environmental barriers that hinders their full and effective participation in society on an equal basis with others [...].

UN Convention on the Rights of Persons with Disabilities
Preamble (e)

Introduction

Globally, around a billion (one thousand million) people live with disability: 15 per cent of the world's population (WHO and World Bank, 2011). Zola (1989) argues that disability must be considered part of the human condition, as 'the entire population is at risk for the concomitants of chronic illness and disability' (p. 401). Yet disabled people, far from living their lives just like other human beings, are more likely to experience poverty, poorer education and employment outcomes, restricted access to public life and denial of their most basic rights. Experience of these common barriers, however, varies across countries, social classes, gender, culture, ethnicity, individual impairments and life course, which is illustrated in the following chapters.

But how is the term *disability* understood and used globally? This chapter aims to review current disability definitions and working models and analyse their implementation in practice. The chapter first presents some of the challenges to define *disability* and introduces the term as it is understood in the Convention on the Rights of Persons with Disabilities (CRPD) (United Nations, 2006). Second, the author provides a description of some of the most influential disability models. The aim in presenting these models is to enable readers to understand the basic differences between the various disability frameworks rather than to fully explore their theoretical foundations. The chapter provides an analysis of two global disability approaches, the human rights-based approach (HRBA) and community-based rehabilitation (CBR). It also illustrates the implementation of models through case examples from the United States of America (US) and Ecuador. The last section of the chapter reflects on the implications of working from a human rights-based perspective in different cultural contexts.

Disability definitions

Disability is a complex, dynamic, multidimensional and contested concept (WHO and World Bank, 2011, p. 3). Human differences and people with impairments have existed for as long as humans have walked this planet (Braddock and Parish, 2001). However, it is only recently that the terms *hand-icap* and, latterly, *disability* were used to refer to the groups of people with impairments. Industrialized countries in the nineteenth and twentieth centuries started to differentiate between disabled and non-disabled people as social policy responses were developed to address the problems faced by those with impairments (Barnes, 2010; Harris and Roulstone, 2011). However, despite firm efforts to standardize the definition and use of the now widely accepted term *disability*, for example by the World Health Organization (WHO) from 1949 onwards, multiple definitions remain which create difficulties in categorizing and comparing disability both across and within countries (European Commission [EC], 2002). Altman (2001) proposed a classification of disability into legal and administrative definitions (used in legislation and/or policy), clinical definitions (used in medical settings) and scholarly definitions (used in academia). However, disability definitions vary according to purpose (Fujiura and Rutkowski-Kmitta, 2001), and countries often have more than one definition in each of Altman's categories. For example, in anti-discrimination legislation most European countries use an administrative definition that focuses on the act of discrimination towards the person on the basis of disability, whereas in the same countries a social policy definition focused on the work (in)capacity of the person is often used (EC, 2002). As the example illustrates, these variations open up the possibility of a person being classified as disabled and non-disabled simultaneously depending on the definition used.

The CRPD (UN, 2006), a landmark international treaty in the history of disability rights, provides a framework for the understanding of disability to all its signatory countries: a total of 158[1] countries in the eight years following its adoption. The CRPD identifies 'persons with disabilities' as those

> [w]ho have long-term physical, mental, intellectual or sensory impairments which in interaction with various barriers may hinder their full and effective participation in society on an equal basis with others.

This description, however, has been referred to as a 'non-definition' as the negotiators of the CRPD failed to agree on whether and, if so, how impairment and disability should be defined (Schulze, 2010). Thus, a description

---

[1] The Convention was open for signature on 30 March 2007, and since then it has been signed by 158 countries of which 147 have also ratified it as of 29 July 2014. The Optional Protocol has been signed by 92 and ratified by 82, accessed 29 July 2014 from http://www.un.org/disabilities/.

rather than a definition was included in the final document. About 50 definitions were considered in trying to come up with one to include in the CRPD document (Schulze, 2010). One of the arguments considered in favour of not providing a definition was that a conclusive definition may leave out people in need of protection. Consequently, any definition is then left to national legislation, along with identifying who qualifies as disabled and who does not, which again may lead to the exclusion of certain people whose rights should be protected (Schulze, 2010). The description, nonetheless, refers to the social model of disability as it breaks the direct link between impairment and disability by introducing 'various barriers' – referring to the social, environmental and attitudinal factors which in interaction with the impairment cause disability. Although we address specific context issues later on in the chapter, a note of caution should be introduced here about the validity of universal definitions. As Grech (2012) states, 'If contexts and circumstances vary and are not static, so the meaning of disability is fluid, dynamic and shifting, constantly (re)negotiated' (p. 58).

Disability models

The description of disability provided by the CRPD further refers to four components: impairment, interaction with barriers, participation in society and equality. These point to different ways of understanding disability, either singly or in combination, in the form of what are termed 'disability models'. Figure 2.1 summarizes the main models of disability that feature throughout the book.

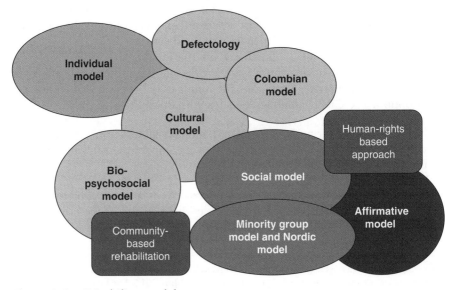

Figure 2.1.   Disability models

Such models can help our understanding of disability by providing systematic organizations of its conceptual elements and the relationships between or among them (Altman, 2001). Models are not theories in themselves, but simple representations of concepts that help understanding and facilitate decision-making. Goodley, Hughes and Davis (2012) argue nonetheless that the social model of disability (see below) develops in close reading of historical materialism and therefore has deep theoretical roots.

Conceptual models of disability are closely linked to society's understanding of impairment and disability throughout history. For example, Barnes (2010) suggests that the domination by medical professionals of all aspects of disability originated in Britain in 1845 when British society identified medical professionals as the main authority to deal with disabled members of society. The official establishment of an individual/medical model of disability in Britain therefore could be situated at that point in history. By contrast, the social model, Nordic model and minority group models developed in the second half of the 20th century, when disability activists and academics started to challenge welfare responses to disability in the United Kingdom (UK), US and Nordic countries (Barnes and Mercer, 2010). Despite differences across Western and non-Western societies, the most influential models internationally have been gestated in the UK and the US or in contexts highly influenced by these countries, such as the WHO and the United Nations (UN). These models have been translated, adapted and used across countries in all continents. The concept of 'glocalization' – mixing globalizing and localizing forces through the active modification of global processes to fit particular cultures – may explain how models of understanding are adopted and implemented in local contexts to fit their own culture in order to ease communication and application (Giddens and Sutton, 2013). Little is known, however, about alternative narratives of disability that originate from non-Western and non-English speaking countries from the Global South (Grech, 2012). These indigenous models will have a critical impact in non-Western countries, although they are often overlooked as disability models in English language textbooks.

This chapter reviews a number of existing models. As illustrated in Figure 2.1, the models are presented in different colour shades indicating three types of models: the individual model; the social model including a further development (affirmative model) and similar developments in other world regions (the minority group model and the Nordic model); and other hybrid models, which employ individual and social analyses to explain disability, such as the bio-psychosocial model, the cultural model and two additional models developed and used in particular geographical regions, defectology and the Colombian conceptual model of disability and social exclusion. We shall now look at each of these in more detail. Table 2.1 summarizes the core message and main critique of each model.

The individual model

The individual model of disability understands disability as a problem located in the individual, caused by cognitive or physical impairments. A clinical

Table 2.1. Disability Models

	Core Message	Main Critique
Individual	Disability is a problem of individuals with impairments that needs to be cured by medical and rehabilitation professionals.	It fails to acknowledge the role of the environment and diminishes people's knowledge of their own experience in favour of professionals' expertize. A disproportionate expense is made on technology to cure disability.
Social	Disability is a problem of society which, through the environment and institutions, disables individuals with impairments. Distinction is made between disability (social disadvantage) and impairment (biomedical limitation).	Individual experience of impairment is overlooked. Impairment is defined in biomedical terms. It assumes disabled people are oppressed and believes in a barrier-free utopian society.
Minority group	Disabled people are citizens with equal rights to non-disabled citizens and other minority groups. Emphasis is placed on independent living, anti-professionalism, de-institutionalization and normalization.	It relies on individual self-advocacy skills; it fails to differentiate between impairment and disability; disabled people are powerless in adverse political and economic circumstances.
Nordic	Disability is a person–environment mismatch; it is contextual; it is relational/relative to the environment.	It fails to differentiate between impairment and disability; it focuses on professional practice and service delivery rather than building on disability activism.
Affirmative	Disability is a positive quality of the disabled person; it is a reason for pride and positive identity; it promotes determination, identity and culture.	Affirmation of identity can be understood as compliance with the status quo; not all disabled people have a positive attitude towards disability; disability identity is limited to recognize the complexity of disabled persons.

Human rights-based approach (implementation)	Operationable way of working in the field from a social model perspective. Disability is inherent to the human condition; disabled individuals' contributions help diversify the human experience.	People are still denied basic human rights; human rights are based on a Western understanding of a 'good life' (independence and reason); it marginalizes people who are not agents in the exercise of human rights.
Bio-psycho-social	Disability is the umbrella term for impairments, activity limitations and participation restrictions, referring to the negative aspects of the interaction between an individual (with a health condition) and that individual's contextual factors (environmental and personal factors)	Disability is framed within a health paradigm. The universality of the definition is questioned.
Cultural	Disability is state of being to be interpreted from each culture. Disability is represented and embodied in cultural artefacts.	It is disconnected from disability activism, service delivery and professional practice; it does not focus on political marginalization; and it creates vulnerability within cultural hegemonic contexts.
Defectology	Disability results from the incongruence between the individual's 'defects' and the sociocultural structures.	It has led to institutionalization; it is one of the main barriers to progress towards a human rights-based approach.
Colombian conceptual model of disability and social exclusion	Disability results from (1) the relationship between the individual and the environment; (2) the dilemma of difference – disability can be adapted to specific situations.	Explanations of disability are limited to the particular Colombian context where the model is developed and are disconnected from disability activism.
Community-based rehabilitation (implementation)	A strategy within general community development for the rehabilitation, poverty reduction, equalization of opportunities and social inclusion of all people with disabilities	Unclear what the role of disabled people is in the overall CBR process and whether they should have separate programmes. Lack of evidence on the cost-effectiveness of CBR.

diagnosis of disability means that the person deviates from the biomedical norms of humanity. The disability is identified as the main cause of any secondary problems the disabled person experiences, such as poorer quality of life or social isolation. The disability problem, however, can be addressed by curing it (for example, implanting a Deaf person with cochlear devices), correcting it (for example, using hearing aids or prosthetic limbs) or rehabilitating it (for example, adjusting the person's body to the demands of the home or work environment) (WHO and World Bank, 2011). The individual model of disability considers the person's environment to be neutral and therefore focuses on the individual as the target of change and intervention.

Following the logic of the individual model of disability, professionals are responsible for 'fixing' the disability by curing, rehabilitating or correcting it (as they have the expertize to fix it), and disabled persons become passive recipients of professional services. This is why this model is also known as medical model and in fact shares many of the assumptions of a biomedical model of health (Giddens and Sutton, 2013). Thus, the responsibility of professionals is to alleviate the disability and therefore contribute to an improved quality of life of disabled individuals. Disabled people, as conceived in the individual model, are often perceived by the general population as victims of a personal tragedy; for instance the word suffering is often used. In sum, the individual is seen as responsible for the difference and the tragedy of disability. Within this view of disability, disabled people often become objects of charity. Barnes and Mercer (2010) state that 'the dominant meanings attached to disability in most western industrial and post-industrial societies remain firmly rooted in personal tragedy theory' (p. 11). The individual or medical model is currently the most dominant model both socially and in terms of the amount of money governments spend on support services. It is especially influential in determining welfare benefits in more affluent countries.

Organizations, services, and professionals operating within an individual model of disability have been the focus of widespread criticism by the disability community, disabled scholars and activists. One of the main criticisms is the expertize that professionals claim over disabled people's lives which serves to diminish disabled people's knowledge of their own bodies and experience.

The individual model of disability has also been criticized for the disproportionate expense made on technology and research to 'cure' disability when, first, there is insufficient evidence of the effectiveness of such techniques, and second, investment in improving social conditions for disabled people may have even greater quality of life benefits (Swain and French, 2008). The individual model is presented first in this chapter because of its traditional dominance. It also forms the point of departure for the creation of alternative models that stem from a critique of its premises in order to achieve a proper understanding of disability (Williams, 2001).

The social model

The social model of disability also understands disability as a problem but presents a radical departure from the individual model in that it identifies society as the main cause of that problem. The social construction of disability is at the heart of the social model. The model postulates that disability stems from the environment and social institutions, by the way they are built and operate, which systematically disadvantage individuals with impairments and therefore oppress them. Disability is not something that exists in the individual, but is the result of the interaction between the oppressive and inaccessible environments and individuals with impairments. For example, architectural barriers such as the lack of an entrance ramp to a building (the physical environment) limit the access of wheelchair users. Likewise, social and communication environments can act as barriers for disabled persons. Following this logic, it is society that actually disables the person and generates the problems associated with disability.

This view of disability was first articulated in the UK in the 1960s by disability activists and scholars such as Hunt (1966) and in the 1970s was adopted by the Union of the Physically Impaired Against Segregation based in the UK (UPIAS) (Oliver, 1990). In the UPIAS manifesto, the terms *disability* and *impairment* are differentiated. *Disability* is defined as a social disadvantage imposed on people with impairments, whereas *impairment* is used in its biomedical sense and in a similar way to how the term is understood according to the individual or medical model: namely, as a deviation from biomedical norms. British disability scholar and activist Mike Oliver was the first to coin the term *social model*, in contrast to the individual model (Shakespeare, 2010). In his seminal work *The Politics of Disablement* Oliver (1990) draws from historical materialism to account for the foundations of the social model.

The social model of disability was the 'big idea' of the British disability movement (Shakespeare, 2010). It has led to a change in the general public's perception of disabled people from victims of a personal tragedy to politically active members of society. It identifies disability as a source of oppression, and puts *disablism* – discrimination on the basis of disability – on a par with other forms of oppression such as racism, sexism and so on (Barnes and Mercer, 2010). The social model has been embraced by several international disability organisations and governments who acknowledge society's role in creating disablement and the need then to incorporate social factors as a target of intervention to improve the life of disabled persons (for example, accessibility of the built environment).

Although the idea of disability as socially constructed is widely accepted (Bickenbach, 2009), impairment is also a cultural construct. Oliver (1990) argues that impairment does not happen randomly, but is conditioned by social and economic factors such as poverty, working conditions, poor health or a lack of safe water. Poor people are more likely to develop impairments and indeed higher numbers of people with impairments – such as blindness or deafness – are concentrated in low-income countries (WHO and World Bank, 2011).

The social model has been criticized for an almost exclusive focus on the social environment, diminishing the importance of the impairment experience for the individual, and for its undue disregard of the bio-medical interpretation of impairment, in a very similar way that the individual model ignores social influences. Further criticisms of the social model include the assumption that disabled people are oppressed and the belief in a barrier-free utopian society as the solution to disability (Shakespeare, 2010). Social model supporters have argued in response to these criticisms that the aim of the social model is to shift the focus towards social barriers while acknowledging that impairments can have psycho-emotional effects for disabled people (Thomas, 2002).

Similar developments to the social model in other world regions

At the same time as the social model developed in the United Kingdom, scholars and activists in North America and the Nordic countries challenged individual and medical responses to disability and developed further conceptualizations as to how disability can be understood in the minority group model and the Nordic model, respectively (Barnes and Mercer, 2010; Bickenbach, Chatterji, Badley and Üstün, 1999).

The minority group model

The minority group model identifies disabled people as members of a minority group who have equal rights as consumers of disability services. Supporters of this model have advocated for equal rights and opportunities like those due to other minority groups, but with an emphasis on independent living, anti-professionalism, de-institutionalization and normalization. Bickenback and colleagues (1999) attribute the political strategy of the minority group model with a widespread change in attitudes towards disability and the passage of landmark anti-discrimination legislation.

However, the adequacy of this model has been criticized on the basis that disabled people require solid self-advocacy skills; it also fails to differentiate between impairment and disability, and leaves disabled individuals powerless in adverse political and economic circumstances (Goodley, 2011).

The Nordic model

From the 1960s there was a critique in the Nordic countries about welfare responses to disability, such as institutionalization and medical approaches, together with a concern for shifting the focus from individual impairment to society and the environment as targets of intervention (Barnes and Mercer, 2010). The Nordic model, rather than a single concept, is a family of ideas about disability which emphasizes that disability is a person–environment mismatch; it is situational or contextual rather than always present; and it is relational/relative to the environment (Tøsseboro, 2004). Although the social model aligns with the Nordic model of disability, multiple approaches and theories are used in understanding disability in the Nordic countries (Traustadóttir, 2004). For example, 'normalisation' (Nirje, 1969), latterly called 'social role valorization' developed in the Nordic countries with the basic premise that disabled people would be treated more normally if they enjoy ways of life as close to non-disabled people as possible. Wolfensberger (1985) reconceptualized 'normalisation' to the use of culturally valued means to enable people to develop and sustain valued social roles.

However, the following have been identified as negative effects of the Nordic model: a failure to differentiate between impairment and disability and a continuing focus on professional practice and service delivery rather than building on disability activism (Goodley, 2011).

A further development of the social model: Affirmative model

The affirmative model is considered a development of the social model of disability (Goodley, 2011). In this model, disability is not understood as a problem or negative aspect of the person, but rather as a positive quality of the disabled person. According to this model, disabled people traditionally were all subjected to a tragedy view of disability. But the affirmative model reverses that dominant view and promotes disability as a reason for pride and positive identity (Swain and French, 2008) in a similar way to other marginalized groups such as gay pride. The affirmative model replaces ideas of dependency and abnormalcy (held from an individual/medical model of disability) with those of determination, identity and culture (Swain and French, 2008). This model strongly opposes the dominant tragedy model of disability and its related assumptions about disabled people. The affirmative model is intricately related to disability arts and culture movements found in the UK and US and increasingly in other parts of the world. These movements have been created around the central argument that disabled people contribute with their talents, experiences, bodies and minds to the creation of an aesthetic and culture where difference stemming from disability is a key factor to the richness of the human experience and society (Sutherland, 2008).

The affirmative model has its critics. First, affirmation of identity can be understood as acceptance of the status quo despite the oppression that disabled people experience within that status quo. Second, some disabled people may find affirmation difficult, and therefore not all disabled people may have a positive identity. And third, a disability identity is limited and does not recognize the complexity of disabled people's aspirations and views of themselves. Swain and French (2008) have responded to these criticisms by acknowledging that identity is increasingly understood as a complex process and that the affirmative model is not the end result. Rather, the affirmation of disabled lifestyles is a critique that challenges the dominant discourse that even if disabled people find it difficult to affirm their disabled identity, the point is that they do not have to adopt a tragedy view. This model opens a channel for resistance that people with disabilities may wish to exercise to a greater or lesser extent.

Hybrid models

Thus far, we have emphasized the distinctions among models with opposing ways of understanding disability, the individual model and the social model including similar developments (Nordic and minority group model) and the affirmative model. Facets of the individual and the social models, however, combine into other models to convey hybrid understandings of disability. These models focus on the body as well as society or culture in their analysis of disability. Here we will describe four such models.

The bio-psycho-social model

The bio-psycho-social model of disability aims to provide a 'workable compromise' between the individual and social model (WHO and World Bank, 2011, p. 4) and is best exemplified in the International Classification of Functioning, Disability and Health (ICF) proposed by the WHO (2001). The ICF has a strong emphasis on the role of the environment on the experience of disability (WHO and World Bank, 2011). This model

> understands functioning and disability as a dynamic interaction between health conditions and contextual factors, both personal and environmental. Disability is the umbrella term for impairments, activity limitations and participation restrictions, referring to the negative aspects of the interaction between an individual (with a health condition) and that individual's contextual factors (environmental and personal factors).
>
> (WHO and World Bank, 2011, p. 4)

The model identifies three areas of functionality, namely: impairments (for example, visual, mobility), activity limitations (for example, self-care) and participation restrictions (for example, lack of access to education) (WHO and World Bank, 2011). It emphasizes the role of the environment in the social participation of disabled people (for example, physical accessibility, information access, poverty conditions, policies). Disability arises from difficulties experienced in any one or all of the three areas of functioning, but it also measures positive aspects of a person's functioning in the three areas. It does not distinguish between the type and cause of disability. Rather, it identifies health conditions such as diseases and injuries, along with disorders and impairments that result from problems in body functions or structures (see Chapter 10 for a presentation of the ICF in relation to inclusive health). It is considered a universal model because it covers all human functioning and treats disability as a continuum on which everyone can be placed rather than as a dichotomous variable of the disabled/non-disabled. A primary aim of the ICF is to generate consistent and comparable measures of disability internationally (WHO and World Bank, 2011).

However, the bio-psycho-social model of disability has been criticized on the grounds of continuing to frame disability within a health context (Barnes and Mercer, 2010). Moreover, disability scholars question the universal validity of the classification as it takes insufficient account of cultural influences on people's lives and development (Barnes and Mercer, 2010; Ingstad and Reynolds Whyte, 2007).

The cultural model

Devlieger (2005) explains that underlying the cultural model of disability is the idea that disability does not exist in the natural context, but its meanings are instead assigned within and across a range of cultural traditions, moral frameworks and religion. For example, from a religious perspective, God is considered as the cause of impairment, which can be a result of wrongdoing, or on the contrary, impairment can be understood as a gift given to special people (several examples in the following chapters illustrate this point). The location of disability is situated in meaning, information and communication (Devlieger, 2005).

Cultural analyses of disability also turn to the relationship between biology and culture (Goodley, 2011). Davis's (2010) historical account of the concept of 'normalcy' provides an example of such analysis. Davis (2010) suggests that the word 'normal' and the idea of 'the norm' as we know them today entered the English language over the period 1840–1860. The concept of normalcy developed linked to statistics, industrialization and eugenic thinking. Statisticians such as Francis Galton developed techniques that made coincide what was considered to be the best human traits in the likes of hair colour or height, according to the eugenic ideology of the time, with the statistical 'norm'. For instance, white skin, tall height and high intelligence were considered normal (even desirable), whereas darker skin, medium or low height and moderate intelligence were considered below (sub-) normal. In other words, people whose traits were considered below the established normal were perceived and labelled as deviants from the norm. Disabled people fell into the latter category alongside ethnic minorities, gay people and arguably even women in a male-dominated society.

In Chapter 5, Gargett and colleagues discuss culture as representational and embodied. The analysis of disability in cultural representations focuses on products such as film, novels or art portraying images of the disabled body and exposing discourses on disability. The examination of cultural embodiment, according to Gargett and colleagues, centres on the belief and value systems which conform to a culture. These belief and value systems, on the one hand, shape individuals' understanding of disability in that culture. Individuals' own belief and value systems about disability, in turn, contribute to shape the culture (see for example Mitchell and Snyder, 2001).

Goodley (2011) has summarized the negative aspects of the cultural model as being disconnected from disability activism, service delivery and professional practice; and focusing on cultural constructions rather than political marginalization and vulnerability of disabled people within cultural hegemony.

To complete the picture, two further models are described that are most relevant in the cultural contexts where they have been developed and applied: namely, defectology, which has dominated thinking in Russia and former Soviet states, and the Colombian conceptual model of disability and social inclusion.

Defectology

Notwithstanding its name, defectology can be seen as falling halfway between the medical and the social models of disability. This approach was developed by Lev Vygotsky within Soviet Marxism philosophy and understands disability as a disconnect between a child's biological and cultural development which is directly influenced by the cultural organizations where the child interacts, lives, and develops (Bøttcher and Dammeyer, 2012). According to this model, any primary biological *defects* (sensory, physical, intellectual impairments) affect the ability of the child to participate in social and cultural activities, which are mostly adapted to normally developing children. They do not support children to develop in any other way, which results in their development being impaired. According to the defectology model, a limitation of the biomedical (individual) model is that it takes no account of the development of the child in a social context whereas defectology perceives disability being corrected through appropriate services. In Vygotsky's (1993) words, 'the development and education of a blind child have to do not so much with blindness itself as with the social consequences of blindness' (p. 19).

Defectology is an academic discipline governing the care and treatment of children with disabilities in Central and Eastern Europe and the Commonwealth of Independent States (CEECIS) (UNICEF, 2012). According to a UNICEF report (2012), teachers in this region are trained in defectology models, and it is the main model used to assess disability and the educational capabilities of the child. Intrinsic to the model is the idea that impairments can be corrected through pedagogical methods so that children can be returned to society (Kalinnikova and Trygged, 2014). In practice, when defectology has been applied by certain political regimes, children were classified into educable and non-educable and the latter placed into institutional care. Reduced contact between Russian scientists and disability specialists in other countries may explain why challenges to the hegemony of institutions in post-Soviet Russia came later than in the rest of the European Union (Kalinnikova and Trygged, 2014).

In the recent past, defectology has been blamed for leading to the systematic institutionalization and segregation of children and adults with certain impairments from the rest of society (see Chapter 8). Indeed, UNICEF (2012) identified defectology as one of the main barriers to moving towards a human rights-based approach in the CEECIS.

The Colombian conceptual model of disability and social inclusion

The Colombian conceptual model of disability and social inclusion (Cuervo Echeverri, Pérez Acevedo and Trujillo Rojas, 2008; Pérez Acevedo, 2012) arose from the idea that disability is a phenomenon directly influenced by external factors, and therefore it cannot be conceptualized by a unique definition of disability. According to this model, disability is a complex phenomenon and reality that results from the interaction of two strains: (1) relationship or interactivity between an individual, with or without physical limitations, and the environment; and (2) the dilemma of difference. The first strain refers to the fact that disability appears, disappears, grows or diminishes in direct relationship to the human and non-human environment. The second strain – dilemma of difference – means that disability is a fluid concept that can be transformed in order to adapt to specific situations. Cuervo Echeverri and colleagues (2008) use the figure/background analogy to explain the fluidity of the concept: sometimes disability can be seen, and sometimes it cannot be seen.

The model includes the following:

(1) Four perspectives on the understanding of disability: human capacity and technology studies (for example, medicine, public health, psychology, education, industrial engineering, architecture); public studies (for example, law, economics, human geography); cultural studies (for example, anthropology, humanities, sociology); and ethical-philosophical studies (for example, philosophy, religion). The four perspectives encompass the concepts and understanding of disability that representatives and professionals from different disciplines use in making disability policy and implementing public action.

(2) The Colombian context which recognizes that the perspectives and understanding of disability are entangled and the context can be enabling or disabling. The enabling and disabling characteristics of the environment, therefore, become critical in understanding disability. For example, disabling characteristics of the Colombian environment are the strong relationship between disability and poverty, and health and education exclusion. Among the enabling characteristics are the increased political interest in disability, the research that has been conducted, economic investment in local development and the growing organization and advocacy of disabled people.

The relationships network created among all of the above components explains some of the complexity of disability. Disability can be studied from each of the four perspectives and from the intersections among them, along with the interactions of each of these perspectives with the environment and resolutions around the dilemma of difference. Hence different approaches to disability may be accepted or rejected in particular contexts and circumstances.

There are no published critiques, to the author's knowledge, on this model. The model offers explanations of disability limited to the Colombian national context, and therefore it may be only applicable to other contexts with similar socio-economic circumstances. The model is disconnected from disability activism.

Disability models in practice

In this section, I turn to examine the implementation of disability models through two global approaches: the human rights-based approach (HRBA) and community-based rehabilitation (CBR). The HRBA sets out a global policy agenda on disability, whereas CBR operates in almost a hundred countries in the Global South. Two further examples illustrate the implementation of disability models in the US and Ecuador.

Global disability approaches

Human rights-based approach

The disabled people's movement in Britain, the disability rights movement in the US and social conceptualizations of disability – the social model and minority group model, respectively – developed together out of disabled people's struggle against an individual/medical approach to disability (Barnes and Mercer, 2010; French and Swain, 2007). This struggle has resulted in the shift since the 1990s of international human rights instruments from an individual/medical to a social view of disability, for example, the Standard Rules on the Equalization of Opportunities for Persons with Disabilities (UN, 1993) and more recently the CRPD (UN, 2006). The HRBA has provided disabled people with an operationalizable way of working in the field of disability from a social model perspective (Lawson, 2006). Disability is framed as a human rights issue in the HRBA, with the basic premises that difference is inherent to the human condition, that contributions from different members of society help diversify the range of the human experience and that society should provide for equal opportunities to all its members to realise their rights (Rioux and Carbert, 2003). The European Commission's 2003 'Equal Opportunities for People with Disabilities: A European Action Plan (2004–2010)' drew on this model and included the following as its operational objectives: anti-discrimination legislation and human rights (to combat discrimination on the basis of disability), accessibility (the implementation of universal design or access for all) and mainstreaming (including disability perspectives across policies rather than developing separate disability policies) (Lawson, 2006). The European Disability Strategy (2010–2020) in turn, has at its core that disability is a human rights issue and builds on the CRPD.

Rioux and Carbert (2003) suggest that a rights-outcome approach develops an analysis of both the barriers that disabled people experience to the realization of their rights and the changes that need to be made to society to remove those barriers. For example, disabled people have the right to work on an equal basis with others. However, unemployment is a reality for many disabled people in the world. Using a rights-outcome approach, barriers to employment could be identified: for example, a lack of accessibility in the workplace and employers' negative attitudes towards disabled people. The approach could be used to identify changes needed, such as these: first, accessibility of the workplace or provision of reasonable accommodations to increase the accessibility of the workplace and, second, disability equality training programmes to change employers' attitudes.

One of the most useful tools in the implementation of the HRBA is the CRPD, firstly to develop policy and legislation, and secondly to enable civil society – both non-governmental organizations and institutions representing the interests of citizens – in monitoring its implementation (Lawson, 2006). The role of civil society participation in the monitoring of the CRPD is further explored in Chapters 3 and 4.

The following case offers an illustration of how the HRBA has been used among some groups of disabled people in Tunisia, where international organizations are pressing for the human rights-based approach to become the dominant disability model (see Box 2.1).

Box 2.1. Tunisia: Transition to a human rights-based approach to disability

Tunisia serves as an illustration of the shift taking place in disability paradigms from an individual care model towards a human rights-based approach.

Tunisia is an Arab country that, along with other countries in the region, has experienced, in the last few decades, the pressure to introduce a human rights-based approach through international human rights plans and tools – such as the World Programme of Action Concerning Persons with Disabilities (UN, 1982), the Standard Rules on the Equalization of Opportunities for Persons with Disabilities, and the Arab decade of disabled people (2004–2014) (Al Thani, 2006; Kabbara, 2013). This approach to disability has been reflected in the signature of the CRPD (UN, 2006) by 16 countries in the region in the eight years following its adoption by the UN (Kabbara, 2013).

Nonetheless, the individual model of disability still dominates in Tunisia and the Arab region as a whole (with the exception of some countries and initiatives) (Al Thani, 2006; Kabbara, 2013). However, disabled Tunisians were very active during the Arab Spring to ensure the disability cause was included in the revolution (Kabbara, 2013). For example, the revolution inspired Tunisian disabled citizens to form the Tunisian Organisation for the Promotion of the Rights of Persons with Disabilities. According to its president, Imed Ouertani, training on a human rights-based approach provided by Handicap International and the International Disability Alliance contributed 'to the building of our advocacy platform and skills, and helped us to seize the day to ensure that the Arab Spring would equally bear fruit for persons with disabilities in Tunisia' (International Disability Alliance, 2013).

Tunisia was the first Arab country to be reviewed by the CRPD Monitoring Committee, in 2011. This review recommended the adoption of legislative measures to ensure disabled persons can exercise the right to vote and participate in public life (see Chapter 3 for a discussion on the CRPD reporting mechanism). This became the focus of the Organisation for the Promotion of the Rights of Persons with Disabilities, and its first target was to implement measures such as physical access to polling stations and the provision of sign language interpretation. An ordinance was adopted establishing measures to facilitate the exercising of the right to vote of disabled voters. However, Article 6 of the ordinance outlines the distinction between degrees of disability and their corresponding capacity to vote and therefore fails to comply with the CRPD.

Other organisations have also used the Arab Spring events as a platform for disability activism. For example, a group of visually impaired Tunisians forced the resignation of the non-disabled management board of the National Federation of the Blind in Tunisia, which had been constituted by the president and his executive office. This revolutionary effort culminated with the emergence of a young and disabled leadership who took on the control of the Federation in 2011. A second example is provided by the Cultural Animation Association for the Deaf in the coastal city of Soussa, which claimed to be the first to openly join the revolution. The association signed and widely publicized a manifesto proclaiming their change from an individual (persons with impairments) to a collective approach (a group of disabled people) of young disabled people to support the youth revolution; their commitment to regaining freedom and dignity; their belief in being partners and not burdens; their experience of double injustice (undemocratic regime and discrimination on the basis of

(continued)

Box 2.1.   Continued

---

disability); and their shared dream for a people's homeland (mo3aq-news.com, 2011). An extract of the manifesto illustrates the collective consciousness of disability and youth claiming respect and equality:

> We decided to go down to the square to participate with you, hand in hand so the blood of the martyrs and honourable people who paid their blood as a price for the love of their nation, will not be wasted. We will not limit ourselves to a sentimental, nor to an individual participation; we participate with you now collectively on the ground and we are speaking in the voice of more than 150 Deaf involved in the association in order to realise the dream in a nation and in a system that respects dignity and respects the disabled. We are partners with you, not burdens.

(mo3aq-news.com) (Translation by Mariana Saad)

Tunisia's example illustrates that a shift in disability paradigms has been occurring in recent years, bolstered by the work of international organizations on human rights. The human rights discourse has been taken up by groups of disabled people in the context of a wider democratic revolution, the Arab Spring. Time still needs to demonstrate, however, whether implementation of the HRBA is effective, in the long run, in changing the lives of disabled Tunisians for the better.

Indeed, some are critical of the human rights-based approach. A commonly held view questions the validity of human rights as a means to achieve equality and full participation when, more than 60 years after the 1948 UN Universal Declaration of Human Rights, notwithstanding significant achievements, all over the world people, disabled and non-disabled, continue to experience challenges to the exercise of their basic human rights, including access to food and shelter, health, education or employment. More specifically, Johnson (2013) argues that the CRPD, with a Western understanding of a 'good life' based on independence and the exercise of reason, marginalizes groups of disabled people such as intellectually disabled people and people with dementia who may not be (or choose not to be) agents in the exercising of their rights. The involvement of people who may not be able to articulate their views in government consultation processes, as well as economic constraints for social change (for example, cuts to services and benefits), create additional barriers to the implementation of the CRPD and therefore to a human rights-based approach (Johnson, 2013).

Community based rehabilitation (CBR)

CBR is currently implemented in over 90 countries. It has evolved from using an individual model of disability to a human rights-based approach in the provision of rehabilitation services. Since 1978, and following the

International Conference on Primary Health Care, the WHO started to develop CBR programmes in order to provide access to rehabilitation to disabled people in developing countries. CBR is defined as 'a strategy within general community development for the rehabilitation, poverty reduction, equalization of opportunities and social inclusion of all people with disabilities' (WHO, 2010, p. 24).

The CBR matrix was developed in 2004 to provide a common framework of understanding for CBR programmes. The matrix consists of five components: health, education, livelihood, social and empowerment (see Figure 2.2). Programmes in particular countries or districts can select the components that best suit their needs, priorities and resources. Furthermore, CBR programmes need to develop collaborations with other sectors not addressed by the programme to ensure that disabled people have access to them and can fully participate in them. Underlying this multi-component framework is an understanding of disability as a multi-dimensional condition which needs to be addressed on multiple fronts. In 2010, the International Labour Organization (ILO), United Nations Educational, Scientific and Cultural Organization (UNESCO) and WHO published the CBR Guidelines which will remain valid until 2020, with the aim to provide direction, a common understanding and an approach to CBR. The CBR Guidelines used the CBR matrix as the framework for their development. The Guidelines are proposed as a practical strategy for implementing the CRPD and supporting community-based inclusive development.

In their review of CBR, Barnes and Mercer (2010) highlight the changes it has undertaken from its beginnings which focused on medical rehabilitation and short-term approaches, towards more community development and

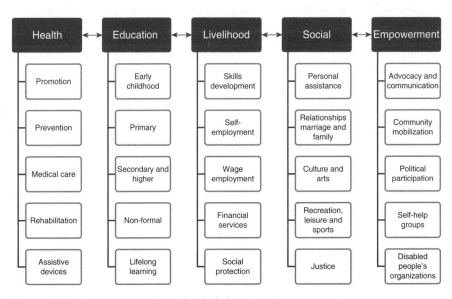

Figure 2.2.   Community-based rehabilitation (CBR) matrix

promotion of equal rights. They point at some unresolved issues in relation to whether CBR is cheaper than other options and whether disabled people should have separate programmes or be included in the overall CBR process. Further information on CBR is provided in Chapters 10 (inclusive health), 12 (livelihoods) and 16 (professional training).

Implementation of disability models

In this section, we present two examples of how disability models are implemented in practice as illustrations of the current realities globally. One pertains to a high-income country, the United States (see Box 2.2), and one to a middle-income country, Ecuador (see Box 2.3). Despite the differences and sometimes-irreconcilable tensions between models, the next two examples illustrate how various models often operate simultaneously in practice.

Box 2.2.   Implementation of disability models: United States

Disability services in third-level or university education in the US operate from an individual model perspective, whereas their overall mission claims the position of equality and the human rights-based approach (HRBA) (Guzmán and Balcázar, 2010). For example, the registration of students in disability services is often dependent on the provision of medical proof of disability (individual model of disability). Furthermore, the provision of access accommodations (such as a note taker, a sign language interpreter) is generally executed on an individual basis, singling out disabled students rather than using universal design (design for all, as in lectures that are regularly signed) to cater for students with different needs (bio-psycho-social model). Still, the overall aim of disability services is for the provision of supports to modify environmental gaps (HRBA/social model). This example shows how a single service simultaneously operates using different conceptualizations of disability.

Box 2.3.   Implementation of disability models: Ecuador

Ecuador is the only Latin American country with constitutional provisions for the political participation of disabled people, which on the one hand reveals the political invisibility of disabled people in the rest of the region and on the other the progressive stance of the country (Stang Alva, 2011). In total, the Constitution of Ecuador includes 21 articles referring to vulnerable groups of which disabled people is one. This shows how Ecuador is very committed to ensuring the equality of its disabled citizens and therefore demonstrates its alignment with the HRBA. At the same time, the Government of Ecuador has conducted a medical assessment with doctors and specialists of 294,166 people with physical, mental, intellectual or sensorial disability in Ecuador (individual model of disability). The assessment allowed the government to provide disabled people with 77,000 technical aids, coverage for medical expenses and medicines (wheelchairs, evacuation chairs, walking canes and so on) (bio-psycho-social model of disability). The disability assessment revealed that some people with

(continued)

Box 2.3.   Continued

disabilities lived in inhumane conditions, left on their own for long periods of time while their family members were away working, due to other socio-economic reasons (social model of disability) (Government of Ecuador, 2011). This example illustrates how different models are used to inform the same national disability plan.

The examples provided in Boxes 2.2 and 2.3 suggest that firstly, different disability models co-exist and are concurrently implemented; secondly, that a single disability model may not be sufficient to conceptualize and address all needs of disabled individuals; and thirdly, that implementation of disability models may result in paradigms that are less clear-cut in practice (see Table 2.1). Models arise in a particular context, and that context helps shape their application. This is even more relevant when models are applied to other contexts different from the one in which they arose.

Implementing the CRPD: Cultural considerations

According to Stein (2007), a disability human rights paradigm aims at 'recognizing all individuals' potential, and at ensuring that they receive the means through which to develop latent talent' (p. 31). However, homogeneity should not be assumed across cultures, disability groups or individuals within disability groups. Working from a human rights approach, it is important that the language of universal human rights is open to dialogue with the local culture(s) in what De Sousa Santos (2002) identifies as multiculturalism. He states that the concept of universal human rights has been developed within Western culture. Through the work of international cooperation and development, it is likely that such a deep-rooted ideal as universal human rights is imposed on non-Western cultures from a top-down approach as a 'globalised localism' (De Sousa Santos, 2002). This is when an idea that has been developed in Western culture (such as universal human rights) is made global by being available to all cultures in the world, without being adapted to the context of each specific 'recipient' culture. A globalized localism can be avoided when dialogue about human dignity (the goal of human rights) involves both approaches to human rights and various cultural understandings of human dignity (see for example Chapter 9 on education and Chapter 13 on independent living).

De Sousa Santos gives the example that in religious traditions such as Hinduism and Islam, other aspects, beyond what are considered individual human rights, are important for human dignity, for example the connection to the cosmos, to others and to nature – matters that are not necessarily covered in different international human rights instruments. *Ubuntu*, which means belonging to a bigger whole, provides one of such worldviews in the southern African region (see Chapters 9 and 12). Ingstad and Reynolds Whyte (2007) state that

[s]eeing disability in context implies understanding disability not (as it once did) in one particular isolated cultural setting, but in contexts in which

modern ideas about rights for persons with a disability co-exist with possibilities, constraints, and beliefs imposed by the local, physical, social, economic, and cultural setting. (p. 250)

Ingstad and Reynolds Whyte (2007) alert us that full participation and
equality for all people are far from being achieved, given the contextual
circumstances of poverty, armed conflict and underdevelopment, particularly in rural areas. The authors recommend that it is not only important to
consider what goals are attainable, but which are desirable, in whose eyes,
and in accordance with what ideology. It is critical therefore that professionals operating within a human rights framework engage in a dialogue with
disabled people about their personal experience and goals, including what
is important in achieving human dignity and *if* and *how* a human rights
approach can help in achieving it.

Conclusions

Disability is an evolving concept explained through a variety of models
in different parts of the world. Although there is a global trend towards
the adoption of social and human rights-based approaches, individual and
tragedy models still dominate in many societies and communities where
programmes and services for disabled people are developing. Furthermore,
the application of models in policy reform, practice, and service provision
results in further variations of these models. The CRPD plays a critical
role in raising awareness about the rights of disabled persons and promoting the agenda of ensuring disabled people have full access to mainstream
services as well as specialist provision. However, the sociocultural contexts
in which models are put into practice are of critical importance and need
to be considered by professionals when intervening, to avoid a top-down
approach to the implementation of their services and preconceived ideas
about disability.

Although much has been achieved in our understanding of disability as a
global issue and how models are used in practice, unresolved matters remain
for the future, such as tensions between global models and local practices
and the effective enforcement of human rights for disabled people regardless
of their country of origin. Following up on the implementation of the CRPD
in the 147[2] countries where it has been ratified will provide further additional
insights to help advance our understanding of what it means to be disabled
and of responses that societies make to disability.

------

[2] The Convention was open for signature on 30 March 2007, and since then it has been ratified by
147 countries as of 29 July 2014. The Optional Protocol has been ratified by 92. Accessed 29 July
2014 from http://www.un.org/disabilities/.

Summary of key points

- Disability is a global phenomenon, and different definitions of disability exist across and within countries; however, there is no unified definition of disability.
- There is a variety of existing models internationally. A basic classification of models separates them into (1) the individual model; (2) the social model (and those that adopt similar positions such as minority group and Nordic models) and the affirmative model; and (3) hybrid models such as the bio-psycho-social model, the cultural model, defectology and the Colombian conceptual model of disability and social inclusion. Although tensions and radical differences between models exist, they are simultaneously applied in practice.
- Disability models have been developed in Anglo-centred countries and contexts, and they tend to ignore non-Anglo cultural dimensions of difference.
- Two global approaches to disability dominate the development of policies, legislation, and programmes, the human rights-based approach (HRBA) and community-based rehabilitation (CBR). Both approaches are currently used to implement the CRPD.
- In a globalized world, professionals need to consider the role of context and the inclusion of disabled people in articulating their work, to avoid imposing a human rights discourse into local understandings of disability and human dignity.

STUDY QUESTIONS

1. Find out and compare disability definitions used in your country's national legislation, social policy and clinical settings. What models of disability can you identify?

2. Find out stories about disability told by disabled people in your country. What models of disability can you identify in the stories? Can you identify more than one model in the stories? Which ones? What terminology is used?

3. Find out whether your country has signed and ratified the CRPD. If it has ratified it, at what stage of implementation is your country? What are the cultural barriers and facilitators to implementing the CRPD? If it has not ratified it, what, if any, positions are put forward against and in favour of the adoption of the CRPD?

Further reading and resources

J. Bickenbach, S. Chatterji, E.M. Badley and T.B. Üstün. (1999). 'Models of disablement, universalism and the international classification of impairments, disabilities and handicaps', *Social Science and Medicine*, 48(9), 1173–1187.

L. Bøttcher and J. Dammeyer. (2012). 'Disability as a dialectical concept: Building on Vygotsky's defectology', *European Journal of Special Needs Education*, 27(4), 433–446.

C.L. Cuervo Echeverri, L. Pérez Acevedo and A. Trujillo Rojas. (2008). Modelo conceptual colombiano de discapacidad e inclusión social. Universidad Nacional de Colombia (Bogotá). ISBN: 9789587191035.

L. Davis. (2013). *The End of Normal: Identity in a Biocultural Era* (Ann Arbor: The University of Michigan Press).

P.J. Devlieger. (2005). 'Generating a cultural model of disability', paper presented at the 19th Congress of the European Federation of Associations of Teachers of the Deaf (FEAPDA).

D. Goodley, B. Hughes and L. Davis, (Eds.). (2012). *Disability and Social Theory: New Developments and Directions* (London: Palgrave Macmillan).

International Disability Alliance (IDA). IDA's Human Rights Publication Series http://www.internationaldisabilityalliance.org/en/idas-human-rights-publication-series.

A. Lawson. (2006). *The EU Rights based Approach to Disability: Some Strategies for Shaping an Inclusive Society* (Cornell University ILR School, Gladnet Collections), accessed 31 January 2014 from http://digitalcommons.ilr.cornell.edu (home page).

M. Oliver. (1990). *The Politics of Disablement* (New York: St. Martin's Press).

M. Schulze. (2010). *Understanding the UN Convention on the Rights of Persons with Disabilities* (New York: Handicap International).

J. Swain and S. French. (2008). 'Affirming identity'. In J. Swain and S. French, (Eds.), *Disability on Equal Terms* (London: Sage).

J. Tøsseboro. (2004). 'Understanding disability: Introduction to the special issue of SJDR', *Scandinavian Journal of Disability Research, Special Issue: Understanding Disability*, 6(1), 3–7. DOI: 10.1080/15017410409512635.

WHO. (2010). *Community-Based Rehabilitation Guidelines*, http://www.who.int/disabilities/cbr/guidelines/en/.

WHO and World Bank. (2011). Understanding disability. In *The World Report on Disability*, pp. 3–17.

Acknowledgements

Seamus Hegarty, Jessica Kramer and Laura Arnau reviewed earlier drafts of this chapter and provided constructive feedback.

The UN Convention on the Rights of Persons with Disabilities: Implementing a Paradigm Shift

3

Peter Mittler

> *The purpose of the present Convention is to promote, protect and ensure the full and equal enjoyment of all human rights and fundamental freedoms by all persons with disabilities, and to promote respect for their inherent dignity.*

**UN Convention on the Rights of Persons with Disabilities
Article 1: Purpose**

Introduction

> *Central to this Convention is the paradigm shift in the treatment of persons with disabilities from being objects of the law to being subjects of the law with the same rights as everybody else.*

(MacKay, 2014, Chair of CRPD Drafting Committee, 2005–2006)

> *The Convention on the Rights of Persons with Disabilities is only as good as its implementation. And even though countries are competing with each other in a race to ratification, its implementation thus far is abysmally poor.*

(Javed Abidi, Chairperson, Disabled Peoples' International, 2014)

The United Nations Convention on the Rights of Persons with Disabilities (CRPD) (United Nations, 2006) provides a unique opportunity to improve the quality of life of a billion people. In parallel with the development of the United Nations post-2015 sustainable development goals (SDGs), it calls for fundamental reappraisals of policy and practice by governments, members of professional and voluntary organizations, service planners and providers, the research community and, in the last analysis, by society as a whole.

By ratifying the CRPD, most of the United Nation's member states have entered into a commitment in international law to translate its principles into both policy and practice. The nature and quality of implementation now depend on the strength of the demand for a matching government response from a united national disability movement, strongly supported by the academic and professional community and by civil society. This is essential in the context of a global economic crisis which has already exacerbated the exclusion of people with disabilities in many countries and now constitutes a major threat in all.

Taking full advantage of these opportunities requires a major paradigm shift not only in thought but in actions directed to the translation of aspiration to achievement. Fundamental to this paradigm shift is the full and equal involvement of persons with disabilities as principal stakeholders and change agents at every stage of the process, in partnership with relevant government representatives, service providers and professionals.

Amongst the many differences between the CRPD and earlier UN conventions is that it is the first to include representatives of potential beneficiaries as equal partners with governments in negotiating each of its principles and articles. It is also a landmark in the history of the disability movement because international disabled people's organisations (DPOs) representing different constituencies have succeeded in working together as a coalition, as well as in partnership with politicians and officials, despite fundamental differences in policies and priorities (see Chapter 4 on advocacy and lobbying). Their successful participation is clearly reflected in the application of the social model of disability (see Chapter 2) to identify obstacles to the expression of human rights and in the formulation of specific recommendations on how these can be overcome. Illuminating perspectives on the difficulties encountered in achieving this positive outcome have recently been brought together in a groundbreaking volume by Sabatello and Schulze (2014).

The high level of participation of people with intellectual disability who previously had been ignored by the wider disability movement is a notable feature of the CRPD. They were successfully represented in the CRPD drafting committee by Inclusion International, whose negotiation team always included self-advocates who continue to be active in its global campaign for implementation (MacQuarrie and Laurin-Bowie, 2014). Inclusion International, together with Down Syndrome International, was also a founder member of the International Disability Alliance (2010), which has since worked in partnership with UN agencies to promote CRPD implementation, and was one of the first NGOs to provide regular newsletters and training courses for its 200 national member societies to this end (Inclusion International, 2008, 2014) (www.inclusion-international.org; www.inclusion-europe.org).

Global opportunities: The Convention on the Rights of Persons with Disabilities

Ratification of the CRPD commits the member state in international law to a number of fundamental general principles which permeate articles on specific domains such as right to life, equal recognition before the law, education,

---

Box 3.1. General Principles in CRPD

- Respect for inherent dignity; individual autonomy, including the freedom to make one's own choices; and independence of persons (Art. 3a)
- Equality and non-discrimination (Art. 5)
- Full and active participation and inclusion in society (Art. 3c)
- Respect for differences and acceptance of persons with disabilities as part of humanity (Art. 3d)
- Accessibility (Art. 9)
- Equality between men and women (Art. 6)
- Respect for the evolving capacities of children with disabilities and the right to preserve their identities (Art. 7)

---

health, employment, independent living, participation in political and public life, culture, recreation, leisure and sport (see Box 3.1).

General obligations

Even the minority of governments that have so far only signed the CRPD (e.g. the United States) have thereby made a commitment to respect the following general obligations

- Modification or repeal of laws, customs and practices that discriminate directly or indirectly against people with disabilities
- Inclusion of disability in all relevant policies ('mainstreaming')
- Refraining from any practice inconsistent with the CRPD
- Consulting with people with disabilities and their organizations in implementing the CRPD
- Making 'reasonable accommodations' to all relevant aspects of the environment so as to enable people with disabilities to exercise their rights (Art. 2)

The full text of the CRPD and Optional Protocol, as well as regular updates and newsletters, is available on the UN Enable and International Disability Alliance websites (www.un.org/disabilities; www.internationaldisabilityalliance .org).

Reporting to the UN human rights bodies

Although the CRPD is not legally enforceable in an international court, the UN Office of the High Commission on Human Rights (OHCHR) (2012b) constitutes a powerful means of holding governments accountable to the international community and providing a springboard for national advocacy (www.ohchr.org).

An essential first step required by CRPD Article 33 is the establishment of a high-level focal point within government, of which DPOs must be full and equal members from the outset, preferably in the office of the head of state or prime minister, with complementary focal points in individual ministries. Its remit is to develop a national implementation programme for the CRPD, with clearly-defined targets and timelines for implementation, as well as responsibility for preparing data-based progress reports to the OHCHR CRPD Committee.

In recognition of the reality of each country having a different starting point for implementation, the CRPD requires ratifying governments to provide concrete evidence of 'progressive realisation' of a national plan of action over a given period of time. Ground rules for the submission of reports by governments make it clear that government implementation plans must specify action under each article, identify responsible actors and be linked to measurable objectives within a stated time frame (OHCHR, 2009).

An important advocacy tool is provided by the Optional Protocol to the CRPD, which enables individuals who complain of infringement of their rights to make direct representations to the CRPD Committee. Because it requires separate ratification, it follows that a high priority for DPOs is to ensure that the 65 governments that have so far failed to ratify the Optional Protocol as well as the Convention should be put under pressure to do so.

The work of the CRPD committee

Following ratification, the government is required to submit a detailed progress report to the CRPD Committee of the OHCHR after two years and then every four years on actions taken to implement the general principles and specific articles of the Convention (www.ohchr.org/disabilities). The Committee consists of 18 elected members, of whom 17 are currently persons with disabilities. Because of delays caused by the backlog of reports, the number of week-long meetings has now been increased from three to five per year, and more preparation time has been made available to its members.

DPOs and other non-governmental organisations have the right to submit independent reports to the Committee. Guidance documents and a toolkit for NGOs provide detailed guidance on the preparation of evidence, as well as suggestions for follow-up actions at national level (OHCHR, 2010, 2012). Useful practical guides to monitoring and advocacy have also been published by the International Disability Alliance (2010), Inclusion International (2008), Disability Rights Promotion International (2011) and Leonard Cheshire International (2013).

After making a detailed study of relevant information from all available sources, a committee member designated as country rapporteur draws up a 'list of issues' which require further explanation or information from the government. The full Committee then engages in 'constructive dialogue' with the government delegation and later publishes its Concluding Observations and Recommendations on the OHCHR website and in a press release.

Examination of the Committee's published conclusions and recommendations on the 13 countries where its work has been completed reveals that the most effective submissions have come from a coalition of DPOs, but with professional support from specialists where appropriate. Alternative reports from Australia, Austria, Hong Kong, Hungary and Spain provide particularly instructive models both of detailed preparation and effective advocacy. For example, in response to the Austrian government's somewhat complacent report on inclusive education, the Committee expressed its concern that 'progress towards inclusive education in Austria is stagnant ... the number of children in special schools is increasing and ... insufficient efforts are being made to support inclusive education of children with disabilities' (www.ohchr.org/disabilities). Independent reports have highlighted problems in other federal administrations such as Australia and Germany where policy and practice may differ from state to state.

A detailed study by Brehmer-Rinderer, Zigrovic, Naue and Weber (2013) focuses on the response of the CRPD Committee to government and NGO reports from Spain and Hungary in respect of Article 1 (definition and scope) and Articles 25 (health) and 26 (rehabilitation). The Committee raised concerns about the exclusion of people with psychosocial and age-related impairments from CRPD implementation in Hungary, and Spain is criticized for not providing data on access to generic medical services by persons with intellectual disabilities. The study also provides background information about the reports submitted by other European governments and NGOs which are awaiting scrutiny.

It is important for national DPOs to ensure that maximum publicity is given to the Committee's conclusions in the media and that they are debated in Parliament. The OHCHR toolkit suggests that DPOs need to be ready to counter government objections to the CRPD committee's concluding observations as out of date and overtaken by later implementation measures (OHCHR, 2012b). Advantage can be taken of the publication of the committee's report to ask to meet ministers and parliamentarians in order to discuss each recommendation. If this is refused, they are encouraged to organize a public meeting or launch an Internet or social media campaign to enlist public support.

In addition to its main task of monitoring implementation, the CRPD Committee has also published exemplary thematic studies on employment, equality before the law, women with disabilities, legal capacity and access to justice, participation in political life and international cooperation. Disability is now also included in the remit of all other OHCHR human rights committees as well as in its regular Universal Periodic Reviews of all human rights at national level. In addition, the United Nations hosts an annual conference for governments that have ratified the Convention. All these events provide opportunities for civil society to make representations and to submit and publicize independent reports. A recent guide to the work of the OHCHR for civil society includes many examples drawn from its work on the CRPD (OHCHR, 2012a).

System-wide United Nations resources

The adoption of the Convention has led to a system-wide recognition of the rights of people with disabilities across all UN agencies, as well as by key international development agencies such as the World Bank (Mittler, 2012).

The United Nations Development Group (2011), which coordinates the work of 25 UN agencies, has issued detailed guidelines to ensure that disabled people are explicitly included in the whole range of UN-sponsored aid and development programmes, as well as in humanitarian disasters, civil conflicts and as refugees. WHO's comprehensive *World Report on Disability* (WHO and World Bank, 2011) and UNICEF's (2013) *State of the World's Children: Children with Disabilities* provide strong foundations for national CRPD implementation by summarizing current knowledge and highlighting examples of good practice, particularly in low- and middle-income countries. The social model of disability is also reflected in the *International Classification of Functioning, Disability and Health* (WHO, 2001), which was developed in association with DPOs and is now being incorporated into the 11th revision of the *International Classification of Diseases*.

Despite the general perception that all UN agencies are centralized in New York, Geneva and Vienna, some of its most effective work is taking place at regional level in its Economic and Social Commissions for Africa (Addis Ababa), Asia and Pacific (Bangkok), Europe (Geneva), Latin America and Caribbean (Santiago) and Western Asia (Beirut). For example, the Asia Pacific region, which has recently launched its third Decade of Disabled Persons, played a major part in the drafting of the Convention and is providing detailed information on its implementation (Economic and Social Commission for Asia and the Pacific [ESCAP], 2010). The Latin America and Caribbean region (Economic Commission for Latin America and the Caribbean [ECLAC], 2011; ECLAC and UNICEF, 2013) is halfway through its Programme of Action for a Decade of the Americas for Persons with Disabilities. New initiatives are also under way under the auspices of the Economic Commissions for Africa (Chataika, McKenzie, Swart and Lyner-Cleophas, 2012) and Western Asia (Economic and Social Commission for Western Asia [ESCWA], 2012).

The 46 states constituting Europe already have their own Human Rights Convention and Court. The European Union is the only regional body to have ratified the CRPD and is now working to ensure that disability is mainstreamed into EU legislation and reflected in the policies of its 28 member states. It has funded the Academic Network of Experts in Disability (ANED) to construct a comprehensive database of detailed information on CRPD implementation for each European country (http://www.disability-europe.net) and also supported DPOs, including Inclusion Europe (2010), who have provided training workshops as well as information and monitoring resources in frequent newsletters (www.inclusion-europe.org).

The post-2015 sustainable development goals

The Convention has now to be set in the wider context of the post-2015 SDGs which have generated worldwide consultations resulting in the recognition of disability as a cross-cutting issue, alongside gender, age and minority status. This is reflected in a unanimous UN General Assembly resolution on the need for urgent action

to ensure that all development policies, including those regarding poverty eradication, social inclusion, full and productive employment and decent work and access to basic social services, and their decision making processes take into account the needs of and benefit all persons with disabilities, including women, children, youth, indigenous peoples and older persons who can be subject to violence and multiple or aggravated forms of discrimination.
(United Nations Secretary General (2013).
General Assembly Resolution A/68/L.1)

Although the needs of people with disabilities were not mentioned in the first round of millennium development goals (MDGs) or in the indicators for assessing their progress, a summary of achievements and failures as summarized by a multi-agency UN report (United Nations, 2012) provides starting points for the realization of more inclusive goals in the next 15 years.

Achievements
- The proportion of people living in extreme poverty has been halved at the global level.
- Over 2 billion people gained access to improved sources of drinking water.
- Remarkable gains have been made in the fight against malaria and tuberculosis.
- The hunger target is within reach.

Failures
- There is less aid money overall, with the poorest countries most adversely affected.
- Environmental sustainability is under severe threat.
- Access to antiretroviral therapy and knowledge about HIV prevention must expand.
- Most maternal deaths are preventable, but progress in this area is falling short.
- Fifty-seven million children are still denied primary education, one-third of whom are children with disabilities (adapted from United Nations, 2012).

All these goals are profoundly relevant to the world's 1 billion persons with disabilities who have been characterized as 'the poorest of the poor' in all continents, but especially in low- and middle-income countries. It follows that their inclusion in all future poverty-related goals is fundamental to the realization of their basic rights as citizens (see Chapter 6 for a discussion on poverty and social exclusion).

Empowerment by Internet

In three short years, the Convention became a land-mark several times over. It is the first human rights treaty to be adopted in the twenty-first century; the most rapidly negotiated human rights treaty in the history of international law; and the first to emerge from lobbying conducted entirely in the Internet.

(UN Secretary General, address to the General Assembly after the unanimous adoption of the CRPD, December 2006)

The potential of the Internet to achieve change at global level has been powerfully demonstrated in the testimonies of the individuals representing a wide diversity of disability organizations who were part of that lobby (Sabatello and Schulze, 2014). The need to negotiate with a single, united voice could not have been met without constant electronic sharing of draft texts between and within NGOs both before and during meetings of the UN CRPD drafting committee. The Internet and social media were also used to lobby individual members of government delegations during the course of the negotiations, often with positive outcomes.

Accurate information is the essential foundation for informed advocacy in the public domain. Rapid advances in information and communication technology increasingly empower ordinary citizens to make their voices heard and to join with others in speaking out against discrimination and oppression by society and its institutions (see Chapter 11 on assistive technology). In most countries, anyone with access to the Internet can now sign a petition to the head of state to call for a change of policy or practice, and increasingly to any organization to request information. In Italy, a new political party entirely created and run through the Internet obtained a quarter of the votes in the last national elections, and its 164 Deputies and Senators now constitute the main opposition to the coalition government (http://en.wikipedia.org/wiki/Five_Star_Movement). Mass demonstrations have been mobilized through the Internet to protest against injustices. Major cities have been brought to a halt by public protests about the price of bread and public transport and authoritarian as well as democratic governments have been brought down by sheer force of public opinion.

A recent global example of the power of the Internet is provided by a petition from the 27 million worldwide membership of Avaaz (www.avaaz.org) following the attempted assassination of Malala Yousafzai, calling for education for the world's 57 million out-of-school children, and presented to the president of Pakistan by Gordon Brown as UN Global Education Envoy. The president responded by signing an order to fund school places for 3 million of Pakistan's 5.5 million out-of-school children. The Internet now provides the means to hold his government to account for implementing this policy.

These developments have profound implications for the disability movement. A vigilant national or regional disability lobby might have used the Pakistan petition to press for the inclusion of a million children with disabilities. An opportunity was also missed when a similar commitment was made by Nigeria, which has more than 10 million of the world's 57 million out-of-school children.

Together with the social media and the growing availability of mobile phones, the Internet could provide a powerful tool in concerted national campaigns for the full implementation of the CRPD and the post-2015 goals.

Campaigns on the rights of persons with disabilities now need to be scaled up in all countries, and involve a wider constituency, including the general public, service providers and volunteers, with the aim of bringing about the radical changes made possible by the Convention. Furthermore, the post-2015 commitment to reduction of inequalities provides opportunities for DPOs to make common cause with other groups marginalized by poverty and discrimination.

Most national disability NGOs have neither the time nor the human resources to study the wealth of relevant information now available on the Internet. Nevertheless, there is scope for links with universities and for the use of student volunteers to keep a watching brief on relevant websites, as well as articles in professional and research journals in order to highlight information which could be used for monitoring and advocacy.

Obstacles to implementation

Lack of political will and commitment by national governments to develop a time-tabled roadmap for CRPD implementation article by article

Criticisms of the nature and quality of government implementation as 'abysmally poor', made by the chairperson of Disabled Persons International at the quotation at the start of this chapter are reflected in concerns expressed by the OHCHR CRPD Committee in their last biennial report to the UN General Assembly (OHCHR, 2012b). These include

- limited opportunities given by governments to DPOs to participate in the development of national action plans;
- implementation plans lacking targets and timelines;
- the persistence of charity, welfare and medical perspectives at the expense of the social model of disability;
- a disproportionate emphasis on earlier achievements and future intentions;
- commitment to segregated provision or two-tiered systems described as inclusive in some high-income countries; and
- particular shortcomings in the implementation of articles on education, employment, independent living and equality before the law.

Some countries committed to ratification have encountered strong obstacles presented by long-established practices reflected in national legislation fundamentally inconsistent with specific CRPD articles. A recent report from Ireland (Doyle and Flynn, 2013) illustrates the difficulties posed by Article 12 on legal capacity, which requires supported decision-making in place of long-established ward of court procedures which remove all decision-making rights from many individuals with intellectual disabilities (Inclusion International, 2014).

Similarly, Article 24 on inclusive education presents a challenge to countries with a strong tradition of segregated education (see Chapter 9). Although Article 24 does not call for the closure of special schools, the United Kingdom is the only government to have entered a formal reservation, because it sees 'special schools as part of the spectrum of inclusive education', consistent with the present government's commitment to 'remove the bias towards inclusion'. This contrasts with Germany, which ratified the CRPD despite having a much higher proportion of children with disabilities in special schools than the United Kingdom but, like the United Kingdom, would be able to provide evidence of 'progressive realisation' towards inclusive practice, at least in some parts of the country.

The fact that a government has put relevant legislation in place does not necessarily mean that people with disabilities will benefit. The problem can be acute in federal states where responsibility for key services such as health, social care and education is devolved to provincial or state level. Public community services for people with disabilities need to be planned and delivered by service agencies with clearly defined responsibilities and channels of communication, which have proved difficult to create and sustain. Moreover, many services are now delivered by the private sector, which tends to be resistant to monitoring and regulation by statutory quality assurance agencies.

Constraints on national disabled people's organizations

The International Disability Alliance has provided strong leadership at the global and regional level in negotiating the CRPD and in continuing advocacy and information. Although some national DPOs have formed strong coalitions in preparing independent reports to the OHCHR CRPD Committee, it is not yet clear whether other national disability movements will be in a position to provide the level of leadership and resources envisaged by the Convention.

An encouraging example of exemplary support of DPOs by governments is provided by the Japanese Disability Forum, which persuaded the government to delay ratification until it had completed a radical programme of harmonization of existing legislation with the CRPD. DPOs have chaired the prime minister's Committee for Policy Reform, made up half its membership and also became paid staff members of the Secretariat responsible for policy development, which achieved many of these changes in a very short time (Osamu, 2013). Commitment to the prior harmonization of legislation has also been made by Finland, Netherlands and Ireland.

By way of contrast, the following extract from a recent paper by one of the founders of the UK disabled peoples' movement could well be relevant in other countries.

> The disabled peoples' movement that was once united around the barriers we had in common now faces deep divisions and has all but disappeared, leaving disabled people at the mercy of an ideologically driven government with no-one to defend us except the big charities who are driven by self-interest. As a consequence of this, most of the political campaigning that has taken place in defence of our benefits and services have forced disabled people back into the role of tragic victims of our impairments and has

involved others undertaking special pleading on our behalf. In fact it has taken us back more than 30 years to the time before the social model came into existence.

(Oliver, 2013)

Oliver's paper makes no mention of the rights conferred by the CRPD. His pessimism is confirmed by the absence so far of any evidence of a unified report to the OHCHR from UK DPOs, as well as by the lack of reference on the websites of the main disability NGOs to the existence or the potential of the CRPD to achieve change. The Equalities and Human Rights Commission, which has a statutory remit to promote and monitor all human rights and published an excellent CRPD toolkit (EHRC, 2010), has recently launched a national consultation in preparation for submitting an alternative report with maximum participation by people with disabilities.

The United Nations has strongly encouraged the development of national human rights institutions (NHRIs) to promote and protect a range of human rights, including those of persons with disabilities. These are intended to operate under the widely accepted 'Paris Principles', which include independence from government, the power to monitor and publicize human rights violations and to submit independent reports to the OHCHR. Regional NHRIs in Asia Pacific and Europe have been powerful sources of disability advocacy (Byrnes, 2014).

Lack of awareness and research

Lack of awareness of the potential of the CRPD and post-2015 goals on the part of organizations and individuals resulting in 'business as usual' policy and practice has affected most governments and major sectors of the disability movement whose participation lies at the heart of the CRPD.

Of immediate concern in the present context is the near-invisibility of these developments not only in the media and among the public but also in the professional and academic literature (see Chapter 16 on professional training). In addition to the book on the negotiation of the CRPD by participants from DPOs (Sabatello and Schulze, 2014) and the first analyses of the results of OHCHR monitoring for two countries (Brehmer-Rinderer et al., 2013), a search of all issues of 13 English-language academic journals concerned with disability since 2008 resulted in some 20 articles focusing on aspects of the CRPD, only a few of which have collected or analysed data.

These can be grouped as follows:

- core concepts: Stainton and Claire (2012); Fyson and Crombie (2013); Shogren and Turnbull (2014); Groce (2014).
- awareness and implementation: Harpur (2012); Mittler (2012).
- regional and country reports: Africa (Chataika, McKenzie, Swart and Lyner-Cleophas, 2012); Asia (Perlin, 2013); India (Cobley, 2013); Ireland (Quinn, 2009; Doyle and Flynn, 2013); Japan (Osamu, 2013); New Zealand (Moriarty and Dew, 2011); Egypt (Gobrial, 2012).

- assessment, monitoring and evaluation: Verdugo, Navas, Gómez and Schalock (2012); Luckasson and Schalock (2013); Aznar, González Castañón and Olate (2012); Stainton and Clare (2012); Roberts, Townsend, Morris, Rushbrooke, Greenhill, Whitehead, Matthews and Golding (2013); Brehmer-Rinderer, Zigrovic and Weber (2014); Sherlaw, Lucas, Jourdain and Monaghan (2014).
- access to CRPD by persons with intellectual disabilities and additional mental health needs: Evans, Howlett, Kremser, Simpson, Kayess and Trollor (2012).
- voting rights: Redley, Maina, Keeling and Pattni (2012).
- CRPD action research by self-advocates: Ollerton and Horsfall (2013).

Lack of data for monitoring and evaluation

Although CPRD Article 31 commits ratifying countries to data collection, there is no evidence of compliance with such data being 'disaggregated, as appropriate, and used to help assess the implementation of States Parties' obligations under the present CRPD and to identify and address the barriers faced by persons with disabilities in exercising their rights' (United Nations, 2006).

The lack of relevant and reliable data on people with disabilities in most countries now constitutes the major obstacle to monitoring the implementation of the CRPD and the post-2015 goals. People with disabilities are often not included in Household and Social Surveys which are used by all UN and international monitoring agencies, nor can they be counted without a birth certificate or are if they are excluded from school or health and social welfare provision. Not to be counted can be considered as an extreme form of discrimination.

Although several groups are collecting useful data on children and adults with disabilities in a range of countries, these studies were not originally designed for monitoring of the CRPD or post-2015 goals. Examples include the well-established work of the UN Washington Group on Disability Statistics (United Nations Economic Council, 2012) and the UNICEF-supported Multiple Indicator Cluster Surveys (Gottlieb, Maenner, Cappa and Durkin, 2009; Llewellyn, Emerson, Madden and Honey, 2012).

Of particular concern is the absence of a clearly identifiable disability element in the work of groups developing comprehensive indicators for the monitoring of the SDGs between 2015 and 2030. These groups include:

- The UK Overseas Development Institute for the UN Development Programme (Melamed and Sammans, 2013).
- The Centre for International Governance on Post-2015 Goals, Targets and Indicators (Carin and Bates-Earner, 2012).
- The UNESCO World Inequalities Data Base on Education (WIDE) which does not seem to be planning to collect disability-disaggregated data on the same basis as for gender, poverty, rural or urban location and language of instruction (UNESCO Institute of Statistics and UNICEF, 2012).
- The Organisation for Economic Co-Operation and Development (OECD) proposal to extend its Programme for International Student Assessment (PISA) and other indicators for SDG monitoring (OECD, 2012, 2013).

In adopting the report of the High Level Meeting on Disability and Development, the UN General Assembly resolution gave high priority to the overriding need for

> ... the collection of internationally comparable data and statistics disaggregated by sex and age, including information on disability ... and to strengthen and support, in coordination with academic institutions and other relevant stakeholders, research to promote knowledge and understanding of disability and development ...
>
> (United Nations Secretary-General, 2013)

Although this resolution was unanimously adopted by government representatives, it is already clear from OHCHR reports that governments in all regions and at all levels of development have been unable to respond to the CRPD requirement to provide disability-disaggregated data in reporting progress in implementing the Convention.

In preparation for the 2014 CRPD conference for member states and NGOs, the United Nations is now looking for guidance on monitoring the inclusion of persons with disabilities in the post-2015 goals by asking them, 'How can a new framework best address inequalities, including specifically those faced by persons with disabilities, in relation to all relevant emerging goals, for example, relating to poverty reduction/eradication, health and education?' (www.un.org/disabilities) (United Nations, 2014a).

A paradigm shift

The CRPD has reached a critical watershed. Following ratification by most governments, action now needs to be taken at all levels, from grass roots to the United Nations, to translate policy into practice in ways that will directly benefit persons with disabilities and their families. Although persons with disabilities must by definition be at the centre in this process, responsibility for taking action rests with all sections of civil society, including the research community.

The proposition that the CRPD constitutes a paradigm shift can be considered in the light of a recent paper by Whitehouse and George (2014), which applies Kuhn's (1970) original concept of paradigm shift to major developments in the reconceptualization of Alzheimer's disease. Scientific paradigms were defined as 'universally recognized scientific achievements that provide model problems and solutions to a community of practitioners', paradigm shifts occurred 'when enough contrary evidence to the dominant way of thinking accrued to force a major qualitative shift in understanding how to approach a scientific problem' (*ibid.*, p.1).

Whitehouse and George use the term 'meta-paradigm' to refer to a conceptual model not of a scientific field, but of the relationship between that field and society. Their concept of a meta-paradigm involves 'a cultural re-examination of the role of science and technology in society, the processes of ageing of themselves, and the very nature of what it means to be a human being in community in the 21st century'. They give examples of meta-paradigm shifts which raise questions about the extent to which responsibility for change rests with professionals, politicians and ordinary citizens.

Issues relating to paradigm shifts in the reconceptualization of the social model of disability are also being actively debated among disability scholars, some of whom have themselves been actively involved in knowledge translation. Following a period of secondment to WHO as the senior editor of *The World Report on Disability*, Shakespeare (2014) aims to indicate 'how an alternative approach to disability might reconcile different factors, avoid the perils of either biological or social determinism and serve as the basis for a progressive politics'.

The CRPD itself can be said to constitute a meta-paradigm shift both because persons with disabilities are seen as the primary stakeholders and as equal partners in the development of policy and planning and because the CRPD now provides access to international law and established human rights mechanisms.

Recent research and practice on quality of life for persons with disabilities can also be considered as a reflection of a meta-paradigm shift because the most recent developments in this field have been found to be generalizable far beyond disability, to cover mathematical difficulties, emotional disturbance, mental health, sensory loss and the needs of older people (Brown and Faragher, 2014).

The time has come for all of us as individuals and as organizations to reconsider the assumptions which have guided us in our different journeys and to reflect on the intellectual and professional baggage which we have been carrying, in order to meet the challenges which face us in the immediate future and in coming decades.

In this context, David Felce has rightly reminded us that

> [s]ervice developments never bring the scale of change that advocates of reform say they will have in advance and that negative effects inevitably occur that are not foreseen or countenanced. Professional opinion, the voice of service analysts and campaign bodies championing reform, the advocates of certain approaches, the voice of service users and the opinions of families all influence direction.
>
> (Felce, 2010, p. 97–99)

On the other hand, constructs such as 'research to practice' and 'knowledge translation' may need to be rethought in the implementation of a CRPD in which persons with disabilities are the major stakeholders in determining their own futures and the nature and quality of the supports and services they require as individuals and as family members. The meta-paradigm shift reflected in the CRPD raises questions about the extent to which the role of the researcher in meeting the needs of people with intellectual disabilities might now go beyond Felce's characterization of that role as

> a questioning stance, investigating the important issues that are before us, measuring effects as comprehensively as we can and doing our best to communicate what we find out honestly to those who need to know it.
>
> (*ibid.*)

There may be scope for a more proactive stance in which the research community offers to work in a collaborative partnership with other groups who are working to make a reality of the CRPD, such as national and international DPOs (see Chapter 17). They may well welcome support from universities, national research centres and individuals with relevant knowledge and experience of persons with disabilities. In the last analysis, taking advantage of the unique opportunities now available to make a difference to the day-to-day lives of people with disabilities comes down to a choice of both personal and professional priorities and values. In this context, it seems fitting to conclude with quotations from Amartya Sen, one of the world's leading philosophers, and Gerard Quinn, a world pioneer in putting disability rights on the international map.

> If the demands of justice have to give priority to the removal of manifest injustice ... rather than concentrating on the long-distance search for the perfectly just society ... then the prevention and alleviation of disability cannot but be fairly central in the enterprise of advancing justice.
>
> (Sen, 2009, p. 259)

> The UN CRPD is a mirror to society. It makes us face up to our own values and it forces us to acknowledge the large gap that still exists between the 'myth system' of our own values ... and the 'operations system' of how these values are dishonoured in daily practice. Thus the Treaty is a force for rationality as well as a vehicle for carrying these values squarely to the heart of the disabilities field.

> As with all mirrors, we can refuse to look into them or we can look at them but ignore their reflection or we can take notice of our reflection and commit to a process of change.
>
> (Quinn, 2009)

Summary of key points

- Implementation of the UN Convention on the Rights of Persons with Disabilities, together with the new UN commitment to ensure the inclusion of people with disabilities in the post-2015 development goals, should now be considered an over-arching priority by organizations and individuals committed to improving the quality of life of persons with disabilities.
- The CRPD can be considered as a paradigm shift because it is a potential catalyst for a radical reappraisal of policy and practice affecting society as a whole and the research community in particular.
- Opportunities now available to translate principles to practice include
  o the General Principles, Obligations and specific Articles of the CRPD;
  o full access by civil society to the accountability mechanisms of the UN Human Rights Bodies;

- o system-wide recognition of disability rights across all UN agencies and particularly in planning for the post-2015 development goals; and
- o the potential of the Internet in providing access to information and the tools for advocacy.
- Obstacles to change include
  - o lack of commitment by governments to implement the CRPD article by article;
  - o constraints on national disabled people's organizations;
  - o lack of awareness of the CRPD and its potential for change by the general public and in sectors of the academic and the research community; and
  - o absence of essential data for monitoring and accountability.
- Suggestions are made for ways in which scientific and professional bodies might work in partnership with DPOs in a combined effort to make a reality of the Convention and the emerging post-2015 development goals in a new dynamic of sharing of knowledge and experience.

STUDY QUESTIONS

1. Why is a Convention on Rights specifically needed for people with disabilities?

2. Not all countries have ratified the Convention on the Rights of Persons with Disabilities. What actions can be taken to encourage national governments to ratify it?

3. How could the post-2015 sustainable development goals contribute to significant improvements in the lives of people with disabilities globally?

Further reading and resources

Peter Mittler talks about the convention at https://www.youtube.com/watch?v=7KXG3n2Xy1c.

Office of the High Commission on Human Rights. (2010). *Monitoring the Convention on the Rights of Persons with Disabilities: Guidance for human rights monitors.* Professional Training Series 17. Geneva: OHCHR. (www.ohchr.org/disabilities).

Office of the High Commission on Human Rights. (2012). *The Convention on the Rights of Persons with Disabilities Training Guide.* Professional Training Series No. 19. www.ohchr.org/Documents/Issues/Disability/OHCHR_TrainingGuideCRPDandOP.doc

M. Sabatello and M. Schulze (Eds.). (2014). *Human Rights and Disability Advocacy* (Philadelphia: University of Pennsylvania Press).

United Nations. (2012). *Realising the Future We Want for All.* Report to the Secretary General by the UN Task Team on the Post-2015 UN Development Agenda (New York: United Nations).

Acknowledgements

This chapter is largely drawn from the author's article in the *Journal of Policy and Practice in Intellectual Disabilities,* volume 12(2), 2015. Our grateful thanks to the editor, Mathew Janicki, and publisher, Wiley, for permitting it to be included in the book.

Advocacy and Lobbying: The Road Map from Charity to Human Rights

Joshua T. Malinga
Trynos Gumbo

In the development and implementation of legislation and policies to implement the present Convention, and in other decision-making processes concerning issues relating to persons with disabilities, States Parties shall closely consult with and actively involve persons with disabilities, including children with disabilities, through their representative organizations.

**UN Convention on the Rights of Persons with Disabilities
Article 4(3): General obligations**

Civil society, in particular persons with disabilities and their representative organizations, shall be involved and participate fully in the monitoring process.

**UN Convention on the Rights of Persons with Disabilities
Article 33(3): Statistics and data collection**

Introduction

For ages, people with disabilities have largely been victims of social neglect, prejudices and exclusion (Govt SA, 1997; Wiman, 1997). In recent years, disabled persons have advocated for their participation in the social and economic development of their communities and nations (Charlton, 1998; Coleridge, 1993; Finkelstein, 1980). Meaningful participation is only possible through the enjoyment of equal access to public services, education, employment and recreation – all according to disabled people's own choices and abilities. However, prejudices hinder such participation, as they are difficult to eradicate and are largely rooted in culture, religion and tradition. The emerging disability mainstreaming agenda, which aims for the inclusion of the disability dimension in all socio-economic, political and cultural activities of the general population, calls for people and organizations to effectively influence power and move resources in favour of persons with disabilities. It is here where advocacy and lobbying come into play, and this needs to be an international endeavour (DPSA, 1993).

This chapter focuses on these two related processes, advocacy and lobbying in disability issues. In the first part of the chapter, we summarize the global achievements of the disability rights movement by outlining the road map of disability human rights over a period of about six decades, from the 1950s to 2008. The second part of the chapter examines advocacy and lobbying in more detail and provides a brief analysis of these activities in connection to the CRPD. Case studies are provided of the China Federation of Disabled Persons and the advocacy of persons with intellectual disabilities. The concluding part of the chapter examines political representation of disabled persons in Africa and how they have influenced legislation in South Africa and Zimbabwe.

A long journey to disability rights legislation: 1948–2008

Shifting perceptions about people with disabilities

Throughout the history of civilization, people with disabilities have traditionally been discarded and disrespected (Bullock and Mahon, 2000). From time immemorial, disability has rarely been accepted as a natural human phenomenon, to be treated humanely. Nowadays, people with disabilities often continue to be outcasts. In some cultures, disability is commonly seen as a punishment from the gods and ancestors, or as retribution for past deeds of ancestors and parents. Disability has often been seen as a bad omen and been linked with witchcraft and evil spirits (see Chapter 5).

People with disabilities have been further segregated from their communities. The growth of institutions following the Industrial Revolution represented another form of social exclusion in Western countries, as did the founding of residential schools for children with physical and sensorial impairments in developing countries by well-intended missionaries. This effectively introduced 'separate education' globally and built a culture of difference and an inferior quality of education (see Chapter 9). The last decades, however, have seen a sea change in perceptions of disability.

The disability rights movement

The development of strong disability movements during the 1970s onwards has made possible the promotion of the human rights of people with disabilities. These emerged from the conditions of charity, discrimination and isolation that were, and still are, prevalent around the world. Learning from the successes of the earlier women's right movement, and the civil rights movement in America in the 1960s, disabled people saw an opportunity to break from the oppressive and non-participatory methods of the past.

Several international, regional, continental and national conferences of disabled people were organized to call for recognition of the challenges faced by disabled people. The agenda for promoting the human rights of disabled persons was initiated after Winnipeg 1980, where Disabled People's International (DPI), a multi-disability international organization, controlled by a majority of disabled people (51 per cent) at the board and membership levels, was conceived to fight for disabled people's rights and self-determination. The DPI manifesto asserted the basic rights of people with disabilities as citizens of the world, just like able-bodied persons, with rights to education, rehabilitation, employment, independent living and income security (Driedger, 1989).

Arguably, the influence of national disability organizations became all the stronger when international alliances were formed. In order to foster and promote unity amongst disabled people's organizations (DPOs), DPI organized disabled people around cross-disability issues that affect them on a daily basis, such as discrimination, oppression, under development and exploitation. In 1999, all international organizations of disabled people combined to form an International Disability Alliance (IDA) – a global coalition to spearhead and provide leadership during the negotiations and debates around the need for the CRPD. The IDA is a powerful voice that operates at United Nations and regional levels and is credited with helping the convention to be created in a short period. IDA is comprised of four regional and eight international member organizations. The regional organizations include the Arab Organization of Persons with Disabilities, the European Disability Forum, the Latin American Network of Non-Governmental Organizations of Persons with Disabilities and their Families (RIADIS) and the Pacific Disability Forum (PDF), and the international organizations cover all the main impairment conditions. The full membership of IDA is given at the end of the chapter. Further details of each organization can be obtained from the IDA website (http://www.internationaldisabilityalliance .org). The ensuing changes became a paradigm shift, moving the conceptualizing of disability from a charity and welfare issue to a human rights and development issue. There are individuals and groups which are not part of any alliance, sometimes purely due to the diversity of disabilities. However, it behoves the disability movement, through its networks, alliances and affiliations that have been built over the years, to provide a wide platform to ensure that people with all types of impairments fully benefit from advocacy efforts.

People with disabilities had to have rights to influence governments and decision-making processes, and DPOs had to be accorded decisive influences in regard to all decisions affecting people with disabilities (see Box 4.1). The rights movement of disabled people fought for self-representation, self-help and self-development as well as for the right to participate in every sphere of society, by rejecting all forms of segregation and refusing to accept lifetime isolation in special institutions.

The disability rights movement (DRM) spurred the promulgation of various human rights instruments in the years following its inception. In 1981,

---

Box 4.1.   Organizations of and for disabled people

There is a crucial difference between organizations *of* and organizations *for* disabled people. Organizations of disabled people are those run and controlled by disabled people themselves, and they are vehicles of self-expression, self-representation and self-development. They spearhead the liberation of disabled people, and their main objective is to campaign and fight for the rights of disabled people and for inclusive development, which would ensure that disabled people are part of every aspect of societal activities. Organizations for disabled people are run by professionals, and they are responsible mostly for the provision of services and care to disabled people. Organizations of disabled people define disability from a social model perspective in which environmental barriers limit the participation of people with disabilities in society. The medical model, on which many organisations for disabled people are based, identifies disability as an individual problem that needs to be cured.

---

the UN declared the International Year of Disabled Persons (IYDP). A major outcome at the end of that year was the World Program of Action Concerning Disabled People and the new principle of Equalisation of Opportunities to Disabled People rather than the 'cradle to the grave' rehabilitation approach. The World Program of Action was a policy document implemented during the UN Decade of Disabled People (1983 to 1992) and the Asian (1993–2002) and African (2000–2009) Decades of Disabled People. These opportunities created an environment that was exploited by disabled people to promote the promulgation of laws at national level and, with time, that of the CRPD.

The World Program of Action Concerning Disabled People was the first UN policy document to have active input from disabled people and their organizations. In this policy document, disabled people were referred to as citizens with rights, first and foremost, and then clients of social services. The document was universal in its implementation. Although pioneers of the Disability Rights Movement such as Henry Enns, Ron Chandran Dudley, Bengt Lindqvist, Joshua T. Malinga and Rachel Hurst, as well as many others, were involved in the development of these documents and initiatives (see Figure 4.1), both the IYDP and the UN Decade may not have resulted in dramatic changes in attitudes towards disabled people. They did, however, provide opportunities for disabled people to meet and exchange ideas and information, thereby unifying and solidifying the DRM. The most important outcomes at the end of the UN Decade of Disabled People were the UN Standard Rules on Equalisation of Opportunities for Disabled People and the International Day of Disabled People, to be celebrated on the 3rd of December each year. The Standard Rules did not, and do not, bind any country or anybody, but they enjoy substantial moral and political support, and have been used to formulate policies and legislation by many countries.

Figure 4.1. Pioneers of the Disability Rights Movement meeting the secretary general of the UN Boutros Boutros Ghali[1]

[1] T. Malinga, World President of DPI, meeting the Secretary General of UN Boutros Boutros Ghali (right), Henry Ennis, Executive Director of DPI (left), and Rachel Hurst, World Council Member (1995).

As soon as the DRM became effective, it adopted a two-pronged (or twin-track) approach in its advocacy and campaigning for human rights. One route was to make all human rights instruments applicable to the disabled, and the other route was to fight for a disability-specific convention. In Box 4.2, we give examples of human rights instruments that existed before and after the disability rights movement was formally constituted in 1980.

Box 4.2.   Examples of human rights instruments

- The United Nations Universal Declaration of Human Rights (1948)
- The International Convention on Civil and Political Rights (1966)
- The International Covenant on Economic, Social and Cultural Rights (1966)
- The United Nations Declaration on the Rights of Mentally Retarded Persons (1971)
- The United Nations Declaration on the Rights of Disabled Persons (1975)
- The UN Convention against Torture and other Cruel Inhuman or Degrading Treatment or Punishment (1984)
- The Convention on the Rights of the Child (1989)
- The Principles for the Protection of Persons with Mental Illness and for the Improvement of Mental Health Care (1991)
- The Standard Rules for the Equalisation of Opportunities for Persons with Disabilities (1993)

The human rights instruments in Box 4.2 included international reso-lutions, declarations, and recommendations – which were supposed to establish international standards and international customary laws. There are also over 20 or so multilateral treaties of human rights that are legally binding to countries that have ratified them; these are called conventions, covenants and treaties. Disability is now seen as a political, developmental, socio-economic and human rights issue supported by a paradigm shift from treating disability as a welfare and medical issue to a socio-economic and political issue. Through this new paradigm, people with disabilities are no longer seen as sick people who need perpetual treatment, rehabilitation and institutionalization, but as citizens with rights, first and foremost, and clients of social services last. We now turn to the two core activities of the DRM, advocacy and lobbying.

Conceptualizing advocacy and lobbying

Advocacy and lobbying have been used to help design and implement both long- and short-term intervention strategies to ensure the inclusion of disabil-ity in a range of areas, such as socio-economic development issues. Advocacy and lobbying have brought to the fore the negative impacts of attitudes, traditional beliefs, institutionalisation and segregated education, and pro-posed solutions, such as mainstreaming and inclusion, for building equality and respect for disabled people. Advocacy and lobbying interventions must be solution focused and may include national, regional or local campaigns that include disabled people from the implementation to the evaluation stages (Chalken, Seutloadi and Sadek, 2009). A review of the two concepts is made, first by providing definitions and then by comparing and contrasting them and their application.

Advocacy

Advocacy involves the practical use of knowledge for purposes of social change, largely, but not exclusively, by directing this at decision makers. It is an act of supporting an issue or idea, and the assurance that the provider or the complainant should be able to act to support that issue being advocated (Invalidnost, 2010). Advocacy also has a legal connotation and background, in which an advocate fights for one's cause in court. It involves helping peo-ple to find ways that can influence both thinking and practice. As Sharma (2001) observes, advocacy is largely about drawing attention to an issue that is important, directing decision makers to a solution, influencing decision mak-ers at various levels and mobilizing members of the community for a cause. In this regard, advocacy means standing by someone's cause, or speaking out for someone's rights. In terms of persons with disabilities, an advocate helps them to get recognition from government departments, at work, school or college, with accommodation and transport, or other services to enable them the exer-cise of their rights. Advocacy therefore means supporting a cause or a group of persons from a passionate, non-judgmental point of view.

Advocacy can take various forms.

- *Self-advocacy and empowerment* – an individual or group of persons are encouraged, trained and supported to speak up for themselves. It involves empowering persons or capacitating them, especially those previously marginalized, so that their voice is heard (GovtSA, 2002). For people with intellectual disabilities, self-advocacy needs to be carefully nurtured, as too often these individuals are used to others speaking for them, such as parents and professionals. Nonetheless, self-advocates with intellectual disabilities can be found in many countries around the world (see Box 4.3).

Box 4.3. Self-advocacy of people with intellectual disabilities in the United States

People First is the umbrella term for organizations of self-advocates, run by and for them. It started in Oregon (United States) in 1974. It has chapters in a number of countries including the United Kingdom, the United States and Belgium. The goal of People First is to provide self-advocacy platforms for people with intellectual disabilities to speak up for themselves, advocate for their rights, and become decision makers in their lives.

A chapter of People First in Chicago is hosted at El Valor, an organization providing lifelong services to people with intellectual disabilities and their families, mostly of Latino ethnic origin. This People First chapter, as many others, initially functioned as a social outlet for service users of the organization. The chapter received funding from the State to pay for two advisers: one member of staff from the organization and one volunteer external to the organization; both supported People First members (García Iriarte, Kramer, Kramer and Hammel, 2009). Over the years, the chapter shifted the emphasis from social to self-advocacy activities.

Testimony of that change is the newsletter the chapter published, where members advocated for issues such as immigration and disability pride; told their personal stories of love and grief; and gave updates on important issues to them, such as accessibility of public places. Furthermore, they spoke at disability conferences and gained a more salient voice in the organization (Kramer, Kramer, García Iriarte and Hammel, 2011). Members with intellectual disabilities gradually gained control from advisers over meetings and activities. Over one year, People First members used a basic questionnaire (Who did what?) to help identify who was in control of meeting tasks such as 'opening the meeting', 'thinking of issues to include in the agenda', or 'organising transport' (García Iriarte et al., 2009). Aggregate data gave members with intellectual disabilities an overall picture of the control they had over the meetings. This analysis prompted them to take control over some of the tasks which the advisers previously had managed and led them to an increased feeling of ownership of the chapter. Further details are provided in:

E. García Iriarte, J.C. Kramer, J.M. Kramer and J. Hammel. (2009). '"Who did what?": A participatory action research project to increase group capacity for advocacy', *Journal of Applied Research in Intellectual Disabilities*, 22(1), 10–22.

J.M. Kramer, J.C. Kramer, E. García-Iriarte and J. Hammel. (2011). 'Following through to the end: The use of inclusive strategies to analyze and interpret data in participatory action research with individuals with intellectual disabilities, *Journal of Applied Research in Intellectual Disabilities*, 24, 263–273.

- *Representative* – this is when someone stands in place of the beneficiaries. However, one has to take note of the principles and ethics of legitimacy and principles of advocacy which guide this representation. This is particularly important with people who have communication difficulties. Their representatives must be encouraged and motivated to support the person's struggle and take actions to fulfil his or her goals.
- *Mobilization* – this is another advocacy type that includes others so that they are encouraged or motivated to support what you struggle for and take actions to fulfil set goals. Mobilization means expanding the support base, and it helps to bring change through popular opinion and public awareness.

As Box 4.4 illustrates, advocates have a range of tools they can use, which as Hansen and colleagues (2005) noted, include community and public awareness of the advocacy effort, civic education and the use of media as a tool of advocacy.

Whatever form advocacy takes, the purposes are the same, foremost of which is the empowerment of people with disabilities. This is why, for example, the National Council of Disabled Persons of Zimbabwe (NCDPZ) pointed out that collective action brings self-confidence, emboldens the most disadvantaged, motivates the pessimists, stirs to action and leads to influencing the thinking and actions of targeted audiences (Mbewe and Lee, 1991).

Advocacy aims to effect social change, and this can only be effective through teamwork, coalitions and communication. In its most basic form, advocacy aims to change an existing situation that is unfavourable to a group of people by applying sufficient pressure on those who control the situation, so they will not maintain the status quo (Hansen et al., 2005). Hansen and colleagues went further, to point out that the public policy objectives of advocacy, and in this case disability advocacy, is to improve the quality of life of the less powerful and vulnerable; those who have been excluded and stigmatized.

Box 4.4. Advocacy tools

- Awareness campaigns, engaging the public through roadshows or public meetings.
- Information workshops targeting civil society organizations and even decision makers and their influences.
- Engaging the media through additional pieces, letters, or producing short stories or films highlighting issues being advocated. In this case, highlighting a disability-friendly culture characterized by mainstreaming.
- Street marches, posters and face-to-face visits.
- Using mobile messages such as T-shirts to send the message to all areas.

Lobbying

Lobbying is a form of advocacy with the intention of influencing decisions made by a government or legislators (Gauger, 2006). Kallonga (2001) defines lobbying and advocacy as processes of influencing what other people feel, think and believe, so that specific changes can happen. Whilst the terms *lobbying* and *advocacy* have sometimes been used to mean the same thing, namely influencing individuals and institutions to support a cause, it is important to give a clear distinction from a scholarly point of view that can be applied within the disability rights movement.

UNICEF (2003) defines lobbying as a deliberate and sustained effort to influence decision makers to take appropriate or certain policy measures. Hence, lobbying is largely directed at achieving specific policy/legislative outcomes, such as crafting or adopting a piece of legislation (see Box 4.5). Lobbying can be done by various people or groups, called advocacy groups or interest groups. Those who lobby therefore serve as a resource for providing information for decision makers, and lobbying can include all activities that impact on decision makers to come to a decision. It is therefore an attempt to court support, sympathy or commitment.

Parliaments are the single most important institutions to lobby, even though it may also be necessary to lobby other government departments, civil service and even non-governmental organisations (NGOs) that work with persons with disabilities, as well as various donor agencies. From this perspective, lobbying can be considered a form of advocacy specifically targeting increased political support.

Box 4.5. illustrates that in lobbying, the techniques move from a soft to a more radical approach, from providing information, sharing experiences, using newsletters, newspaper publications or memoranda, to public demonstrations with placard-carrying groups.

Box 4.5.   Lobbying activities

- Submitting position papers or memos to parliamentary committees and governmental officials, explaining political points and giving justifications for the lobbyists' position.
- Making oral presentations to parliamentary committee hearings.
- Conducting research and collecting data to back up proposals made in the lobbyists' submissions.
- Monitoring parliamentary debates, government pronouncements and commenting appropriately.
- Writing letters to specific legislators or influential persons, soliciting their support.
- Signing and delivering petitions. (DPSA, 1993)

The cycle of advocacy and lobbying

It should be noted that advocacy and lobbying are an unending process. One can take an abolitionist or radical approach, or a reformist engagement approach, though in the end, the approach should be constructive.

Advocacy works hand in hand with lobbying because in order to bring about a comprehensive change, there might be the need to persuade politicians to introduce a new piece of legislation or a new policy, followed by lobbying for its implementation and then reviewing its impact. Lobbying and advocacy therefore should take place concurrently or simultaneously, and at the same time, systematically. Figure 4.2 illustrates the unending and cyclical nature of the two processes. The need for advocacy permeates all levels and steps in development and decision making. As continuous changes occur, new challenges will arise which need attention, and advocacy is needed to raise awareness of them, alongside lobbying for actions to address the challenges.

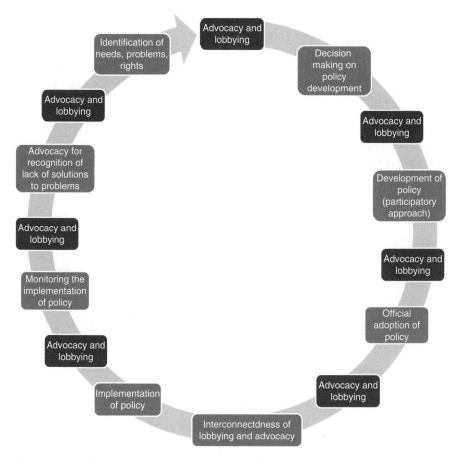

Figure 4.2.   The interconnectedness of lobbying and advocacy[2]

[2] Adapted from O'Connell (2007) and Roebeling and De Vries (2011).

The DRM successfully engaged in this process, which resulted in one of the most critical achievements for people with disabilities at the international level, the adoption of the CRPD by the United Nations.

The Convention on the Rights of Persons with Disabilities (CRPD): conditions for nurturing advocacy and empowerment

The coming into force of the CRPD was a very crucial event in the history of disability rights in the world, as the family of nations undertook to recognize and respect the rights of persons with disabilities at a higher level (see Chapter 3). With the CRPD, the DRM has now been equipped with a relevant document from which to advocate and lobby for better living conditions for persons with disabilities, and on the other hand, governments, as well as non-governmental organisations and inter-governmental bodies, have a comprehensive guide which can help them in the crafting of meaningful legislative and policy frameworks for the development and protection of persons with disabilities. It is important to note here that the CRPD does not seek to treat a person with a disability as a different human being with different rights, but rather expands on already existing international human rights instruments, elaborating them to highlight the accessibility and inclusion angle of all human rights (Schulze, 2010).

'*Nothing about us without us*' is a phrase that has been repeated in disability circles, often with few tangible results. The CRPD, however, is repeatedly inspired from that aspiration. Article 4(3) encourages the consultation and active involvement of persons with disabilities, including children with disabilities, in the formulation and implementation of laws and policies to operationalize the CRPD. Article 33 on the national implementation and monitoring of the CRPD also calls for the involvement of organizations, and representatives of persons with disabilities, to be a crucial part of the implementation and monitoring processes. It is on the basis of such provisions that disability rights activists can begin to lobby for more involvement and inclusion of persons with disabilities, not only as recipients of policies but also as policymakers. The CRPD calls on the state to 'adopt immediate and effective measures' to raise awareness at all levels (Article 8, 'Awareness-raising'). These awareness campaigns should be aimed at dealing with prejudices against persons with disabilities and discouraging harmful practices against persons with disabilities. The CRPD also makes provisions for accessibility, education and employment, areas in which State parties undertake to ensure that persons with disabilities are given equal opportunities. According to Article 31, 'Statistics and data collection', states commit to collect statistical data on disability that can be used for purposes of planning (see Chapter 17 on research). Disaggregating population data on disability, which should be made available to development partners, is crucial for policy formulation and implementation. All these are lobbying points for disabled people and their organizations to take forward. Organizations of disabled people have indeed sprung up all over the world, and disabled people are organizing locally, nationally, regionally, continentally and internationally. One of the largest, globally, is the China Disabled Persons' Federation (see Box 4.6).

Box 4.6.   China Disabled Persons' Federation

Established in March 1988, the China Disabled Persons' Federation (CDPF) is the largest disability organization globally. It is a national umbrella organization of and for persons with diverse disabilities. CDPF's mission is to promote the full participation of persons with disabilities in society on an equal basis with others, ensure that persons with disabilities share in the material and cultural achievements of society, as well as to foster humanitarianism in society.

CDPF performs three key functions: to represent the common interests and safeguard the rights of persons with disabilities; to provide comprehensive services to persons with disabilities; and, as commissioned by the Government of China, supervise the administration of disability-related affairs. CDPF is the Secretariat of China's State Council Working Committee on Disability.

In a statement to the UN Committee on the Rights of Persons with Disabilities when considering China's First Compliance Report, the Chinese delegation stated: 'China is the country with the greatest number of disabled people of about 85 million – beyond the national population of many countries. We face tremendous difficulties and challenges in this regard'. The following examples are taken from a report on China by the International Labour Organization:

- The gap of living conditions between disabled persons and others is growing bigger. Poverty remains a key obstacle in the development of disabled persons.
- People with disabilities lack opportunities to access employment, education, vocational training and social security.
- Disabled persons have lower education and skills. They are disadvantaged in the labour market. The quality of employment, including wage levels and conditions of work, needs to be improved.
- Employment services for disabled persons are just at the initial stage. The quality of these services is insufficient to assist disabled persons in finding jobs.

China was one of the first signatory countries to the CRPD. The Standing Committee of the National People's Congress of China approved the Convention in June 2008, and the Convention went into effect in China in September 2008. The Law on the Protection of Disabled Persons (enacted in 1991 and amended in 2008) is of significant importance in safeguarding the rights of people with disabilities as it addresses issues of rehabilitation, education, employment, cultural life, welfare, access, and legal liability.

The Chinese spokesperson ended her statement to the UN Committee by giving this pledge:

> The Chinese government will continue to fully implement the Convention … we are bent on making every child with disabilities educated, every adult employed, and every old person provided for, so that all persons with disabilities can live a happier life with more dignity. We strive to gradually realise the lofty goal of 'equality, participation and sharing' for persons with disabilities!

Further Information: China Disabled Persons' Federation: http://www.cdpf.org.cn/english/home.htmhttp://www.ilo.org/wcmsp5/groups/public/---asia/---ro-bangkok/---ilo-beijing/documents/publication/wcms_142315.pdf.

Case studies of political representation and disability legislation in Africa

In this concluding part of the chapter, we give examples of how disabled people in Africa have become involved in government and the influence they have had on legislation. This is a reminder that advocacy and lobbying do not happen only at a local level – important as that is – but that they must reach the highest levels within government so that the potential then exists to improve the lives of all citizens with disabilities.

Participation in government across Africa

Full participation and equality, which was the theme of the International Year of Disabled Persons (IYDP) in 1981, has been the 'war cry' of the DRM from its inception. In general terms, this means a close involvement in the economic, social, cultural and political processes that affect disabled persons' lives. In political terms, particularly, it means freedom to choose and be elected at any level of governance, from village to national levels. This is happening in some countries in Africa.

Disabled people in Zimbabwe have been campaigning for self-representation since the inception of the movement in 1975. This resulted in the first author of this chapter, and two other disabled people, becoming members of the Constitutional Review Committee in 1999. Unfortunately, this constitution was rejected by the people through a referendum. From 2009, the first author, as one of the Constitutional Review Committee chairpersons, and other disabled people were also appointed to the committee to write the constitution, up to the final draft, in 2013. In Zimbabwe, there were no special constitutional provisions for disabled people to be members of parliament until 2013, when the constitution made a provision for two senators in the upper house to be elected by an electoral college comprising equal representatives of charities and grass roots organizations of disabled people. The Disabled Persons Act made a provision for a director to be appointed in 1992, although up to now the incumbent has not been appointed.

Uganda elects a minimum of five Members of Parliament representing disabled women, people with specific impairments (sensory and physical) and albinos, in addition to over 45,000 disabled people's representatives at county and sub-county levels. At executive level, there is a Minister for Disabled People, who reports to a senior Minister for Labour and Social Welfare. The Ministry of Disabled People has no direct budget and is poorly resourced, however; most of the resources come from donors.

In South Africa, disabled people are included on party lists, and the electoral system is based on proportional representation. The umbrella organization of disabled people and its affiliates recommend a certain number of disabled people on party lists. At executive level, there is an Office on The Status of Disabled People manned by a director who reports to the Minister in the Presidency and is charged with the responsibility of mainstreaming disability into all societal structures. At cabinet level, there is a minister who combines issues of disabled people, children and women, and which is supported by provincial directors. There are also focal points in every ministry, department and office of government on the status of disabled people.

In Malawi, there is a stand-alone minister who represents disabled people at cabinet level, and in Namibia there is a special advisor within the presidency.

Experience suggests that stand-alone Ministries for Disability are like departments of the 'Bantu' in apartheid South Africa. They have no power to promulgate instructions that fall under the remit of other departments. There is general ineffectiveness with all the mechanisms that have been described above, with the exception of the South African situation, which is supported by a great deal of political will and is buttressed by strong democratic institutions like the South African Human Rights Commission, Gender Commission and others. The Continental Plan of Action for the African Decade of Persons with Disabilities (1999–2009) recommends that an office to service the interests of disabled people should be housed in the presidency and be buttressed by focal points in every other ministry, office and department, so that whoever is given the responsibility carries the clout of the presidency when seeking to influence other members of the cabinet. Disabled people in Africa have been campaigning for a ministry of the disabled ever since the early stages of the movement. The only countries that have made concrete progress in this direction are Botswana, South Africa, Namibia and Malawi.

Disability legislation in Zimbabwe and South Africa

Countries in Africa, as elsewhere, have taken different approaches to disability legislation. For example, Zimbabwe and South Africa adopted different strategic routes in formulating and implementing legislation to improve the rights of people with disabilities.

Zimbabwe. From 1975 up to the 1990s, disability activists from Zimbabwe were responsible for organizing disabled people all over the world, for example in the United Kingdom, South Africa, Botswana, and Malawi. Zimbabwe was the first country to introduce human rights legislation in relation to disability in Africa. The Disabled Persons Act 1992 (Chapter 17.1) as amended in 1996 is an omnibus act intended to cover every aspect of a disabled person's life. The formulation of this act was based on the UN Standard Rules and the principle of equalization of opportunities, but it has outlived its usefulness because of its being out of sync with international best practices and disability jurisprudence. The act is governed by the Department of Social Welfare, which is saddled with many issues of destitution, including poor people, squatters, widows, ex-prisoners, detainees, war veterans, refugees, disadvantaged and vulnerable people. The department is completely overloaded and overwhelmed, with a very small budget.

In 2004, the Zimbabwe Government made disability a constitutional issue by including disability in the bill of rights clause, stating that every citizen has the right to freedom from discrimination based on a number of social criteria, including disability. In the new 2013 constitution, there is a section on national objectives to create a disability-inclusive development policy and another section on services and rights of disabled people. Unfortunately, the language in the constitution is based on the welfarist and medical model and is non-committal because it states that all services for disabled people will depend on the availability of funds. In this new constitution, disabled people have been allocated only two seats in the Senate and nothing in the National Assembly and other tiers of government. Ironically, these two people are supposed to represent 2 million disabled people in Zimbabwe. It is important also to note that Zimbabwe ratified the CRPD as late as 23 September 2013 and also that on two occasions, in 2012 and 2013, the International Day of the Disabled was not officially celebrated. This shows a great lack of political will and ignorance of the importance of disabled people as an important constituency whose rights are also human rights! The disabled community are campaigning for the CRPD to be translated into national legislation and policy at parliament. They demand at least 15 per cent representation at all levels of governance from village to parliament (national level). The advocacy and lobbying still continues to vigorously campaign for more seats.

South Africa. South Africa took a different route altogether to disability legislation, which was via its constitution. The South African 1996 Constitution guarantees fundamental rights to all citizens. It includes, in the equality clause, the right to freedom from discrimination based on a number of social criteria. Non-discrimination based on disability is specifically mentioned, and disabled people are thus guaranteed the right to be treated equally and to enjoy the same rights as all other citizens. The first constitution-making organ, the Convention for a Democratic South Africa (CODESA), involved disabled people and they made sure that the non-discrimination clause includes the rights of disabled people. The Disabled People South Africa (DPSA) umbrella body was also involved in the writing up of the constitution.

Various pieces of sector legislation and policies derive from this constitutional dispensation, such as the Employment Equity Act, South African School Act, Mental Health Care Act and the Child Care Act. The Disability Desk is housed in the office of the president, which is the highest authority in the country, giving it clout and the ability to influence changes in governance.

The desk is also headed by a disabled person, with focal persons in every office, department and ministry. There is a great deal of political will, which was cultivated over a long period of apartheid rule and the associated violence, when disabled people were part of the struggle and 'chaos'. Those who were injured in the political struggle found a home in the DRM, thereby raising the status of disabled people. Disabled people are represented at all levels of governance; from village to national levels and also in every governmental, quasi-government bodies and various statutory bodies like South African Broadcasting Cooperation. South Africa has got one of the best-integrated national disability strategies and policies in the world. The DRM in South Africa has made a lot of gains, and the current Minister of Justice and Correctional Services is a disabled person and the Minister of Social Development is a disabled woman.

Conclusions

In conclusion, disabling attitudes towards disabled people have existed for millennia, and sadly very little had changed until disabled people organized and fought for their rights. Politicians, civil servants, professionals and the public listen to organized people, and organized people are visible through the vehicles of organizations. Those who understand the nature of the problem are able to provide a solution to the problem. The struggle for disabled people is not a struggle for able-bodied people who can jump in and out of policy making: it is a struggle for disabled people, and all they need is support for the cause. The roadmap clearly shows the role disabled people and their organizations played, up to the ultimate goal of achieving an instrument that will address their rights and provide guidance to all players in the field of disability – including governments which ought to provide services to disabled people just as they would for non-disabled people. Other factors at play include political will, socio-economic advancement and the involvement of those concerned in formulating legislation and policies. Examples of how these factors interplay are to be found in South Africa and Zimbabwe, where disabled people were included in constitution-making processes. Advocacy and lobbying are therefore processes that do not operate in a vacuum.

Summary of key points

- The disability rights movement (DRM) has been actively advocating and lobbying for the rights of people with disabilities since the 1960s, effectively shifting interventions from a charity to a human rights-based approach.
- There are a number of international disability rights organizations that unite national and regional disabled people's organizations. The International Disability Alliance (IDA) includes membership of eight international organizations and four regional organizations. The mission of the IDA is the advancement of human rights of disabled people, using the CRPD.
- Although several human rights instruments have been developed over the last decades, the most important accomplishment of the DRM advocacy and lobbying efforts is the adoption of the Convention on the Rights of Persons with Disabilities by the United Nations.
- Advocacy is a process of supporting a cause and can take various forms such as self-advocacy, representative advocacy and mobilization.
- Lobbying is a deliberate and sustained effort to influence decision makers to take appropriate or certain policy measures. Both advocacy and lobbying work as part of a cyclical process.

STUDY QUESTIONS

1. To what extent have disability practices been transformed from the traditional/ charity model to the rights-based developmental model in your country?

2. Are political, societal and economic environments accommodative of the equal treatment of disabled people in your country?

3. How have global and regional disability instruments and provisions, such as the CRPD, helped to improve the situation of people with disabilities in your country?

Further reading and resources

African Disability Rights Yearbook (2013). http://www.pulp.up.ac.za/pdf/2013_07/ 2013_07.pdf.

African Journal on Disability – www.ajod.org.

I.J. Charlton. (1998). *Nothing about Us without Us: Disability Oppression and Empowerment* (Los Angeles: University of Certification Press).

P. Coleridge. (1993). *Disability, Liberation and Development* (Oxford: Oxfam).

Community Based Rehabilitation Africa Network – http://www.afri-can.org.

Consortium for refugees and migrants in South Africa. Available from http://www .cormsa.org.za/advocacy-and-lobbying/.

Department of Psychology Stellenbosch University, South Africa – http://sun025.sun .ac.za/portal/page/portal/Arts/Departments/psychology.

Disability in Africa – www.disability-africa.org.

Disabled People South Africa (DPSA): Pocket Guide on Disability Equity – African Decade of Disabled Persons 1999–2009.

Disabled People's International (DPI) – www.dpi.org.

Disabled People of South Africa (DPSA). Available from http://www.dpsa.org.za/.

GovtSA. (2002). Advocacy Training Manual. Disabled Persons South Africa. Cape Town, South Africa.

M. Mbewe and P. Lee. (1991). 'The SAFOD Development activists Handbook'. Bulawayo: Zimbabwe.

S. Miles. (1996). 'Engaging with the Disability Rights Movement: The experience of community rehabilitation in Southern Africa. *Disability and Society*, 11(4), 27–29.

W. Rowland. (2004). *Nothing about Us without Us: Inside The Disability Rights Movement Of South Africa* (Pretoria: Unisa Press).

School of Health and Rehabilitation Science, Faculty of Health Sciences, University of Cape Town – http://www.health.uct.ac.za/fhs/departments/shrs/about.

Southern Africa Federation of the Disabled (SAFOD) – www.safod.org.

Status of Disability Rights in Southern Africa, Open Learning. – http://www.osisa.org/ sites/default/files/disability_open_learning_-_overview_final.pdf.

The Secretariat of African Decade of Persons with Disabilities (SADPD) – www .africandecade.co.za.

United Nations Human Rights – Office of the High Commissioner for Human Rights – http://www.ohchr.org/EN/Pages/WelcomePage.aspx.

B. Watermeyer, L. Swartz, T. Lorenzo, M. Schneider and M. Priestley (Eds.). (2006). *Disability and social change: A South African agenda* (Cape Town: HSRC).

Zimbabwe Disability Inclusive Development Forum Launch Report – http://www
.academia.edu/5263737/Zimbabwe_Disability_Inclusive_Development_Forum
_Launch_Report.

Annex: Members of the International Disability Alliance

The *Arab Organization of Persons with Disabilities (AOPD)* is an independent non-profit organization founded in 1998 in Cairo, Egypt. It is a regional organization composed of DPOs operating in the different Arab Countries. AOPD's main objectives are to promote the rights of people with disabilities, to empower people with disabilities and to represent Arab people with disabilities in the world at large.

The *European Disability Forum (EDF)* is an independent European non-governmental organization (ENGO) that represents the interests of 50 million disabled people in the European Union and stands for their rights. It was created in 1996 and is based in Brussels.

The *Latin American Network of Non-Governmental Organizations of Persons with Disabilities and their Families (RIADIS)* is a network formed by organizations of persons with disabilities from 19 countries in Latin America and the Caribbean. Formed in 2002, RIADIS represents more than 60 national organizations as well as several NGOs acting as technical collaborators.

The *Pacific Disability Forum (PDF)* is the regional response to addressing disability issues in the Pacific. The PDF was established in 2002 and officially inaugurated in 2004, to work towards inclusive, barrier-free, socially just, and gender-equitable societies that recognize the human rights, citizenship, contribution and potential of persons with disabilities in Pacific Island Countries and territories.

IDA members include a range of international organizations, many of which started as national associations but came together globally to promote greater advocacy for their cause. Most are based around specific impairments with one notable exception, *Disabled People's International.*

Established in 1981, the International Year of Disabled Persons, DPI was the world's first successful cross-disability endeavour to convert the talk about full and equal participation of persons with disabilities into action. Over 30 years later, DPI continues to be the world's *only* cross-disability global disabled people's organisation (DPO). Headquartered in Canada, it has a presence in more than 130 countries through its Member National Assemblies (MNAs) spanning across seven regions: Africa, Arab, Asia-Pacific, CIS, Europe, Latin America and North America, and Caribbean. The MNAs are focused on capacity building, and empowerment of people with disabilities in their countries, and over half of them are based in the developing world.

The other members of IDA span the range of impairments.

Inclusion International (II) is a grass roots organization of persons with intellectual disability and their families which advocates in all aspects of their communities for the inclusion of people who have an intellectual disability.

It is based on shared values of respect, diversity, human rights, solidarity and inclusion and has member societies in over 115 countries.

Down Syndrome International (DSI) is the international organization promoting the rights of persons with Down syndrome through their organizations at regional and national level. Its members include people with Down syndrome, parents, family members and friends, carers, professionals, practitioners, researchers, organizations and people who are just interested in Down syndrome from all over the world.

International Federation of Hard of Hearing People (IFHOH) is an international non-governmental organization of national associations of and for hard of hearing and late deafened people. IFHOH provides a platform for cooperation and information exchange among its members and interested parties. As an umbrella organization and through its individual organizations, IFHOH works to promote greater understanding of hearing loss issues and to improve access for hard of hearing people worldwide. Likewise the *World Federation of the Deaf (WFD)* is the international non-governmental organization representing Deaf people worldwide. WFD works for human rights and equal opportunities for Deaf people everywhere.

The *World Blind Union (WBU)* advocates for human rights of persons who are blind and partially sighted and seeks to strengthen their organizations and advance the participation of all persons who are blind and partially sighted.

The *World Federation of the Deaf and Blind (WFDB)* is a representative organization of national organizations or groups of deafblind persons and of deafblind individuals worldwide. The aim of WFDB is to be a forum of exchange of knowledge and experiences amongst deafblind persons and to obtain inclusion and full participation of deafblind persons in all areas of society.

The *World Network of Users and Survivors of Psychiatry (WNUSP)* is a democratic organization of users and survivors of psychiatry that represents this constituency at the global level.

(Adapted from the website of the International Disability Alliance (IDA): http://www.internationaldisabilityalliance.org/en.)

Global Cultures and Understandings of Disability

Alexandra Lewis Gargett
Rebecca Barton
Gwynnyth Llewellyn
Antoni Tsaputra
Sai Kyi Zin Soe
Sainmili Tawake

The States Parties to the present Convention (are) concerned about the difficult conditions faced by persons with disabilities who are subject to multiple or aggravated forms of discrimination on the basis of race, colour, sex, language, religion, political or other opinion, national, ethnic, indigenous or social origin, property, birth, age or other status.

**UN Convention on the Rights of Persons with Disabilities
Preamble (p)**

State Parties undertake (b) To combat stereotypes, prejudices and harmful practices relating to persons with disabilities, including those based on sex and age, in all areas of life; (c) To promote awareness of the capabilities and contributions of persons with disabilities.

2 (c) Encouraging all organs of the media to portray persons with disabilities in a manner consistent with the purpose of the present Convention.

**UN Convention on the Rights of Persons with Disabilities
Article 8: Awareness-raising**

Introduction

Disability is a global phenomenon that occurs in every country around the world. However, as the *World Report on Disability* (WHO and World Bank, 2011) makes clear, the lives of people with disabilities vary considerably depending on the country where they live, their age, their gender, their socio-economic status and city or rural location. This is the case for the over 1 billion people globally who experience disability. For example, internationally somewhere between 250,000 and 500,000 people incur a spinal cord injury each year (WHO, 2013). How individuals with a spinal cord injury are able to participate in their community varies from culture to culture, and from country to country, and may vary according to different cultural groups within a country. Different outcomes after spinal cord injury are not so surprising when disability is understood as resulting from the interaction between the individual and his or her environment, which includes attitudinal, social and cultural as well as physical factors.

Understanding cultural dimensions of disability is a critical part of the work of practitioners, policy makers, and service providers. This knowledge will help bring about a better future for people with disabilities, grounded in knowledge about culture and disability. This chapter is structured in two sections. In the first section, we discuss current discourses about disability and culture. In the second section of this chapter, we discuss three concepts to help develop a more nuanced understanding of culture and disability. These are: (i) disability as arising from interaction between individuals in their particular cultural contexts; (ii) culture as embodied and representational; and (iii) the lived experience of disability as the embodiment and instantiation of culture in everyday lives. We include a case study from Indonesia to illuminate these three concepts.

Disability as person–environment interaction

The United Nations Convention on the Rights of Persons with Disabilities (CRPD) Article 1 states that persons with disabilities include 'those who have long-term physical, mental, intellectual or sensory impairments which in interaction with various barriers may hinder their full and effective participation in society on an equal basis with others'.

The description of disability contained in Article 1 of the CRPD demonstrates that disability comes from an interaction between a person and his or her environment. Cultural understandings of *ability* and *disability* form a large part of how individuals experience disability. It is a truism to note that, worldwide, disability is more likely to be regarded negatively. This has led some disability studies theorists to propose the concept of ableism to help explain why this is so. Ableism is said to come from the positive values given to being able bodied, which then results in a belief that people with disabilities are inferior (Campbell, 2009). In other words, the 'normative' body – the able-body – functions as the normative comparison standard. This helps to explain why people with disabilities remain disadvantaged and discriminated against around the world. For example, people with disabilities are less likely to be employed than their non-disabled peers, experience poorer health, and are less likely to develop social relationships and participate fully in their societies (WHO and World Bank, 2011).

The global picture of disability described in the opening paragraph demonstrates that disability is part of the human condition. That does not mean however that all societies react to and treat disability in the same way. The lived experience of people with disabilities is quite diverse across countries and cultures (Ingstad and Reynolds Whyte, 1995; Langness and Levine, 1986; Priestley, 2001). Disability may accompany an impairment or illness which is present at birth or due to a health condition, impairment, illness or injury that occurs during the course of one's lifetime. However, as the CRPD makes clear, disability *results* from barriers and attitudes in the community that limit participation. In other words, people with impairments, health conditions or illnesses are disabled by the society in which they live. This international understanding of disability informs the work of the international agencies of the United Nations system, such as the World Health Organization, International Labour Organization, UNICEF and the World Bank.

The CRPD is a paradigm shift in thinking about disability, moving from a model where persons with disabilities were treated as objects of medical treatment or charity and social protection to a model where persons with disabilities are recognized as people with rights (see Chapter 2, for a discussion on disability models). This new human rights-framed thinking about disability is increasingly being incorporated into legislation and policy in many countries around the world. This is because governments are recognizing the need to advance the interests of people with disabilities and their families and carers. For example, *Fulfilling Potential: Building a Deeper Understanding of Disability in the UK Today* (Department for Work and Pensions, 2013) is about making the CRPD a living reality for disabled people in Britain. In Australia, the National Disability Strategy (2010–2020) commits all governments in Australia to a national approach which supports people with disability to maximize their potential and participate as equal citizens in Australian society (Commonwealth of Australia, 2011).

Culture as a pervasive force in society

The Oxford English Dictionary (2014) defines culture as 'the distinctive ideas, customs, social behaviour, products, or way of life of a particular nation, society, people, or period'. This is a broad definition of culture as commonly understood. As with other aspects of society, the concept of culture has been interrogated by critical theorists. Ideas such as culture as a 'political process of contestation over the power to define key concepts, including that of "culture" itself' (Wright, 1998, p. 14) are helpful in understanding that in many 'cultures' people with disabilities are excluded from the everyday rituals and ways of life that derive from those in the more powerful positions in society. We are often not aware of how cultural ways of thinking and behaving are embedded in our everyday lives until we experience a clash of cultural values. Then we realize the distinctive ideas, customs, or social behaviours that are features of culture.

This is not to say that culture is static. We frequently see that ideas, behaviours and ways of life within cultural groups change over time. Developments in society can produce changes in cultural understandings of disability. For example, when countries change from primarily agrarian to industrialized societies, people with cognitive impairment may have increasing difficulty because participating in society requires being able to read and write and do numbers.

Many people in countries of the North and the South may not yet understand that disability is a product of the person–environment interaction. Instead, disability may still be considered the 'problem' of the individual and believed to have come about, for example, as a consequence of an individual's actions or behaviours either in their present or past life, or as an act of a supernatural or spiritual being. Globally, disability is often regarded as a consequence of the individual's or his or her family's negative behaviours, thoughts or wrong doings. These cultural understandings of disability evolve under the influence of factors such as religion, traditional practices or political regimes. The cultural beliefs and values that accompany these understandings are often deep seated and subconscious.

The dynamic nature of culture means that cultural attitudes towards disability can change, and change for the better. There need to be both changes in values and increased understanding at all levels of society, as well as a focus on those social and cultural norms that can bring about false and inappropriate myths about disability (Pacific Islands Forum Secretariat, 2014).

Understanding culture and disability

No matter how disability is understood in a particular culture, the CRPD requires that people with disabilities are respected for their inherent dignity and are able to equally enjoy all human rights and fundamental freedoms. This requires attention to many matters such as employment, right to life, health, education, full access to justice and non-discrimination. Realizing the right of people with disabilities to be respected as equal members of their society also requires an understanding of the diverse – and valued – roles and contributions that individuals make across varying cultural contexts, as provided for in Article 30(2) of the CRPD.

How disability is understood within a culture can be explored in several ways. This can be through the lived experience of people with disabilities, by examining community attitudes toward people with disabilities and by how disability is represented in stories and myths, newspapers and other media as well as in cultural products such as art, theatre or film.

Disability – interaction between individuals and cultural context

As Bickenbach (2009) argues 'it is not difficult to agree that concepts like "disability" are socially constructed ... What it means to be disabled, in short, fundamentally includes what it means to be *viewed as disabled* by others, and this is contingent on features of one's society, system of economic exchange, culture, language and many other things besides' (p. 1112). To understand disability in a cultural context requires consideration of the distinctive set of beliefs, moral values, traditions and laws (within religion and in politics) that define a particular culture, and also the influences of institutional factors, country and cultural histories and changing perspectives on social roles (Trollope-Kumar and Last, 2002). Religion, political and institutional factors, social roles and multiculturalism are discussed in more detail below.

Religion

Many aspects of culture are positive and ensure peaceful and productive outcomes *but at the same time* can exclude persons with disabilities. An example of this comes from the Pacific, which is rich in its diversity of cultures and religions. The uniquely Pacific traditions and customs, blended with Christianity and other religions, portray tolerance and respect but can also be exclusionary. Christianity in its many forms, Hindu and Muslim faiths, and traditional religions or beliefs are of enormous influence – magnifying both the potential challenges and opportunities for people with disabilities and their families. The challenge for persons with disabilities, particularly women with disabilities, is to find and maintain positive aspects of tradition and culture while confronting the entrenched patriarchal views of persons with disabilities and the role of women and cultural beliefs about the causes and effects of disability.

There are many religions globally. Each has its own explanation about how disability should be regarded spiritually. In many places disability has been thought of as delivered by a higher entity such as fate, deity or karma. Also common is the belief that disability is a result of behaviour that has failed to show due respect to supernatural and spiritual forces, such as ancestors or black magic. According to Miles (2002), the commonality in these belief systems is that 'disability is given by an agent' (p. 124). When disability is thought of as given, it leads to negative views. Disability is seen as a punishment or an 'inescapable consequence' of actions undertaken or beliefs held by individuals, society or, more broadly, by humankind. Behaviours thought to cause disability include sinful, ignorant, foolish or accidental actions; mistaken beliefs too can occasion disability either in the present life or a previous existence.

Miles (2002) also noted, however, that disability can be viewed as an opportunity, and not always negatively. From this perspective, Miles (2002) suggests disability is an

> open ended challenge for the strengthening of a person's soul, as a specific lesson to be learnt to enable the soul to make progress, as a challenge to the disabled person's family or other carers, as an opportunity for the deity's power or love to be demonstrated, or as an opportunity for individual or neighbourhood charitable action. (p. 125)

This view, though seemingly more positive, still contributes to the continuing power imbalance between non-disabled people and people with disabilities. Non-disabled people are viewed as strong, rich and successful (and able to bestow goods), whereas the receiver, who is a person with a disability, continues to be viewed as vulnerable, weak or poor, and as a burden or challenge to the normal or ideal state of being.

Religion can play a positive and important role in how individuals respond to and handle the challenges that can accompany disability. Parents of children with disabilities have reported that their spiritual beliefs provide strength and peace to adapt to the life difficulties and changes introduced through having a child with a disability (Poston and Turnbull, 2004). Tarakeshwar and Pargament (2001) demonstrated a link between religious coping strategies (prayer, seeking guidance and seeking peace) and positive adjustment to life stressors in parents of children with disabilities. A review of the literature on religion and disability (Johnstone, Glass and Oliver, 2007) explored some of the theoretical bases for the positive effects of religion on individuals' coping with disability. Their findings show that a belief in and reliance on a higher power can help to reduce feelings of anxiety over loss of control and dependence. Another explanation comes from the theory of psycho-neuroimmunology, which posits that a positive frame of mind can influence how the body responds to stress.

Language

Language and cultural understandings influence and shape each other (Underhill, 2012). Accordingly, when cultures use positive and constructive language to describe individuals with disabilities, it is more likely that people with disabilities can be integrated into the society (Scheer and Groce, 1988). Conversely, cultures that use negative or demeaning language to describe people with disabilities are more likely to reject disabled members of their societies that have disabilities (Boylan, 1991). For example, in various languages disability is translated as 'deficient', 'less than human', 'innately inferior', which justifies the social exclusion of persons with disabilities. They may also be seen as dangerous people being possessed by evil spirits or punished by God due to their past-life sins or bad deeds of their forefathers, and are often shackled and isolated from the rest of society. When society as a whole discriminates against persons with disabilities or particular types of impairment, their families are also affected. This forces the person with a disability to live in isolation and become more vulnerable, with direct consequences to society, to his or her family and, of course, to him or herself.

Political and institutional factors

The political governance structures of nation states determine society's laws, regulations and policies. These structures interface with religious beliefs and cultural perspectives and thereby 'determine' the fate of people with disabilities. So, for example, if people with disabilities are culturally understood as sick or ill, society's responses are more likely to focus on health and medical curative practices. On the other hand, if people with disabilities are culturally understood as a subclass of unfortunate citizens, responses to people with disabilities may vary from their being worthy of charitable actions to being marginalized and ignored as undeserving (see Box 5.1).

> ### Box 5.1.   Policy and disability – an example from Myanmar
>
> Political and institutional responses to disability are dynamic and change over time as effects of legislation or policy outcomes become evident within society. Myanmar presents an example of this. Myanmar has a fairly long history of promoting equality for people with disability in the Mekong region. In 1958, Myanmar enacted a law on equal employment opportunity for persons with disability. This law required state-owned enterprises, as a priority, to employ people with disabilities. Later, people with disabilities came to be seen as 'special people' or 'a special case' that were afforded much more flexibility in relation to productivity and performance than others without disabilities in the same workplace. This led to people with disabilities becoming demotivated and less responsible workers, leading others to conclude – at all levels of society – that people with disabilities were not employable and are unproductive. This cultural perspective on people with disabilities driven by political and institutional frameworks has now become a major barrier to promoting equal employment opportunities for people with disabilities in Myanmar.

Social roles

Although the roles dedicated to people with (usually) observable differences may vary with cultural context, they do share similarities across contexts and time. So for example, Schur and colleagues (2013) observe that 'people with disabilities have been considered sources of ridicule and entertainment' (p. 1) in many places and over time. This is illustrated by the roles that people of short stature have filled throughout history and across the globe. This includes court jesters in ancient China and slaves for the wealthy during the Middle Ages in the Roman Empire and in Europe.

The roles that men and women play in society are also culturally determined. In particular, there is good evidence that women with disabilities are 'doubly handicapped' within and across most cultural contexts (Deegan and Brooks 1985; Priestley, 2001). New terms such as *multiple* or *intersectional discrimination* reflect the growing body of knowledge about the disadvantage experienced by women with disabilities in all aspects of their lives compared to their male peers (for example, Ortoleva and Lewis, 2012; Schur, Kruse and Blanck, 2013) (see Chapter 6, section on gender as cause of social exclusion). The evidence in high-income countries, summarized by Schur et al. (2013), shows that women have lower levels of education or no education at all, lower levels (or no means) of employment, fewer opportunities to learn skills to gain a job, lower disability income benefits and are more likely to live alone and be the victims of assault and abuse.

Throughout the Pacific region, in both urban and rural communities, women and girls with disabilities face multiple and compounding forms of discrimination. They are targets of discrimination not only because of their disability but also their gender. In addition, they are often poor and/or face various challenges which others do not have. They often experience discrimination and further prejudice, based on common assumptions and widely held beliefs about their status and capacity both as females and as people with disabilities (Stubbs and Tawake, 2009). This is why the Incheon Strategy to 'Make the Right Real' for Persons with Disabilities in Asia and the Pacific 2013–2022, has, as one of its ten goals, ensuring gender equality and empowerment for women with disabilities (DINF, 2012).

Multi-culturalism

In multicultural countries, there is increasing interest in understanding the experiences of people with disabilities from culturally diverse (usually minority) groups. It is widely reported that these 'minority' groups experience greater disadvantage and difficulties accessing services and supports due to a range of factors including language barriers, poverty and social isolation, racial discrimination, and lack of knowledge about services and systems (Azmi, Hatton, Emerson and Caine, 1997; Hatton and Emerson, 2009; Jegatheesan, 2009; Stevens, 2010). People from culturally diverse backgrounds are likely to encounter cultural, religious, social and institutional values and practices living in the majority culture that is not their own. This can include different perceptions about the cause and meaning of disability (Heer, Larkin, Burchess and Rose, 2012), conflicting ideas about 'normal' roles, and varying perspectives on the roles of people with disabilities and how they should be 'treated' (Mandell and Novak, 2005).

People from minority groups face an ongoing task of making sense of the cultural differences they encounter from the majority culture. This includes navigating services and systems that are fundamentally shaped by different values and beliefs (Sham, 1996; Hatton, Azmi, Caine and Emerson, 1998; Hon, Sun, Suto and Forwell, 2011). Often this results in people with disabilities and their families experiencing difficulty in accessing services, including health care, disability services and schools or further education. They may feel strongly that services and systems are not responsive to their needs or understand their cultural values and beliefs, thereby leading to further marginalization.

People with disabilities from culturally diverse minority groups also engage in a process of renegotiating their identity in relation to both disability and their cultural values (Atkin and Hussain, 2003; Hussain, 2005; Stevens, 2010). This process of navigating and negotiating difference is largely left to the person with disability rather than being seen as the responsibility of the service system, creating additional barriers to participation.

Culture as embodied and representational

The previous sections have emphasized what might be called a helicopter view of disability and its intersection with cultural context. From this bird's eye view, it is evident that the interaction of cultural context and cultural understanding is dynamic, changes with historical time and is influenced by political, religious and social perspectives.

Culture as embodied

Culture is, as the OED definition explains, '... a way of life of a particular nation, society, people, or period (Oxford English Dictionary, 2014). Culture is a persistent influence determining the opportunities, life chances and restrictions on all citizens. Culture is not an external force distant from, or separate to, everyday lives and experiences. Culture is both generated by and embodied within all who are part of culture. This is a two-way process. This means that the shared beliefs and values of any culture are adopted by and embedded within individuals as part of their own value and belief systems. At the same time, the belief and value systems of these individuals contribute to and shape the cultural beliefs and values of the culture of which they are part. Individuals combine the shared values and beliefs of their culture with their own experiences to develop and re-develop over time their own ways of making sense of the world. Their life experiences including their own and their family beliefs, values and goals contribute to and influence their individual actions and behaviours. This means that there will also be individuals who do not accept or actively flout cultural standards. Individuals' perspectives also influence the shared values of the broader groups in which they participate.

Culture as representational

Article 8 of the CRPD, 'Awareness-raising', declares that States parties shall encourage 'all organs of the media to portray persons with disabilities in a manner consistent with the purpose of the present Convention'. Examining the language and representations of disability in 'cultural products' such as literature, arts, media or sport reveals a lot about disability beliefs within a cultural context (Kuppers, 2003) (see Chapter 2, cultural model of disability). There are at least three aspects to this. The first involves attitudes towards people with disabilities at particular points in time. One example of this is found in Thomson's (1996) examination of the 'freak' show. These travelling shows put people with disability on display, portraying them as almost inhuman, as not one of us (Braddock and Parish, 2001). In contrast, children's TV shows such as Sesame Street and Debenham's inclusivity campaign portray people with disability as role models. Although this campaign is heralded as groundbreaking in the world of fashion, Driscoll (2013) noted that there is some way to go before disability and difference are widely accepted as normal. Similarly, Davis (2013) argues that diversity is the new "normal", which again, fails to include disability.

In cinematic 'products', Darke (1998) has proposed a 'normality genre' for films which include a disability plot. According to Darke, this genre exists because cinemagoers want to see a story that reaffirms what they already think about disability. Darke argues that in films in this genre, the person with a disability 'destabilizes' normality or 'introduces chaos'. To overcome this, the person with a disability then seeks to normalize his or her presence in the story line by fulfilling roles that are expected of others; if failing to do so, the character is regarded as less worthy or good. If, despite the person's best efforts, he or she is unable to achieve this re-stabilization, the story is thought of as tragic.

Cultural representations of disability provide insight into *how* disability is understood in different cultural contexts, but not necessarily *why*. Shildrick (2012) suggests we need to know more about why there is (almost) veneration of bodies as able. An example comes from Goggin and Newell (2005), who examine the place of sport as a key feature of cultural identity in Australia, asking, 'If sport tells us important things about what Australians value and believe, how does disability relate to such national symbolism?' (p. 76). Their analysis is about the 2000 Sydney Olympic Games. They observe that although media coverage of these Olympic Games was extensive and widely televised, media coverage of the Paralympics, which occurred three weeks afterwards, was minimal. They suggest this is a reflection of an Australian 'cultural norm that only tolerates disability as long as it stays in the margin' (p. 85). They go on to suggest that the appeal of watching sport is about viewing bodies in their peak physical form performing at their pinnacle. Disability does not conform to this and therefore is not as interesting to the spectators.

Interestingly, however, as Goggin and Newell (2005) note, Paralympians do receive attention when they are successful, fulfilling the national reputation of performing well on the world stage, bringing home the gold medals. These athletes are represented as bravely overcoming the odds 'earning' the admiration awarded to other 'able-bodied' athletes through hard work, bravery and success. This was exemplified in Fiji during the 2012 London Olympic and Paralympic Games – hailed by many as the greatest Games ever. It was at these Games that the Pacific scooped its first ever gold medal, and this was won by Iliesa Delana, a Fijian with a disability, who competed in high jump.

The whole of Fiji celebrated this great achievement. A big event was hosted in Suva, with a grand parade through the city by people of all ethnicities, school students, women and men, young and old. Iliesa Delana was accorded the highest traditional welcome only accorded to a Fijian high chief and honoured with 50 gun salutes by the military government in a public organized celebration. Iliesa Delana's gold medal leap at the Paralympic Games was worth $90,000, and counting – the biggest payout to any individual in the history of amateur sports in Fiji. Furthermore, for his great achievement, his winning jump is engraved on Fiji's 50 cents coin. For more than five decades, Fiji has been sending teams of non-disabled people to the Olympic Games, but it was a person with disability who garnered not only the first gold medal for Fiji but also the first for the Pacific. It was also the first time an athlete with a disability from Fiji was able to compete in the Olympic Games as such.

Lived experience of people with disabilities

The lived experiences of people with disabilities are presented by way of a case example through the story of Vino, a young boy from Indonesia (see Box 5.2).

Box 5.2.   Lived experience of people with disabilities in Indonesia: Vino's story

In Indonesia, which ratified the CRPD in 2011, a 20-year-old young man named Vino Pratama, with a severe physical disability, has changed his immediate family's views about disability from being a burden to a blessing in disguise. Although his mother is still alive, Vino has been living with his aunt and her family in Padang, West Sumatra, since he was two years of age. It was not Vino's decision to live with his aunt, or that should she become his full-time carer. Vino's father passed away when he was only a few months old, and at two years of age, his mother, citing his severe disability, asked her older sister to take care of him. It is still very common in some areas of Indonesia to feel shame at having a child with severe disability who, it is believed, will have a bleak future and become a burden to the family.

Vino's aunt thought that looking after Vino, a disabled child abandoned by his own mother, was her obligation as a family member and that it was an *ibadah* (good deed) as a pious Muslim. But because she also had her own children to feed and her husband's income was limited, she could not afford to provide Vino with a proper education or take him out into the community. Vino, not knowing differently, thought that he should be grateful to his aunt for caring for him and that he should not demand more from her than what she had already done for him. Vino set out to learn to read by himself, which he did at age ten, and later to write, when he received a smartphone as a gift when he was 15.

Vino almost never left his house and only interacted with people through social media. Last year, however, he met people with disabilities through social media. They were involved in a disabled people's organisation (DPO) in his city. Since then, this DPO has actively engaged Vino in advocacy activities. Through these activities, Vino has learned about disability rights and advocacy. He now believes he has the right to make his own decisions. He no longer accepts things as the way they are, and his aunt and other members of his family are now supporting him in his dream to achieve a bright future.

Conclusions

In this chapter, we have drawn attention to the ways in which disability is understood in different cultural contexts. Fundamentally, this occurs because, as Bickenbach (2009) reminds us, disability is a socially constructed concept. Social constructions are contextually situated. In this chapter, we discussed culture and cultural contexts to help understand culture and disability in the context of global cultures and understandings of disability. Three concepts underpinned our discussion of culture. The first was the understanding of disability as person–environment interaction, which is now widely accepted through the international recognition of the CRPD. The second was the concept that culture is developed from, absorbed within and represented by all who are part of a culture. This concept is fundamental to our understanding that we are all people of our culture, as the Oxford English Dictionary (2014) reminds us, sharing a way of life with distinctive ideas, customs and social behaviours. Cultures do not remain fixed, however, and this offers promise for coming to greater global understanding and implementation of 'the full and equal enjoyment of all human rights and fundamental freedoms by persons with disabilities' (Article 1, CRPD).

We have seen that culture is highly inter-relational. Cultural understandings derive from and drive individuals' beliefs and value systems and therefore their thoughts, actions and behaviours. Cultures as inter-relational phenomena, as we have seen, develop answers to questions such as what it is to be human and how others are to be regarded, and these answers change over time. This offers promise for positive change in cultural understandings of disability and responsibility to contribute to positive change. As Shildrick (2012) has written 'all of us – regardless of our own individual morphology – are participants in the socio-cultural imaginary that pervasively shapes the disposition of every-day attitudes and values – and we all therefore have a responsibility to inter-rogate it' (p. 36).

Summary of key points

- Disability arises from interaction between individuals in their particular cultural contexts. Therefore, understanding disability in a cultural context requires consideration of the distinctive set of beliefs, moral values, trad-itions and laws that define a particular culture, as well as the influences of institutional factors, country and cultural histories and changing perspec-tives on social roles.
- Culture is not an external force distant from, or separate to everyday lives and experience, but rather, through a two-way process, is generated and embodied within all members of a particular culture.
- Article 8 of the CRPD, 'Awareness-raising', declares that States parties shall encourage 'all organs of the media to portray persons with disabilities in a manner consistent with the purpose of the present Convention'.
- Examining the representation of disability in cultural products such as newspaper articles, film or theatre helps to illuminate how different cul-tures understand disability.
- Learning about the lived experience of people with disabilities provides insight into how culture and cultural understandings of disability influence people's everyday lives and life opportunities.

STUDY QUESTIONS

1. As Bickenbach (2009) stated, the meaning of disability is socially constructed and culturally contingent. Consider how the meaning of disability is constructed in your culture and how this influences your attitude towards people with disabilities.

2. The media and advertising are powerful forces in creating cultural understandings. Consider how people with disability are portrayed in the media or through adver-tising in your country and the effect this has on you and others.

cont.

3. People's life experiences tell us a lot about the culture in which they live. What does the lived experience of people with disabilities illuminate about how disability is understood in your culture and how you understand disability?

Further reading and resources

Accentuate UK (http://www.accentuateuk.org/homepage) – an independent programme which challenges perceptions of disability by providing opportunities to people with disabilities to participate in the cultural sector. Their vision is summarized in Tom Shakespeare's video presentation *Raising the Game*. https://www.youtube.com/watch?v=vjm8dn5X0Xc.

Bad news for disabled people: How the newspapers are reporting disability – research report from the University of Glasgow on how the media in the UK reports on disability and the subsequent impact on public attitudes. http://www.gla.ac.uk/media/media_214917_en.pdf.

End the Cycle – a movement to 'end the cycle' of disability and poverty. The website includes a collection of videos and stories of people with disabilities living in some of the world's poorest countries. http://www.endthecycle.org.au/.

Ortoleva and Lewis (2012) describe evidence of violence and abuse towards women and girls with disabilities worldwide. Their work can be found on the website of Women Enabled, an advocacy group working to advance the human rights of women and girls, especially women and girls with disabilities. http://www.womenenabled.org.

Pacific Sisters with Disability – a report of the challenges women with disabilities face in the Pacific. http://www.wwda.org.au/wp-content/uploads/2013/12//pacificsisters1.pdf.

Stella Young Tedx Talk. (2014). *Inspirational porn and the objectification of disability*. Stella discusses the perception of people with disabilities as objects of inspiration in the Australian context. https://www.youtube.com/watch?v=SxrS7-I_sMQ.

Women with Disabilities Australia (WWDA) work to improve the lives and life chances of women with disabilities. The WWDA website has many useful resources about women with disabilities. http://wwda.org.au/.

Young Voices – a movement of young people with disabilities across the globe who advocate for the rights of people with disabilities. A number of research and activity reports that reflect the lived experience of young people with disabilities are available on the website: http://youngvoices.leonardcheshire.org/.

Disability, Social Exclusion and Poverty

Subharati Ghosh
Sarah Dababnah
Susan L. Parish
Leah Igdalsky

The majority of persons with disabilities live in conditions of poverty, and in this regard (State Parties) recognizing the critical need to address the negative impact of poverty on persons with disabilities.

**UN Convention on Rights of Persons with Disabilities
Preamble (t)**

States Parties recognize the right of persons with disabilities to social protection and to the enjoyment of that right without discrimination on the basis of disability, and shall take appropriate steps ... to ensure access to

(a) ... clean water services, and to ensure access to appropriate and affordable services ... for disability-related needs;

(b) ... in particular women and girls with disabilities and older persons ... to social protection programmes and poverty reduction programmes;

(c) ... assistance from the State with disability-related expenses, including adequate training, counselling, financial assistance and respite care;

(d) ... to public housing programmes;

(e) ... retirement benefits and programmes.

**UN Convention on Rights of Persons with Disabilities
Article 28(2): Adequate standard of living and social protection**

Introduction

Worldwide, the numbers are chilling. People with disabilities experience higher rates of poverty across the lifespan. In both developed and developing countries, people with disabilities experience social exclusion and poverty. Globally, people with disabilities make up about 15 per cent of the world's population (WHO and World Bank, 2011). Although there is no consensus on how many people with disabilities live in poverty around the world, 80 per cent of people with disabilities worldwide live in developing countries (UN, 2011b). Even in developed countries, people with disabilities count among the poorest and are more likely to be poor than non-disabled people. In the United States, for example, 28 per cent of people with disabilities lived below the poverty level defined by the country's federal government in 2012, compared to 12 per cent of people without a disability. Clearly, people with disabilities experience higher levels of poverty around the world. Furthermore, the relationship between disability and poverty is probably undercounted in these figures, because income-based poverty measures do not account for all of the material and social costs of living with disability (Emerson, 2007; Parish et al., 2008).

Disability is not an individual phenomenon. It impacts both the individual with disability and his or her family, and often has intergenerational effects on the economic well-being of families. In this section, we discuss the complex interaction among disability, poverty and social exclusion. We also examine some of the factors other than poverty that systematically operate to exclude people with disabilities from various life chances, in both developed and developing countries.

Our understanding of the meaning of poverty has evolved over time. Historically, poverty was conceptualized with a deprivation approach, which led to the measurement of income and whether basic human needs were met (Lipton, 1997; Streeten, 1984). These frameworks have been supplanted by Amartya Sen's (1999) capability approach, which is widely used today to understand the multidimensional nature of well-being and deprivation. Sen referred to poverty as capability deprivation, where poverty is not understood as the accumulation of an individual's goods, but whether an individual has the required personal characteristics to convert the goods to fulfil ends. Sen (1999) used the situation of people with disabilities to illustrate his capabilities framework, defining the relationship between disability and poverty using the concept of 'capability deprivation'. According to Sen (1999, p. 88):

> Handicaps, such as age or disability or illness, reduce one's ability to earn an income. But they also make it harder to convert income into capability, since an older, or more disabled, or more seriously ill person may need more income (for assistance, for prosthesis, for treatment) to achieve the same functioning (even when that achievement is not possible). This entails 'real poverty' (in terms of capability deprivation) may be, in a significant sense, more intense than what appears in the income space.

Capability poverty is a particularly relevant measurement for people with disabilities because it underscores the impact social exclusion has on income as well as functioning. The term *social exclusion* primarily refers to the involuntary exclusion of groups or individuals from full participation in social, political, economic and other societal processes of the society in which they live (UN, 2010a). According to Sen (2000), there is a bidirectional relationship between social exclusion and capability poverty. In his words, 'Social exclusion can, thus, be constitutively a part of capability deprivation as well as instrumentally a cause of diverse capability failures', and as such could be placed in a variety of situations; in this case, in the study of disability.

Social exclusion

Over time, social exclusion encompasses people who are socially disadvantaged through the systematic exclusion of individuals, groups or communities from opportunities, rights and resources that are key to social integration and are typically available to others in society. Social exclusion is multidimensional (Sen, 1999), incorporating components of social justice and considering multiple factors that act together to disadvantage groups and communities (Room, 1995; Levitas et al., 2007). Although the evolution of the term *social exclusion* is Eurocentric and has primarily been used in industrialized nations, it has wide applicability in the assessment of exclusionary processes in developing countries (Gore and Figueiredo, 1997).

Based on our review of the existing literature, people who are socially excluded could be broadly categorized as belonging to these three groups: (i) those who are socially excluded because of health conditions and/or disability; (ii) those who are excluded based on their economic status; and (iii) those who are excluded due to socio-structural factors (for example, gender, race, ethnicity, citizenship). Some people with disabilities are at greater vulnerability to social exclusion because of their income, income poverty, old age, unemployment or underemployment and/or limited education (WHO and World Bank, 2011). Individuals can exclusively belong to one of these three groups or may share attributes from each of the groups, for example, a woman with a disability may be socially excluded both because of her disability as well as due to her gender. In other words, many people with disabilities often carry a double or triple burden of exclusion.

The opportunities from which people may be excluded include education, stable income, employment, housing, welfare or social insurance benefits, citizenship, civil rights, security, justice, mobility, social and political participation, and information and communication (Silver, 1994; UN, 2010a). People with disabilities are often simultaneously deprived of multiple sets of opportunities.

However, the concept of social exclusion has been criticized for two primary reasons. First, there is no uniform or precise definition of the term (Atkinson and Hills, 1998) and the concept lacks clarity and empirical validation (UNDP, 2006). Still, there is some underlying consensus of what it truly means. For example, the World Health Organization defines social exclusion as

dynamic, multi-dimensional processes driven by unequal power relationships interacting across four main dimensions – economic, political, social
and cultural – and at different levels including individual, household, group,
community, country and global levels. It results in a continuum of inclu-
sion/exclusion characterized by unequal access to resources, capabilities
and rights, which leads to health inequalities.

(Popay et al., 2008)

By contrast, the International Labour Organization's definition focuses on
needs and deprivation:

a state of poverty in which individuals cannot access the living conditions
which would enable them both to satisfy theory essential needs (food, education, health, and so on) and participate in the development of the society
in which they live.

(Smelser and Baltes, 2001)

Various other definitions which are often context specific also have been delineated, particularly with regard to developing countries (Saith, 2001).

Due to this lack of clarity and variable definitions, there is no universally
accepted definition of the term *social exclusion*. For example, the term *inclusive education* for children with disabilities is contested (WHO, 2012) (see
Chapter 9 for a further discussion on inclusive education). Therefore, countries and international organizations have discretion to define or even address
inclusionary policies in their political, social and economic agendas (Mathieson et al., 2008). A possible source of this lack of clarity and uniformity arises
from the value-laden nature of the concept (Silver, 1994), which largely reflects
how a given society views and treats marginalized, disadvantaged people.

The second critique of the concept of social exclusion arises from its quantitative and qualitative components, which cannot be measured easily because
the causes of social exclusion vary between and within countries. Quantifying
and standardizing values, intentions, and resources that are necessary for full
participation and are comparable across countries and over time is a daunting
task (UN, 2010a) that has not been achieved to date. Measurement is further impeded by the complex, multidimensional and dynamic nature of social
exclusionary processes. Despite these limitations, the importance of the concept is evident from research conducted on social exclusion experienced by
people with disabilities both in developing and developed nations.

Causes of social exclusion among people with disabilities

In this section, we discuss some of the causes of social exclusion experienced
by people with disabilities. Poverty is a significant determinant of social exclusion, but it is only one cause. Therefore, a systems approach is necessary to
assess the factors that might lead to the social exclusion of people with disabilities. However, one caveat is that these systems are mutually interactive.
As such, we describe the factors and not the processes, which are inherently

dynamic and complex, and beyond the scope of this chapter. In addition, most of the data we report here are drawn from developed countries. There is a paucity of evidence from the developing world, and further research is needed to fully understand these issues.

We also use a life course perspective to guide this discussion because it frames the understanding of a range of exclusionary processes experienced by individuals with disabilities at each life stage. This approach suggests that risk factors build over time and has been characterized as a 'risk trajectory' in which one risk factor reinforces another, leading to poor outcomes in adult life (Rutter, 1990). This phenomenon has also been explained as the 'downward spiral of cumulative disadvantage' (Gallie and Paugam, 2000). The scope of the chapter leads us to discuss some of the factors associated with the social exclusion of people with disabilities. These factors include impairment type, gender, age, race and ethnicity.

Type of impairment

The large global population with disabilities has heterogeneous impairments, and there is evidence that people with different types of impairment are at greater or lesser risk for experiencing social exclusion. People with cognitive disability or mental illnesses experience significantly higher levels of disadvantage compared to people with sensory or motor impairments (Roulstone and Barnes, 2005). Furthermore, disadvantage varies by severity of impairment, and those with the most severe impairments are typically the most excluded (Grech, 2008; Grammenos, 2003). These individuals experience difficulty in securing and maintaining employment (WHO, 2011). For example, according to the American Community Survey (2012), individuals with hearing and visual impairments reported the highest rate of employment (37–49 per cent), whereas individuals with ambulatory and cognitive disabilities had much lower rates, at 23–24 per cent. In other words, it is not only the status of disability, but the type and severity which jointly determines the extent of social exclusion.

Gender and disability

A significant body of research in both developed and developing countries has explored the role of gender as an important determinant of social exclusion. Although disability and poverty impacts men and women, long-standing gender-based discrimination faced by women in most societies compounds the impact (Welch, 2002). There is extensive evidence that the social exclusion of women with disabilities in both developed and developing nations often includes systematic rape and mental and physical abuse, which often endures through their lives (Baladerian, Coleman and Stream, 2013; de Silva de Alwis, 2010). It is therefore likely that women with disabilities often face double or triple burden by belonging to two or more socially excluded groups.

Gender is also an important determinant of health status. This is especially true in countries where women experience discriminatory practices that make them vulnerable to disabilities and long-term health consequences. These practices include inability to access health care without being accompanied by a trusted male (Groce, 1997); discriminatory health care spending; and food consumption patterns, such as eating less or eating last, after the entire family has eaten (Pacey and Payne, 1985).

In developing countries, girls with disabilities begin experiencing discrimination at birth (Economic and Social Commission for Asia and the Pacific [ESCAP], 1995). Those who do survive may be denied medical treatment, sometimes food and are often victims of abuse (ESCAP, 1995). In addition, children, and especially girls with disabilities, are denied educational opportunities. According to UNICEF, only 1 per cent of girls with disabilities are literate in developing countries. In India, for example, dropout is much more prevalent among girls with disabilities than it is for boys with disabilities. And even among girls who do attend school, only one-quarter of girls with disabilities expressed an interest in pursuing higher education (Census of India, 2012). This pattern is particularly troubling given that education is often a critical pathway to escape social exclusion.

As adults, women with disabilities are disadvantaged in multiple ways. In the United States, they are more likely to be poor and to experience deprivation compared to women without disabilities. Furthermore, deprivation persists even among women with higher income (Parish, Rose and Andrews, 2009). Their social exclusion can be exacerbated by their status as single mothers as well as by challenges related to poverty (Magaña, Parish and Cassiman, 2008).

The situation is worse for women in cultures where they occupy low social positions (Groce, 1997). Women with disabilities are less likely to marry in contrast with other women (Dhungana, 2006; Nagata, 2003; Rao, 2004), which often limits their access to economic resources of spouses. In some instances, women with disabilities are prohibited from inheriting because of their impairments and their gender (Yeo, 2001; Groce, London and Stein, 2013). Women with disabilities thus experience a range of barriers in marriage, education, employment, income and property ownership. For many women living in countries that lack disability-related social welfare programmes, these barriers translate into extreme poverty and social exclusion (Groce, London and Stein, 2013).

Age and disability

Age can impact social exclusionary processes for individuals with disabilities, which can be characterized as a double burden. Improved public health measures and medical care have extended the lives of people with disabilities. However, this increasing longevity has increased the prevalence of age-related diseases, such as Alzheimer's and dementia. In general, impairments are more prevalent in older adults who live in low-income countries compared to high-income countries, and this is especially the case for women. This pattern points to the possibility that health risks accumulate over the lifespan, especially for women in low-income countries (Australian Institute of Health and Welfare, 2004).

Several of the social exclusionary processes experienced in old age are a continuation of social exclusions experienced in early life. This phenomenon is particularly true for people with lifelong disabilities like intellectual and developmental disabilities or mental illness (see also Chapter 14 for an in-depth analysis of ageing people with intellectual disabilities). Ghosh and Magaña (2009) found co-morbidities experienced by older adults with developmental disabilities and severe mental illnesses are often preventable at mid-life, yet the health care system inadequately addresses them. For example, people with severe mental illness are rarely screened for drug and alcohol abuse (Dixon et al., 2001) but do receive regular health checkups (Roberts, Roalfe, Wilson and Lester, 2007). Similarly, adults with developmental disabilities are less likely to be regularly screened for common, preventable health conditions (Beange, McElduff and Baker, 1992; Janicki, Dalton, Henderson and Davidson, 1999; Barr, Gilgunn, Kane and Moore, 1999). Ghosh and Magaña (2009) conclude that the lack of knowledge and training by health professionals in how to meet the needs of ageing adults with disabilities is largely to blame for these health disparities. Research from Chile and Uruguay has found younger people with disabilities are faring better in education and employment compared to older cohorts, which is likely due to better access to education and resources available to the younger cohort (Contreras, Ruiz-Tagle, Garcés and Azócar, 2006; cited also in WHO and World Bank, 2011).

Older adults with disabilities, and especially those with intellectual disabilities and mental illnesses, also experience social exclusion in the dearth of appropriate housing. The existing systems of elder care are not equipped to support the needs of older adults with these disabilities (Ansello and Coogle, 2000; Bigby, 2002, 2010; Rice and Robb, 2004). Further, the growing population of older adults with developmental disabilities is caught between the ageing and disability service systems, which are fragmented and reject responsibility for these individuals (Cleaver, Hunter, and Ouellette-Kuntz, 2009; Stainton et al., 2006). Overall, ageing adults experience exclusion in multiple domains.

Race, ethnicity and disability

Race and ethnicity are important determinants of social exclusion. People with disabilities often bear a double burden if they also experience racial or ethnic discrimination in education, employment, and health care. Magaña and Ghosh (2013) found these individuals to be disadvantaged in multiple domains. First, older US adults from ethnic minorities who also had developmental disabilities and severe mental illness were likely to receive worse medical and psychiatric treatment than their white counterparts (Lagomasino et al., 2005; Satre, Campbell, Gordon and Weisner, 2010; Heller and Factor, 1991). Further, people of Latino and African-American ethnic origin had more frequent unmet service needs than their white peers (Pruchno and McMullen, 2004). In terms of employment, education and poverty, adults with disabilities who are of African-American or Latino ethnic origin have higher rates of poverty, less education, and low rates of employment compared to their white counterparts (American Community Survey, 2011).

Material hardship, deprivation, and marginalization

We turn now to a consideration of deprivation. Although poverty and social exclusion are often used interchangeably, they are different concepts (Atkinson and Hills, 1998). Unlike social exclusion, as noted above, poverty is directly related to income and a lack of assets or other economic resources, which often leads to deprivation.

Deprivation is not the same as social exclusion, yet very often researchers use measures of deprivation as a proxy for social exclusion (Barnes, 2005). Deprivation emphasizes the inability to achieve a minimally adequate living standard, secure needed material resources and have diets and amenities that prevent people from engaging in 'the roles ... relationships and ... customary behavior which is expected of them by virtue of their membership of society' (Townsend, 1993). Deprivation is thus a narrower concept than social exclusion, which includes additional domains of relational importance such as participation in cultural activities, social life, citizenship, power and politics. Deprivation is typically quantified by housing instability, food insecurity or hunger, the inability to pay bills and living in unsafe or toxic environments (Boushey, Brocht, Gundersen and Bernstein, 2001; Parish et al., 2008). Over the past few decades, the United States and European Union countries have been collecting these supplemental measures of hardship in addition to the traditional income poverty measures.

Finally, marginalization and exclusion are two different concepts. Marginalization means being able to participate, but at the margins. For people with disabilities, who are typically left completely out of mainstream education, employment and legal and social engagements, the reality is most often exclusion rather than marginalization (Peters, 2009).

In conclusion, social exclusion incorporates components of social justice, inequity and human rights, in contrast to concepts such as traditional income poverty, deprivation and marginalization, which are predominantly measures of disparities.

Relationship between poverty, disability and social exclusion

We begin this section of the chapter with a case example that illustrates the relationships among poverty, disability and social exclusion (see Box 6.1).

This case describes a situation that is all too common in many areas of the world, where political realities hamper already struggling economies and individuals' access to services. Although Israel is a signatory to the CRPD, how can the CRPD be employed in the West Bank, given the shared control between Israel and the Palestinian Authority? Furthermore, in this case, CBR workers played a significant role in the identification of individuals with disabilities. How can their work be expanded for the most vulnerable and impoverished communities across the globe? Lastly, this case illustrated the tremendous financial and emotional toll placed on the family of the twins.

Box 6.1.   Relationship between poverty, disability and social exclusion in the West Bank: The case of Abu Rami and his family

Israel and Jordan surround the West Bank, which owes its name to its location on the western side of the Jordan River. The Oslo Accords established three areas of control in the West Bank, the largest of which (Area C) is fully ruled by the Israeli government. The Palestinian Authority and the Israeli Government control the remaining two non-contiguous areas either fully or in part. Internal checkpoints and security barriers often obstruct access to services within the West Bank.

The economy in the West Bank is weak. Nearly one-fifth of the population has poverty-level income and nearly one-fourth of adults are unemployed (US Central Intelligence Agency, 2012). Furthermore, almost one-third of the West Bank population in 2012 was undernourished (UN, 2014b). Ongoing political turmoil throughout the region makes the area vulnerable to future economic instability (Vishwanath and Serajuddin, 2012).

Abu Rami and his family live in a rural Palestinian village in the West Bank near an Israeli settlement. Abu Rami is a 45-year-old father to five children ranging in age from 8 to 20 years old. He has been unemployed since he was injured 15 years ago. He inherited his home and a bit of land from his father. His only income is from renting a small field to a local farmer, and he struggles to provide his family with food and other necessities.

Abu Rami has been a widower since his wife passed away during the birth of his twin girls eight years ago. His wife unexpectedly went into premature labour at 27 weeks, and the local midwife was unable to deliver the babies at home. Eventually, the family was able to arrange transportation to take Abu Rami's wife to the nearest hospital, about 30 minutes away. Unfortunately, by this time, the doctors could not save the mother's life. The babies spent a month in the hospital. The hospital stay proved to be too expensive for Abu Rami, and he decided to take his daughters home against the doctors' advice.

The twins, Fatima and Hadeel, never seemed 'right' to Abu Rami. Abu Rami's oldest daughter, Samira, who was ten years old when the girls were born, assumed primary responsibility for the twins' care, but they ate poorly and grew slowly. Community Based Rehabilitation (CBR) workers, who encouraged him to take the twins to a specialist, visited Abu Rami every other month. However, he resisted because of the difficulty in travelling to the nearest town, and the costs of travel and medical care. By the time the twins were age 4, the CBR workers were quite concerned that they were not yet speaking, and arranged for an evaluation by a paediatrician. Both twins were diagnosed with autism, stunting and malnourishment. The CBR workers could not locate any autism-specific services in the area, and the local public school and the local agency serving children with developmental disabilities both refused to accept the twins because of the severity of their impairments. Abu Rami and his family have struggled emotionally and financially, as the twins' behaviour has become more challenging over time. They neither speak nor respond to verbal commands. Hadeel, in particular, is sensitive to fabric on her skin, and thus removes any clothing she can. A number of times she has left the home alone without clothing and has been found running in the village. After the latest incident, Abu Rami began to lock Hadeel up in a room all day, where she often injures herself trying to escape.

(continued)

Box 6.1. Continued

Abu Rami reports feelings of intense shame regarding the twins' behaviour. He says his neighbours refuse to speak to him. Furthermore, he is estranged from his family because they blame his wife's death and twins' disabilities on a 'curse' on him from God (see Chapter 5). His eldest daughter, Samira, dropped out of school in the eighth grade because of her responsibilities as the twins' caretaker. Abu Rami acknowledges he has developed severe depression and rarely leaves his home. He remarks, 'I know there are great services to help the twins in Europe, but I cannot even afford to go to Ramallah'.

Relationship between disability and poverty

The relationships among poverty, disability and social exclusion are multi-dimensional, and each concept shares a bidirectional relationship with the others. Therefore, it is necessary to address them simultaneously, rather than individually, if we are to eliminate social exclusion and poverty of people with disabilities in order to improve their lives (Yeo, 2001; Parnes et al., 2009; Trani et al., 2010). We first describe the bidirectional relationship between poverty and social exclusion. Poverty refers to 'capacity deprivation', meaning low income or resources (Sen, 1999) or limitation of resources (material, cultural and social) that are inadequate and result in people being denied minimally acceptable living conditions (European Council of Ministers, 1985).

There is mounting evidence that the relationship between poverty and disability is bidirectional (Elwan, 1999; Emerson and Hatton, 2009; Fujiura and Yamaki, 2000; Parnes et al., 2009). People with disabilities and their families consistently report higher rates of income poverty than other families (Elwan, 1999; Barron and Ncube, 2010; Emerson and Hatton, 2009; Fujiura and Yamaki, 2000). These families also report less income, savings, assets and possessions compared to households that do not include people with disabilities (Eide and Loeb, 2006; Parish, Rose and Swaine, 2010), with some evidence showing a long-term impact of raising children with disabilities on savings when parents are followed longitudinally into mid-life (Parish, Seltzer, Greenberg and Floyd, 2004). Further, families that include people with disabilities are more likely to report material hardship and deprivation, such as food insecurity, inability to pay regular expenses, unmet health care, compared to households without people with disabilities (Emerson and Hatton, 2009; Parish et al., 2008). Unlike for other families, hardship and deprivation occur in families that include people with disabilities, irrespective of household income level, even after controlling for a range of background characteristics (Parish et al., 2008; Ghosh and Parish, 2013). Families of people with disabilities need resources over and above what is needed by other families with similar income, to attain the same level of well-being. These findings echo Sen's (1999, p. 74) example of disability as capability deprivation, in which 'a person who is disabled may have a larger basket of primary goods and have less chance to lead a normal life (or to pursue her objectives) than an able bodied person with a similar basket of primary goods.'

Pathways of increased vulnerability to poverty

We describe several possible pathways through which disability increases vulnerability to poverty. The first pathway involves the impact of disability on education and later employment. Due to stigmatizing attitudes, discrimination and often outright legal exclusion, children with disabilities are often precluded from obtaining an adequate education or any education at all. Young adults with disabilities then face limited employment options, and again encounter stigma and discrimination in the workforce (see Chapter 12 on livelihoods). Taken together, inadequacies in education and employment limit life chances and reduce families' financial well-being. Disparities start early in the life of children with disabilities and persist throughout life, with long-term consequences for their financial well-being in adulthood.

Worldwide, children with disabilities are five times more likely to have never enrolled in schools, compared to children without disabilities (Braithwaite and Mont, 2009). In developing countries such as India, for example, only 10 per cent of people with disabilities had completed secondary education, and just 3 per cent had a graduate degree. Dropout rates among people with disabilities range around 52 per cent overall, and at every education level the dropout rates for people with disabilities were significantly elevated compared to those without disabilities (Census of India, 2012).

Similarly, significant disability-based disparities in educational outcomes have also been reported in developed countries such as the United States. There is recent evidence of significant, persistent gaps in the four-year graduation rate between children with and without disabilities. Another study found that in three US states, more children with learning disabilities dropped out than graduated (Cortiella, 2013; Samuels, 2014).

These disparities that originate in childhood subsequently translate into under- or unemployment and poverty in adulthood (see Chapter 8 on children). In the United States, in contrast to same-age non-disabled adults, working age adults with disabilities were less likely to be employed, less likely to have completed college, earned significantly less, and had much higher rates of poverty, compared to their non-disabled peers (American Community Survey, 2008; Centers for Disease Control and Prevention, 2011). This pattern is evident both in other developed and developing nations (WHO and World Bank, 2011).

A large body of research has confirmed persistent, troubling disability-based disparities in education, employment and poverty. However, few studies have investigated the dynamic processes through which disability impacts poverty. One compelling longitudinal study from the United Kingdom found that the onset of disability was accompanied by a precipitous decline in employment and income. Although income started recovering over time, it never closed the gap and reverted to pre-disability levels (Jenkins and Rigg, 2003). These findings suggest that barriers to employment and education, both measures of social exclusion, possibly mediate the relationship between disability and poverty.

The second pathway through which disability increases vulnerability to poverty comes from the high costs of living with impairment borne by care-giving families or individuals with disabilities themselves (see Chapter 15). Adults with disabilities and family caregivers bear the direct costs of disability in the form of out-of-pocket expenses for things like treatment, medical care, medication, home modifications, assistive devices, therapies and transporta-tion. In addition, people with disabilities and family caregivers generally incur indirect costs too, in the form of lost employment, taking time off or working part-time (Parish et al., 2004; Porterfield, 2002; Newacheck and Kim, 2005; Parish and Cloud, 2006; Chen and Newacheck, 2006; Perrin, 2002; Parish, Shattuck and Rose, 2009). These patterns of reducing or foregoing employ-ment are particularly prevalent among mothers raising children with disabil-ities in developed nations.

Thirdly, poverty can cause disability. Living in impoverished circumstances exposes children and adults to unhealthy and unsafe environments and lim-its their access to adequate nourishment and medical care, including prenatal care. These conditions in turn increase the likelihood that an individual will acquire a disability (Brooks-Gunn and Duncan, 1997; Elwan, 1999; Emerson and Hatton, 2009; Evans, 2004; Palmer, 2011; WHO and World Bank, 2011). UNICEF (2008) has found that children who experience discrimination have poor access to social services, are stunted or underweight and have an elevated risk of acquiring disabilities. Further, poverty increases the probability of get-ting other health conditions that lead to disability (for example polio, tuber-culosis, HIV). We next discuss the bidirectional relationship between disability and social exclusion.

Relationship between disability and social exclusion

People with disabilities have been excluded from opportunities historically because of stigma, fear and societal assumptions about normality. Cultural ideolo-gies of the meaning and manifestations of disability shape political ideologies because politics reflects the needs of the larger society (Dye, 1981) (see Chapter 4). Finally, people who are socially excluded experience a range of curtailed life opportunities, which might heighten their vulnerability to acquiring disabil-ities. For example, being poor and socially excluded may delay access to early intervention and health services, which may cause disability, leading to further exclusion and exacerbation of existing disability (Burchardt, 2003) (see Chapter 10 on inclusive health).

We conclude that poverty, social exclusion and disability are enmeshed in a web of causality. According to the Asian Development Bank (2000), poverty and disability reinforce one another, leading to exclusion and increased vulner-ability. To reduce social exclusion, conditions that lead to impairment should be prevented, and barriers to participation must be eliminated. Similarly, to reduce poverty among people with disabilities, social exclusion must be eradi-cated. In other words, to break the cycle of disability, social exclusion and poverty, all three must be addressed simultaneously.

International strategies to eradicate poverty

As discussed in Chapter 3, the United Nations Convention on the Rights of Persons with Disabilities (CRPD) holds considerable promise to advance the human rights of individuals with disabilities. The CRPD contains specific language to address the disproportionate levels of poverty experienced by those with disabilities. Furthermore, the CRPD utilizes a framework of the social model of disability (see Chapter 2), in which societal barriers and isolation facing individuals with differences are the primary causes of disability.

The CRPD is a tremendous step towards recognizing the societal roots of disability, which contribute to the endemic poverty among people with disabilities worldwide. The preamble recognizes that '[t]he majority of persons with disabilities live in conditions of poverty' and Article 28, 'Adequate standard of living and social protection', recommends explicit measures to be taken by State parties to alleviate the poverty experienced by disabled persons. Taken together, CRPD and one of the largest anti-poverty campaigns in history, the United Nations Millennium Development Goals (MDGs) create the potential to make direct and lasting reductions in poverty among individuals with disabilities. Yet, the MDGs have done little to explicitly confront the specific challenges faced by people with disabilities and their families. Below, the MDGs are examined in more detail, along with a summary of key international reports on global disability issues. Finally, this section will briefly discuss international efforts to incorporate individuals with disabilities into the post-2015 United Nations development agenda.

The Millennium Development Goals (MDGs) represent the United Nations' current foremost international effort to create global partnerships to achieve eight specific action-oriented development goals by 2015. Anti-poverty measures are a central focus of the MDGs. In addition, the MDGs address universal primary education, maternal health, gender equality, child mortality, malaria and the HIV/AIDS epidemic, international partnerships and the environment. Each goal has one to three targets, with an objective for completion by 2015.

United Nations agencies, governments, and regional and community partners are tasked with implementing, monitoring and evaluating programmes which specifically tackle these targets. In addition, the United Nations and their partners invest heavily in social awareness campaigns to mobilize communities on the eight key development goals.

The MDGs were designed to reduce poverty among the world's most vulnerable and marginalized individuals. The multi-pronged action plan required the engagement of communities, local and international organizations, and governments. Yet, despite strong evidence of the interrelationships among poverty, social exclusion and disability, the MDGs, including all eight goals and their associated targets and indicators, are silent on any disability-specific issues (Table 6.1 provides an adaptation of the MDGs and targets including disability). This is troubling since, as highlighted in the CRPD, societal barriers and marginalization play a large part in contributing to the 'disability' of persons with limited access to resources and support. By ignoring people

Table 6.1. Millennium development goals and targets (adapted to include disability)

Goal	Targets
(1) Eradicate extreme hunger and poverty	Halve, between 1990 and 2015, the proportion of people **with disabilities**[1] whose income is less than $1.25 a day. Achieve full and productive employment and decent work for all, including **people with disabilities**, women and young people. Halve, between 1990 and 2015, the proportion of people **with and without disabilities** who suffer from hunger.
(2) Achieve universal primary education	Ensure that, by 2015, children everywhere, boys and girls alike, **with and without disabilities**, will be able to complete a full course of primary schooling.
(3) Promote gender equality and empower women	Eliminate gender **and disability** disparity in primary and secondary education, preferably by 2005, and in all levels of education no later than 2015.
(4) Reduce child mortality	Reduce by two-thirds, between 1990 and 2015, the under-five mortality rate.
(5) Improve maternal health	Reduce by three-quarters the maternal mortality ratio. Achieve universal access to reproductive health **for women with and without disabilities**.
(6) Combat HIV/AIDS, malaria, and other diseases	Halt by 2015 and begin to reverse the spread of HIV/AIDS. Achieve, by 2010, universal access to treatment for HIV/AIDS for all those who need it. Halt by 2015 and begin to reverse the incidence of malaria and other major diseases.
(7) Ensure environmental sustainability	Integrate the principles of sustainable development into country policies and programmes, and reverse the loss of environmental resources. Reduce biodiversity loss, achieving, by 2010, a significant reduction in the rate of loss. Halve, by 2015, the proportion of the population without sustainable access to safe drinking water and basic sanitation. Achieve, by 2020, a significant improvement in the lives of at least 100 million slum dwellers.
(8) Develop a global partnership for development	Develop further an open, rule-based, predictable, non-discriminatory trading and financial system. Address the special needs of least developed countries. Address the special needs of landlocked developing countries and small island developing States. Deal comprehensively with the debt problems of developing countries. In cooperation with pharmaceutical companies, provide access to affordable essential drugs in developing countries, **for people with and without disabilities**. In cooperation with the private sector, make available benefits of new technologies, especially information and communications, **for people with and without disabilities**.

[1] The official website of the Millennium Development Goals is http://www.un.org/millenniumgoals/.

with disabilities in the planning and implementation of the MDGs, the United Nations missed an important opportunity to make meaningful improvements in the lives of people with disabilities who live in poverty worldwide.

Eleven years after the General Assembly adopted the Millennium Declaration, the United Nations (2011a) released a report which addressed the considerable omission of disability issues in the MDGs. In this report, the authors integrated data from multiple sources, including the World Health Organization/World Bank *World Report on Disability* (2011), and argued all of the eight MDGs are relevant to individuals with disabilities. Although gender equality has now been widely recognized as a 'cross-cutting' issue affecting development as a whole, disability has not garnered the same attention. This omission persists despite wide recognition of the prevalence of poverty and inequality in this population. Indeed, the cyclical nature of poverty and disability pervade every MDG. For example, as described above, children with disabilities are often denied the right to primary education, which results in severe and lasting consequences on their future economic stability and social inclusion.

The report proposed 'mainstreaming' the issue of disability throughout the MDG initiative – from planning programmes to evaluating outcome data, and offered the following four recommendations: (1) Embed disability issues into every MDG programmes and operational activity; (2) include persons with disabilities in MDG awareness and mobilization campaigns; (3) monitor, collect and analyse data specific to persons with disabilities in MDG programmes; and (4) integrate key stakeholders in the disability community into ongoing MDG efforts.

In fact, the 2011 United Nations report contended that without explicitly including individuals with disabilities in all MDG processes, the entire MDG initiative would be unable to completely meet its targets at all.

In reality, the shortfalls of the MDGs related to disability issues are nearly moot given the 2015 deadline. Looking ahead, the United Nations has proposed an ambitious post-2015 development agenda. United Nations Secretary-General Ban Ki-moon spearheaded discussions to revisit development goals and engage more stakeholders in future MDG efforts. A website, the World We Want 2015 (http://www.worldwewant2015.org/) serves as a platform for individuals and communities to contribute their suggestions for the post-2015 agenda.

The possibility of the increased visibility of persons with disabilities in the post-2015 MDGs is promising: in 2010, the Secretary-General released a report, *Keeping the Promise: Realizing the Millennium Development Goals for Persons with Disabilities towards 2015 and Beyond.* It offered recommendations to improve data collection and analysis, accessibility and equal participation related to persons with disabilities. In their 2011 report, the United Nations offered strategies for disability issues to gain 'entry' into the MDGs. Primarily, these entry points will be made by stakeholders in the global disability community: individuals with disabilities and their families, community-based advocates, and disability agencies and organizations. The report highlights the work of three efforts dedicated to including disability issues in current and future MDG discussions: Include Everybody Campaign (http://www.includeeverybody.org/); UN Department of Economic and Social Affairs

'Enable' website (http://www.un.org/disabilities/); and Inclusion International (http://www.inclusioninternational.org/en/ii_priority_areas/mdg/index.html).

In conclusion, no concentrated efforts were made early on in the MDG process to include persons with disabilities. Nonetheless, the present decade has seen a number of important efforts to increase awareness of the importance of including disability-specific issues into all aspects of the MDG process. Perhaps these endeavours will serve as a model for future collaborations and initiatives across the globe to improve the outlook for those challenged by poverty and disability.

Conclusions

Worldwide, people with disabilities experience high rates of poverty and social exclusion. The evidence suggests a bidirectional relationship between poverty and disability. Thus, efforts to improve the well-being of people with disabilities must focus on poverty and the social exclusion that supports high poverty levels. Four complementary approaches are needed to tackle these complex issues. First, anti-poverty initiatives, including the UN Millennium Development Goals, must fully include people with disabilities and their family caregivers. True inclusion is imperative for poverty to be eradicated among disabled people. Second, data collection and surveillance efforts must be strengthened to provide real-time information about not just the well-being of people with disabilities but also the barriers they face to full social, economic and educational inclusion. Third, the CRPD must be implemented and assertively enforced in every nation on earth, and monitoring of implementation efforts must be scrupulous. Finally, assiduous efforts must be made to prevent impairment. These prevention efforts must improve public health and medical care globally, including effective prenatal care and adequate nutrition, and must provide access to education and employment opportunities for all children. This ambitious agenda is imperative if we are to create a just world that honours and fully includes every person in all aspects of community and civic life.

Summary of key points

- The relationships among poverty, disability and social exclusion are bidirectional. Each of these factors causes the other.
- To improve the lives and living conditions of people with disabilities and their families, aggressive public health, education and anti-poverty campaigns are needed.
- The preamble of the CRPD recognizes that 'The majority of persons with disabilities live in conditions of poverty'. Article 28, 'Adequate standard of living and social protection', recommends explicit measures to be taken by State parties to alleviate the poverty experienced by disabled persons.

- The UN's Millennium Development Goals did not include the needs of people with disabilities and their families. The world will not make meaningful progress in the fight against poverty if people with disabilities are excluded.
- Post-2015 MDGs must fully include people with disabilities in the planning and implementation of development strategies.

STUDY QUESTIONS

1. In your country, what actions have been taken to reduce poverty and social exclusion of people with disabilities? Have these been effective? Why or why not?

2. If you had the chance to advise the United Nations on how to improve its post-2015 MDG strategies, and to ensure that people with disabilities are included, what would your advice be?

3. In developed countries, to what extent do social security payments perpetuate poverty among persons with disabilities?

Further reading and resources

Rangita de Silva de Alwis. (2010). *The Intersections of the CEDAW and CRPD: Putting Women's Rights and Disability Rights into Action in Four Asian Countries* (Wellesley, MA: Wellesley Centers for Women, Wellesley College).

Ann Elwan. (1999). *Poverty and Disability: A Survey of Literature.* Social Protection Discussion Paper Series No. 9932. World Bank, Washington, DC.

Eric Emerson and Chris Hatton. (2009). 'Socioeconomic position, poverty and family research,' *International Review of Research in Mental Retardation*, 37, 97–129.

Amartya Sen. (1999). *Development as Freedom* (New York: Alfred A. Knopf. Inc).

Peter Townsend. (1993). *The International Analysis of Poverty* (London: Harvester Wheatsheaf).

United Nations. (2011). *Disability and the Millennium Development Goals: A Review of the MDG Process and Strategies for Inclusion of Disability Issues in Millennium Development Goal efforts*, http://www.un.org/disabilities/documents/review_of_disability_and_the_mdgs.pdf.

War and Disability: Stories of Dread and Courage

Fabricio E. Balcazar
Daniel Balcazar

> *States Parties shall take, in accordance with their obligations under international law, including international humanitarian law and international human rights law, all necessary measures to ensure the protection and safety of persons with disabilities in situations of risk, including situations of armed conflict, humanitarian emergencies and the occurrence of natural disasters.*
>
> **UN Convention on Rights of Persons with Disabilities**
> **Article 11: Situations of risk and humanitarian emergencies**

Introduction

The history of disability has long been closely connected to instances of war and conflict, as very often those who survive the violence of war end up with an acquired disability. Since ancient times, we hear stories of individuals who acquired disability through war, most commonly resulting in some type of physical, sensory and/or mental impairment. In addition, advancements in the medical treatment of victims of war violence during the last half-century have reduced the historically high rates of mortality and significantly increased the number of survivors with disabilities (Gerber, 2006). However, physical and psychological injuries are not only impacting on the soldiers engaged directly in the war but also on large civilian populations located in or near the conflict zones. In fact, attacking and terrorizing the civilian population has long been a strategy utilized by those engaged in war and conflict. The more recent introduction of weapons of mass destruction has greatly increased the risk of casualties and injuries among the civilian population. For example, Gerber (2006) mentions that there were at least 87,000 civilians killed and 41,000 injured by the American firebombing campaign of Tokyo in 1945 and more than 200,000 deaths in Hiroshima and Nagasaki, with countless injured survivors, the majority of them civilians.

Most industrialized countries started their welfare programmes and services to help war veterans with disabilities, particularly after the First and Second

World Wars. Examples include the introduction of medical and rehabilitation services, pensions, housing, education and other support services and benefits for war veterans. Cohen (2006) mentions how Germany established the Weimar Republic's National Pension Law in 1920 to give war veterans with disabilities not only a pension but also occupational retraining and free medical care for all their service-related injuries. Cohen adds that after WWII, the German model was followed by most of the countries participating in the conflict. In the United States, rehabilitation programmes, designed to help veterans return to work, predated the introduction of such services for civilians with disabilities by almost 50 years.

Gerber (2006) also pointed out that '[t]here has been an evident reluctance to come to terms with the price that military conflict has exacted on the bodies and minds of both participants and bystanders' (p. 1621). In fact, little attention is paid to the civilian victims of war, often referred to in current media reports as 'collateral damage', language which attempts, in part, to mitigate the public's negative perception of acts of war that injure or kill 'innocent bystanders'.

The purpose of this chapter is to examine disability in relation to acts of war and armed conflict, illustrated by several case examples from recent conflict zones from around the world, including those of Syria, the Democratic Republic of Congo, Bosnia and Colombia, and from war veterans from the United States. We draw conclusions from the examples with regards to the plight of people with disabilities exposed to armed conflicts and efforts to address their needs.

The Convention on the Rights of Persons with Disabilities (CRPD), adopted by the United Nations General Assembly in 2006, is a good starting point for understanding the current relationship between acts of war and disability (see Chapter 3 for an in-depth discussion on the CRPD). The CRPD defines persons with disabilities as those who have long-term physical, mental, intellectual or sensory impairments which, in interaction with various barriers, may hinder their full and effective participation in society on an equal basis with others. Given that the main purpose of the CRPD is to 'promote, protect and ensure the full and equal enjoyment of all human rights and fundamental freedoms by all persons with disabilities, and to promote respect for their inherent dignity' (Hendricks, 2007), Article 11 of the CRPD states that:

> *Situations of Risk and Humanitarian Emergencies:* States Parties shall take, in accordance with their obligations under international law, including international humanitarian law and international human rights law, all necessary measures to ensure the protection and safety of persons with disabilities in situations of risk, including situations of armed conflict, humanitarian emergencies and the occurrence of natural disasters.
>
> (Hendricks, 2007)

The CRPD seeks to ensure that persons with disabilities are protected under situations of armed conflict. The intentional or unintentional use of force to terrorize military or civilian populations is covered under other United

Nations treaties, like the Universal Declaration of Human Rights of 1948 and the Geneva Convention of 1949. Intentionally inflicting harm on captured soldiers or civilians is a crime against humanity. Unfortunately, such brutality is common. See for example the case of Patrick Lahai, a double amputee who lives in Bo, Sierra Leone's second-largest city:

> We were all captured in the village. Some were killed, some were burned alive and some had their hands chopped off. If you were lucky they would only chop off one hand. I was the last boy they cut; they ended up chopping off both my hands and now I am a double amputee.
>
> (Feika, 2013)

In the following sections, we are going to examine various armed conflicts from around the world and consider how such conflicts affect people with disabilities. In the last section, we will consider the relative effectiveness of some of the humanitarian responses to the crises and interventions trying to address the unmet needs of the affected civilian or military populations.

The Syrian civil war

The Syrian civil war is at the time of writing this chapter an ongoing conflict between the Syrian government led by President Bashar Hafez al-Assad and his Ba'ath party against several groups seeking to dismantle his government. The war began in April of 2012 and was catalysed by popular nation-wide protests against Assad regime, which eventually turned into an armed conflict. As of March 2014, the death toll was calculated to be more than 100,000, with many more injured. The conflict has also spurred the departure of over 2 million Syrians to nearby countries like Jordan, Lebanon, Turkey and Iraq, and there are almost 4 million citizens internally displaced and 6.8 million Syrians who require some form of humanitarian assistance, half of those being children (United Nations High Commissioner for Refugees [UNHCR], 2013).

The United Nations Committee on the Rights of Persons with Disabilities (CRPD), recently reported that '[l]iving in the midst of conflict is physically and emotionally distressing, but all the more so for persons with disabilities who face the same if not greater barriers in times of armed conflict' (United Nations Office of the High Commissioner for Human Rights [OHCHR], 2013). The Committee also voiced grave concern about the plight of persons with disabilities who have fled the fighting and are now in refugee camps in neighbouring countries:

> Many persons with disabilities have been affected by the Syrian conflict; there is clearly a large number of refugees and internally displaced persons who are disproportionately at risk of being neglected, excluded or even abused because of their impairments and traumas, particularly the most vulnerable women and children with disabilities.
>
> (CRPD, 2013)

Box 7.1. Syria: The case of Hadi

Hadi and his family are Syrian refugees who fled their home after a bomb exploded on their home. Hadi is a 3-year-old boy partially paralysed by shrapnel lodged in his spine from the explosion. The family is currently living in an unfinished cement housing development in a remote area of the Bekaa Valley in Lebanon. The family lacks contact with a proper rehabilitation facility. A Handicap International Mobile Team including a social worker and a physical therapist visited Hadi and his family last winter and brought a small walker to teach Hadi to walk and stand again. Because of their location, it is difficult for rehabilitation aid to reach Hadi. This highlights a problem happening in Syria as well, with aid teams having trouble giving consistent aid to persons with disabilities in areas of heavy fighting. (Handicap International, 2013)

There is also grave concern for refugees who have been displaced to neighbouring countries and are in need of assistance. Handicap International reports that 18 per cent of Syrian refugees in Jordan and Lebanon (well over 250,000 people) have at least one impairment (i.e. physical, sensory, or intellectual) and are unlikely to receive the services they need (Handicap International, 2014).

A recent United Nations report from the High Commissioner for Refugees (UNHCR, 2013) detailed that the continuing conflict in Syria has produced an outflow of some 570,000 refugees and other displaced persons to Lebanon. The number is expected to reach 1 million by the end of the year. Refugees in Lebanon are being hosted in over 1,200 locations across the country, straining the capacities of local responders and putting severe pressure on public services and jobs. The living conditions of refugees and other displaced persons are increasingly difficult, and with the crisis entering its third year, the resources of both displaced and host communities are diminished. The report also argues that '1.3 per cent of the expected refugee population (approximately 13,000 persons) is estimated to have some form of disability, yet only about half of them will have access to medical care and about a third will be assisted with rehabilitative services' (p. 108). The report adds that services for physically and mentally disabled individuals and supports for longer-term care will not be available in all areas of the country, particularly in the South and Mount Lebanon. Available equipment and materials (e.g. hearing and visual aids) are unlikely to meet the needs, and rehabilitation centres will continue to lack skilled and trained staff (UNHCR, 2013).

The war has resulted in thousands of amputees, but exact figures at the time of writing this manuscript are currently unknown. Kassar (2012) asked the Medical Health Commission for the Syrian Revolution about the estimated number of either temporary or permanently disabled people resulting from military operations, and they responded. 'We can't tell,' or 'We don't know.' One of the doctors said, 'I have seen many persons lose eyes, hands, feet or arms as a result of war and other random acts of violence, and the families lack the fundamental infrastructure to care for the people – the men, women and children who become disabled' (Kassar, 2012). The Disability Rights Syria (DRS) report added:

> The need is beyond our capacity, but through coordination and cooperation with other national, regional and international agencies working on the ground, we need to start a program that will expand and develop to become a sustainable program for supporting war victims and persons with disabilities during the revolution, during the transition period and until we have a new Syria that is capable of providing protection and a sustainable rehabilitation program for all its citizens.
>
> (Kassar, 2013)

Although there is a lack of concrete data on the war's effects in relation to disability, there are data on selected populations that serve as a microcosm. From November 2012 to October 2013, Handicap International (2014) conducted 1,847 interviews with displaced persons in Syria, in the areas where the organization is working to provide them with physical care and psychological support. Almost half (913) of those interviewed had sustained injuries related to the current conflict. One in five of these people were aged below 17 years old. Of those numbers, '89 per cent declared they had not received satisfactory access to rehabilitation services when initially interviewed' (p. 2). Also, 25 per cent of those hurt from explosive weapons (60 per cent of interviewees) have undergone amputations, 21 per cent suffered peripheral nerve injury, and 7 per cent suffered spinal cord injuries (p. 4). Alarmingly, 17 per cent of those faced with severe or permanent impairments are heads of their households, with an average of over seven dependents (Handicap International, 2014).

As the conflict in Syria continues, the number of people injured and displaced by the conflict will continue to increase (see Box 7.1). The efforts of organizations like Handicap International, DRS and UNICEF are critical for assisting individuals with disabilities and their families, although the resources available are not nearly enough to meet the demand for assistance and support (see Chapter 6).

Bosnia

The Bosnian war was an ethnically-rooted armed conflict that took place between 6 April 1992 and 14 December 1995. The war began after the collapse of the former republic of Yugoslavia. At the time, the predominant ethnic groups in the area were the Muslim Bosniaks (which represented 44 per cent of the population), Christian Orthodox Serbs (31 per cent) and Catholic Croats (17 per cent). All three groups claimed Yugoslavia as their ethnic homeland. Yugoslavia began unravelling in 1980 when the former communist president Josip Broz Tito died. He had kept the ethnic tensions from escalating, and after his death nationalist movements began to sprout. In Bosnia, Croats and Bosniaks formed a tactical alliance to gain political power over the Serbs. As war started on multiple fronts, the Serbs claimed control over half of Bosnia.

Serbian ethnic cleansing became widespread in 1992, and the Bosniaks and Croats began fighting.

The total number of casualties from the war was never established, but a report from the Bosnian Institute for Public Health (cited by Burg & Shoup, 1999) estimated that approximately 146,000 people died (about 40 per cent civilians, the majority from the Muslim and Croat territories), and 175,000 were left injured or disabled (e.g. as many as 5,000 people lost limbs and required prostheses).

The World Bank funded the War Victims Rehabilitation Project for Bosnia and Herzegovina from 1996 to 2001 in order to help approximately 40,000 war victims with disabilities (World Bank, 2000). The project was designed as an emergency response to address post-war medical needs and as initial support to the health sector reform in the Federation of Bosnia and Herzegovina. In this context, the project had the main objective of helping to reintegrate people with war-related disabilities into productive life. Secondary objectives were to introduce a more cost-effective approach for dealing with disabilities and to support the development of local and regional capacity to manage and deliver rehabilitation services. There were three main components of the project: The largest component was *community-based rehabilitation* (CBR) (see Chapter 10 for a discussion on CBR and health), which provided for the establishment of locally-based physical and psychosocial rehabilitation centres (CBRs) within or appended to existing health centres. The CBRs were designed to provide a continuum of essential diagnostic and treatment services for individuals with physical or mental disabilities (e.g. post-traumatic stress disorder, or PTSD). Prior to the war, services for these individuals had been provided only at centralized facilities, which would require that patients reside in or near the facilities for the course of treatment (which meant institutionalization). Local CBRs, in contrast, are enabling rehabilitation patients to continue to live and work in their own homes and business places without the disruptions that would occur in the previously existing system. The project planned to fund the development and operation of a network of 30 CBRs for physical rehabilitation. In addition, the project planned to fund the development and operation of 30 CBRs for the treatment of post-traumatic stress disorders and other psychosocial disorders as well as professional training in community-based psychosocial rehabilitation. Parallel financing would establish an additional eight CBRs for physical rehabilitation and eight for psychosocial rehabilitation, for a total network of 76 CBRs.

The project also included a *Prostheses Production* component, which was to support three main production units and five maintenance/service units. Through this component, training was also to be provided to approximately 75 existing and new technicians in prosthetic manufacturing. A third component, *Orthopaedic and Reconstructive Surgery*, planned to upgrade essential orthopaedic and reconstructive surgical services in three clinical centres (in Sarajevo, Tuzla and Mostar) and in four cantonal hospitals (in Zenica, Travnik, Livno and Bihac). This component planned to provide limited civil works, surgical instruments, supplies and pharmaceuticals to enable the effective functioning of the selected surgical units. The component planned also to provide training abroad to approximately 50 professionals involved in ortho-paedic and reconstructive surgery.

The operations of CBRs for mental health were delayed due to the lack of local expertize in community mental health and multidisciplinary services. The progress report from 1998 noted that 80 per cent of the mental health CBRs were not operational at that time due to the lack of trained psychiatrists or spe-cialized professionals. Two years later, 70 per cent of the mental health CBRs were operating as intended. The University of Sarajevo is also developing, with assistance from the Soros Foundation, a curriculum for the treatment of post-traumatic stress disorders. A total of 3,000 permanent prostheses were pro-vided to amputees. Approximately 2,100 prostheses were purchased through the project, and the Government of Iceland donated an additional 600. The report found that all the patients identified as needing prostheses have been fitted and supplied over the past three years. The Government informed the World Bank that project investments resulted in a greatly increased cap-acity for and quality of surgical procedures, and decreased waiting times, but detailed information on the number and types of surgeries undertaken was not available. There has only recently been progress in establishing a system to track patients and services, through the development and installation of man-agement information software. Despite these shortcomings, the project was successful in strengthening local capacity to provide rehabilitative services and therefore in decentralizing the health care system (see Box 7.2).

Box 7.2.   Bosnia: The case of Vahid

Vahid was born in 1961 in Tuzla, Bosnia and Herzegovina. He fought in the Bosnian war from 1992 to 1995 and at one point was injured by a grenade shell. His pros-tate gland, urinary tract and intestines were damaged, as were the peripheral nerves of his right leg. The injury greatly decreased his mobility. Along with these physical implications, he developed PTSD. After 1996, he was unable to continue to work at a shoe factory and received a pension from the government. He got outpatient therapy from one of the CBRs providing mental health treatment. He is glad he was not hospitalized because he was able to continue to receive the support from his friends and family. Vahid joined the disability rights movement to advocate for the rights of persons with disabilities because he was angry over the amount of discrimination and stigma he experienced. He eventually became the president of 'Fenix' (Phoenix), or the Association for Mutual Support in Mental Distress, in the Tuzla Canton. 'We have our own place where our members can meet. We also own a van, a wood-processing workshop and a greenhouse for vegetables. One of our main objectives is to raise awareness about mental health and the problems encountered by mental health ser-vice users.' He concluded: 'Since members of the organization have begun to talk openly about their problems, more of us have become engaged in socially beneficial activities and the issue of mental health has begun to take its rightful place in public awareness. I have found an inner energy that was always there, but which I had no access to before. Now I use that energy for my own good and the good of my com-munity'. (World Health Organization, 2014)

The Democratic Republic of Congo

The Democratic Republic of Congo (DRC) has been at war since 1998, which has devastated the country and involved nine African nations and at least 20 armed groups. Despite the signing of peace accords in 2003, fighting continues in the east of the country to date. The civil war is infamously known for its human rights abuses, including the use of systematic rape, child soldiers, mutilation, displacement and genocide. The war is the world's deadliest conflict, killing an estimated 5.4 million people since 1998 (Coghlan et al., 2007). More than 90 per cent of the dead were not killed in combat, but died instead from malaria, diarrhoea, pneumonia and malnutrition, especially among displaced populations living in unsanitary and over-crowded conditions that lack access to shelter, clean water, food and medicine. Forty-seven per cent of those deaths were of children under five. To save lives, improvements in security and increased humanitarian assistance are urgently needed. Conflict for control of the mineral wealth in Congo is behind some of the most violent atrocities in the Eastern Kivu states.

Aldersey (2013) reported that the Congolese government is generally absent from the affairs of people with disabilities, but people with disabilities do not accept or excuse their absence. Rather, 'Disability advocates continue to call for increased governmental presence in the affirmation and implementation of the rights of people with disabilities' (p. 795) (see Chapter 4 for a discussion on advocacy and lobbying in African countries). 'There are roughly 9.1 million people with disabilities in Congo, 11 per cent of the total population of almost 75 million,' said Patrick Pindu, coordinator of the National Federation of Associations of People Living with a Disability in Congo (quoted by Bakiman, 2012). Due to the lack of a stable central government, international aid agencies are the primary vehicles of assistance for persons with disabilities in the country. Mr. Pindu added: 'Amongst people with disabilities, 90 per cent are illiterate, 93 per cent are jobless and 96 per cent live in an unhealthy and inhumane environment' (Bakiman, 2012).

Jolie Apelo is one of around 350 members of the Kikwit Association of Disabled Persons. 'As you see me here, I don't eat properly due to a lack of financial resources. I'm unable to buy clothes so I can present myself like a human being worthy of the name, even if I am a member of an association' (quoted by Bakiman, 2012). Apelo's association is one of 226 that are part of an institute working for the defence, promotion and protection of the rights of the disabled in the DR Congo. 'We set up the National Training Institute for People with Disabilities more than three years ago, where they can learn appropriate technology for the production of soap, perfume, bread and so on. This helps them to care for themselves,' said Jean Etienne Makila, the institute's director general, who is also a person with a disability. 'In the Bas-Congo Province (west of the country), the provincial government has, for the first time, released two million Congolese francs (around 2,180 dollars) to create micro-credit facilities dedicated to associations of people with disabilities,' Mr. Makila said. 'If I couldn't fend for myself selling the bread I make at the market, I wouldn't be able to provide food for my children,' said Madeleine Murakupa, a disabled mother of two (quoted by Bakiman, 2012). Despite these efforts, however, the situation for people with disabilities in the DRC remains very worrying given their large numbers across the country.

There is one policy that is benefiting some people with disabilities, allowing them to pay less taxes and fees on each package of goods transported across the river in the crossing between the capitals of Kinshasa (DRC) and Brazzaville (Republic of Congo). The policy allows them to be 'hired' by able-bodied merchants to transport goods across the river, and some of them work as traders themselves. This policy has benefited many previously unemployed persons with disabilities to work as self-employed traders and use their disability to make a living (Radio Netherlands Worldwide Africa, 2014). The cost of a return trip across this 2-mile river stretch varies widely, as fees are randomly applied, and corruption is rampant on both sides. 'There are several ways of doing business. If you simply want to cross, you can recruit a blind man or another disabled person and be his guide,' a policeman explained. 'Your ticket will be half as expensive as the full price and you give a part of what you saved to the disabled person,' the policeman said (Radio Netherlands Worldwide Africa, 2014). Baggio Ngama Bamba of Kinshasa, who has a deformed leg, also uses his disability to make a living, but he said the stresses of trading across this hectic river are becoming unbearable for him. 'We buy produce in Kinshasa and we sell it here in Brazzaville. When we make a profit, we give money to those who help us,' he said. 'But now there is too much hassle, taxes and outgoings. It's too much' (Radio Netherlands Worldwide Africa, 2014).

These are examples of how people with disabilities have to fend for themselves and try to make a living in the absence of a government able to provide supports and services and in the midst of a civil war (see Chapter 12 on livelihoods). Resilience is what characterizes people facing desperate situations. People would do what is necessary to survive (see Box 7.3).

Box 7.3. The Democratic Republic of Congo: The case of Riciki

Riciki is a 19-year-old Congolese woman who, two years ago, on her way back from school, was stopped by a rebel soldier and raped. She managed to escape her attacker but in retaliation was shot multiple times while running away. She suffered gunshot wounds to her neck and legs. Riciki's mobility was severely affected; she is unable to bend her leg, and she now uses crutches. Although she struggles to walk the distance to school, Riciki is determined to finish her schooling and learn to become a seamstress. Given that she lives in her family farm, at an isolated village, she does not receive consistent rehabilitation services. She continues to do chores and work, even with her impaired mobility. (International Criminal Court, 2013)

Colombia

Colombia has been involved in a constant state of civil war that dates back to the 1948 assassination of a popular Colombian Liberal Party candidate. The assassination started clashes in a conflict that lasted ten years, involving paramilitary groups of the conservative and liberal parties. This conflict gave root to the ongoing (1968 to present) guerrilla insurgency between the FARC (Revolutionary Armed Forces of Colombia) and the Colombian government. The FARC evolved from one of the original Liberal paramilitary groups when some members embraced communist ideals and decided to fight on behalf of poor peasants in Colombia. However, in recent years, their ideological foundation has crumbled, and domestic support lessened because of their involvement in kidnappings and drug trafficking (Peace Direct, 2014).

Land owners developed their own paramilitary groups in the 1980s in order to combat the leftists insurgents, but those groups ended up engaged in extortion, drug trafficking and peasant massacres. Recent efforts to promote paramilitary demobilization have been successful in many, but not all, areas of the country. The government is currently engaged in peace negotiations with the FARC in Cuba. However, the armed conflict is fuelled by drug-related violence, organized crime and tensions with neighbouring Ecuador and Venezuela, which have been accused of supporting rebel groups. Relations with Venezuela, in particular, have worsened over recent months (Peace Direct, 2014).

Measuring the casualties of this long war is difficult, but a recent report from the Centro Nacional de Memoria Histórica (2013) found that 220,000 Colombians were killed between 1958 and 2013. Of that number, 176,000 were civilians – a ratio of eight civilians for every ten deaths, or about 80 per cent. Since 1981, paramilitaries have been the biggest perpetrators of violence. In the past three decades, there were 1,983 massacres, which have cost the lives of more than 400 children. The paramilitaries were responsible in 59 per cent of the cases, the guerrillas in 17 per cent, and state officials in 8 per cent of the cases. The war has also generated a very large population of displaced farmers – almost 4.7 million (Centro Nacional de Memoria Histórica, 2013).

One of the main side effects of the armed conflict in Colombia has been the proliferation of landmines. Colombia has the second-highest number of landmine victims in the world, after Afghanistan – 10,189 (Salcedo, 2013). These mines are generating thousands of lost limbs among those lucky enough to survive. Army sources say outlawed insurgents on both the left and the right were sowing about 26,000 new devices each year during the 1990s (Penhaul, 2001). Unfortunately, the prospects for mine-removal programmes are remote as long as the fighting continues. UNICEF works closely with the Colombian Campaign Against Landmines, setting up workshops and self-help groups to warn civilians of the risks from landmines.

The Colombian Integral Rehabilitation Centre has pioneered treatment for mine victims (see Box 7.4). The clinic treats children and adults who became disabled by landmines. Most of the clients are civilians, but occasionally the clinic

---

Box 7.4.   Colombia: The case of Edgar

Edgar lost his left leg to a landmine in 1992 while herding cows in a northwest province of Colombia. He was fortunate enough to survive the initial impact, which took his left leg and badly burned his right leg. He was driven on the back of a beer truck for two and a half hours to the nearest hospital that had the equipment to treat his wounds. Edgar struggled a lot after the incident; his girlfriend left him, and his hopes of joining the military were now impossible; he spent the months after his accident getting drunk and doing odd jobs. Now Edgar has kicked his alcohol habit and is working at the same clinic that fitted him with an artificial leg – the Colombian Integral Rehabilitation Centre. He moulds and polishes prostheses for other landmine victims and people experiencing physical disabilities. (Penhaul, 2001)

---

fits police agents and even former guerrillas with artificial limbs. The majority are desperately poor, so the clinic has developed functional low-cost alternatives to imported prostheses. The clinic specializes in providing affordable prosthetic legs for its patients. An artificial leg produced in its workshops costs between US$360 and US$700, compared to about US$2,200 for an imported one. The clinic's services for landmine victims and their families include psychological counselling and opportunities to meet other survivors (Penhaul, 2001).

The Colombian conflict is not ending yet, but the people in the country are tired of this endless war. People with disabilities are also getting organized and are fighting for their rights. The Colombian government ratified the CRPD on 10 May, 2011. 'Colombia has made progress in improving disability laws and policies and has many active organizations of people with disabilities;' in addition, 'Colombia now has an opportunity to lead on disability rights by ensuring these laws translate into real change for people with disabilities,' said Shantha R. Barriga, disability rights advocate at Human Rights Watch (Human Rights Watch, 2011).

United States war veterans

The United States has a long history of involvement in wars and conflicts around the world. In comparison to the previous countries mentioned, it also boasts a superior Disabled Veteran Assistance Program. Although the total number of veterans in the United States is decreasing due to the passing of WWII and Korean War veterans, the costs for the government to support veterans is projected to dramatically increase. The number of veterans with any type of disability in 2008 was 5.5 million. According to a recent report, 'In the federal fiscal year 2012, the U.S. spent a total of $46.9 billion on compensation and pension benefits paid to disabled veterans; of that amount, $43.5 billion was spent on disability compensation, while $3.4 billion was spent on disability pensions' (Houtenville, 2013).

One of the primary reasons the number of veterans with disabilities is so high is that in previous wars many soldiers experiencing severe injuries would die, whereas now – thanks to improvements in medical treatment – soldiers with severe injuries are likely to survive. The cost of compensating them is also high, as technology and rehabilitation treatments are expensive, and many soldiers are injured at an early age and have a long life expectancy.

The system for evaluating disabled veterans consists of giving wounded veterans a rating from 0 to 100 per cent based on the severity of their injury. Annual benefits run from $1,404 for a veteran rated at 10 per cent to about $30,324 for those rated at 100 per cent. In extreme cases, the annual compensation can easily reach upwards of $30,000. Compensation rates are dependent on whether the veterans are married and on the number of dependents they have. A disabled veteran with a disability rating of 100 per cent (the maximum) with a spouse and children is entitled to $3,134.32 per month (Veterans Health Care, 2013).

The most recent veterans from the ten-plus-year wars in Iraq and Afghanistan are statistically the group with the highest average frequency of impairment. A staggering 45 per cent of the 1.6 million veterans from these wars are seeking compensation for service-related injuries. That proportion is more than double the number of veterans that sought compensation from the Gulf War, which was 21 per cent (The Associated Press, 2012). Soldiers are returning with higher rates of mental health issues and more severe types of physical and other injuries than in the past.

A recent report to Congress (Fischer, 2014) indicates that during the conflicts of the last 14 years, a total of 6,775 service members died, and 51,809 were wounded in action. A total of 152,986 soldiers were diagnosed with PTSD, and 287,911 were diagnosed with traumatic brain injuries (TBI). Up to 1,588 soldiers underwent major limb amputations; at least 156 are blind, and thousands of others have impaired vision; more than 177,000 have hearing loss, and more than 350,000 report tinnitus or constant ringing in the ears. Thousands are disfigured, and as many as 200 soldiers required face transplants.

Overall, despite significant advancements in medical technology, weapons, armour and training, many soldiers are injured and experience severe functional limitations (see Box 7.5). The United States is choosing to be the 'police force of the world', yet the cost is heavy, not only fiscally but also in loss of human lives and function. Thousands of young men and women are now living with disabilities resulting from their war exposure. Many of these individuals come back to communities that are not ready to provide them with much needed rehabilitation and mental health services. As a society, we must have a national dialogue to examine the human cost of all these wars. Is it worth it for us to engage in distant conflicts that have very little direct impact on our own security or economy? Are we ready to provide the supports and opportunities that disabled veterans need and deserve, regardless of their cost? These are questions that should be openly discussed but are seldom mentioned or debated in the public sphere.

Box 7.5.   United States: The case of Kortney

Before the war, Kortney was a junior college football player and track athlete at East Mississippi Community College. He was just about to finish his 2-year tour as a combat medic in the 1st Cavalry Division when he went to the aid of a soldier whose Humvee had been blown off a dirt road outside Baghdad by an insurgent's bomb. He was readying the wounded soldier for a helicopter evacuation when a second bomb nearby killed three fellow medics and blew away his right leg from above the knee. Kortney spend the next ten months at a military hospital in Germany. After fully healing the burns and wounds to his body, he began the slow process of rehabilitation using a prosthetic leg. After going through a rough time of depression and self-pity, he re-emerged a driven man. He was the first Iraq war veteran to qualify for the US Paralympics team and compete at the Beijing Games running with a prosthetic limb. He also graduated from Penn State University with a degree in therapeutic recreation. (Davies, 2009)

Conclusions

Debating whether war is evil or necessary is beyond the point of this chapter. However, it draws the worst in human behaviour and has multiple consequences, including physical, cognitive and mental impairments for many survivors. As shown in this brief review of some of the recent and current conflicts around the world, the consequences for both combatants and bystanders can be disastrous.

One notable aspect of the various war scenarios we examined is their contextual and cultural differences and how the different countries of the world respond to the conflicts. The people in Africa appear to be getting the least attention – although they have experienced the greatest losses in lives. The government of Colombia has received more than 5 billion dollars from the US government since 2000, to combat the communist insurgency and the drug trade. The Bosnians got a lot of international help and so do the Syrians. There is no argument that people engaged in war of any kind experience a great deal of suffering. So why do the countries or institutions with the resources to help appear more willing to help in some areas of the world rather than others? Are the African people being discriminated against?

Another important contextual difference has to deal with the capacity of the central government to deliver supports and services to people with disabilities after the conflict. Of course, the degree of decimation of the infrastructure plays a critical role because it exacerbates the cost of re-establishing the service delivery systems (e.g. transportation, health care or education). It is important to notice how international organizations can play a critical role in restoring those services, as described in the case of Bosnia and Syria. The World Bank, agencies like UNICEF and even volunteer organizations like Doctors Without Borders can play a critical role. It is also important to acknowledge how volunteer organizations like the advocacy group called Disability Rights Syria

(DRS), made up by Syrian health professionals, doctors and advocates supporting the insurgency, are already actively engaged in the process of helping the refugees and the injured. They are not waiting for the end of the conflict to start their work. In fact, the group identified multiple areas of need in order to help individuals with disabilities either displaced by the conflict or injured by the war (Kassar, 2013). The DRS generated the list below, which is actually applicable to most war-torn countries and includes the following priorities:

- Availability of mobility and prosthetic equipment
- Treatment for individuals with post-traumatic stress disorder (PTSD)
- Capacity building to deliver medical and rehabilitation care
- Establishment of information management systems to keep medical records and coordinate information among various providers
- Special education services for children and youth with disabilities
- Support services to assist veterans with disabilities re-enter their communities after serving in the war (e.g. housing accommodations/accessibility, job placement, transportation, assistive technology/devices, mental health services and caregiving when needed).

The UN Office of the HCHR (OHCHR, 2013) has criticized the efforts made to ensure the safety and treatment of persons with disabilities in several countries currently engaged in warfare. Their concerns include the following: (a) All parties to the conflict must stop the deliberate targeting of civilians, and must, in their actions, take all precautions to avoid death or injury to civilians; (b) it is vital that humanitarian agencies be allowed to operate without restrictions throughout the country to provide the assistance needed by persons with disabilities, those with impairments acquired before the conflict and as a result of the conflict; and (c) as the humanitarian emergency response increases in the war regions, it is essential that there be inclusive protection and assistance programmes for all, in order to guarantee access to human rights and minimum standards of treatment for persons with disabilities.

Unfortunately, as Kassar (2013) pointed out, the fundamental rights of persons with disabilities are consistently violated in states at war, and few organizations, if any, are capable of providing needed rehabilitation and support services for people with disabilities under war conditions. In effect, the needs are always much greater than the system's capacity to respond. The human cost of war is always great, but the plight of people with disabilities before and during combat operations is often ignored. Only after surviving combatants end up with serious disabilities does society start paying attention.

People with disabilities from around the world have the same aspirations and dreams as anyone else. They have to overcome many physical and attitudinal barriers in order to succeed. States at war not only increase the number of people with disabilities in need of services, but services for people with disabilities are often disrupted by the conflict. We all need to be vigilant and willing to denounce abuses and discrimination of people with disabilities whenever we see it. It is through acts of solidarity that we all help each other. We cannot be silent about these stories of dread and courage.

Summary of key points

- The purpose of this chapter was to examine disability in relation to acts of war and armed conflict, illustrated by several case examples from recent conflict zones from around the world, including those of Syria, the Democratic Republic of Congo, Bosnia and Colombia, and from war veterans from the United States.
- One notable aspect of the various war scenarios we examined is their contextual and cultural differences and how the different countries of the world respond to the conflicts. The poor people in Africa appear to be getting the least attention – although they have experienced the greatest losses in their lives. The government of Colombia has received more than 5 billion dollars from the US government since 2000, to combat the communist insurgency and the drug trade. The Bosnians got a lot of international help, as did the Syrians.
- Article 11 of the CRPD, 'Situations of risk and humanitarian emergencies', seeks to ensure that persons with disabilities are protected under situations of armed conflict.
- International organizations can play a critical role in restoring services for people with disabilities and their families, as described in the case of Bosnia and Syria. Agencies like UNICEF and volunteer organizations like Doctors Without Borders can play a critical role.
- The United States is choosing to be the 'police force of the world', yet the cost is heavy, not only fiscally but also in loss of human lives and function. Thousands of young men and women are now living with disabilities resulting from their war exposure.
- States at war not only increase the number of people with disabilities in need of services, but services for people with disabilities are often disrupted by the conflict. We all need to be vigilant and willing to denounce abuses and discrimination of people with disabilities whenever we see it.

STUDY QUESTIONS

1. What has been the historical relationship between disability and war?

2. What are common elements you find among the cases from Syria, Bosnia, Congo and Colombia? How do the experiences of people with disabilities from those countries contrast with the experiences of American soldiers returning from war zones?

3. What are three examples of important services that could be provided to individuals with disabilities displaced or directly affected by war violence?

Further reading and resources

Syria

Article: 'Syrian Civil war'. Background information on the Syrian civil war, http://www
.britannica.com/EBchecked/topic/1781371/Syrian-Civil-War.

Article: 'Persons with disabilities "forgotten victims" of Syria's conflict – UN committee'. Contains quoted statements regarding situation in Syria concerning persons
with disabilities from the UN Committee on the Rights of Persons with Disabilities
(CRPD), http://www.ohchr.org/en/NewsEvents/Pages/DisplayNews.aspx?NewsID=
13736&LangID=E.

Article: 'Photo essay: The uncounted Syrian tragedy'. From Al Jazeer news outlet, contains some case brief stories and overview of impact war has had on Syria's health
infrastructure, http://america.aljazeera.com/watch/shows/america-tonight/america-
tonight-blog/2013/9/12/photo-essay-the-uncountedsyriantragedy.html.

Report: 'Causes and types of injuries encountered by Handicap International while
working with Internally Displaced Persons in Syria'. Has statistics regarding types
of injuries happening in Syria and their effects, http://www.handicap-international
.org.uk/where_we_work/middle_east/syria/stories/20140122-study-shows-legacy
-disability-explosive-weapon-use-Syria.

Newspaper article: 'Rapid assessments of the needs of war victims with disabilities in
Syria', http://www.english.globalarabnetwork.com/2013020212810/Culture/rapid
-assessments-of-the-needs-of-war-victims-with-disabilities-in-syria.html.

Organization's website: Syria American Medical Society. Has statistics on effects war
has had on the destruction of Syrian health infrastructure, http://sams-usa.net/.

Bosnia

Article: 'Government institutions in Bosnia and Hercegovina'. Contains policy and
laws in Bosnia that are helping persons with disabilities, http://en.dat-see.com/
institutions-and-legislations/government/government-bih/.

Report: World Bank Report: War Victims Rehabilitation Program. Explains the logistics
of a rehabilitation programmes that lasted from 1996 to 2001, developed to help
war victims return to public life and become productive members of the economy,
http://www.worldbank.org/projects/P044424/war-victims-rehabilitation-project?
lang=en&tab=overview.

Report: Situation report on organisations of disabled people in Bosnia and
Herzegovina (BiH). Discusses problems that arose after the war regarding persons
with disabilities (International Federation of Persons with Physical Disability),
http://www.fimitic.org/content/situation-report-organizations-disabled-people
-bosnia-and-herzegovina-bih.

DR Congo

Report: Democratic Republic of Congo. Gives background information on the Congo
civil war, http://www.globalpolicy.org/security-council/index-of-countries-on-the-
security-council-agenda/democratic-republic-of-congo.html.

Radio Transcript: 'Congo's Beach port is haven for disabled traders'. Contains
information about disabled traders using Congo River trade and giving permission not to pay taxes, http://www.rnw.nl/africa/bulletin/congos-beach-port-haven
-disabled-traders.

Colombia

Report: Memories of War and Dignity: Report on Victims of Colombia's conflict. Contains statistics on casualties, deaths, and victims of landmines from the Colombian civil war, http://justf.org/blog/2013/07/25/memories-war-and-dignity-report-victims-colombias-conflict.

Website: Insight Direct: Colombia: Guide to the conflict and Peace-Building in Colombia. Contains multiple stories and blogs about the Colombian conflict. Published by Peace Direct, http://www.insightonconflict.org/conflicts/colombia/.

Website: Fellowship of Reconciliation Colombia Program. A project of FOR's Task Force on Latin America and the Caribbean, http://www.forcolombia.org/conflict.

United States

Article: 'The shocking cost of war: Afghanistan and Iraq veterans are "the most damaged generation ever" with almost HALF seeking disability benefits'. Contains statistics with per cent veterans seeking compensations and brain trauma, http://www.dailymail.co.uk/news/article-2150933/The-shocking-cost-war-Afghanistan-Iraq-veterans-damaged-generation-HALF-seeking-disability-benefits.html.

Report: Annual Disability Statistics Compendium. Contains statistics on veterans, compensations and pensions paid to disabled veterans, http://disabilitycompendium.org/compendium-statistics/veterans.

Report: VA Disability Compensation Rates. Contains statistics on exact compensation rates for disabled veterans, http://www.military.com/benefits/veterans-health-care/va-disability-compensation-rates.html.

Report: U.S. Military Casualty Statistics: Operation New Dawn, Operation Iraqi Freedom, and Operation Enduring Freedom. Contains statistics on casualties, including brain injury, amputees, PTSD, http://www.fas.org/sgp/crs/natsec/RS22452.pdf.

Children's Rights and Disability

Robbie Gilligan

1. States Parties shall take all necessary measures to ensure the full enjoyment by children with disabilities of all human rights and fundamental freedoms on an equal basis with other children.

2. In all actions concerning children with disabilities, the best interests of the child shall be a primary consideration.

3. States Parties shall ensure that children with disabilities have the right to express their views freely on all matters affecting them, their views being given due weight in accordance with their age and maturity, on an equal basis with other children, and to be provided with disability and age-appropriate assistance to realize that right.

UN Convention on the Rights of Persons with Disabilities
Article 7: Children with disabilities

Introduction

'Children should be seen and not heard' was a popular saying right into my parents' generation in Ireland, and no doubt also in many other places. Although in part it related to certain notions at the time of politeness and good manners in family life and public space, this saying also gives insights about beliefs then held quite widely about childhood and children. The ideal child should be present, but silent. In recent decades, we have learned that silencing children may carry many costs. Children who are silenced may not be able to be heard when they wish to draw attention to bad experiences in their lives. Silencing children excludes a substantial proportion of the population from playing their full part in every society. Silencing children may habituate them to silence when they become adults. Only with a voice can children claim a full presence in social life.

Although many children across the globe increasingly find their voice and claim their presence, the picture is much more complicated for children with disabilities. They may often face a 'double silencing'. They may find it hard to be seen *and* to be heard. In many communities, children with disabilities may remain hidden in family homes or institutions because of family shame in response to negative community attitudes about disability. Children with disabilities may also not be heard because too little attention is paid to their voice and views. This silencing and marginalization may carry an especially high price for a child with a disability.

For a long time, children were seen as the possessions of their parents. Indeed, in many societies the mother and children were seen as the chattels of the husband and father. It has only been as the result of a very long process that both women's rights and children's rights have begun to be seen and articulated as crucial parts of the broader project of human rights. Only gradually have we begun to see children as active persons and citizens capable of views and actions on their own behalf. Even more slowly, are we beginning to recognize the rights, capacity – and voice – of children with disabilities.

The International community first gave special recognition to the rights of children in the UN Declaration on the Rights of the Child in 1959. The ten principles of the Declaration included one on children with 'handicap', then the term in common usage:

> The child who is physically, mentally or socially handicapped shall be given the *special treatment, education and care* required by his particular condition. [italics added]

Although no doubt a step forward in its time to include reference to disability, the phrasing of the Declaration's principle about disability sounds somewhat naïve in today's terms. The words seem to hint at or imply a singularity or simplicity of response. They almost suggest that each handicapping condition calls for its own separate response, whereas now we see more clearly, thanks to the social and other models of disability, that even children with the same condition will actually need a more diverse range of possible responses, depending on the social and other circumstances. There is also the issue that the word 'special', though doubtless well intentioned, also carries within it the approval of segregation – a point to which we will return.

In time, the Declaration gave way to an international treaty – the UN Convention on the Rights of the Child, which came into force in 1990. At the point of writing, only three countries in the world have not ratified the Convention to date (in alphabetical order, Somalia, Southern Sudan and the United States of America[1]). By signing and ratifying this Treaty, countries agree to live by its standards and participate in its procedures. The standards are set out in the 54

---

[1] The United States has signed (signalling support of principles) the UN Convention on the Rights of the Child. It has not ratified the Convention (signalling willingness to be legally bound by it) because of internal political conflict about whether the UNCRC goes too far in eroding US sovereignty (or freedom in deciding its own laws) (see *The Economist Explains* (2013)).

separate articles contained in the text. These are interpreted, as necessary, by an elected committee of 18 international experts. The procedures linked to the Convention include a regular reporting mechanism in which countries periodically submit progress reports for review to this committee.[2] Although countries may vary in the level of their attention to this overall process of review and follow-up, it seems clear that the general mechanism of reporting has had an impact at national and international levels. The international scrutiny and accountability involved in the reporting mechanism helps create conditions more favourable to reform.

The UN Convention on the Rights of the Child has a number of important provisions relevant to children with disability. Before exploring these, however, it is important to highlight some key general features of the Convention and its focus on promotion of rights, protection, participation and prevention. The Convention asserts very clearly the fundamental rights of every child. These rights are unconditional and apply in *all* circumstances to *all* children – no ifs, no buts. It stresses a range of ways that the rights of children must be protected. More specifically, it highlights the needs for policies and services which support children and families and which protect children from harm. In terms of participation, the Convention calls for respect for children's experience and pays special attention to giving children a voice in matters affecting them. The Convention addresses the issue of prevention at two levels: preventing harm and also promoting a least restrictive approach in which care and support are provided to a child in order to *prevent* removal from home, placement in institutions and so on (see Box 8.1).

As Box 8.1 describes, key phrases in Article 23 include reference to a 'full and decent life' for the child with disability, the expectation that a child should have 'active participation in the community' and 'the fullest possible social integration and individual development, including his or her cultural and spiritual development'.

The Convention on the Rights of the Child is almost 25 years old at the time of this writing, and there is no doubt it has been a major success. But in the passage of time, a number of issues have become clearer. The work of scholars across the broad field of childhood studies in this period has highlighted the important point that there is no single childhood that captures the reality of children across the globe. Instead, there are many different *childhoods*, reflecting a range of (sometimes overlapping) social contexts

---

[2] This process is mirrored by a parallel reporting process in which a country's NGO sector has an opportunity to present an alternative (and often more revealing and critical) report on realities for children in the country at the point of review (Kilkelly, 1996). With the two reports and questioning of witnesses from the country, the Committee can get a fuller picture with which to make its own assessment and report, which is then fed back in a transparent process to the country concerned. The Committee uses its previous reports on a country as a way of benchmarking progress since the last review of the country's performance. All the key documents are accessible on the Committee's website, http://www.ohchr.org/EN/HRBodies/CRC/Pages/CRCIndex.aspx.

Box 8.1. Convention on the Rights of the Child – Article 23

1. States Parties recognize that a mentally or physically disabled child should enjoy a full and decent life, in conditions which ensure dignity, promote self-reliance and facilitate the child's active participation in the community.
2. States Parties recognize the right of the disabled child to special care and shall encourage and ensure the extension, subject to available resources, to the eligible child and those responsible for his or her care, of assistance for which application is made and which is appropriate to the child's condition and to the circumstances of the parents or others caring for the child.
3. Recognizing the special needs of a disabled child, assistance extended in accordance with paragraph 2 of the present article shall be provided free of charge, whenever possible, taking into account the financial resources of the parents or others caring for the child, and shall be designed to ensure that the disabled child has effective access to and receives education, training, health care services, rehabilitation services, preparation for employment and recreation opportunities in a manner conducive to the child's achieving the fullest possible social integration and individual development, including his or her cultural and spiritual development.
4. States Parties shall promote, in the spirit of international cooperation, the exchange of appropriate information in the field of preventive health care and of medical, psychological and functional treatment of disabled children, including dissemination of and access to information concerning methods of rehabilitation, education and vocational services, with the aim of enabling States Parties to improve their capabilities and skills and to widen their experience in these areas. In this regard, particular account shall be taken of the needs of developing countries.

---

and social characteristics. Being a little girl in a slum in Mumbai is likely to be very different from being a little girl in a wealthy part of New York City. Being a 12-year-old boy in rural Norway is likely to be very different from being a boy soldier in Northern Uganda. Being an ethnic minority child in a poor family from the remote hill tribes of Vietnam will be a different experience from growing up in a white middle-class family in Melbourne, Australia.

All of these examples serve to underline the point that there is not one child, not one childhood. There are many children, many childhoods, with many diverse experiences. Our thinking, our language, our responses need to reflect that range. The notion of the singular *child* as reflected in the Convention's title now seems too constricting. Singling out *the child* for attention in a UN Convention on the Rights of the Child was a huge step forward in a context where the world gave too little attention to the experience of the child, where the child was to be seen not heard. But now, partly due to the Convention's success, and therefore an often deeper attention to children's lives, it seems that the Convention might be more aptly entitled the Convention on the Rights of *Children*. Increasingly, we realize that we must see the child not as a discrete child, but the child as the child in context, the child in relationship to others, the child as a link in a set of intergenerational relationships.

UN Convention on the Rights of Persons with Disabilities and its approach to children

Although the previous view that children, in general, should be seen and not heard may have changed, it is arguable that the picture has not altered so much for children with disabilities. Indeed, in many places it seems that the attitude to children with disabilities, as observed earlier, still remains more exclusionary: too often it seems that they should be both not seen *and* not heard. However, the Convention on the Rights of Persons with Disabilities (CRPD) further serves to promote a climate where diversity of populations, diversity of experience and diversity of response have to be respected and included in the frame of imagination and practice (see Chapter 3).

Article 7 of the CRPD focuses on 'Children with disabilities'. Key phrases in the article highlight the child's right to the 'full enjoyment' of 'all human rights' and 'on an equal basis with other children'; the 'best interests of the child'; right to 'express their views' and to have 'disability and age-appropriate assistance to do so'. The two Conventions leave absolutely no doubt that children with disabilities must be treated equally when compared to children without disability, must be able to express their views (and get relevant support to do so) and have full attention given to the key issues in their lives (see Box 8.2).

The challenge for children with disabilities and for those promoting their interests is to insist that their issues get onto the agenda and ensure that those issues are tackled (see Box 8.2). The first step in recognizing rights is recognition, and this often proves not to be a simple matter. An important initiative in support of a comprehensive and coordinated approach to children

---

Box 8.2. Convention on the Rights of Persons with Disabilities – Article 7

1. States Parties shall take all necessary measures to ensure the full enjoyment by children with disabilities of all human rights and fundamental freedoms on an equal basis with other children.
2. In all actions concerning children with disabilities, the best interests of the child shall be a primary consideration.
3. States Parties shall ensure that children with disabilities have the right to express their views freely on all matters affecting them, their views being given due weight in accordance with their age and maturity, on an equal basis with other children, and to be provided with disability and age-appropriate assistance to realize that right.

> **Box 8.3. The Global Partnership on Children with Disabilities (GPcwd)**
>
> The Global Partnership on Children with Disabilities (GPcwd) is a network of more than 240 organizations, including international NGOs, national and local NGOs, disabled people's organisations (DPOs), governments, academia and the private sector, working to advance the rights of children with disabilities at the global, regional and country levels. With a rights-based approach, the Partnership provides a platform for advocacy and collective action to ensure the rights of children with disabilities are included and prioritized by both the Disability and Child Rights Movement.
>
> This network, established in March 2011, led to the inaugural forum, which was held on 14–15 September 2012 at UNICEF House in New York. Discussions were held to advocate for an inclusive post 2015-agenda. Four task forces were formed to influence the mainstreaming of disability rights into global child-focused agendas (http://www.unicef.org/disabilities/index_65319.html).

and disability issues globally is The Global Partnership on Children with Disabilities (GPcwd) and its four task forces (nutrition, education, humanitarian action and assistive technology) (see Box 8.3).

Capacity

If one view of children was that they were to be silent – and/or invisible – another familiar (and related) notion is that they lack capacity to make decisions. A further reason, therefore, for not listening to children was the commonly held view that they lacked the understanding to formulate or articulate their views on their own situation and experiences. This implied a view that children not only lack a capacity for, but also an entitlement to, having a voice that must be heard. This perceived lack of capacity then clearly justified adults unilaterally stepping in to decide and speak on the child's behalf. The reader will recognize strong echoes here of the experiences of people (adults and children) with disabilities. Indeed, if children generally were thought to lack the capacity, and adults with disabilities were/are thought to lack capacity, how much more was/is this the case with *children* with disabilities? Although recognizing the voice of the child may have different support in different contexts, there are also social characteristics that may serve as barriers (or facilitators) to recognition in those contexts. Assumptions about 'capacity' relating to age, socio-economic status, ethnicity, dis/ability and so on would be influences. The views and experience of a child from a poor minority family might be accorded less attention in the wider society than the child from a well-connected, prosperous family, and this may prove even more so in the case of a child with disability.

Yet, as has been discussed, it is widely and increasingly recognized that *all* children have rights and that children have capacity to exercise *agency* (that is make their own individual appraisals, choices, influences, preferences) towards securing those rights. Children may express these views and preferences through words and/or actions; by their ease in certain situations, their unease in others. The challenge for adults is to listen and observe discerningly. It should also be noted that when capacity is used in the legal sense, it is unconditional: legal capacity resides automatically in every individual regardless of his or her cognitive or other competence.

The influence of such new thinking about children's agency and capacity means that people will see these ideas about children and their capacity being tested and applied in many arenas: families, schools, communities, courts and so on. Children with disabilities may face many physical and social obstacles, but it is also clear that it should be assumed that they have the *capacity* (exercised directly by themselves or with sensitive support by appropriate others on their behalf) to lay claim to their rights and assert their interests. Children can help to shape their circumstances as well as be influenced by them. This is not yet the universal picture, but even if such examples still only occur occasionally, these exceptions serve as vital case examples that the pool of exceptions can be expanded, and send a clear message about the way things are moving across the globe.

In discussing notions such as 'laying claim to rights' or 'asserting their interests', this does not mean the child's interests or rights automatically trump those of others, that they have instant priority. The issue is that the child's views and experience should have respect and recognition: children's rights should receive *due consideration* in the relevant context. And this must also mean that *due consideration* is given to the experiences, wishes and preferences of children with disabilities.

Translating rights on paper to rights in reality

In one sense, rights are words written on paper. They require action to come alive and have effect in real lives. In the case of children, and children with disabilities, children are heavily reliant on adults to breathe life into their rights. These adults are both those close to them and those who create the laws, policies and decisions that shape children's opportunities. On a day-to-day basis, children may be heavily dependent on parents and other carers to make their case, to lay claim to their (the child's) rights. One example is Kathy Sinnott, who took a legal case on behalf of her son against the Irish government, to insist on the right of all children to a primary education, regardless of level or range of disability (see Chapter 9 on education). But can children with disabilities always depend on those close to them to lay claim to their rights? Parents and teachers may want what they think is best for the child. But there is the rub: what the *adult* thinks is best. And ideas about what is best may be coloured by many other influences beyond human rights, child rights or disability rights. Parental, wider family and community attitudes can all influence views and expectations of the child with disability, and of how the messages they pick up from those around them shape the identity and sense of possibilities for the young person. Thinking of these attitudes along a continuum, there may be views which effectively serve to exclude and discourage and at the other end views which include and encourage. Inevitably, the reality is much more complex, with competing views interacting and mutually influencing each other.

Globally, there remains in many cultures, as noted earlier in this chapter and elsewhere in the book, a widespread view that childhood disability is a source of retribution or threat (see Chapter 5). In parts of Pakistan, for example, it is reported that a child's disability is seen as 'God's punishment for a parent's sin' (Hussain, 2012). Social pressure may thus lead to the child being kept hidden.

Negative views of the child with disability are also to be found in other regions. Citing a range of research work Atilola, Omigbodun, Bella-Awusah, Lagunju, and Igbeneghu (2014) argue there is considerable evidence that in the case of Nigeria and West Africa more widely, many mothers and teachers may attribute 'the cause of childhood epilepsy, neurological deficits and intellectual disability in children to possession by evil spirits, witchcraft or virulent contagion'. Such ideas may again lead parents to hide their child to avoid community criticism, or even to harm the child in an attempt to appease the unhappy spirits which caused the disability. Bayat (2014) reminds us that such ideas once held sway in Europe also and are more likely in communities with lower access to education.

Role of parents – navigating between overprotection and independence

Most parents want the very best for their children, and it is no different in the case of parents and their child with disability. Parents may interpret differently, of course, what is best and how to achieve it. They may be influenced to a greater or lesser degree by messages they pick up about disability from their wider family and the community. Even more crucial perhaps may be the messages that parents receive from professionals, whether explicitly or sensed in more subtle signals. These may go on to have a lifetime effect on the parents and young person and their interaction on the issue of the disability. Expectations that parents have of children and young people growing up and their potential roles and opportunities, may be deeply coloured by conversations with and (even casual) comments by professionals. And the child may internalize these messages that become, effectively, relayed by the parents. Professional training and the messages professionals themselves absorb about disability and about conditions will inevitably colour the messages they transmit. There is a world of difference, for example, in the messages professionals trained in the principles of human rights will transmit, as compared to professionals immersed in the more traditional model of rehabilitation (see below and Chapter 2, disability models).

Within the overall group of parents of children with disability, there will inevitably be many differing notions of risk, with consequent implications for the range of opportunities or sense of freedom accorded to the child. Parents may vary in how they respond to the presence of disability in their child's life. They may take considerable time (possibly over many, many years) to come to terms (or not) with the implications of the condition: for the child's daily reality growing up, for the specific employment and social prospects of the disabled teenager, and for the reaction of the wider community to the presence of disability in the household. Negative views of disability held in some cultural or community contexts may mean that the child and family pay a high price in terms of stigma, and the child, also, in terms of his or her prospects for autonomy and inclusion.

Parents will generally seek to find the best advice and support available: from their extended family, friends and families with experience of relevant disability, where they can find them, or from professionals with necessary expertize who may, of course, often be thin on the ground. Professional attitudes and knowledge about disability in general and specific conditions in particular may also differ considerably. Informed by messages from professionals or community attitudes, some parents may come to have lowered expectations for the prospects of their young person. Others may be determined to ensure that their young person should have a 'normal' life in which the disability is accommodated, but not dominant. The level of impairment may, of course, have a bearing on prospects and aspirations. Some parents may be reinforced in such a positive approach by other parents with children with disability who share their experiences. Some other parents may adopt an overly protective approach to what they see as the extra vulnerability of their child. Meaning well, they may, however, impede the social development and opportunities of the young person. In some ways, parents have to find their own response to the challenge of how large the issue of disability is to loom in the life of the child and family. And each partner may also have different views personally which may have to be somehow reconciled. Everyday life poses many questions for them: where the choice is available, should their child go to a mainstream school or a 'special' school? Should their young person with disability be allowed to use public transport unaided when that is available? Should their young person be able to make his or her own choices about a social life independent of home and parents?

The response of the parents to such questions is likely to prove very influential in shaping young people's identity and their understanding of their disability, its implications for them and their sense of possibility in their own life. Parents who are overly preoccupied with the impact of the disability may transmit such an outlook to their young person. On the other hand, parents determined to allow the young person to have as a full a life as possible alongside disability may succeed in instilling confidence and a sense of independence in the young person. For one set of parents, 'Be careful' may be the recurring advice. In another case, the message may essentially be: 'There is nothing you cannot do'. In reality, of course, parental responses may shift over time in the light of experience and may also have to adapt to the realities of life around them. It may be easier to promote the idea that 'There is nothing you cannot do' when external factors such as accessible and safe public transport and public spaces reinforce and support such messages.

Parents may also become caught up in a dilemma where certain labels or diagnoses may open up access to services or close down a sense of possibility for their child. In some places, where service providers ration services in the face of demand and shortages of resources, they may determine that eligibility for certain supports is dependent on children having obtained an explicit diagnosis related to eligibility conditions. This may seem an objective and fair way of determining eligibility, but there may be many adverse effects to such a policy. In the aggregate, it may serve to inflate figures of a condition and distort the actual reality. In the case of an individual child, acquiring a label such as Attention Deficit Hyperactivity Disorder (ADHD) may open up entitlement to certain support, but it may also colour how educational and other professionals view the child and his or her prospects in the future, as well as changing the child's self-perception.

What happens when parents can't play their part – due to death, poverty or other reasons?

In most countries, a certain proportion of children live apart from their families because of a range of factors. In the case of a particular child, these reasons may include one or more of issues such as family poverty, abuse, neglect, parental death or special needs of some kind. There is generally a clear social gradient in the risk of such placement away from the family happening. Children from poor families, children from ethnic minorities or children with disabilities are at highest risk, and conversely, those most privileged, at lesser risk. Put simply, poorer children face greater risk of bad things happening to them (see Chapter 6). Of these three groupings, it seems that children with disabilities may be the social grouping who most often face the *greatest* risk of being placed outside their family in a residential centre.[3] Take the example of the Central and Eastern Europe/Commonwealth of Independent States region, where one in three children placed away from their family in residential care is a child with disabilities (UNICEF, 2013). This proportion represents an estimated *17 times* greater risk of being placed in residential care settings for children with disabilities in that region compared to the rate of placement for those without any disabilities. Ireland is another case in point. Despite a long-standing policy favouring community support rather than institutional care, recent research has found that the rate of placement of children away from home was considerably higher for children with intellectual disability compared to children without. Children and young people aged 10–19 with intellectual disability were *14 times* more likely to be placed away from home than children without intellectual disability and less likely to be placed with foster families (McConkey, Kelly and Craig, 2012).

---

[3] The one exception in certain places may be the somewhat greater rate of placement of children from the Roma community.

The rate of placement for children with disabilities globally may vary, but the broad point holds true across different regions of the world – children with disabilities seem to be at much greater risk than other children for living in institutions. There are complex reasons for this difference between the risks of being placed in institutions for children with and without disabilities. Poverty is clearly a significant influence, as it makes it more difficult for parents to cope with the extra demands of rearing a child with a disability. A related issue is the social stigma that attaches to a child with disability in many cultures and which can put families under extra pressure. Cultural attitudes may cause children with disabilities to be seen as unworthy or scary. There is also the legacy (in the relevant countries) of the Soviet Union era concept of 'defectology' (see Chapter 2) and how it came to be interpreted in practice under that political regime (Kalinnikova and Trygged, 2014). This paradigm led to an over-medicalized, or 'white coat', approach to disability which regarded (intellectual) disability as a defect and the details of that 'defect' as the primary focus for attention. Instead of care of the child with disability by 'lay' people such as family, the necessary response *to disability* was conceptualized by the authorities or professionals as 'treatment' that was beyond the competence of lay people such as parents. Echoes of this thinking may also be found in other countries beyond the continuing influence of the old Soviet system.

In such a climate of medical dominance, parents were expected to submit to pressure to hand their child over to what was represented as the superior care of medically-led teams. For parents already heavily pressured by poverty, this notion had some appeal, not that those parents were in a strong position to argue either way. The influence parents could exert in such circumstances might have been further limited by barriers related to language, inadequate education and social status.

The failure of institutions

Besides being at greater risk of being placed outside their family, children with disabilities are also at higher risk of being placed in institutions rather than in foster families, and of remaining in such institutions even where reform efforts are being made to move children from institutions to more community-based alternatives. There are many reasons for the international effort to close institutions for children especially and oppose their development. Institutions represent a one-size-fits-all response when the need for more diverse and community based responses is increasingly recognized. The main function of institutions is to segregate. This is at the heart of their failing. Segregation also means that residents – and staff – are cut off from the normal scrutiny of daily interaction with the wider community.

Institutions are very challenging to run well, and to do so requires a level of investment and expertize that cannot be guaranteed – or easily justified for use in that way. The history of institutions is littered with episodes of neglect and abuse. Typically, under-resourced institutions offer an environment that is risky, cold, impersonal and harsh. Because they are mostly hidden away, the reality of life in institutions rarely touches the lives of ordinary people. Occasionally, journalists or television producers succeed in drawing attention. One powerful example is Kate Blewett's BBC television series *Bulgaria's Abandoned Children* in 2007, which focused on Mogilino Institution in Bulgaria. It shocked viewers across Europe and led to major political pressure for the closure of such institutions in a range of countries. The programme vividly portrayed a neglected setting with poor physical and emotionally barren conditions, overstretched and under-trained staff, occasional abusive practices by staff, the social isolation of residents and staff, repetitive self-comforting behaviours of residents adapting to the boredom and harshness of their lives, and all of these things seemingly set to continue indefinitely.

The international community – in the form, for example, of the European Community, the United Nations system (mainly through UNICEF) and donor governments (such as the United States Agency for International Development USAID) – seek to promote alternatives to institutions with varying degrees of success. The idea is to close harsh, impersonal and often geographically remote institutions and replace them with forms of care that are emotionally richer and closer to the home and the everyday realities of the ordinary person, child or adult. Two lessons can be drawn from the experience of these efforts. The model of institution is remarkably tenacious, and in some cases funds for reform have actually been found to have been spent in remodelling the institution sometimes on site, sometimes in a new setting, thus thwarting the intended reform. The second lesson is that the last children and young people in the queue for transfer from institutions to more community-based alternatives seem often to prove, in practice, to be children and young people with disabilities, as the case studies illustrate (see Box 8.4).

Although institutional care is heavily embedded in the landscape of provision in Eastern Europe, there are emerging signs of efforts to develop alternatives. One example is from Moldova, where there are projects to provide family support or long-term care though foster placement, or to help children move back to the care of their parents (Banos Smith, 2014). Such exemplars are very important since in many countries there may be considerable professional or community resistance to the feasibility or desirability of family based alternatives to institutional provision for children with disabilities.

Box 8.4. Nigeria and Eastern Europe: Case examples

Ibadan, Nigeria. A recent study shows that 22.4 per cent of the children and young people placed in a residential centre (officially entitled a 'remand home') had an intellectual disability; 19.4 per cent had epilepsy; and 18 per cent had a neurological impairment (Atilola et al., 2014). These conditions were more common for children admitted to the centre for abuse/neglect reasons than for those admitted under the criminal code for offences. The authors speculate about the risk of such centres (of which there are reported to be 24 across Nigeria) becoming 'a dumping ground for children with unrecognized or unattended neurological or intellectual disabilities'.

The quality of life of children with disabilities living apart from their families depends on the quality of care, which in turn depends on the training and commitment of the carers. It also depends on the transparency of care practices and the role of independent advocates and researchers in highlighting the needs and experiences of children and young people at an individual and aggregate level (Carpenter and McConkey, 2012).

Tackling social exclusion

Achieving real and plentiful opportunities for children with disabilities to engage in everyday life remains a considerable challenge. It is about closing institutions; it is about taking children with disabilities out of the shadows of shame in their home and communities. Even more, it is about moving to a point where the supports are there for children with disabilities to take themselves out of the shadows and to enable them to be active participants in peer groups, classrooms, clubs and neighbourhood life. Easily said, but not so easily achieved. The barriers are many – sometimes beginning with the attitudes of parents, of community members, professionals, peers and of the young people themselves. There are also, of course, physical barriers and levels of impairment which may be aggravated by lack of adequate rehabilitation or support facilities. There may also be well-intentioned but naïve attempts to transfer ideas and practices about promoting inclusion from the 'developed' minority world (Srivastava, De Boer and Pijl, 2015). Enduring progress will require thoughtful actions – and frequently resources – across a range of settings and systems, including education, health, social protection and public attitudes.

For many children, access to and experience of daily life in school is perhaps the most immediate issue in terms of inclusion or segregation in wider society. Disability may impact on the educational opportunities and outcomes of individual children. It may also affect their friendship experiences within and beyond school. The CRPD holds that people with disabilities should be entitled to 'accommodation' within service provision, meaning reasonable adjustment of mainstream provision to their personal circumstances. In the school, reasonable 'accommodation' is about promoting a physical and social environment, an overall climate that helps the child with disabilities to thrive academically and socially. Teachers need to be sensitized through training and support to the support needs of children with disabilities. Getting the climate right also means attending to the critical issue of peer relationships and the potential for good and harm that may flow from these. However, a four-country study in Bulgaria, Romania, Croatia and the Former Yugoslav Republic of Macedonia concluded that 'negative public opinion appears to be a significant barrier to educational reform in all four countries, where the populace tends to doubt the benefits of education for persons with disabilities' (Phillips, 2012). Among some teachers and educational policy makers, there may also still be a view that children with disabilities are ineducable or represent a low priority in educational provision. Yet even where the need for educational reform for inclusion is accepted, it may not be so clear how to achieve that. An important issue is to ensure that debates, appraisal of existing provision and attempts at reform are informed with the perspectives of children with disabilities. Why is inclusion important? What harm does exclusion cause? How well does inclusion as attempted currently work from the perspective of the young people with disabilities? Which parts work well, which parts not? What are barriers and facilitators in terms of positive daily and longer-term experience for the young person? These are questions that have to be addressed, with children's participation, in each local context.

Relations with non-disabled peers – support or victimization?

Although we may hope for the best in peer relationships, it is prudent to plan for the worst. A study across 11 Western countries found that in all countries children with disabilities or chronic illness reported higher rates of having experienced peer victimization at school than did their non-disabled peers (Sentenac et al., 2013). A harsh reality for children and young people is that they may sometimes pay a high price for seeming different to their non-disabled peers. A young person who is not well connected in the peer group and who displays some characteristic(s) of what is perceived as negative difference may be vulnerable to one or more forms of victimization – shunning, ridicule or outright physical abuse. Children with disabilities who are new to the peer group or who lack champions or supporters in the group may easily become victims of such peer hostility. Confronted with this scenario, victims may choose silence or seek support. Victims are also often faced with the dilemma that drawing adult attention may seem likely to make the problem worse. There is also the risk that, when alerted, adults may not respond well. They may discount the report, or respond clumsily, in a way that ultimately weakens the position of the victim. An effective adult response needs conviction, consistency and clarity. An ineffective response leaves the victim even more vulnerable and isolated, and the perpetrator(s) even more confident of their invincibility.

It should also be noted that, like their non-disabled peers, children with disabilities, face the risk of abuse beyond the school setting, and not just by peers but also by adults. The nature of such abuse may include sexual abuse.

Protecting vulnerable children

It is widely accepted that children with disabilities are at greater risk of experiencing child abuse in its different forms – physical abuse, sexual abuse, emotional abuse and neglect. Child abuse may cause considerable harm to the child in the short or longer term, especially where the abuse involves betrayal of trust by those close to the child. There are a range of reasons why children with disabilities are at heightened risk of abuse. They may be less able to draw attention to difficulties, or when they do so, they may be less likely to be heeded by others. Segregation at home or in institutions may render them more vulnerable to harmful behaviours by others. A frequently poor fit between needs and supports may generate stress for caregivers that may flare into abusive behaviours by the carer at times. Awareness of the risks of abuse and constant vigilance are important elements of child protection, especially in the case of children with disabilities. Good practice in this regard should include constant public education aimed at families, children and young people, professionals and the wider public. It should also promote the message that adult relations with children with disability should be transparent at all times – secretive or hidden contact by adults should be seen as risky and unhealthy. The most important sources of protection are hopefully those closest to the child. Where this proves not to be the case, it falls to others – in many countries, social workers and other professionals – to investigate and provide social and legal follow-up as necessary. In some cases, it may be necessary to contemplate removal of the child to a safe place, possibly on a long-term basis. This is a major step, and will normally require careful consideration and the legal approval of a court (unless parents consent).

Children as carers of people with disabilities

The impact on other children within the family of having a disabled sibling or parent also needs consideration (see Chapter 15, supporting family carers). Depending on the circumstances and the composition of the household, a child (with or without a disability) may be drawn into a lot of practical caring roles in support of the parent or sibling, or in carrying out caring tasks and responsibilities on behalf of, or in place of, the person with disability. This is quite apart from any emotional energy demanded as the young person may worry about how the person with disability or the family may cope with unfolding situations. Pressed into such a role as carer, it is well established that a young person may, as a result, pay quite a high price. The health of such children may suffer or their normal educational progress may be impeded. They may literally have to miss out on large parts of normal school life to provide daily care. Or they may only be able to attend or devote home time to study intermittently, either of which may inevitably have an adverse effect on their educational attainment or prospects. Home duties may also mean that they have less time to spend interacting with friends or participating in sporting or other interests.

The actual social or educational impact of the demands of the carer role may depend on the nature of the condition and the level of other support available. An episodic condition such as a recurring mental health issue may leave long periods without difficulty. The overall demands on the carer may thus be reduced and may have less overall impact. Similarly, having other people available to share the day-to-day caring load may greatly reduce the impact on the children or young people, as they step in at certain points to fill gaps rather than having to carry the full burden on their own. It is one thing to be one of the people in reserve to be called on occasionally. It is quite another, for example, to be in effect or actually the head of household. The impact of AIDS may mean that in cases of the absence or inability of parents chronically ill with or eventually taken by the disease, the eldest sibling may have to take responsibility as head of household for the younger siblings, who may on occasion include a young person with a disability.

How the role and responsibilities of carer, adult or child, is understood may vary in different cultural contexts. Although notions of individualism in Western thinking may emphasize the issue of burdens, recent Korean research (Hwang and Charnley, 2010a, 2010b) highlights a different perception among siblings of children with disabilities. In Korean culture, family ties, honour and responsibilities are highly valued within the broadly Confucian ethos of society. The flip side is that provision of support services by the state remains underdeveloped because of the dominant role of the family. The collectivist spirit emphasizes the role of the individual in contributing to overall harmony within and beyond the family. In this context, siblings of children with disabilities are expected and willing to make sacrifices on behalf of their disabled sibling and the honour and harmony of the family. The sacrifice delivers practical and reputational gains.

Conclusions

Children with disabilities must no longer be silent and invisible. That vital message is gradually reaching every community, no matter how remote or traditional. Achieving visibility and voice for children with disability needs to be sought for all children with disabilities, and not just those with more visible or 'conventional' disabilities. It is particularly important that children with intellectual disabilities receive their share of attention. The universal symbol of the wheelchair for disability is very much a mixed blessing in this regard.

Disability is part of the child's story, not the whole story, or at least that is what we must strive for. We also must not presume what that story means to the child or family. Meaning will depend on the context of the experience over time. Whatever the meaning ascribed to the child's disability, there is (unfortunately) no iron law that says that disability will be the only issue facing the young person. Some young people may be faced with additional challenges in daily life – poverty, domestic violence, parental heavy drinking – a point that further underlines the importance of context.

The needs of children and young people may differ in important ways from those of adults. Listening carefully to the experiences and needs of children with disabilities can help us remember that one size does not fit all. Children will need a different response from that for adults, and each child needs a response fitted to their circumstances.

The people closest to children are family members and teachers, so influencing their attitudes and behaviours with positive messages and expectations is important. This is especially important in the case of children with disabilities, where the cultural burden of negative associations may otherwise be very heavy. Household membership and family life are fluid and subject to (often very sudden) change over time. Parents may become ill and dependent, or they may despair in the face of various pressures, natural disaster or war that may wreak havoc.

It is important that our approach to promoting the rights and serving the needs of children and young people with disabilities is well informed by good-quality evidence gathered and disseminated in a range of ways. High-quality qualitative research and good-quality journalism that investigates and illuminates the experiences of children with disabilities will be very important in helping raise awareness. In this way, the public, families and professionals who work with children with disabilities can learn more about responses and forms of service that respect and cultivate the individuality and agency of each child, and in this context, especially, children and young people with disabilities.

Summary of key points

- Each child is unique with his or her own experiences, views, preferences. Children have rights – as children and as human beings. These rights apply unconditionally to all children.
- Children with disabilities are children first; they bear the same unconditional rights as any children. Disability is part of their lives, but not the whole story.
- There is great diversity in circumstances and experiences of children with disabilities.
- Responses to the needs of children with disabilities need to respect this diversity and the rights and views of the children.
- Stigma and segregation severely damage the lives of children with disabilities and must be fought at every turn.
- Poverty aggravates the challenges for children and families posed by society's response to disability.
- The UN Conventions on the Rights of Children and Rights of Persons with Disabilities (Article 7) are powerful frameworks for promoting the rights of children with disabilities.
- Parents and families need support in providing well for their child with disability.
- School is a very important place in the life of every child, and especially so for children with disabilities. It is here that inclusion or exclusion truly begins.
- Professionals and policy makers must learn to listen carefully to the experiences of children with disabilities and their families in making their decisions and plans.
- Ensure policy and practice listens to the experience of children – and their families.

STUDY QUESTIONS

1. How do we involve children more fully in influencing decisions and policies affecting them?
2. How do we create greater public awareness of the diversity of experiences and capacities of children with disabilities?
3. How do we ensure professionals working with children with disabilities follow the principles of children's rights in their daily work?

Further reading and resources

J. Carpenter and R. McConkey. (2012). 'Disabled children's voices: The nature and role of future empirical enquiry'. *Children and Society*, 26(3), 251–261.

T. Curran and K. Runswick-Cole (Eds.). (2013). *Disabled Children's Childhood Studies: Critical Approaches in a Global Context*. (London: Palgrave Macmillan).

A. Graham, M. Powell, N. Taylor, D. Anderson and R. Fitzgerald. (2013). *Ethical Research Involving Children*. (Florence: UNICEF Office of Research – Innocenti). http://childethics.com/.

P. S. Pinheiro. (2006). *Rights of the Child. Report of the Independent Expert for the United Nations Study on Violence Against Children* (Geneva: United Nations Secretary-General's Study on Violence against Children).

M. Sentenac, A. Gavin, S.N. Gabhainn, M. Molcho, P. Due, U. Ravens-Sieberer, M. de Matos, A. Malkowska-Szkutnik, I. Gobina, W. Vollebergh, C. Arnaud and E. Godeau. (2013). 'Peer victimization and subjective health among students reporting disability or chronic illness in 11 Western countries'. *The European Journal of Public Health*, 23(3), 421–426.

M. Srivastava, A. de Boer and S.J. Pijl. (2015). 'Inclusive education in developing countries: a closer look at its implementation in the last 10 years'. *Educational Review*, 67(2), 1–17.

UNICEF. (2013). *The State of the World's Children – Children with Disabilities* (New York: UNICEF), http://www.unicef.org/sowc2013/report.html.

Access to Education: Experiences from South Africa

Nithi Muthukrishna
Pholoho Morojele
Jaqueline Naidoo
Antoinette D'amant

> *States Parties recognize the right of persons with disabilities to education. With a view to realizing this right without discrimination and on the basis of equal opportunity, States Parties shall ensure an inclusive education system at all levels and lifelong learning.*
>
> **UN Convention on the Rights of Persons with Disabilities**
> **Article 24(1): Education**

Introduction

Education is one of the most important basic rights delineated in the Convention on the Rights of Persons with Disabilities (CRPD) under Article 24 (UN, 2006) (see Chapter 3). The right to education is foregrounded in this article and the right to equity, participation and inclusion in the education system as part of that right. Yet access to education still poses significant challenges to governments of the Global South (Bines and Lei, 2011). There are many areas of neglect in policy and provision, and disability remains a significant factor in exclusion from schooling (Croft, 2010).

In countries of the South, fewer than 5 per cent of children with disabilities reach the Education for All (EFA) goal of primary school completion. In 2007, only 10 per cent of children with disabilities in Africa were attending school (World Vision UK, 2007). Children with disabilities, according to the *World Report on Disability* (WHO and World Bank, 2011) have lower participation in school, which includes attendance, completion and promotion within school and achievement outcomes. Further, some estimates show that approximately 90 to 98 per cent of children with disabilities in the South do not attend school, and 99 per cent of girls with disabilities are illiterate (UN, 2007). Youth with disabilities are at risk of remaining illiterate, which can most likely result in limited access to further education, employment and income generation.

Thus, having a right to education does not automatically mean that disabled people and their families have the power to take up such a right. There are various influences that have a direct or indirect impact on the disabled individual's capability to seize the right to education. Economic, political, social, environmental and cultural factors impact access to education and may create pervasive barriers to realising the right of education of persons with disabilities.

This chapter firstly examines access to education for individuals with disabilities from primary to post-secondary levels in the Global South in order to provide a background to the chapter. Secondly, the chapter presents an analysis of inclusive education policy implementation in South Africa within a cluster of schools and their communities, and explores the co-existing successes, tensions and contradictions. The chapter will argue that the role of context in shaping responses to policy is critical to policy implementation.

Access to education in the Global South: Policy imperatives

In the last two decades or so, as the world has grown to be increasingly globalized, education policy and practices in countries of the South have been shaped by international trends, debates and international policy instruments. In 1990, the World Conference on Education for All (EFA), in Jomtien, placed disability as significant to the commitment to EFA (UNESCO, UNDP, UNICEF and World Bank, 1990). The Salamanca Statement (UNESCO, 1994), the Dakar Framework for Action (UNESCO, 2000), the Millennium Development Goals (UN, 2010c), the EFA Flagship on Education and Disability (UNESCO, 2004) and the CRPD (UN, 2006) have committed governments to equity in education for individuals with disabilities. Thus, a rights-based agenda and the social model of disability have resulted in increasing commitment to access and participation in education for children and youth with disabilities.

Most countries in the Global South have ratified these international conventions and policy instruments, and have included their embedded principles and commitments in local constitutional provisions, and in social and education policies (for example, Ghana Education Service (GES), 2005). In Uganda, the Constitution guarantees affirmative action in favour of people with disabilities to ensure they attain their full status as individuals (Republic of Uganda, 1995). In India, the Persons with Disabilities (Equal Opportunities, Protection of Rights and Full Participation) Act was promulgated in 1995 with a social rights agenda as opposed to a welfare approach, which provides for education, employment, creation of barrier-free environment and social security. In the Tenth to Twelfth Five-Year Plans, disability is foregrounded as a major concern in education, and a commitment is made to ensure access to education, health and nutrition for children with disabilities. Education of children with disabilities is a legal obligation up to age 18 (Government of India, 2002, 2007, 2012).

Access to higher education increases the chance of employability, ensuring a dignified life for persons with disabilities. At the tertiary level, there have been developments in policy in many countries of the Global South to protect the right to access for students with disabilities. For example, the policy frameworks put in place by the South African Government to drive inclusion in higher education are the *South African Higher Education Act 101 of 1997* (Republic of South Africa, 1997a); *White Paper 3: A Programme for the Transformation of Higher Education* (Republic of South Africa, Department of Education, 1997); *White Paper 6 on Special Education: Building an Inclusive Education and Training System* (Republic of South Africa, Department of Education, 2001a); and the *National Plan for Higher Education* (Department of Education, 2001b). In Brazil, affirmative action policies in higher education started in the year 2003 and have encouraged increased diversity among students, welcoming groups that have been virtually absent from higher education such as poor people, black people, native people, and people with disability (Oliven, 2012).

In many country contexts of the South, there has been a commitment to extending advocacy programmes to address discriminatory and exclusionary attitudes; expand education provision for children and youth with disabilities; improve the quality of services, infrastructure and provision; upgrade the professional training of teachers; and create inclusive education and training systems (for example, Republic of South Africa, 2001a; Government of India, 2012). However, despite commitments in legislation and policies, research shows that the journey to educational access for children and youth with disabilities and learning difficulties has been a difficult one. We illuminate some of the inherent complexities of this journey in selected contexts of the South in the section below.

Struggles in accessing quality education and training

Studies emanating from the South show that children with disabilities face significant obstacles to accessing quality education (for example, Moyi, 2012; Singal, 2009). Despite rights based legislation and policies in many countries, parents and families face exclusionary pressures as they try to access quality education and support for their children (for example, Muthukrishna and Ebrahim, 2014; Swart et al., 2005). Studies have shown that often the everyday experiences of disabled children and their families in the Global South lie outside the grasp of human rights instruments. In many country contexts, disabled individuals and their families have limited political power and knowledge of their rights and how to access services such as education, social welfare and health.

A key issue is that inequalities within and across countries of the South entrenched by globalization and capitalist ideologies have resulted in the oppression and marginalization of individuals with disabilities from mainstream social life. The neglect of the education of individuals with disabilities, for example, is rooted in structural inequalities and exclusionary social processes, making it virtually impossible for them to access rights embedded in government education policies and legislation. Children with disabilities face limited opportunities (due to lack of qualified teachers, an inflexible curriculum, inaccessible buildings, and so on), negative attitudes and low expectations about their ability to participate in teaching and learning (Singal, 2011) (see Chapter 8).

Scholars of the South have questioned the assumptions that underpin the social model of disability and the human rights-based approach (see Chapter 2, disability models). It is acknowledged that a solely medical understanding of disability reinforces difference, exclusion and marginalization, and creates barriers to accessing educational opportunities available to the majority (Singal, 2009). For example, in many countries of the South, high levels of resources continue to be channelled to special schools, irrespective of the likelihood that such settings may entrench exclusion from mainstream society and reinforce life on the margins of society (Miles and Singal, 2008; Singal, 2009).

However, a key concern regarding an over-emphasis on the social model has been the tendency to underplay the relationship between innate impairment and disability. Scholars have argued for the need to bring impairment back into focus in policy and practice debates alongside the social model with its focus on social, attitudinal and structural barriers to inclusion in society. Impairment cannot be de-emphasized when examining disabled individuals' lived experience, particularly in respect of access to education. Disability has to be conceived as a dynamic interaction between impairment and context, and this process impacts access to quality education. The impact of health and impairment on the social reality of individuals is experienced regardless of structural barriers, especially in contexts of poverty and underdevelopment. Further, disability is not a homogeneous category, as impairments vary in degree and type, and therefore the barriers to participation faced in society may be diverse, depending on context. In poor countries, disability support services, assistive technologies and transport to access educational institutions are severely limited or even non-existent (for example, Hayden, 2013). A further criticism of the human rights-based approach is that the social and cultural context of disablement is often neglected. For example, the language of 'rights' makes the assumption that individual rights are a priority in all societies of the Global South, whereas in many societies community and collective rights may be prioritized (for example, Miles, Merumeru and Lene, 2014).

Grech (2011) and Kozleski, Artiles, Fletcher and Engelbrecht (2009) further suggest that local values, histories, knowledge and practices are silenced when Western models and epistemologies are transferred to the South uncritically. In fact, the social model has been contested for ignoring the lived experiences of individuals with disability and their families in contexts of poverty. In such contexts, 'opportunity' such as access to quality education is seldom equitable. Developing the capabilities of individuals with disabilities and their families is critical if they are to access opportunities available to them.

Educational outcomes for individuals with disability continue to be an area of concern in the Global South. The trend in most countries is lower transition rates resulting in low levels of grade attainment which may be due to limited resources, lack of sound assessment techniques and processes, poorly trained teachers, and limited parental involvement and support (Moyi, 2012; UNESCO, 2010). Donor-funded education projects are rarely sustained as most countries generally lack the human and administrative capacity that is required to maintain and support programmes. Lei and Myers (2011) suggest that inclusive policies are often not translated into implementable education sector plans.

In the higher education sector, disability remains a source of inequality that has not received significant policy or research attention in the Global South. Morley and Croft (2011) provide an analysis of this neglect in Ghana and Tanzania. Other studies show that the rights agenda in higher education policy in the Global South has not translated into access for students with disabilities to higher education. Some of the reasons for this include infrastructural facilities within institutions, access to new technology, attitudes towards persons with disabilities, transportation facilities and lack of support services (Jameel, 2011; Matonya, 2012; Obiozor, Onu and Ugwoegbu, 2010).

Since the 1990s, the inclusive education movement has become the cornerstone of policies to advance access to education for children with disabilities in many countries of the South. Influenced by international instruments, the commitment to inclusive education agendas is evident in many countries of the Global South. Inclusive education is recognized as part of the human rights agenda in which a student has a right to access education as well as equitable rights within education. The notion of inclusive education has become a key element of Education for All (EFA) debates and critical to educational access for children with diverse learning needs, including those with disabilities. However, internationally, implementation of the inclusive education policy agenda has been a complex issue with inherent tensions and struggles (for example, Väyrynen, 2005; Anthony, 2011; Kalyanpur, 2011; Muthukrishna and Morojele, 2014).

Recently, a critical concern has been around the danger of trying to emulate Western models that do not align with local demands and priorities (for example, Richard, 2014; Grech, 2012). A further concern is that there are many competing discourses that have resulted in diverse conceptualizations, meanings and understandings. Thus, inclusive education philosophies, models and practices differ from context to context. In response to these debates, Maudslay (2014) argues for more sustainable and context-appropriate policies and practices in countries of the South. She questions the way in which donor-led interpretations of inclusive education are imposed on countries, with little attempt to analyse local ways of knowing and responding to disability issues. Le Fanu (2013, p. 42) has argued for the notion of 'grounded inclusionism' to acknowledge the situated expertize of local stakeholders.

Often, there is a lack of political will and accountability mechanisms at all levels of government, including national, provincial, district and local levels (Peters, 2004; Croft, 2010). In many contexts, serious consideration is not given to whether there are resources to support expanded educational provision and services to create inclusive schools and communities and decide where these resources are channelled as well as create accountability systems, good governance structures at all levels of the system, sound professional development and capacity building of school management and teachers. Calls have been made in the last decade for the reorientation of education systems towards an inclusive approach, stressing the need for re-shaping education departments at various levels and sectors; school practices, cultures and policies; the curricula; and the cultures and communities of local schools to make them more responsive to learner diversity (Le Fanu, 2013). Such transformation would create possibilities for ensuring that all students are present, participating and achieving, including those with disabilities. In many countries, there is a continued marginalization of the issue of education for disabled children from the mainstream EFA agenda (Lei and Myers, 2011).

Despite these challenges, there are emerging inclusive education practices in many country contexts in the Global South (for example, Hayden, 2013; Pather, 2011; Lynch, McCall, Douglas, McLinden and Bayo, 2011; Grimes, Sayarath and Outhaithany, 2011; Vaillant, 2011). However, there is need for in-depth analyses to explore these questions: How is the goal of inclusive education understood and realized within local contexts? How does local need determine how inclusive education policies are played out in practice?

Inclusive education policy implementation in South Africa

In 1994, emerging from the history of segregation and oppression, the South African government viewed education as a critical conduit for the transformation of society. This is evident in various education legislative frameworks and policies that emerged in the ensuing years (for example, the *South African Schools Act 84 of 1996* [Republic of South Africa, 1996]; *White Paper on the Integrated National Disability Strategy* [Republic of South Africa, 1997b]). *Education White Paper 6 (EDWP6) Special Needs Education – Building an Inclusive Education and Training System* (Republic of South Africa, Department of Education, 2001a) is the key policy document that provides a framework for access to education for *all* learners, irrespective of diversity, within an inclusive education and training system. According to EDWP6, inclusive education is viewed as an approach for establishing enabling education structures, systems and learning methodologies to meet the needs of all learners. EDWP6 acknowledges diversity in the learner population, including socio-economic status, culture, language, ethnicity, religion, ability/disability and race, among others.

A key concept in EDWP6 is 'barriers to learning', which shifts the focus to broader issues than disability (Republic of South Africa, Department of Education, 2001a). Four categories of barrier experienced within the system are delineated in EDWP6: systemic barriers to learning (overcrowded classrooms; inaccessible school buildings, policies and procedures; and so on); societal barriers to learning (poverty; lack of safety and security in schools; the impact of HIV/AIDS; abuse in schools, including bullying; and so on); pedagogical barriers to learning (unqualified or under-qualified teachers, inappropriate teaching and assessment methodologies, inadequate and inaccessible teaching and learning materials, and so on); intrinsic barriers to learning (neurological, sensory, physical and intellectual disabilities; behavioural and emotional problems; and so on). Thus, inclusive education is not about disability solely, but about a wider range of barriers to learning.

EDWP6 proposes that within each province there will be schools and structures that offer varying levels of support to learners to meet the diversity of needs and ensure access to quality education. The following are key components of support:

The Special School as Resource Centre (SSRC) is designated to provide high-level support for students who experience severe barriers to learning. A SSRC provides on-site support for students with high-level learning needs, as well as providing support to neighbouring schools and communities.

The Full-Service School (FSS) provides a moderate level of support and serves as a resource and referral centre for mainstream surrounding schools and communities. These schools have slightly greater resourcing and staffing than mainstream schools and are able to address barriers to learning caused by moderate physical and mental impairments as well as socio-economic barriers.

The mainstream school provides low levels of care and support. Teachers at these schools can refer students to the Full-Service School and the Special School as Resource Centre when additional support is necessary. In addition, mainstream teachers receive training and support from teachers and therapists at the Full-Service Schools and Special School as Resource Centres.

The Institution Level Support Team (ILST) is a school-based support team whose main responsibility is to identify and address support needs, and to assist teachers and the school to access support from within the school, the local community, the district and so on.

The District-Based Support Team (DBST). The DBST's core responsibility is to plan, budget and programme for the additional support needs of the district. Further, the DBST's task is professional development of school management and teachers and other support staff.

Since 2001, there have also been various EDWP6 implementation strategies and strategy documents that have directly impacted the education system (for example, *National Strategy on Screening, Identification, Assessment and Support (SIAS) – Operational Guidelines* [Republic of South Africa, Department of Education, 2008]; Guidelines for Responding to Learner Diversity in the Classroom through Curriculum and Assessment Policy Statements [Republic of South Africa, Department of Education, 2011]). However, the reality in South Africa is that the implementation of inclusive education is still at its infancy almost 13 years since the release of EDWP6. Despite encouraging emerging practices, some of the challenges to policy implementation have been around funding pressures, sustainability of pilot projects, inadequate teacher development and support, weak education management at the district level, a lack of collective knowledge about inclusive education policy and its implementation, persistence of exclusionary school cultures and practices, systemic inequalities, inadequate school leadership to support policy implementation, lack of accountability mechanisms and limited parental/caregiver and community involvement (see for example, D'amant, 2012; Eloff and Kqwete, 2007; Perumal, 2005; Swart et al., 2005; Wildeman and Nomdo, 2007). There continues to be inadequate provision for students with disabilities in higher education (Howell, 2006; Matshedisho, 2007).

In the context of the above inclusive education policy developments in South Africa, we present a qualitative case study research project that was undertaken in a rural context of the province of KwaZulu-Natal (see Muthukrishna and Morojele, 2014). The case study focused on institutions that are the key focus of the inclusive education strategy in South Africa: SSRC, FSS, and one mainstream school. The FSS and the mainstream school have enrolled children with disabilities, including those with mild to moderate intellectual disabilities and hearing impairment. Further, teachers have indicated that there are many learners who are experiencing difficulties in learning and are not functioning at grade level, particularly in numeracy and literacy. The SSRC caters for learners with physical and visual disabilities. The cluster of schools is supported by the DBST.

The aim of the study was to examine how school management and teachers engage with the process of creating inclusive schools that are responsive to the needs of all learners, irrespective of diversity. These were the key research questions: How do teachers and school management establish enabling structures, systems and learning methodologies to meet the needs of all learners? What skills, competencies, attitudes and knowledge are required for teachers to be effective in inclusive schools and classrooms? What are the influences that shape and limit the policy enactments of teachers? What are the different policy positions and actions that are evident in teacher enactments?

The theoretical framing of this study was influenced by policy research undertaken by Stephen Ball and his team at the London Institute of Education in schools in the United Kingdom. Their work enables a grounded analysis of the complexities of the interface between policy and practice in the education arena (Ball, Maguire, Braun, Hoskins, 2011a, 2011b). In this case study (see Box 9.1), selected concepts and ideas from this work were used to make sense of teachers as enactors of inclusive education policy. Data generation involved individual interviews; focus group interviews; a participatory technique, photo-voice; document analysis; and classroom observations.

Teachers as enactors of inclusive education policy

In this sub-section, we engage in analysis of key trends that are emerging in the policy implementation journey of teachers (including the school principals) within the case study schools.

Making meaning of the notion of 'inclusive education'

The study examined the meanings of inclusion and inclusive education constructed by the various participants in the different school contexts. The

---

Box 9.1.   Case study: Rainbow primary school – a full-service school

Rainbow Full-Service School is a primary school with 1,427 learners from grade R (preschool) to grade 7. The school is situated in a rural area about 45 km southwest of the city of Durban, in the province of KwaZulu-Natal. The communities surrounding the school face a myriad of complex and intersecting social problems, including crime, unemployed youth, drugs and alcohol abuse, HIV/AIDS and teenage pregnancy. In line with the policy proposals of EDWP6 – *Special Education: Building an Inclusive Education Training System* (July 2001), Rainbow School was selected for conversion into a Full-Service School. The Department of Education in 2012 allocated Rainbow 3 million for the construction of a Care and Support Centre on the school grounds to facilitate the outreach activities. The school has the support of two Learning Support Educators (LSEs) who are part of the DBST. The Full-Service School serves as a resource and referral centre for surrounding schools and communities.

The Rainbow Primary School was converted to a Full-Service School on grounds that school management and teachers were already agents for change and were engaging with the proposals of EDWP6 in their own nuanced ways. The school has an ethos that is welcoming and affirms diversity. Learners who experience a range of barriers to learning are enrolled at the school, including those with mild to moderate intellectual disabilities. According to teachers, there are many learners who have learning difficulties, particularly in literacy and numeracy. Two 'remedial', or 'transition' classes have been established in order to provide these learners with high-quality support in literacy and numeracy to facilitate their progress to grade level. Teachers are highly motivated to achieve this goal, and believe that this initiative is highly successful.

Teachers, management teams, local businesses, taxi organizations, the unions, social workers, parents (or guardians), the Department of Education, local hospitals and clinics, community health workers, youth organizations, medical doctors and nurses are some of the key stakeholders who play a significant role in supporting the Full-Service School, and work as a unique learning community.

There is emerging leadership at various levels in the school to support and enhance inclusive practices. Staff are willing to share their expertize and provide leadership to schools in the community on matters relating to inclusive education practice. The ILST has had training from the DBST on inclusive policies and practices, and on the role of a Full-Service School in the community. The agency of school personnel is reflected in the staff development process that is largely initiated and led by staff, driven by what they perceive to be their needs. The LSE based at the school undertake funding drives to support their Inclusion Outreach project – an advocacy initiative in the community. The ILST indicated that priority areas in which they would have to access outside intervention are curriculum differentiation and inclusive assessment procedures. Skills development in addressing the needs of learners with severe disabilities would be an area for future development, according to teachers.

---

teachers interviewed in all three school contexts were aware of EDWP6 on inclusive education. In three school contexts, teachers interviewed were aware that inclusive education is not about disability only, but involves a wider range of barriers to learning. Their staff narratives revealed that they engage with systemic barriers, pedagogical barriers and intrinsic barriers. There was strong evidence of a rights-based agenda in teacher narratives. Teachers foregrounded learners' right to quality education, access and participation, equity in education and right to full participation in society beyond the schooling phase. That schools should be responsive to the community and inculcate a sense of belonging also emerged as important principles for inclusion in this context.

As shown in the studies by Stephen Ball and his team (2011a, 2011b), as policy subjects, teachers may be eloquent in policy language and may be able to articulate policy imperatives and values. However, as policy actors *and* subjects, teachers may exhibit incoherence which becomes evident in the course of the policy implementation process. Various contradictions were evident that seemed to be located in competing discourses of disability. For example, language associated with medical/deficit discourse tends to operate alongside a social rights discourse, for example, 'learners with severe psychological barriers', 'learners with learning barriers', 'remedial learners', 'slow learners', 'normal vs disabled learners'. Internationally, the deficit gaze underpinning educational responses for children with disabilities has proven to be resilient and resistant to change. This finding suggests that teacher professional development programmes need to challenge and disrupt deficit thinking as a moral imperative.

Teacher values and beliefs in educating for diversity

In countries of the South in the last two decades, there has been a proliferation of research on teacher attitudes towards inclusion (for example, Bothma, Gravett and Swart, 2000; Eloff, Swart and Engelbrecht, 2002; Nel et al., 2011). Much of this literature is about integrating children with disabilities into regular classes, and teacher attitudes towards and willingness to accommodate the needs of students with disabilities in an ordinary class. An analysis of studies shows that epistemologically such research often tends to operate from a medical/deficit discourse, which many would argue is a violation of the rights of learners with disabilities. Would the question around attitudes be posed and examined if the issue involved other categories of diversity such as gender, race, immigrant children or children living in poverty? In contrast, we were interested in how teacher personal histories, values and belief systems shape their responses to diversity. This was the question explored: How do teacher values align with or conflict with the policy imperatives and undermine or promote them?

Many teachers believed strongly that the academic facet of teaching and learning cannot be divorced from the psychosocial realities in their schools and local communities. The data revealed numerous stories of teacher agency as they respond to learner and community needs in the everyday lives of being teachers. Stories of care, compassion, and support to learners and the embracing of parents and caregivers emerged in the data.

In the case of many teachers, their commitment and passion for inclusion is linked strongly to their personal histories, cultural and religious beliefs. The philosophy of Ubuntu, Christian and Hindu values were voiced by participants and linked to the rights-based discourse of inclusion. Ubuntu is a humanistic worldview that emanates from southern Africa. It is the essence of being human. A person with Ubuntu has allegiance to and affirms one's fellow human beings, has a sense of community, compassion, and shared concern for the rights of others. To oppress, humiliate or diminish others is not Ubuntu (Tutu, 1999) (see also Chapter 12 for Ubuntu in relation to livelihoods).

Working to create responsive support structures

In all three schools, school management and teachers as policy subjects have taken up the policy imperative of establishing ILSTs and are trying to perform the roles and practices set out in policy guidelines. It is evident that training initiated by the DBST and the national guideline documents have played a critical role in this development (for example, Republic of South Africa, Department of Education, 2007) (see Chapter 16 on professional training). Teachers across the three schools shared stories of how they had undertaken various school-based initiatives to address contextual barriers to learning and participation.

The FSS and the mainstream schools on their own initiative have structured the work of the ILST around certain portfolios, for example whole school development, teacher support and learner support. Members of the ILST are responsible for the different portfolios in a shared manner of working. The study shows that the ILST as a micro-system does not operate in isolation, but interacts with other systems inside and outside the school to harness the psycho-educational and psychosocial support for learners. Members are able to build networks and partnerships to harness human and social capital. An ILST member from the SSRC provides insight of this:

> What is also lovely and important is empowering the community, disability advocacy is huge priority. We have had such amazing opportunities empowering these parents, teaching them about the disabilities and going to companies and helping them understand disabilities so that they are open to the learners actually working there or volunteering there.

Reflexivity and openness to continuous learning on the part of all ILST members are key elements that emerged in the study. The ILSTs have had training from the DBST, and there is evidence of self-initiated teacher development and capacity building. At the FSS School, staff development occurs once a fortnight, initiated by the teachers. The agency of teachers is reflected in the focus group interview below, when they were questioned about who takes the lead:

> Anyone among us who has the knowledge. If you have the knowledge and the skill in a particular aspect, we allow him or her to develop the teachers.

Teachers did, however, indicate that in-depth skills development to capacitate them to address the needs of learners with severe disabilities was an important area for future development.

At the FSS, teachers are willing to share their expertize and provide leadership to schools in the community on matters relating to inclusive education practice. However, the enthusiasm of teachers is dampened by lack of funding to support their new role. The outreach Centre for Care and Support that has been built at the school is not fully resourced as yet. No funding has been allocated for workshops for teachers from neighbouring schools. The two Learning Support Teachers who are part of the DBST undertake funding drives to cover the cost of their Inclusion Outreach project – an advocacy initiative in the community. Although accessing funding is a struggle, they remain completely dedicated to goals and objectives.

Networking and partnerships

The case study shows that the ILSTs and the DBST in the three schooling contexts are committed to building networks and partnerships in the community to access human and social capital for the creation of inclusive schools and communities (see Chapter 12, livelihoods). Grech (2011) has argued that social programmes in the Global South are strengthened if they build on the strengths and resiliencies of families, communities and social networks.

The LST in the DBST are active members of a large and very active Stakeholders Forum in the district, a special initiative supported by the Office of the Premier in the province. Membership includes seven non-governmental organisations (NGOs) that work in the district; key provincial departments, including Health, Social Welfare, South African Police Services, Environmental Health, Human Settlement and Education. The key imperative of the forum is addressing barriers to learning and participation and monitoring the health and well-being of learners and families. In the context of community vulnerability in the face of HIV/AIDS and poverty, this support is invaluable to schools.

Teachers in the Full-Service School are deeply involved in responding to community needs that impact children's learning, health and well-being, for example by working with the Department of Social Welfare to assist families to access government social grants such as disability grants and child support grants. Local businesses are partners with the school. A local business donated water bottles to each child in the school in support of the school's 'save water' initiative. The mainstream school is renowned for an exceedingly successful vegetable garden project supported by local farmers which is seen as a strategy for poverty alleviation amongst learners and their families.

The data yielded stories of innovative initiatives as well as networking and partnerships across the three schools to build support in the community and protect and enhance child well-being, development and learning. What was powerful in the data is the reflexive nature of the responses of teachers that emerge in grounded manner. The photovoice narratives of the Learning Support Teachers provided insight into an Inclusive Education Outreach project, Disability Awareness Day and Grandma's Day (to affirm grandmothers who care for vulnerable children, including children with disabilities).

Creating curriculum access and inclusive pedagogies

In line with EDWP6, the main focus for DBST is to provide *indirect* support to learners through supporting teachers and school management. This indirect support is in the form of a 'consultancy'. A secondary focus would be to provide *direct* learning support to learners where necessary and possible, where institutional-level support teams are unable to respond to particular learning needs. The two Learner Support Teachers as members of the DBST play these important roles at the FSS and the mainstream school. In view of the lack of funding to support the work of the SSRC, the DBST's role at this institution is in its infancy.

Teachers in the three schools have a broad understanding of what the concept 'an inclusive curriculum' entails. They were able to articulate their actions in engaging with meeting the diverse needs of learners and in adapting the curriculum to suit particular learner needs. It was evident that their pedagogical practices and cultures are influenced by inclusive attitudes, values and beliefs. However, a mixture of didactic, teacher-centred teaching practices and learner centredness approaches play out in the schools. It is likely that contextual complexities such as large classes and limited material resources influence pedagogic decision making.

An important part of curriculum planning is the *National Strategy on Screening, Identification, Assessment and Support (SIAS)* (Republic of South Africa, Department of Education, 2008). The majority of teachers have been trained on the SIAS and are using it in different ways to meet the needs of the context. Various school documents provided evidence of assessment of systemic barriers, intrinsic barriers and contextual barriers to learning. The Learning Support Teacher plays a pivotal role in training teachers and directly modelling inclusive practices, when necessary.

Post EDWP6, the National Department of Education prioritized the issue of curriculum differentiation and inclusive pedagogy in the context of the national curriculum, and the aim of one curriculum for all. Two guideline documents have emerged, *Guidelines for Inclusive Teaching and Learning* (Republic of South Africa, Department of Education, 2008); *Guidelines for Responding to Learner Diversity in the Classroom through Curriculum and Assessment Policy Statements (CAPS)* (Republic of South Africa, Department of Education, 2011). However, professional development of teachers on these guidelines, which target curriculum differentiation, has not occurred as yet at the three schools. The study showed that teachers are constructing their own meanings of curriculum adaptation in respect of what learners learn (content), how learners learn (process) and how learners demonstrate what they have learned (product).

A grade 2 class at the mainstream school has a child who is hearing impaired and wears a hearing aid. The teacher identified that the child had a problem at the beginning of the school year. Her agency emerges in this interview:

In the months he was in my class, I found he can't walk properly, he can't hear well, he is a lip reader. When you are talking to him, he didn't hear anything. So I wrote a letter – and told the parents to take the child to the doctor at the hospital. The doctor assessed the child. After he assessed the child, he also found that the child has a hearing problem. So he organized a hearing aid for him just in one ear – because they suspect it is one ear. They asked me to help him in putting it on and taking it out when he goes out for play. Then I tried to teach him how to put it and take it out. But now granny, his caregiver, keeps the hearing aid at home because the doctor told her that it was very expensive and granny fears he will lose it. So I have to work with granny now.

Although the teacher is playing a valuable role, she does need support and further development in how to address the needs of a child who is Deaf, for example the importance of wearing the hearing aid during social play and how to counsel the grandmother. The data here show that the teacher is committed to 'getting it right'. She has an inclusive attitude, but she has to navigate contradictory, precarious and complex influences and social realities. In an isiZulu mother tongue lesson, it was evident that the child was fully engaged in meaningful learning. There was little doubt that the teacher had high expectations for this learner.

However, as Ball and his team (2011a) suggest, policy implementation is never a smooth, linear and predictable process. Teachers are clearly social actors and agents in the mediation and enactment of policy. At the FSS, teachers and ILST members made the decision to begin two 'remedial classes' for learners in grades 1 and 2; and grades 4 and 5 who are not performing at grade level. The principal and teachers stressed that the main aim is to provide the learners with maximum support to address 'gaps' in literacy and numeracy learning, and to facilitate their re-entry into their grade level classes. Ball et al. (2011b) remind us that, as actors of policy, teachers find spaces to perform their agency as they select, interpret and adapt policy to align with their shifting beliefs. The notion of a 'remedial class' may be viewed as a contradiction to inclusive education policy values.

At the SSRC, there are two curriculum streams: an academic and a skills-based curriculum. The national Curriculum and Assessments Statements (CAPS) (Republic of South Africa, Department of Education, 2011) are strictly followed and used as a monitoring tool for teaching and learning. Analysis of learner books and other texts revealed that performance of learners in the academic stream is at grade level or higher. Teachers are steadfast that they are committed to the highest academic performance and high expectations for learners.

The findings in this study raise what may seem a controversial question: What does inclusion mean in a special school? In examining the ethos and culture of this school, the quality of education offered, access to education and the values of teachers, one gains the impression that this is a school striving towards inclusion. For teachers at the SSRC, inclusion is about belonging to society and ensuring that learners can eventually lead an independent life.

Conclusions

The case study shows that most teachers in the schooling contexts are firmly embedded in the prevailing policy space and discourses. Although often overwhelmed and overloaded with work commitments and resource constraints, teachers are engaged. The case study reveals that teachers tend to make sense of policy through the lens of their own values and pre-existing knowledge and practices. As Ball et al. (2011b) explain, teachers as agents interpret, modify, adapt and often alter policy messages as they engage with them. This may explain the diverse and complex ways in which inclusive education policy emerges in countries of the Global South.

Further, the study shows that teachers act towards policy in particular ways that align with their local contexts and circumstances. This foregrounds the role of context in framing responses to policy; for example, the nature of available human and material resources may limit, distort and facilitate policy enactments. The policy journey is shaped by networks of social actors with diverse values, interests and commitments. The findings of this case study have some important implications for teacher education and teacher professional development in the Global South.

Lessons from South Africa

- *Inclusion is a complex concept*, and understanding the ways in which complex local meanings are shaped by historical, cultural, political and economic forces is important.
- The role of context in forming, shaping and hindering responses to policy is critical to policy implementation. Inclusive education policy implementation takes place within the dynamics of *shifting contexts and the inherent multiple interrelationships*.
- Often *competing discourses* of inclusion and disability play out in teachers' enactments of policy. Teacher professional development programmes need to explore creative pedagogies to engage students in interrogating the values that shape their understandings of inclusion and constructions of difference.
- A *values education orientation* component in teacher education programmes is of vital importance to engage students in issues of personal and social morality, and how this shapes their responses to diversity.
- *Teacher reflexivity* in the process of creating inclusive schools and their communities needs to be encouraged. Reflexivity is about finding strategies to question one's attitudes, thought processes, values, assumptions, prejudices and actions.
- Building social capital to create inclusive schools is a skill teachers need to be equipped with, particularly competence in creating networks and civic engagement (Goodwin and Armstrong-Esther, 2004).

Summary of key points

- The right to education is foregrounded in Article 24 of the CRPD, 'Education', and the right to equity, participation and inclusion in the education system as part of that right. Yet access to education still poses significant challenges to governments of the Global South.

- The perpetuation of a universal notion of inclusion and inclusive education reflects narrow notions of schools and their diverse communities. Inclusive models and practices will have limited similarity from context to context because of the heterogeneity of national sociocultural contexts.
- Individual and collective agency is crucial to inclusive education policy implementation – an issue neglected in a deterministic understanding of the social model of disability.
- Inclusion is an ongoing process involving reflexivity and negotiation, and negotiated through historical, material conditions and social relations, and interpersonal actions in local contexts in response to situated needs.
- An over-emphasis on barriers to learning and participation may suggest a deficit construction of schools, learners and their communities. There is need for a shift to exploring the agency of teachers, community members and parents/caregivers who are able to navigate challenging situations in creative ways.
- Teacher enactments of policy implementation are never linear, as teachers are both policy subjects and social actors who mediate policy imperatives in complex ways.
- Creating inclusive schools is about building professional and local learning communities. Such communities provide opportunities for stakeholders across a school system to learn, take risks, build relational trust, share common values and beliefs, and continually build capacity to improve their schools and their practices.
- Thinking from within experiences of inclusive education policy implementation is important for school-based teacher professional development programmes.

STUDY QUESTIONS

1. How does context shape teachers' enactments of inclusive education policy implementation?
2. What do you view as the strengths and constraints of Inclusive Education policy implementation in the case study context?
3. What implications does the case study have for teacher professional development in countries of the South?

Further reading and resources

A. Croft. (2010). 'Including disabled children in learning: Challenges in developing countries. CREATE pathways to access', *Research Monograph*, No. 36, accessed 13 December 2013 from http://files.eric.ed.gov/fulltext.
M. Kalyanpur. (2011). 'Paradigm and paradox: Education for all and the inclusion of children with disabilities in Cambodia', *International Journal of Inclusive Education*, 15(10), 1053–1071.

E. B. Kozleski, A.J. Artiles, T. Fletcher and P. Engelbrecht. (2009). 'Understanding the dialectics of the local and the global in Education for all: A comparative case study', *International Critical Childhood Policy Studies Journal*, 2, 15–29.

G. Le Fanu. (2013). 'Reconceptualising inclusive education in international development'. In L. Tikly and A. Barrett (Eds.), *Education, quality and social justice in the Global South* (London: Routledge), 40–55.

S. Miles, L. Merumeru and D. Lene. (2014). 'Making sense of inclusive education in the Pacific region: networking as a way forward', *Childhood*, 21(3).

S. Miles and N. Singal. (2010). 'The education for all and inclusive education debate: Conflict, contradiction or opportunity?', *International Journal of Inclusive Education*, 14, 1–15.

J. Ngcobo and N. Muthukrishna. (2011). 'The geographies of inclusion of students with disabilities in an ordinary school', *South African Journal of Education*, 31, 357–368.

B. Richard. (2014). 'Families, well-being and inclusion: Rethinking priorities for children with cognitive disabilities in Ladakh, India', *Childhood*, 21(3).

N. Singal and N. Muthukrishna. (2014). 'Introduction: Education, childhood and disability in countries of the South – re-positioning the debates', *Childhood*, 21(3).

Disability and Inclusive Health

Malcolm MacLachlan
Hasheem Mannan
Joanne McVeigh

> *States Parties recognize that persons with disabilities have the right to the enjoyment of the highest attainable standard of health without discrimination on the basis of disability. States Parties shall take all appropriate measures to ensure access for persons with disabilities to health services that are gender-sensitive, including health-related rehabilitation.*
>
> UN Convention on Rights of Persons with Disabilities
> Article 25: Health

Introduction

This chapter explores the relationship between health and disability. Although it is concerned with the health of adults and children with disability, we have a particular interest in children with disability, as they are relatively poorly addressed in the literature. Furthermore, as community-based rehabilitation is the major service delivery mechanism for most people with disabilities in low-income settings, we focus our discussion on access to health through CBR.

Inclusive health

Inclusive health is about health for all humankind, across all ages; it builds on the aspiration for Health for All embraced by the Alma-Ata meeting of 1978 (WHO, 1978). Inclusive health adds new and important dimensions to this ethos; by more explicitly encompassing a rights-based approach to health including children's rights; by more actively promoting inclusion as a verb, requiring a proactive approach to identifying and addressing distinctive and different barriers to inclusion, such as for children with disabilities; by recognizing that new initiatives in human resources for health can offer exciting and innovative ways of health care delivery reaching further than ever before

(MacLachlan et al., 2012). Disability is not a 'health problem', but people with disability have an equal right to the same standard of accessible health care as those without disability. Some people with disabilities may of course have enhanced needs for health care support.

The enhanced health needs of people with disability may be in relation to primary health conditions associated with a disability, for instance, the progressive skeletal muscular weakness associated with muscular dystrophy. Secondary health conditions, which are related to disability but occur in addition to the disability, may include pressure ulcers or urinary tract infections and will require health care intervention. Some health problems may be 'co-morbid' with disability; that is, they occur alongside but are unrelated to the disability, such as diabetes. There are some disabilities that are associated with premature ageing processes, and so diseases of ageing (for example, cardiovascular disease or osteoporosis) may be more prevalent at younger ages. Disability may also restrict lifestyle options, and this may influence the propensity of some people with disability to engage in behaviours that put them at increased risk of developing health problems; such behaviours may include inactivity, overeating or smoking. Stigma associated with disability, lack of social inclusion, lack of opportunities for employment, or the demands of coping with a long-term disabling condition may constitute a chronic stressor and become associated with mental health problems. However disability in itself should not be seen as a 'health problem', as some people with disabilities do not require any more health interventions or treatments than do most people without disabilities. Thus it is important to make health care inclusive of people with disabilities – and other marginalized groups who lack access to health care – rather than seeing disability as being associated with particular and separate health needs. This is the primary reason why we have developed the concept of inclusive health (MacLachlan et al., 2012).

Inclusive Education (see Chapter 9) has become a widely acknowledged and applied concept, whereas Health for All is still contested. For instance, Foreign Policy in Focus (Parsons, 2009) has argued that 'health for all' has become more 'health for some'. It asserts that governments and international bodies are fully responsible for the failure of Health for All by the Year 2000. It cites *The People's Charter for Health* (People's Health Movement, 2009) as indicating that access to health care and other social services have been undermined by neoliberal political and economic policies, and the unregulated activities of transnational corporations. As we show here and in recent reviews of health policies (Amin et al., 2011; MacLachlan et al., 2012; Mannan, Amin, MacLachlan and the EquitAble Consortium, 2012; Mannan, MacLachlan, McVeigh and the EquitAble Consortium, 2012; Mannan, McVeigh et al., 2012; Mannan, Amin, MacLachlan and the Equitable Consortium, 2011), for instance, some sections of society are privileged over others regarding their access to health care. In the context of scarce resources, particularly in low-income countries, competition for such resources can mean that the needs of some groups predominate over the needs of others, often including the less vocal, visible or powerful groups, such as children with disabilities (see Chapter 8). In essence, the idea of Health for All, though clearly desirable, may be seen as too idealistic, politically charged and expensive to be implemented. New thinking is required to develop a more all-encompassing agenda for health, one that resonates with contemporary health systems and related developments, and addresses the marginalizing effects of social dominance within societies. Inclusive health is a concept which more proactively integrates a range of United Nations conventions which recognize the importance of difference – ability, ethnicity, gender, age. For each of these groups, what marginalizes them in terms of health and social welfare provision is not their inherent characteristics, but the hierarchical position into which they are placed by mainstream society – a position that reflects privilege, and the maintenance of it (Burke and Eichler, 2006) and this positioning in itself can serve to further undermine the rights and dignity of these population groups (MacLachlan, Carr and McAuliffe, 2010). Sometimes marginalization is accentuated through dichotomized positioning: mainstream vs marginalized, men vs women, abled vs disabled. People with disabilities, and especially children with disabilities, the majority of whom live in impoverished contexts in low-income countries (WHO and World Bank, 2011), are a clear and poignant example of such a marginalized group and of the need to address their right to health (UN, 2006) (see Chapter 6 for a discussion on poverty and disability).

Both from a systems perspective, and simultaneously the perspective of individuals, the inclusive health ethos is encapsulated by Thomas Jefferson's two-century-old assertion that '[t]here is nothing more unequal, than the equal treatment of unequal people'. Inclusive health challenges such inequity; it sees inequity in health arising not from a poorly implemented and resource-constrained system per se, with unfortunate but unavoidable oversights, but rather, from the often deliberate – sometimes thoughtless – construction of 'mainstream' services to address particular majority needs in particular majority ways. As such, inclusive health challenges the aspiration of 'mainstreaming' for any particular group or issue, as in so doing this only serves to move a group along the exclusion–inclusion dimension rather than rethinking the systems in ways that would be inclusive for all, especially the most vulnerable and marginalized.

However, this idealism requires health services that are efficacious and affordable as well as equitable. Efficacious means that the health services actually work – they produce gains in people's health and well-being, and seek to prevent both disease and social conditions that detract from health (Commission on Social Determinants of Health, 2008). Affordable – both to the individual and the community – means that services are provided in the most cost-effective way possible. Equitable means that services are provided on the basis of people's needs – that those most in need can access the service as easily as those least in need. Inclusive health therefore strongly resonates with the rights-based approach to health – incorporating political, social, economic, scientific and cultural actions that promote health for all humankind (Sen, 2008). In this paper, we are particularly concerned with establishing the case for equitable health.

Inclusive health also recognizes that individuals are not simply members of discrete constituencies of a particular 'vulnerable group', but rather are simultaneously members of inter-related groups. Social identity is 'that part of an individual's self-concept which derives from … knowledge of … membership in a social group (or groups) together with the value and emotional significance attached to that membership' (Tajfel, 1978). People may voluntarily identify with or be identified with (involuntarily, by others) a number of groups or categories of people. Social identification is a critical process through which people come to understand their place in society and develop a view of and value for their self (Bennet, 2011) and perhaps also to question it. In the context of inclusive health, vulnerable groups may be defined as 'social groups who experience limited resources and consequent high relative risk for morbidity and premature mortality' (Flaskerud and Winslow, 1998) and individuals may be a member of several such vulnerable groups, as well as other groups with much more positive connotations.

From the health systems perspective, the idea of inclusion in inclusive health also applies to different service delivery mechanisms. This means allowing for a range of health practitioner cadres (including ones with shorter and more focused training than conventionally trained health professions) to be involved in providing an acceptable quality of care in the most efficient and cost-effective manner. More generally, the inclusive health philosophy promotes more horizontal programmes, preferably under one roof or campus, rather than vertical, segregated and defragmented programmes across various health care facilities. Interestingly, this may actually be more achievable in less specialized and community-based services than in more 'developed' and specialized services in secondary or tertiary health facilities. Likewise, inclusive health care resonates with the idea of inter-sectoral, inter-ministerial and inter-disciplinary working, which is at the core of the Bamako Call to Action on Research for Health (Lancet Editorial, 2008), and recognizes that health and well-being are dependent on a considerable range of services and resources, not just those occurring in hospital or clinics.

Inclusive health policies and children with disabilities

Children with disabilities are among the most vulnerable members of any society; policies to address the needs of such children should be amongst the highest priorities for global leaders (UNICEF and University of Wisconsin, 2008). But how widely are children with disabilities, young people in general or indeed people with disabilities in general actually considered in national health policy documents? *EquiFrame* has been described as 'a theoretical tool that facilitates the integration of human rights concepts into policymaking' (Farmer, 2011). It establishes the extent to which 'policy on the books' – what policies actually say – incorporates 21 Core Concepts of human rights and coverage of 12 Vulnerable Groups, including children with disabilities (Amin et al., 2011; MacLachlan et al., 2012; Mannan, Amin, MacLachlan and the EquitAble Consortium, 2012; Mannan, MacLachlan, McVeigh and the EquitAble Consortium, 2012; Mannan, McVeigh, Amin, MacLachlan, Swartz et al., 2012; Mannan, Amin, MacLachlan and the EquitAble Consortium, 2011). For the purposes of this paper, we focus on just three Vulnerable Groups and five Core Concepts, which are defined in Tables 10.1 and 10.2 respectively.

Table 10.1. *EquiFrame* Vulnerable Groups Definitions

No.	Vulnerable Group	Attributes or Definitions
1.	**Children (with special needs)**	Referring to children marginalized by special contexts, such as orphans or street children
2.	**Youth**	Referring to younger age without identifying gender
3.	**Disabled**	Referring to persons with disabilities, including physical, sensory, intellectual or mental health conditions, and including synonyms of disability

Table 10.2. *EquiFrame* Key Questions and Key Language of Core Concepts

No	Core Concept	Key Question	Key Language
1.	**Non-discrimination**	Does the policy support the rights of vulnerable groups with equal opportunity in receiving health care?	Vulnerable groups are not discriminated against on the basis of their distinguishing characteristics (i.e. Living away from services; Persons with disabilities; Ethnic minority or Aged).
2.	**Participation**	Does the policy support the right of vulnerable groups to participate in the decisions that affect their lives and enhance their empowerment?	Vulnerable groups can exercise choices and influence decisions affecting their life. Such consultation may include planning, development, implementation, and evaluation.
3.	**Family Resource**	Does the policy recognize the value of the family members of vulnerable groups in addressing health needs?	The policy recognizes the value of family members of vulnerable groups as a resource for addressing health needs.
4.	**Family Support**	Does the policy recognize individual members of vulnerable groups may have an impact on the family members requiring additional support from health services?	Persons with chronic illness may have mental health effects on other family members, such that these family members themselves require support.
5.	**Cultural Responsiveness**	Does the policy ensure that services respond to the beliefs, values, gender, interpersonal styles, attitudes, cultural, ethnic, or linguistic, aspects of the person?	i) Vulnerable groups are consulted on the acceptability of the service provided. ii) Health facilities, goods and services must be respectful of ethical principles and culturally appropriate, i.e. respectful of the culture of vulnerable groups.

Figure 10.1 charts the coverage of the selected Vulnerable Groups: Youth, Children (with special needs), and Disabled (all age groups including children) across 51 health policies from Namibia (10), Malawi (14), South Africa (11),

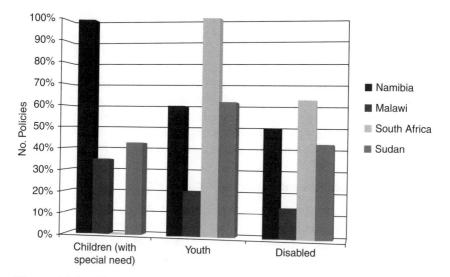

Figure 10.1. EquiFrame coverage of Vulnerable Groups in four African countries

and Sudan (16). It is evident that all Namibian polices referred to Children with special needs, and all South African policies referred to Youth. However, the lack of South African policies referring to Children with special needs, or of Malawian policies referring to people with disabilities, is striking, as is the finding that no country is inclusive of all of these three Vulnerable Groups across the health polices targeted at addressing their greatest burden of disease (MacLachlan et al., 2012).

Figure 10.2 charts the coverage across the same policies of five selected Core Concepts of human rights – *Participation, Non-discrimination, Cultural*

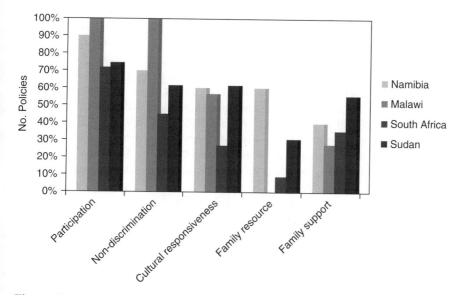

Figure 10.2. EquiFrame Core Concept coverage

responsiveness, *Family resource*, and *Family support*. Although it is evident that the Core Concepts of *Participation* and *Non-discrimination* were explicitly mentioned across all Malawian policies analysed, coverage of *Family resource* across the equivalent Malawian health policies was absent. By and large, Figure 10.2 demonstrates that the selected Core Concepts were not explicitly mentioned across a sizeable percentage of health policies analysed for each country. Regardless of the considerable challenges of policy development and implementation, if 'policy on the books' is not inclusive of vulnerable groups, and observant of human rights, then neither are health practices likely to be.

United Nations conventions and children with disabilities

The United Nations Convention on the Rights of Persons with Disabilities (CRPD) (UN, 2006) provides human rights and moral and legal legitimacy for the inclusion of people with disabilities, including children, in policies (see Chapter 3). Article 7 of the Convention directly concerns children with disabilities.

A similar analysis can be extended to the United Nations Convention on the Rights of the Child (UN, 1990). Article 23 directly concerns children with disabilities. Children with disabilities are thus expressly entitled under the Convention to enjoy all the protection it offers. This provision is vital as it dramatically expands protection of the rights of children with disabilities in a range of areas.

But the mere existence of UN Conventions will not magic their provisions into policy documents in the health and welfare or other sectors. New initiatives for policy revision and development need to be driven by a deliberate focus on more inclusive health. *EquiFrame* provides a tool for facilitating this and benchmarking existing policies in terms of their inclusion of disability, children with special needs and youth and other vulnerable groups, allowing us to highlight some of the barriers to inclusive health at policy level.

From the perspective of health policy promoting early detection of childhood disabilities, we believe that early intervention is critical, and a much more determined effort is required in this domain. Early intervention is the process of providing health, education and social services to support young children and their families. Children who are deemed to have an established condition – those who are evaluated and deemed to have a diagnosed physical or mental condition (with a high probability of resulting in a developmental delay), an existing delay or a child who is at-risk of developing a delay or special need – are the intended recipients of early intervention services. The purpose of early intervention is to lessen the effects of the disability or a developmental delay. In general, services are designed to identify and meet a child's needs in five developmental areas, including physical development, cognitive development, communication, social or emotional development, and adaptive development. However, early intervention is possible only if children are identified as early as possible, and this process of identifying children needs to be a continuous process of public awareness activities, screening and evaluation designed to *locate, identify and refer as early as possible* all young children with disabilities and their families. Early intervention could happen within health initiatives such as nutrition, malaria and immunization programmes. For instance, children in these programmes can be screened for developmental delays and disabilities with provision for early intervention, thus enabling *inclusive health* practices across these horizontal programmes.

Below we present two case studies to illustrate current practice and what the same practice would look like as an inclusive health practice (see Boxes 10.1 and 10.2).

Although much emphasis has been placed on strengthening health systems as a means to promote CBR (Mannan and MacLachlan, 2010), more attention needs to be given to how children and adolescents 'get into' health and inter-related systems that cross-cut children's developmental needs. In practice, this will require the use of basic screening techniques for children at regular intervals in any context in which children, or their parents, come into contact with services. This might be facilitated by the adoption of 'health passports' (McCaw-Binns et al., 2010; Gladstone et al., 2010), for

---

Box 10.1. Current practice and inclusive health practice: Malnutrition

Current Practice (Department for International Development [DFID], 2010): At the Mogolo health centre in western Eritrea, mother-of-five Tsega Berhane receives her monthly ration of DMK, a locally produced food ration consisting of sorghum, chick peas, ground nut, a vitamin and mineral mix, and salt. She'll feed it to her two youngest children – 2-year-old Zahara and 14-month-old Gebriel. Both were found to be moderately malnourished and suffering from diarrhoea on a recent visit to the health centre. Zahara and Gebriel are just two of thousands of children under 5 in Eritrea who are suffering from malnutrition as a result of repeated droughts. Their treatment is part of the DFID-funded Catholic Agency for Overseas Development (CAFOD) Emergency Nutrition Project, which is providing 10,000 moderately malnourished children and pregnant and lactating mothers in Eritrea with a supplementary food ration to prevent severe malnutrition. Zahara and Gebriel have gained weight, and the family is benefiting from the health education sessions Tsega attends as another part of the programme.

Inclusive Health Practice: As part of the screening for signs of malnutrition at the Mogolo health centre, inclusive health practice would also include screening for disabilities and developmental delays, perhaps using a standardized assessment such as the Rapid Neurodevelopmental Assessment Instrument (Khan et al., 2010). In this case, we might imagine that Zahara was identified with a disability, and the Emergency Nutrition Project provided – alongside supplementary food ration to prevent severe malnutrition – early intervention services; or that the project was also networked with other service providers to refer on children as necessary. Consequently, Zahara has gained weight; Gebriel's catching up on his developmental milestones; and the family is benefiting from the health education sessions Tsega attends as another part of the programme.

Box 10.2. Current practice and inclusive health practice: Pregnancy and childbirth

Current Practice: The Averting Maternal Death and Disability Program (AMDD), funded by the Bill and Melinda Gates Foundation, refocused the international community on a critical part of the health system that was absolutely essential to reducing maternal mortality. It is the first global project to directly address the principal factors contributing to maternal death and disability as well as obstetrical complications during pregnancy and birth. AMDD was designed as a demonstration program to show how moderate investments in infrastructure (around $10,000 per facility) in conjunction with human resource capacity development for health care providers in technical procedures and management produces changes in the responsiveness, quality and utilization of services. The interventions include upgrading of infrastructure, ensuring availability of supplies, training of personnel (safe delivery) and improving technical know-how and management systems for improved infection prevention.

Inclusive Health Practice: Pregnancy and childbirth are the primary causes of death, disease and disability among women of reproductive age in developing countries and account for approximately 18 per cent of the burden of disease among this group – more than any other single cause (Caro, Murray and Putney, 2004). For every woman who dies of pregnancy and childbirth-related causes, three more suffer severe morbidities that limit their capacity to earn a livelihood, participate as citizens and care for their children (Caro, Murray and Putney, 2004). Inclusive health practice here would include interventions upgrading infrastructure to ensure physical access, ensuring availability of supplies, training of personnel (safe delivery and assessment of disabilities) (Üstün et al., 2010; Madans, Loeb and Altman, 2011), and improving technical know-how and management systems for improved infection prevention and disability assessment as well as enhancing functioning and participation (WHO, 2001; WHO, 2010).

example those recently launched by the Ministry of Health, Jamaica (Ministry of Health, Government of Jamaica, 2010), where children are required to have regular developmental check-ups stamped as completed on their card. This may, of course require, offering incentives to staff to do this additional screening, the preventative and early detection value of which could be hugely beneficial for children, to the child's family and service providers in terms of diminished service demands later on. One of the greatest practical barriers to such an initiative is, of course, the stigma attached to disability and to children with disability, and this may be especially the case in low and middle-income countries (Maulik and Darmstadt, 2007), where resources are scarce and competition for them intense. Initiatives that promote the valuing of children with disabilities, including by their own parents, for instance the Portage programme (Einfeld et al., 2012), will therefore also be a key ingredient of any intervention that seeks to get children with disabilities 'into the system' and for the 'system' to then appropriately respond to their developmental needs. Programmes such as Portage interface well with the ethos of CBR, as described below.

Inclusive health and conceptualization of disability

The International Classification of Functioning, Disability and Health (ICF) (WHO, 2001) understands disability as an interaction between bodily impairments, activity limitations and participation restrictions. The ICF was an important departure from the 'medical model' of disability which had individualized and internalized how a bodily or mental impairment prevented people from being able to do the things that people without such bodily impairments could do (see Chapter 2, disability models). The ICF acknowledged the social component of disability by stressing that the way in which society is designed also limits the sort of activities that people with disability can engage in. For instance, a lack of ramps may be a barrier for wheelchair users who want to enter buildings. However the ICF goes beyond recognizing physical barriers to also recognizing that social and cultural norms and attitudes can restrict the extent to which people with disabilities are permitted to participate in important activities; such as education, employment or health care. In essence the ICF, while acknowledging that bodily limitations are an important element of disability, also acknowledges that it is often society – factors outside the individual – which actually disables the person with an impairment. The ICF therefore implicitly supports a rights-based approach to disability – seeing that people with disability have the same rights to education, employment or health as anyone else. The ICF is therefore entirely consistent with the concept of inclusive health. Although these arguments extend to all people with disability, we again focus on the ICF in relation to children, as the ICF in children has received much less attention than its application to adults.

The ICF for Children and Youth (WHO, 2007) recognizes that the above definition also interacts in particular ways with the developmental process that children go through, such as learning and establishing, and maintaining new relationships. In fact, child well-being and health must be facilitated by the effective interplay of education, transport, health and other services, as well as opportunities for meaningful employment and engagement with society more generally. There is very little empirical research on using the ICF-CY in low-income contexts (O'Sullivan and MacLachlan, 2009), but we believe that its ethos is complementary to inclusive health because it incorporates a range of factors influencing well-being, and it sees these as systemically related. Figure 10.3 illustrates the use of the ICF-CY to demonstrate how different ICF life domains constitute a 'life-system' with interaction and knock-on effects in the case of a 13-year-old girl from Burkina Faso (O'Sullivan and MacLachlan, 2008).

'Michelle' has a right hemiplegia as a result of meningitis when she was a child (she doesn't know how old she was). However, she has no functional restrictions in that she is fully able to wash clothes and help around the household. She went to school for a little while and liked it, but she had to stop going to school, as she was regularly beaten up and bullied due, at least in part, to her right hemiplegia 'making her different'; her parents worried about this and withdrew her from school. As a consequence, she cannot read or write. Although she still occasionally gets beaten up outside of the school, she does feel that she has some good friends and hopes to become a housemaid in

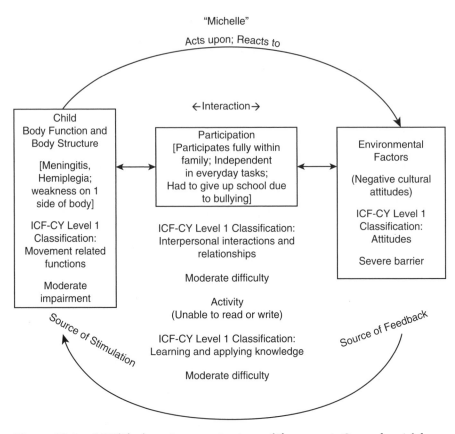

Figure 10.3.   ICF life domains constituting a 'life-system': Case of a girl from Burkina Faso

the future. The diagram illustrates the interaction between distinct but related domains. In the case of this girl, the fear of bullying could for instance prevent her from accessing health care, and her illiteracy may have consequences for her awareness of health promotion and health protection initiatives. An inclusive health perspective would require the active identification of social (stigma), personal (illiteracy) and service provision factors as key barriers to her broader health and welfare, recognizing that the major barrier to health care for many children with disabilities, may fall far outside the remit of health services. Before considering what can be done about such situations, we briefly consider the broader context of childhood disability.

Inclusive health and children with disabilities

Progress on childhood disability has been very slow particularly in low- and middle-income countries, in which it has been argued that knowledge about, recognition of, and activities directed towards childhood disabilities are inadequate, with scant information on existing policies and legislation (Maulik and Darmstadt, 2007). The vast majority of children with disabilities have little or no access to medical and rehabilitation services (Pan American Health Organization, 2008). According to the WHO Regional Office for Europe (2010), children with intellectual disabilities are especially disadvantaged with respect to health care in three ways: (1) they have greater health needs; (2) they experience greater barriers in accessing appropriate health care; and (3) if they are treated, then they are at higher risk of receiving poor care. These barriers may be confounded by the poor knowledge of health professionals concerning intellectual disability issues, communication difficulties, negative attitudes toward intellectual disability and poor inter-sectoral collaboration, as well as a lack of reliable health monitoring data for this population.

Malnutrition

The Strategy for Improved Nutrition of Children and Women in Developing Countries (UNICEF, 1990) was the impetus for UNICEF's work on malnutrition, which was conceptualized in terms of the manifestation of the problem (child malnutrition, death and disability), its immediate causes (inadequate dietary intake and diseases) and the underlying causes (insufficient access to food, inadequate maternal and child-care practices, poor water/sanitation and inadequate health services). Although there is evidence that nutrition programmes have indeed improved child survival rates (UNICEF, 2009), many of the children who have survived also appear to experience recurring illness and faltering growth – diminishing their physical health, irreversibly damaging their development and their cognitive abilities, and undermining their potential to fulfil their capacities as adolescents (UNICEF, 2009). In low-income countries, the number of children under 5 years old who are stunted is close to 200 million. In Africa and Asia, stunting rates are particularly high, at 40 per cent and 36 per cent, respectively. More than 90 per cent of children who are stunted and residing in low-income countries, live in Africa or Asia (UNICEF, 2009). Encouragingly, community-based efforts to improve basic health practices have led to a reduction in stunting levels among these young children (Lechtig, Cornale, Ugaz and Arias, 2009).

Malnutrition is both a cause of and risk factor for developmental disabilities and could be addressed through intervention programmes that include 'feeding programmes as well as rehabilitation services to address the needs of the child and empowerment of the mother and the family' (Durkin and Gottlieb, 2009). Thus the aim of assisting children with disabilities and that of supporting the health needs of children with or without disabilities should go hand in hand. Interventions that have short-term successes by increasing child survival must be followed by interventions that allow them to thrive. For instance, the establishment of new rural clinics, the training of alternative cadre in emergency obstetric procedures or the provision of more hygienic delivery environments can all be expected to increase child survival, including the survival of children with disabilities. Appropriate nutrition, assistive technologies, community supports and accessible education are just some of the features that must be in place in the longer term to allow children born with disabilities to thrive and meaningfully participate in their communities, including having access to appropriate health care.

Inclusive health and community-based rehabilitation

Guidelines on community-based rehabilitation (CBR) (WHO, 2010) were published in 2010, providing a comprehensive and multi-sectoral approach that can contribute to the implementation of the CRPD and to the achievement of inclusive health. The CBR Guidelines arise from a global collaboration between the World Health Organization (WHO), United Nations Educational, Scientific and Cultural Organization (UNESCO), International Labour Organization (ILO) and International Disability and Development Consortium (IDDC), and reflect several years of consultative and highly collaborative work between multiple stakeholders (WHO, 2010). The Guidelines introduce a CBR matrix (see Chapter 2), which gives an overall visual representation of the components of CBR. The matrix also indicates the different sectors which need to work together to create a cohesive and coherent CBR strategy.

The community-based rehabilitation matrix represents an imaginative and radical innovation in service delivery to people with chronic illness and people with disabilities. Its implementation requires a novel skill mix incorporating the inter-sectoral, inter-ministerial and inter-disciplinary ethos envisaged in the Bamako Call to Action on Research for Health (Lancet Editorial, 2008). The Guidelines have modules of direct relevance to children with disability, such as early childhood care and education, and family, recreation and sports. The Guidelines also embrace inclusive health, which it states 'means all individuals can access health care irrespective of impairment, gender, age, colour, race, religion and socioeconomic status' (WHO, 2010). The Guidelines envisage the function of inclusive health being 'to ensure health systems recognize and accommodate the needs of people with disabilities in their policies, planning and services delivery' (p. 7). Although the CBR Guidelines constitute the leading-edge knowledge concerning *what* needs to be done, there is a considerable challenge in working out just *how* this should be achieved, particularly in the context of the extreme shortage in human resources for health (HRH) in low-income countries.

Inclusive health and human resources for health crisis

Two brief case studies below illustrate just how a lack of human resources can affect the lives of people with disabilities (MacLachlan, 2012a) (see Boxes 10.3 and 10.4).

The Joint Learning Initiative Strategy Report of 2004 found that there were 75 countries in the world that had fewer than 2.5 health workers per 1,000 population, which is the minimum number estimated as necessary to deliver basic health services (Joint Learning Initiative Strategy Report, 2004).

Box 10.3.   Lack of human resources: The case of Washeila

Washeila's mother and father were labourers on a wine farm and were paid, in part, with alcohol. Washeila's birth was not planned, and her mother consumed significant amounts of alcohol during her pregnancy. As a result, Washeila was born with an intellectual disability and was not felt likely to benefit from schooling. Washeila's difficulties communicating became increasingly frustrating and were often associated with anger, aggression and self-harming, distressing her parents and siblings. Ultimately, Washeila was admitted to a children's home, on a long-term basis.

Information about risk factors during pregnancy might have prevented Washeila's disability. Advocacy for her right to education might have helped her learn how to communicate more effectively, and facilitation of the development of coping skills for the family could have prevented her subsequent institutionalization. All of these services could have been provided through one worker, but none of these needs were addressed by anybody.

The World Health Organization Maximizing Positive Synergies Collaborative Group (WHO, 2009) estimates a global deficit of trained health workers of over 4 million, and the Global Health Workforce Alliance (Global Health Workforce Alliance and WHO, 2008) estimated that Africa alone needs 1.5 million new health workers to be trained to address current shortfalls in its health systems. The world's poorest countries, with the greatest health burdens, are, of course, also the ones with the fewest health human resources available. The *World Report on Disability* (WHO and World Bank, 2011) also notes with concern the lack of rehabilitation workers – physiotherapists, occupational therapists, rehabilitation physicians and others (see Chapter 16). In

---

Box 10.4.   Lack of human resources: The case of Precious

Precious was born with a 'club foot', which was taken to signify bad fortune, attributable, some people said, to her mother's alleged infidelity. Precious's father left to live with another woman and Precious's mother became reclusive and somewhat resentful towards her. Precious was kept indoors, and her mother, being nonetheless attentive to her needs, had to earn what she could by exchanging sex for food and firewood. A community nurse heard about Precious and was able to arrange for corrective surgery. When Precious went away for surgery, neighbours were told that she had died. After intensive in-patient therapy, Precious was ready to come back home, but her mother felt it was best, both for Precious and for herself, that she did not come back. Social workers could not find Precious's mother and believe that she moved away. Community education about the cause and meaning of disability could have challenged the stigma often associated with community explanations of it. Early screening of children could have prevented Precious's mother struggling so desperately to cope and prevented the disintegration of the family. Had a CBR worker been present in the area, he or she could have addressed the above problems and liaised with the community nurse.

addition to HRH problems, assistive devices are often not available, and there are inadequate systems for their delivery, adaptation and maintenance (Eide and Øderud, 2009; Borg, Lindstrøm and Larsson, 2009). Unfortunately many people working in the disability field have received little or no relevant formal training, and resources are wasted by not involving persons with disabilities, their families and their organizations in the planning of programmes and education (Barnes, 2001).

Resources are unlikely to become available to support the scaling up of training of practitioners along the conventional Western health professions paradigm (Joint Learning Initiative Strategy Report, 2004). It has been argued that a move away from the expensive production of clinically-oriented health professionals to a more pragmatic production of health workers appropriate to a country's 'burden of disease', availability of resources and minimum standards of good care is more realistic and appropriate (Huddart, Picazo and Duale, 2003). This strategy has already been adopted through the use of 'mid-level cadres', such as medical assistants, clinical officers and enrolled nurses in other areas of health care (Buchan and Dal Poz, 2003). These so-called 'mid-level cadre' are generally trained in a more narrowly defined set of tasks, with the training taking considerably less time than is the case for more conventionally trained 'Western' style doctors or nurses, for instance.

Inclusive health and CBR: Towards a global implementation programme

The CBR Guidelines (WHO, 2010) come after decades of the application of CBR in a myriad of fashions, through varied mechanisms and in hugely differing contexts. In consequence, we have very little knowledge of what works well in CBR and what does not work; where it works, how or why. With the recent launch of the Guidelines (WHO, 2010), we urgently need to establish a programme of implementation that allows for organizational, country and contextual differences, while also allowing for the collection of comparable data through the establishment of a range of 'common goods' concerned with CBR training, support, monitoring, evaluation and research (MacLachlan, 2012b).

We suggest implementing the CBR Guidelines through the development of a new cadre of CBR workers; a systematic coordinated global response across the World Health Organization's six regional office zones (Africa, AFRO, Eastern Mediterranean, EMRO, Europe, EURO, South-East Asia, SEARO, Americas, PAHO, and Western Pacific, WPRO) with the intention to address the problem of the crisis in human resources for health in general and human resources in rehabilitation more specifically. The response would entail undertaking country-specific situational analyses, supporting work of existing rehabilitation cadres and development of alternative and additional rehabilitation worker cadres. The cross-sectoral working envisaged in the CBR Guidelines launched in 2010 requires a much broader and more process-focused set of skills than any existing health care cadre or profession is currently trained in, as illustrated in Figure 10.4 (MacLachlan, Mannan and McAuliffe, 2011b).

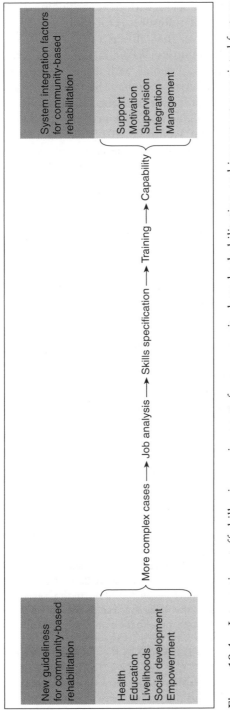

Figure 10.4. Integrative staff skill-mix requirements for community-based rehabilitation and important associated factors for system integration

A systematic coordinated global response to the challenge of implementing the new CBR Guidelines coincides with current thinking described by the Joint Learning Initiative on Human Resources for Health (Joint Learning Initiative Strategy Report, 2004). Given that CBR as a development strategy is currently implemented in over 90 countries (WHO, 2010) throughout the world, a new cadre to address the needs of people with disabilities and their family members could ease the HRH crisis (Mannan, Boostrom et al., 2012) and could contribute to a thought shift by evaluating health services in terms of how well they serve the most vulnerable as a probe of their overall effectiveness (MacLachlan, Mannan and McAuliffe, 2011a): if a measure of democracy is 'how well minorities are treated', then perhaps a measure of a health system could be how well people with disabilities are treated.

Despite an insufficient database attesting to the effectiveness of CBR in general, there are certainly examples of it working well in particular situations. Box 10.5 illustrates an example of a modest and successful CBR intervention in a remote village and the benefits it has had for one child. The project was carried out by Plan in Togo (Magee, 2012) (see Box 10.5).

Box 10.5. Community-based rehabilitation in Togo: The case of Marbelle

'Marbelle was born 7 years ago, in the dusty remote village of Pagala Gare in Central Togo. She was a healthy baby, and a joy to her parents who already had a little boy. Her father also had another wife, with whom he had four children, and the family were very happy with the new baby Marbelle.

'Then when she was three years old, Marbelle had an unexplained fit, resulting in her falling into a coma. Her family were devastated, especially her mother, who was so heartbroken she fled the village, leaving Marbelle and her brother with her husband and his second wife. Marbelle stayed in a coma for two long months. Then suddenly she woke up. But Marbelle had changed. The illness that had struck her down (suspected now to be a strain of cerebral malaria) had left her permanently disabled; unable to walk or talk. For three years little Marbelle remained in her home under the care of her step mother, who didn't understand what had happened to the little girl, and feared it was some kind of sorcery that had affected Marbelle.

'Then last year, Plan and partner organisation Envol came to the remote village, calling village meetings, holding trainings and raising awareness about disabilities and the rights of disabled children. Marbelle's step mother volunteered to join the committee of the new project which was called Community Based Rehabilitation. She received specific training on the rights of disabled children, the causes and consequences of disabilities, and various ways that disabilities can be prevented. The role of the committee was to share this information with the community, and to support two recently recruited CBR village agents, who were starting up specific classes for disabled children in a newly constructed classroom in the local primary school. Marbelle was enrolled in the classes.

'A year later, Marbelle can now walk thanks to the physical rehabilitation she received at the centre. Through her classes three times a week at the primary school,

(continued)

Box 10.5. Continued

not only has she learned to speak, but she can now speak in three languages, a source of immense pride to her step-mother. Marbelle loves the classes, especially music and dance, and she loves being with other children her own age, both in the class and in the primary school, where she goes every day with all the other village children. The CBR agents are delighted with her amazing progress, and hope that next year she can be integrated into the mainstream school. That is her wish also; when asked what she would like to do in the future, she simply stated that she would like to be in CP2 (the equivalent of 2nd class in primary school). A simple wish, but one from the heart of a child who thought she would never have that chance.' (Magee, 2012)

Marbelle's story illustrates how a health problem can lead to bodily impairments, activity limitations and participation restrictions, and how these can be simply addressed with hugely beneficial effects across a number of inter-linked life domains.

Another recent study investigated the experiences of children with disabilities in Gaza who were receiving services from CBR providers (Nasser and MacLachlan, 2012). The aim of this study was to explore the possible benefits associated with a sense of enhanced social inclusion that children may get from CBR programmes. The study involved 100 children with limb amputations, and although it was a correlation study (and therefore unable to demonstrate causal relationships), children who expressed a greater feeling of social inclusion had significantly better mental health, including a stronger belief in their own ability to influence their mental health. In a series of Key Informant interviews conducted by Nasser (Nasser, 2011) with the directors of organizations in Gaza who were providing CBR for children with physical disabilities, one of them commented: 'Through continuous involvement in different social events, we make children with disability stronger than before and enhance their self-insight, which enables them to cope with their new reality'. One of the greatest challenges for providing a robust evidence base for inclusive health and CBR is the development of sensitive, valid and reliable ways to assess the experience of disability and the impact of intervention programmes.

How many children with disabilities could benefit from inclusive health and community-based rehabilitation?

From the perspective of protection and promotion of the right to health for children, there is insufficient evidence regarding the situation of children with disabilities in poor countries (WHO, 2011). In recent years, countries have been collecting prevalence data on disability through censuses and surveys, with many having moved from an 'impairment' approach to a 'difficulties in functioning' approach (WHO, 2011) as promoted by the ICF (WHO, 2001). The lack of accurate worldwide data impedes the development, implementation and evaluation of disability policies and programmes for children. United Nations Children's Emergency Fund (UNICEF) in its Multiple Indicator Cluster Surveys (MICS), for ages 2–9, used ten questions to screen children for risk of disability: between 14 and 35 per cent of children screened positive for risk of disability in 15 of the 20 participating countries (UNICEF and University of Wisconsin, 2008). These studies were found to lead to a large number of false positives – an overestimate of the prevalence of disability (Millennium Development Goals Indicators, 2010). On the basis of the data from industrialized countries, as well as decades of its own research and practice, the European Academy of Childhood Disabilities (EACD) estimates that an average of at least 2.5 per cent of children have a disability (with 1 per cent having serious conditions) (UNICEF, 2005). EACD considers that an additional 8 per cent of the child population has learning and/or behavioural disorders. This makes the overall share of children with disabilities and special needs in any given population about 10 per cent (UNICEF, 2005).

In the United States, household survey data from the *National Health Interview Survey* in the early and mid-1990s found the share of children with functional limitations to be between 6 and 12 per cent (UNICEF, 2005). It is estimated that 1.5 million children – three times as many as a decade ago – receive basic disability supports in the 27 Central and Eastern Europe (CEE) countries, the Commonwealth of Independent States and the Baltic (CIS) countries (UNICEF, 2005). This analysis of data from CEE and CIS countries suggest that greater formal recognition of disability – including an increase in benefit claims by parents – is, by far, the biggest factor in higher rates of disability among children in the region, rather than increases in congenital anomalies and impairments from disease and trauma. It must be noted that not all of the studies used the same set of measures and/or approaches to document disability among children. Therein is the challenge in a true global estimate of children with disabilities and also, as we have argued, in assessing the impact of CBR and related interventions through comparative measures in a systematic fashion on a global basis.

Stigma: The greatest barrier

Goffman (1963) understood stigma as 'the process by which the reaction of others spoils normal identity'. Stigma affects not only people with disabilities but also their caregivers, and can discourage them from seeking the services that are required (Green, 2003) and that they have rights to. Analysis of household survey data from 13 low-income countries indicates that in those countries where there is greater stigma toward people with disabilities, the schooling of children with disability suffers (Filmer, 2008); without comparable health service data, we expect similar findings to apply. In many cultures, the idea that misfortune is motivated or meaningful can serve to protect others from the frightening element of its apparent randomness (MacLachlan, 2006). Disability and health problems can be attributed to retribution for wrongdoing, the actions of malevolent spirits (possibly sent by other people), or many other factors including the will of God (see Chapter 5).

For instance, the loving family of a child with cerebral palsy in Nigeria recently sat up all night to see if the boy would indeed turn into a snake and seek out the boiled egg that their pastor had told them to place in their house's roof space. When the boy failed to do so, the pastor remarked, 'These snakes are clever; he must have known you were watching …'. This is, sadly, an unexceptional story. When we visited the day care centre the boy attended, we also learnt that the Centre had developed a successful community business providing fish to a local hotel. To the hotel management's great regret, they had to cease buying the Centre's produce because its patrons refused to eat the fish once it became known it came from a home for children with disabilities.

In Senegal, it is reported that many women refuse to take children with disabilities on public transport; the families of children with mental or neurological disorders may hide them and keep them out of public view, and some parents disown them (Integrated Regional Information Networks, 2010). Link and Phelan (2001) have shown how perceived differences between stigmatised and dominant groups can lead to their social exclusion, marginalizing them, with reduced power and resources, within society. Stigma is a defining challenge for social inclusion (Cobigo, Ouellette-Kuntz, Lysaght and Martin, 2012), and so for inclusive health to become a reality for children with disabilities, stigma needs to be addressed at multiple levels both within health care and its indivisible interfaces with other social institutions.

Conclusions

Inclusive health embraces the greater complexities that are involved in truly addressing health for all human kind. The ICF (WHO, 2001) recognizes some of these complexities by stretching the definition of disability to reach beyond bodily impairments, incorporating the social model of disability and society's impact in terms of activity limitations and participation restrictions that people with disability may experience. The Guidelines on CBR (WHO, 2010) recognize the importance of a holistic approach to people with disabilities, and these new Guidelines are a cornerstone of inclusive health. The Guidelines also recognize that to implement sustainable gains for people with disabilities requires a new and much broader skill set for practitioners who can work across sectors and Ministries but must also be capable of undertaking or understanding the need for screening and preventative interventions for children with disabilities. Any new cadre for CBR will need to be supported by health policies that identify barriers to health and seek to monitor the effectiveness of measures to combat these. The economic cost as well as the social value of inclusive health needs to be evaluated. As well as the human rights arguments and the morality of promoting social cohesions over inequity, it is also the case that timely and appropriate access to health care for people with disabilities can contribute to the prevention of secondary health conditions and so lead to greater efficiencies in health systems (Lollar and Crews, 2003). This may be especially true for children with disabilities, where early identification and intervention can avert enormous subsequent health care costs, suffering and disadvantage. The financial gains of inclusive health may therefore also provide some momentum for its realization. Our discussion has been particularly concerned with children with disabilities because we feel that their needs are of great concern and have been poorly addressed. However, much of what we have noted applies equally to adults with disability. As children with disability may be even more marginalized and disempowered than adults with disability, the extent to which the needs of children with disability are met by health services may be the most robust test of the inclusiveness of these services.

Recommendations

In order to promote inclusive health and community-based rehabilitation, we make the following recommendations:

1. Replace the concept of 'mainstreaming' particular problems or groups with the idea of actively developing inclusive health, both for children and older people with disabilities, and other types of vulnerabilities that affect the right to health.
2. Undertake a programme of policy review, revision and development so that a full range of vulnerable groups are addressed, and a full range of core concepts of human rights are incorporated in national level health policy documents. In the case of children with disabilities, particular attention should be given to family supports and resources, cultural, participation and non-discrimination issues. This should be applied to both child-related policies and to health policies to ensure they are inclusive of the rights of children with disabilities.
3. Establish a systematic and coordinated global programme for implementing the Guidelines on Community-based Rehabilitation to allow for contextual variation, but facilitating comparable data collection that will contribute to a robust evidence base for policy and practice. Such a programme should ensure that the psychological and social developmental needs of children and adolescents with disabilities feature prominently.
4. Develop a new cadre of rehabilitation workers with shorter training and a broader set of competencies than conventionally trained rehabilitation workers, allowing them to work effectively across professional domains and sectors, and to work across age groups, with particularly sensitivity to the developmental needs of children and adolescents with disabilities.
5. Agree on effective criteria to assess disability, service needs and the effectiveness of interventions, on a comparative global basis, with appropriate contextual variations and incorporating developmental needs at different stages of life.
6. Address stigma by educating people with non-stigmatizing facts about people with disability; legislate against discrimination; and promote community engagement with and by children with disabilities.
7. Establish the cost-saving and the additional costs that will be involved in providing equitable access to health care for children with disabilities.
8. Develop a coordinated programme of early intervention across the health, welfare and educational sectors to promote the early identification, management or prevention of childhood disabilities.

Summary of key points

- This chapter explores the relationship between health and disability, with a particular focus on children with disabilities. As children with disabilities may be even more vulnerable and disempowered than adults with disabilities, the extent to which the needs of such children are met by health services may be the most robust test of the inclusiveness of such services.
- The concept of 'Inclusive Health' seeks to build on the idea of Health for All and to strengthen it through the rights-based approach; to emphasize the need for more active inclusion by recognizing that particular groups have particular needs and that particular barriers have to be overcome to address such needs; and to utilize a much greater range of health care delivery options embodied in a greater variety of human resources for health.
- Community-based rehabilitation (CBR) – a multi-sectoral strategy to address the broader needs of people with disabilities, ensuring their inclusion in society and enhancing their quality of life – is the major service delivery system for the majority of people with disabilities in low-income settings. Therefore, access to health through CBR is a primary focus of discussion.
- A particular focus of this chapter is establishing the case for equitable health, signifying that health services should be provided on the basis of people's needs – that those most in need can access the service as easily as those least in need.
- In the context of scarce resources, particularly in low-income countries, competition for such resources in relation to health can mean that the needs of some groups predominate over the needs of others, often including the less powerful groups, such as children with disabilities.
- Some people with disabilities of course have enhanced needs for health care support. However, disability is not strictly a 'health problem', and people with disabilities have an equal right to the same standard of accessible health care as those without disabilities as stated in Article 25 of the CRPD [Health].

STUDY QUESTIONS

1. Develop a short vignette based on your current work practice in dealing with people with disabilities. Proceed to write a short reflective analysis on whether you consider this practice to be inclusive. (Note: A reflective essay is a piece of writing that expresses your views and feelings about a particular subject. The goal of a reflective analysis is not only to discuss what you learned but also to relay your own beliefs, attitudes and observations. Include any beliefs, attitudes and practice you may change or sustain based on your learning.)

2. Identify a policy document outlining your local government or private providers' services for children with disabilities. Proceed to examine to what extent

cont.

any of the following core concepts of human rights are contained in the policy document:

- Non-discrimination
- Participation
- Family resource
- Family support
- Cultural responsiveness

3. As a group of students/practitioners committed to disability inclusive health and education, outline the content and approach in advocacy material addressing stigma. Consider audio/video/social media opportunities to do so.

Further reading and resources

Nora Ellen Groce, Paola Ayora, and Lawrence C. Kaplan. (2007). 'Immunization rates among disabled children in Ecuador: Unanticipated findings', *The Journal of Pediatrics*, 151(2), 218–220.

Nora E. Groce et al. (2013). 'Inclusive nutrition for children and adults with disabilities', *The Lancet Global Health*, 1(4), e180–e181.

Lilian Mariga, Roy McConkey and Hellen Myezwa. (2014.) *Inclusive Education in Low Income Countries: A resource book for teacher educators; parent trainers and community development workers*. ISBN 978-0-9870203-4-5. Available to download at http://www.eenet.org.uk/resources/docs/Inclusive_Education_in_Low_Income_Countries.pdf.

Acknowledgement

The writing of this chapter was supported by UNICEF and is based on a background paper for the State of the World's Children Report, 2013.

Assistive Technology and Disability

Esther Baños García

(g) State Parties ... undertake to promote research and development of, and to promote the availability and use of new technologies, including information and communications technologies, mobility aids, devices and assistive technologies, suitable for persons with disabilities, giving priority to technologies at an affordable cost.

**UN Convention on the Rights of Persons with Disabilities
Article 4: General Obligations**

2. State parties shall also take appropriate measures: (g) To promote access for persons with disabilities to new information and communications technologies and systems, including the Internet.

(h) To promote the design, development, production and distribution of accessible information and communications technologies and systems at an early stage, so that these technologies and systems become accessible at minimum cost.

**UN Convention on the Rights of Persons with Disabilities
Article 9: Accessibility**

Introduction

In the preface to the *World Report on Disability* (WHO and World Bank, 2011), Chan and Zoellic voice their wish for 'an inclusive world in which we are all able to live a life of health, comfort, and dignity'. In which way can the new information and assistive technologies and their fast-paced advances help this vision to come true? This chapter will try to make a small contribution to answering this question.

People with disabilities often experience difficulties in achieving full integration into the current Information Society on equal terms to their peers. Nowadays there is a huge variety of devices and services to mitigate and overcome these difficulties. The umbrella term *assistive technology* (AT) is commonly used to encompass both types of devices: *assistive* (to help people to perform a given task) and *adaptive* (to help people to modify the environment). In addition, people need support services to facilitate their use (National Assistive Technology Research Institute [NATRI], 2006). Maximum advantage of these new technologies needs to be taken in order to reach a more complete integration of people with disabilities in the environment where they live and work.

This chapter will firstly address the concept of AT by reviewing some definitions, classifications and expectations placed on new technologies and, more specifically, on the information and communication technologies (ICT). We then examine the role of computers and the Internet as the most widely used ICT devices, paying special attention to the accessibility and usability concepts and their key impact in avoiding the info-exclusion of people with disabilities from the Information Society and narrowing the digital divide they currently experience. Complete integration is possible if individualized support systems or profiles are set, including a well-guided usage of AT. Although advances, especially in the use of ICT, are noticeable for people with developmental disabilities and children with special education needs, there is still more to be done when it comes to integrating youths and adults with intellectual disabilities. The chapter ends with a reflection on how technology can help promote inclusive education in the future to allow for the equality of all citizens in the Information Society.

Technology, society and disability

Ever since inventing the wheel, human beings have looked for technological resources which have enabled them to compensate for or overcome their natural deficiencies to survive in hostile physical surroundings and so further control and make their environment better, such as the wheel for easy transport or to reach higher speed, and the lever or the pulley for lifting heavy loads. Thus human history has fostered a parallel progress of humanity through technology.

Assistive technology (AT)

Fortunately, the concept of AT has evolved in parallel with the revised concepts of disability. It is currently used to refer to the broad range of devices and services available in order to support users with different functionalities to overcome the difficulties they find when meeting the demands posed by the environments where they live. These include accessibility to environment, to education and to employment, the improvement of autonomy and quality of life, or the enjoyment of leisure and sport (Roca-Dorda, Roca-González and Del Campo, 2004). The NATRI has categorized these human functions in seven areas: those related to existence, communication, body support, protection and positioning, travel and mobility, environmental interaction, education and transition, and sports, fitness and recreation.

For Cullen, McAnaney, Dolphin, Delaney and Stapleton (2012) 'The field of AT concerns the practical tools that can support functional needs of people who experience difficulties linked to disability or ageing'. A more accurate definition of AT can be extracted from international standards for equipment. So for EN-ISO 9999[1], 2011, AT is 'Any product (including devices, equipment, instruments and software), especially produced or generally available, used by or for persons with disability

- for participation;
- to protect, support, train, measure or substitute for body functions / structures and activities; or
- to prevent impairments, activity limitations or participation restrictions.

These standards set precise bounds to the sorts and types of AT shown in Table 11.1.

In recent years, we have witnessed a growing interest, especially by professionals and AT providers, to find operationally more useful classification systems. A widely used approach has been to put in order all the AT information in a way which is useful for users, families and professionals so as to allow a quick identification of those ATs that best meet their needs. Most of these classifications have been developed following the guidelines of the International Classification of Functioning, Disability and Health (ICF) (WHO, 2001) (see Chapter 2).

Another useful way of categorizing AT is based on its technological level (AtiA, 2014):

- Non-technology: those including special uses of methods and common-use objects such as specific study strategies, types of magnified letters and so on.
- Low-technology: those using adaptations of existing simple devices such as an aid to hold a spoon.

Table 11.1.   One-level classification of ATs (EN-ISO 9999)

Usual ATs[2]
Assistive products for personal medical treatment
Assistive products for training in skills
Orthoses and prostheses
Assistive products for personal care and protection
Assistive products for personal mobility
Assistive products for housekeeping
Furnishings and adaptations to homes and other premises
Assistive products for communication and information
Assistive products for handling objects and devices
Assistive products for environmental improvement and evaluation
Assistive products for employment and occupational training
Assistive products for recreation

---

[1] International standard that establishes a classification of assistive products, especially produced or generally available, for persons with disability.

[2] Information on the classification of ATs is available from https://www.iso.org/obp/ui/#iso:std:iso:9999:ed-5:v1:en.

- Medium-technology: those devices or appliances that, as well as being purposely developed for some functions, require certain technological complexity, like a wheelchair.
- High-technology: those equipment and products of a high technological complexity that are based on ICT, robotics, nano-technology, biomedical engineering and so on, such as adapted optical mice, state-of-the-art communicators, DAISY (digital accessible information system) books for blind and low vision users, and so on.

A further classification is according to the users' impairment (Alcantud and Soto, 2003) – that is, equipment and products for persons with a physical impairment, psycho-cognitive impairment or a sensory impairment.

Irrespective of the classification, all of these various supporting or assistive technologies have always played a key role in facilitating the social integration and the participation of all people, disabled and non-disabled, in the community, trying to equally ensure to all their access to independent living, education and employment. All the supporting products will influence the quality of life of their users, as long as they are tailored to individual and customized necessities of every individual. To that end:

- Their handling should be as simple as possible.
- They must observe aesthetics and be as standardized as possible.
- They should not interfere with the development of the person.
- Value for money needs to be addressed and extra care taken in usage so that the aids can be long lasting.

All of this will have repercussions – on the one hand, economically, in optimizing resources by adjusting public and private spending, and on the other hand, by adjusting and also optimizing the cognitive demands on users who will only have to learn and use those essential technologies which better solve their needs. It is important to note that the high technologies are not always the best solutions; on the contrary, often the simplest solutions are more effective and more accessible.

There are many resources, especially on the Web, designed to assist family, professionals, support staff and also people with disabilities when it comes to selecting and purchasing assistive technology. This is sometimes complicated, as the same individual has several functional, cognitive, sensory and/or physical needs.

These web resources have been developed by a variety of organizations: disability associations; state institutions concerned with social issues; universities or research institutions; companies engaged in the design, manufacture and marketing of these technologies; and even individual parents of children and youths with disabilities who have the ICT skills to create and share these resources. Web pages normally provide assessment services and function as search engines of up-to-date technological aid resources. These web resources also usually facilitate access to guides and training regarding the products they

---

Box 11.1. Web resources

- National Institute of Health (NIH), project 'do2learn': http://www.do2learn.org
- NCTI (National Center for Technology Innovation), project Techmatrix: http://techmatrix.org/
- The Rix Centre: http://www.rixcentre.org/
- CEAPAT (Spain): http://www.catalogo-ceapat.org/acercade
- ONCE Foundation and Technosite: http://www.discapnet.es/
- Citizen Information Board: http://www.assistireland.ie/eng/
- Information for SEN: http://www.sess.ie/
- Parents of a Deaf child: http://www.closingthegap.com/
- ABA (Applied Behaviour Analysis) Educational Resources Ltd.: http://www.disabled-world.com/
- Laureate Learning Systems Inc.: http://www.laureatelearning.com

---

offer, and to do this, they frequently edit magazines and promote webinars, conferences, seminars and so on. A short list of these websites is listed as an example in Box 11.1.

Computers and Internet: interfaces, usability, accessibility and social networks

At present, the computer is the most widely used ICT device. Fortunately, computers and laptops are continuously becoming better and better, more and more powerful, and easier to use; moreover, they offer improved features. This constant progress benefits all citizens, with and without disabilities. We will only have to be sure that the chosen computer for a disabled person has enough number of ports in order to connect the needed peripherals or hardware in the way of technical aids, which allow the person to optimally use the computer.

In addition, the number and variety of peripherals now available, as well as the adjusted software, allow most people with disabilities, including those with multiple and severe impairments, to access computers. These peripherals range from facial mice to all types of products of environmental control for people with specific and multiple impairments (cognitive, sensory and physical) such as different types of keyboards (either as hardware or virtually, for example, on the computer screen), trackballs, joysticks, switches and touchscreens.

In recent years, personal digital assistants (PDAs), tablets and smartphones have gained prominence thanks to their easy handling. Every day, new applications (apps) allowing easy and instant access to solve a large number of everyday situations are launched: educational apps, apps to support communication, service apps (to buy tickets, to plan a trip or to vote), global positioning system (GPS) locators, sign-language guides for Deaf or Quick Response (QR) codes that give detailed product information. Who knows what potential the recently publicized Google Glass will bring?

However, computers, PDAs, tablets, smartphones and even new multitouch screens require an interface to act as mediator in the communication between the user and the computer. The interface is therefore the component that has the most impact on access to ICT for persons with disability. For instance, the user must be able to interpret graphic information such as icons or pictograms, or to read and understand the text on the screen, and to be able to write through typing. They also need to understand audible information such as alarms or voices. In short, the user must have the cognitive abilities to be able to interpret the signs and carry out effective actions on the interface (Marrero Expósito, 2006).

Current browsers and operating systems of computers, tablets and smartphones, thanks to their accessibility options, allow changes in the interface for data input and/or output. When the adjustments provided by the operating systems are not sufficient to find the appropriate interface for the capabilities of a given user, it is necessary to use other options, which can be software, hardware or non-computer-based aids. Nowadays, both the flexibility of computer applications and the development of support products that offer access solutions to standard devices allow for individualized computer access interfaces to be created.

When all other options fail, there are tools which attempt to find suitable interfaces to facilitate access to these computers, such as the interface simulator developed by Biswas and Robinson (2013) that helps to customize interfaces targeting users with different access needs, or the browser Web Trek, which is purposely designed for intellectually disabled people (Davies, Stock and Wehmeyer, 2001).

The World Wide Web

In order to achieve the complete participation of people with disabilities in the Information Society, user-centred 'Universal Design' should be guaranteed not only for software and for hardware but also for web pages on the Internet. Consequently, usability and accessibility standards should be met. We should not confuse both concepts. To put it simply, *accessible* means you can access it and *usable* means you can easily use it.

Even so, there is a large overlap between both accessibility and usability. Improvements in usability make it easier to use a site or page, but an accessibility improvement will make it easier for everyone to view the page. 'Web accessibility means that people with disabilities can perceive, understand, navigate, and interact with the Web, and that they can contribute to the Web' (W3C). A website or page is accessible if it is 'reasonably possible for anyone to access the content. As the level of accessibility increases, the differences in ease of access decrease' (Durham University, 2014).

Web accessibility depends on several components working together. These components include: content of the web page; 'user agents' such as web browsers or media players; assistive technologies such as screen readers, virtual mice, alternative keyboards; users' knowledge, experiences, and in some cases, adaptive strategies using the Web; developers with or without disability;

Box 11.2. The concept of usability

Usability consists of three dimensions:

- **Effectiveness:** Measures of the accuracy and completeness of system tasks performed.
- **Efficiency:** Measures of the accuracy and completeness of resources-related system tasks such as time or human effort, used to perform specific system tasks.
- **Satisfaction:** Measures of comfort and acceptability of the system with regard to its users and other persons affected by its use.

For a product to be usable, the following conditions are implied:

- It can be used in a proper, efficient and successful way by most potential users.
- It is so easy to learn to use, in that it does not require a manual.
- It can be used by people with different abilities or disabilities.
- Anyone, regardless of age or culture, can use it.
- It prevents users from making mistakes.

---

authoring tools and evaluation tools. According to the international standard ISO 9241-11, usability is the 'extent to which a product can be used by specified users to achieve specified goals with effectiveness, efficiency and satisfaction in a specified context of use' (USER Behavioristics, 2014) (see Box 11.2).

In sum, when referring specifically to a usable system or website, we want it to be user friendly, easy to use and easy to learn. The presentation *Usability Testing for People with Disabilities* (Wahlbin and Hunter Utt, 2012) provides tips and tricks for a usability test for people with disabilities.

Social media

For the complete social participation of people with different functionalities, they should be able to use the Internet to learn, study, socialize, work and be entertained. They should also be able to use increasingly common telematic services for management, travel arrangements, purchasing, advocacy or voting (see Chapter 3, use of Internet in the negotiations of the CRPD). They must also be able, through appropriate training programs, to use the Internet in a responsible and safe way, preventing abuse, cyberbullying and cybergrooming.

Although the major social networks – such as Facebook – are not yet adapted to the needs of persons with intellectual disabilities, many people with disabilities find their way to them via forums, blogs or meeting points (García, 2011). People with a disability, along with those who care for them, have also created virtual spaces where they share experiences and interests. For instance, in 2011, a social network named 'Sidiscapacitados', was created in Spain. The 'Anundis' social network is also intended for people over 18 years, with and without disabilities, to promote friendship, relationships, finding information and even matchmaking. Other examples are Special Friends and Australian Livewire.

Information and communication technologies (ICT) and the digital divide

The unstoppable and ever-increasingly rapid technological progress in ICT is leading to significant social changes. The new ICT will provide widespread access to all kinds of information to the majority of citizens, as well as the possibility of interconnection among users from anywhere through networks. Many citizens already have the minimum skills required to use these new technologies (Gómez Pérez, 2004; Sevillano García, 2010).

ICT has given rise to what we know as the 'Information Society' (Ballestero, 2004). The World Summit on the Information Society (WSIS; held in Geneva in 2003 and in Tunisia in 2005) (International Communication Union [ITU], 2006) defines the Information Society as one in which 'everyone can create, access, use and share information and knowledge, enabling individuals and communities to achieve all their potential and to improve their quality of life in a sustainable way'.

Based on this relationship between people and their context, this new model of society takes place in a new environment where the main resource or raw material is information (Rodríguez de las Heras, 2006; Sevillano García, 2010). As happened with other advances, such as the invention of printing, the development of the Information Society is causing differences and inequalities, leaving certain groups of the population disadvantaged and on the fringes of development (McKenzie, 2007; cited by Abbot, Brown, Evett, Standen and Wright, 2011; Maeda, Tsjimura, Sigita, Oka and Yokota, 2009; Gutiérrez and Martorell, 2011).

Although remaining uneven across different regions of the world and even among different groups within one region itself (Echeverría, 2004; Selwyn and Facer, 2007; Orange Foundation, 2012), access to ICT has become a determining factor for countries and social groups in evolving to higher levels of development (Aguilar Tamayo, 2004). The term used to identify the social inequalities arising from unequal access to ICT, and more specifically to the use of computers and the Internet, is the *digital divide*. One of the first definitions of the digital divide can be found in the document 'Understanding the Digital Divide' drawn up by the Organisation for Economic Co-operation and Development (OECD, 2001):

> the gap between individuals, households, businesses and geographic areas at different socio-economic levels with regard both to their opportunities to access information and communication technologies (ICTs) and to their use of the Internet for a wide variety of activities.

Van Dijk (2006) expands on this:

> The digital divide commonly refers to the gap between those who do and those who do not have access to new forms of information technology. Most often these forms are computers and their networks but other digital equipment such as mobile telephony and digital television are not ruled out by some users of the term.

From these definitions we can guess that the broader concept of digital divide involves not only access to a broad range of ICT but also the use made of them by citizens. *Digital illiteracy* is indeed putting at a risk of social exclusion those individuals who are not versed in the use of new technologies, for example by preventing them from developing social and work activities.

As the OECD report (2001) noted, it is therefore necessary to plan and implement programs and training initiatives to facilitate the digital literacy of large segments of our society: elderly persons and unemployed workers who are not proficient in handling computers, people with low education levels and people with disabilities (OECD, 2001). Without being well skilled and literate in the use of ICT, we cannot exist and progress in the Information Society, and we can hardly progress as a social community (Area Moreira, 2010).

The information society, ICT and disability

Access to ICTs is key for the development of people with disabilities because of the opportunities these new technologies bring in terms of training as well as access to culture, information and participation. If this access does not occur, the inequalities will widen the digital divide, resulting in digital illiteracy and, in turn, in the *info-exclusion* and social exclusion of these groups (see Chapter 6 on disability and social exclusion).

But access is only a start. Training in the use of ICTs is a key strategy to bring to an end this growing inequality. This is recognized at a worldwide level, such as in Article 4 ('General obligations') of the CRPD (UN, 2006) and at a European level in the Council of Europe (2006), for example through the 'Action Plan to promote the rights and full participation of people with disabilities in society: Improving the quality of life of people with disabilities in Europe 2006–2015' (p. 1).

Change needs to come at national, regional or even local level, promoted by governments, foundations, associations or NGOs. For example, in Salvador do Bahia (Brazil) the charitable society named Irmã Dulce carries out the Infoesp Program (Computers in Special Education) in a computer and telematic (blend of telecommunications and informatics) environment such as an operating theatre equipped with robots, computers and Internet, in which a surgeon from another country can operate (telesurgery) with all necessary data instantly updated. About 120 students with intellectual and/or physical disabilities (some of them being among the most severe) and/or sensory disabilities (visual and auditory) are involved. The purpose of this program is to promote the development of the cognitive potential of special education students in solving their own problems by effectively using logical deductive reasoning – enabling them to better interact with others and with their environment, plus, in some cases, train them for effective working (Alves and Lopez, 2008).

Support systems for people with disabilities and the role of technology

Cook and Polgar (2008) define the role of assistive technologies in the daily lives of disabled people in their HAAT (Human Activity Assistive Technology) model. This model centres on the interaction among four basic components: the activity, the human factor (operator), assistive technologies and the context in which the interaction occurs.

As a telling example of this model, they explain the case of FAM, aged 40, who needs to write reports. Therefore, the activity is to write reports. The activity is required as part of his work, so the context is employment. As a consequence of a spinal cord injury, FAM cannot use his hands but can speak clearly and precisely. If a speech recognition system is available (technical support, assistive technology) for him, he may use his abilities (oral language, human factor) to write (activity). These elements change as individuals, the activities they perform and the context vary. For another individual, any of the elements could be completely different.

As to the areas where AT becomes most relevant, Cook and Polgar (2008) identified eight major work areas:

1. Training systems: for motor training, incontinence, software-based educational training software, built ad-hoc training, or for training in general.
2. Alternative and augmentative systems of accessing information.
3. Computer access technologies (adaptive technology), hardware and software: access systems (direct input selection systems such as conventional keyboard aids, alternative keyboards, mouse emulators, on-screen keyboards, voice access systems) and input systems by means of sweeping selection.
4. Alternative and augmentative communication systems: communication boards, electronic communicators.
5. Mobility technologies: wheelchairs or the new bionic suit or robotic exoskeleton.
6. Technologies for manipulation and control of the environment, like a page turner.
7. Rehabilitation technologies.
8. Caring technologies: anti-bedsore mattresses or respirators.

Alcantud and Soto (2003) highlighted two components present in the above: the emphasis on functional abilities rather than on limitations, and the component of individualization of the user-support system. But they added two new work areas:

9. Technologies for sport, leisure and recreation.
10. Technologies for daily living not included in previous sections, such as support systems for feeding, adapted furniture and adapted bathrooms.

The AT found in these ten working areas shows that technology not only enhances user skills and competences, but through increased accessibility and use of universal design principles, it adapts the environment to the individual. The intricacies of achieving both outcomes have yet to be investigated. In a case study experiment, Torrente and colleagues (2010), in cooperation with Technosite, a company that belongs to the ONCE group (Spanish National Organisation for the Blind), evaluated the effectiveness of the software program *eAdventure* in order to support game designers when developing accessible games. To do this, they designed a game called *My First Day at Work*, starting from scratch, and then monitored the process needed to make it accessible. The game was aimed at people with all kind of abilities, although more emphasis was placed on user profiles with low or no vision, mobility impairments and cognitive limitations. It proved very difficult to quantify the various efforts involved in adapting the interface and the game for the different users, but it was most complex with users who had cognitive limitations. Alternative versions of most parts of the game had to be designed. Nonetheless, this experience shows how AT can evolve to support people with intellectual disabilities to obtain further integration into the Information Society.

Supportive systems for intellectually disabled people

The planning and provision of supports to persons with disabilities is key to correcting the imbalance between people's skills and the environments where they participate. Although the discussions about such supports have occurred in all living areas, there has been more discussion perhaps on the provision of supports in the field of employment than in other domains related to daily functioning. This discussion has initially focused on the use, definition and viability of natural supports in work environments (see Chapter 12). These might be provided by a job coach or a co-worker. However, the most sustainable form of support has up to now been that provided by an individual. Davies, Stock, and Wehmeyer (2001, 2002) have already suggested, though, that computer-based technologies offer a promising means to enable people with intellectual and other disabilities to become, basically, their own support, functioning by themselves. However, the promises of these new technologies to help in this process remain, on the whole, unfulfilled for many people with intellectual disabilities and their families. Moreover, these new technologies are hardly mentioned in the large amount of literature existing around the assessment, intervention programmes and provision of customized supports.

The ICT supports may consist of different technologies such as a tablet or a PDA showing the steps to complete a work task, or an augmentative communication system to help improve communication skills by means of synthesized speech output from symbol or text input. They can also be given by persons like a housemate who cooperates in social and personal autonomy skills training (Liesa and Vived, 2010) or a bus driver telling a disabled person at which stop he or she should get off. The provision of support should be based on the assessment of the support needs of a person and be always aimed at improving human functioning and/or those desired personal outcomes through individualized supports (Schalock, 2009, Thompson et al., 2010; Braddock et al., 2013).

Lastly, ICT fits well with the person-centred planning approach proposed by the American Association on Intellectual and Development Disabilities (AAIDD) in its latest manual (AAIDD, 2012):

1. Identify the desired goals and living experiences.
2. Determine the pattern and intensity of support needs.
3. Develop an individualized plan.
4. Monitor progress.
5. Evaluation.

Once the desired goals and necessary supports have been identified and prioritized, the technologies that might best help in the individualized plan can be investigated.

Computer-based applications and intellectual disability

Many youths and adults who have access to ICTs tend to use them, and the Internet, mainly for recreational and leisure activities such as listening to music or watching videos (Palmer, Wehmeyer, Davies and Stock, 2012). The potential for ICT to be used for educational and training purposes is still in its infancy. There are a growing number of programs or computer-based applications (CBA) currently on the market that can be used by intellectually disabled people, either for free or via paid access, available on the Internet or in hardware format. Despite the availability of suitable CBA, we can still see these groups of people in their classroom learning with some inadequate child-targeted CBA. The efficacy of CBAs is limited by various factors, however:

- No common pedagogical patterns are used when it comes to accomplishing the idea and the design.
- There is no standardization of terminologies, leading, at times, to confusion.
- Financial and commercial factors have a great influence on the design and marketing of the CBAs.
- Different points of view among developers regarding objectives and approaches. Some favour purposely designed applications for persons with disabilities, whereas others recommend the same general-purpose programs, used by non-disabled peers, but supported by assistive and adapted technologies.
- The growing obsolescence of software when new hardware and devices become available.

At present, we have at our disposal a broad range of programs under the umbrella term of CBA, according to the digital technology used in their design and development: interactive or non-interactive multimedia applications, virtual reality, augmentative reality, artificial intelligence, learning management systems (LMS), learning content management systems (LCMS), intelligent tutorial systems (ITS), hypertext and hypermedia. Although it is true that we can currently find many intellectually disabled people using some of these CBAs, much work remains to be done in order to put these users on the same level as the general public.

It is, perhaps, the field of special education needs (SEN), updated for some as alternative support needs (ASN) (Abbott, 2007) and specially focused on learning-disabled children, in which the usage of CBA is most widespread not only in classrooms but also at home, in leisure facilities and so on (see Chapter 9 on education). Recent years have seen these initiatives extend to independent living skills; shopping skills (Hansen and Morgan, 2008; Waters and Boon, 2011); public transit and road safety (Mechling and O'Brien, 2010); personal daily living activities such as food preparation, personal cleanliness and clothing (Lányi, Brown, Standen, Lewis and Butkute, 2012); social skills (Cheng and Chen, 2010) and employment-related skills (Davies et al., 2002; Savidis, Grammenos and Stephanidis, 2007; Benda, Havlíc̆ek, Lohr and Havránek, 2011).

If we want to take full advantage of CBA, more purposely-designed CBA should be developed for youths and adults with intellectual disabilities that can be adjusted to their age and preferences. To reach this goal, they must be involved in the process of developing the CBA, as the following case example illustrates (Box 11.3).

Box 11.3.   An interactive multimedia application to train in safety and order-at-home issues

In the last decades and especially after joining the European Union in 1986, efforts to improve quality of life and to integrate people with some kind of disability in Spain have grown considerably. Policy measures, promoted programs and funding from state institutions, and especially the work of associations and foundations, have achieved good progress for this group, although a long way still remains to go to place disabled people on equal ground to other Spanish citizens regarding rights such as access to employment or independent living.

At the same time, a growing concern about the inclusion of ICT in all sectors of society has encouraged numerous experiences and research in universities and research centres, quite often promoted by these foundations and associations.

In this context, we designed and evaluated, at the University of Burgos, *Get Used To* (*Habitúate* in the Spanish version), an interactive multimedia application that is purposely designed to assist youths and adults with intellectual disabilities to gain independent living skills (see Chapter 13, independent living). Users of the *Get Used To* application can learn, for example, the steps to use the microwave (see Figure 11.1), do laundry, and practice home safety in an interactive manner. Although several works (both on the use of ICT in education in various educational settings, and on the design of interactive multimedia applications also for educational purposes) had already been developed at this university, this was the first development of CBA in two countries – Ireland and Spain.

(continued)

Box 11.3.   Continued

Figure 11.1.   Screenshot of 'microwave' activity

The principles on which the design was based were motivation, adequate and universal accessibility, quick and easy adaptation to other contexts, flexibility (i.e. a quick and easy adaptation to different abilities) and realism, (i.e. maximum agreement between what users see and training with the environments in which the actions usually happen). The application was tested with a number of groups in both countries. People with intellectual disabilities gave feedback on the interface, accessibility and usability of the application. The active engagement of every participant was crucial for the final design of the application.

Its user-centred design followed the rules of cognitive, physical and geographical accessibility. It was also made available on the Internet. Training in daily and universal activities that demand functionality from users, as well as an easy context adaptation, make it a suitable application to be used in various environments and contexts such as college and home settings.

Users of *Get Used To* improved their performance when they worked under education staff and teachers' supervision. The use of ICT in any computer classrooms, no matter the country, resulted in an equalizing effect.

The number of potential users exceeded expectations. Spanish and English speakers found it a useful medium for learning in each language within simple and familiar contexts. In addition, individuals with other support needs, such as people with Alzheimer's or senile dementia, found *Get Used To* useful as training for both everyday household activities and for the use of computers and ICT. The materials can be accessed at this website: http://www3.ubu.es/habituate/casa_house/E_E.swf.

Conclusions

To conclude, ICT and CBAs hold the promise of increasing the educational and training opportunities for people with disabilities both in schools and in higher education. People with disabilities can take their place alongside non-disabled peers thanks to user-centred design for all, adapted software and interfaces for people with disability, along with assistive technologies. ICT is crucial in developing appropriate educational environments in which well-prepared teachers supply mechanisms for students to access knowledge, in accordance with various disabilities and individual learning objectives. It can offer the opportunity for repeated practice and graded learning while developing the intrinsic motivation of students. The initial capital costs of equipment and software development can be recouped through repeated usage and sharing locally, nationally and indeed internationally. But the success of these initiatives is dependent on adequate training being provided to teachers as well as students. This may be less of an issue with the new generation of professionals who have grown up with ICT and are expert users of it. New political and legislative measures should be taken, and more support should be given to the work that associations and foundations are already doing, by promoting specific programs and research in which people with disabilities participate actively. A brighter future beckons if the promise of ICT is made real for people with disabilities.

Summary of key points

- Assistive technology (AT) is evolving in parallel with the fast-paced advance of technology in general and the new information and communication technologies (ICT) in particular, which are opening up new possibilities for improving the quality of life and the inclusion of disabled people in the current Information Society.
- Universal design, especially for interfaces and browsers, which is user-centred, and seeks a cognitive, physical and geographical accessibility as well as high usability, along with the AT needed to enhance or replace the different functionalities of each individual, will narrow the digital divide which has opened and will facilitate the inclusion of every disabled person in any environment.
- It is essential to include the use of new technologies from the earliest educational stages and provide technology-aided support systems in an inclusive classroom of those children with educational special needs. Hence, adequate training in ICT should guarantee skills for both disabled people and their teachers, educators and families.
- State institutions, associations, foundations and researchers, with and without disabilities, have a crucial role when it comes to fostering, funding and carrying out programs and research to increase and improve AT and their usage.

- The wider digital divide among youths and adults with intellectual disability must be tackled by taking advantage of the equalizing effect that comes from training and working with ICT. The importance of training in the use of ICTs is recognized in Article 4 of the CRPD [General obligations].

STUDY QUESTIONS

1. What experience have you had of using AT or ICT with persons with disabilities? If you have had experience of using it, what barriers and facilitators of use did you find? If you have little or no experience, can you think of ways in which you could use it?

2. How do you think the use of ICT could further social inclusion of persons with intellectual disabilities? What changes would need to happen to bring this about?

3. Get Used To is a computer application that can be included as a training instrument in educational programs or in the provision of personalized support services in independent living settings. How does the use of this application contribute to the implementation of the CRPD?

Further reading and resources

Association for the Advancement of Assistive Technology in Europe (AATE) http://www.aaate.net.

J. Borg, A. Lindström S. Larsson. (2011). 'Assistive technology in developing countries: A review from the perspective of the convention on the rights of persons with disabilities', *Prosthet Orthot Int.*, 35(1), 20–9. Doi: 10.1177/0309364610389351.

Citizens Information Board (Ireland) – Assist Ireland, http://www.assistireland.ie/eng/.

Disabled World, Assistive Technology: Devices, products and information http://www.disabled-world.com/assistivedevices/.

Do2learn – A resource for individuals with special needs, http://do2learn.com/.

Education Development Center (EDC). Learning Transforms Lives http://www.edc.org.

International Program on Disability, Technology and Rehabilitation – University of Washington, http://idtr.uwctds.washington.edu.

National Center for Technology Innovation, Techmatrix project, www.techmatrix.org.

ONCE Foundation and Technosite, http://www.discapnet.es/ (Spanish).

WHO Assistive devices/technologies, http://www.who.int/disabilities/technology/en/.

WHO Global Cooperation on Assistive Health Technology (GATE), http://www.who.int/phi/implementation/assistive_technology/phi_gate/en/.

Access to Livelihoods

Peter Coleridge

> *States Parties recognize the right of persons with disabilities to work, on an equal basis with others; this includes the right to the opportunity to gain a living by work freely chosen or accepted in a labour market and work environment that is open, inclusive and accessible to persons with disabilities. States Parties shall safeguard and promote the realization of the right to work, including for those who acquire a disability during the course of employment.*
>
> **UN Convention on the Rights of Persons with Disabilities Article 27(1): Work and employment**

Introduction

This chapter views disability and employment from the perspective of livelihood and is based on experience and research in developing countries. Some of its points are relevant in an industrialized country like Britain or Ireland, but its aim is to increase understanding of livelihood issues for disabled people in countries where poverty is the main focus of aid and development. However, the main principles of community development outlined are applicable in both the Global South and the Global North.

By using the word *livelihood* instead of *work* or *employment*, the intention is to show that just promoting income generation is not synonymous with enhancing livelihoods or eradicating poverty. Livelihood does not only mean employment or income. It is the way in which we organize our lives not just to survive but also to flourish, as human beings with desires and aspirations. A focus on livelihoods involves creating opportunities to develop one's full potential as a *social* human being with the ability to contribute to the development of one's community and society.

The relationship between disability and poverty

Because disability has not been seen historically as a mainstream development topic, little systematic research has been done on the direct link between disability and material poverty. Academic organizations such as the Foundation for Scientific and Industrial Research (SINTEF)[1] and government donors such as United Kingdom Department for International Development (DFID)[2] are conducting research to obtain both quantitative and qualitative data that can provide prevalence estimates and general links between poverty and disability. However, there is at present scant systematic data on the dynamics of how the presence of impairments affects the economic and social life of people in developing countries. Global figures on the employment of disabled people are problematic and unreliable.

Nevertheless, both common sense and a mass of anecdotal evidence link disability with poverty. Disability is both a cause and an effect of poverty (see Chapter 6 for an in-depth discussion of the relationship between disability and poverty). Classic indicators of poverty such as communicable diseases, poor sanitation, poor nutrition, dangerous work conditions and transport, and lack of medical services especially around birth, all conspire to produce impairments. There is also much evidence that once impaired, a disabled person and his or her family will find it more difficult to escape from absolute poverty, and those who become disabled through accidents at work or other reasons are more likely to descend into chronic poverty. There is strong evidence of a correlation between mental health problems, especially depression, and poverty (Patel, 2014).

However, we cannot measure poverty only by whether basic material needs are met. There are other needs: 'the need to be creative, to make choices, to exercise judgment, to love others and be loved, to have friendships, to contribute something of oneself to the world, to have social function and purpose. These are active needs; if they are not met, the result is the impoverishment of the human spirit, because without them life has no meaning' (Coleridge, 1993). The denial of these needs is a feature of disabled people's lives everywhere, not just in poor countries; but they are not normally measured in poverty statistics (Coleridge, Simonnot and Steverlynk, 2011).

The profile of disability and livelihood in international development

Until the advent of the UN Convention on the Rights of Persons with Disabilities (CRPD), which entered into force in 2008 (see Chapter 3), the employment of people with disabilities was not seen as a mainstream development issue.

---

[1] Unsubstantiated estimates (for example, that 20 per cent of the world's poorest are disabled) are common in the literature, but such estimates are not reflected in any available research data.

[2] Cf. SINTEF studies on living conditions of disabled people in Zambia, Botswana, Malawi, Yemen and other countries. For example, http://www.ii-livinginthecommunity.org/Report_Lesotho_310111.pdf.

But the CRPD has spawned a number of important publications which have raised its profile in international development, including the *World Report on Disability* (WHO and World Bank, 2011), and the *Community-based Rehabilitation (CBR) Guidelines* (WHO, 2010). With the CRPD these make essential contributions to the discussion on livelihoods.

As noted at the start of the chapter, Article 27 of the CRPD, 'Work and employment' states:

States Parties recognize the right of persons with disabilities to work, on an equal basis with others.

Furthermore, the CRPD prohibits all forms of employment discrimination, promotes access to vocational training, encourages self-employment and calls for reasonable accommodation in the workplace, among other provisions.

The chapter on work and employment in the *World Report on Disability* is a comprehensive summary of the factors which combine to limit the employment of people with disabilities and how these disabilities may be overcome. It underlines that the main impediments to employment are discrimination and prejudice in the labour market, and disincentives created by disability benefit systems. Many countries have laws prohibiting discrimination on the basis of disability, but enforcement remains a problem, especially when the majority of the workforce is in the informal sector. 'Quotas, vocational rehabilitation and employment services – job training, counselling, job search assistance and placement – can develop or restore the capabilities of people with disabilities to compete in the labour market and facilitate their inclusion in the labour market. At the heart of all this is changing attitudes in the workplace' (WHO and World Bank, 2011).

In line with the CRPD, WHO spearheaded the production of the *Community-based Rehabilitation (CBR) Guidelines*, published in 2010. At the heart of these Guidelines is the CBR matrix, which makes clear that community approaches to disability cut across all sectors of development: health, education, livelihood, social activities, and empowerment. All are essential for the well-being and fulfilment of the individual. Because it cuts across all these sectors, disability is placed by the matrix firmly in the mainstream of development (see Chapter 2).

The generally accepted broad aim of international development cooperation is the reduction of poverty. The CBR Guidelines view CBR as a strategy whose primary purpose is to contribute to this process. Livelihood is seen as the key to reducing poverty for disabled people and their families.

The CRPD and the CBR Guidelines are seminal documents not just for disability: they use an approach to development which challenges the conventional paradigm of international development. They do this in two ways. First, as the CBR matrix illustrates, disability is not a discrete topic, the preserve of specialists; it is a universal human condition and needs to be incorporated into mainstream development thinking.

Second, they challenge the conventional paradigm of international development itself. There is much fully justified criticism of the values, ethics and practice of international development cooperation when viewed as a global phenomenon (see Maren, 1997; Calderisi, 2007). All these criticisms can be summarized under the headline of 'unequal relationships'. The central problem is that if a system is based on unequal relationships, it will fail in human terms. A system defined primarily by the presence of donor and recipient is inherently one of unequal relationships characterized by dominance and subservience, and the distortion of self-image in both donor and recipient.

Furthermore conventional international aid generally uses a needs-based approach to community development. In this approach agencies external to the community generate needs surveys, analyse problems and identify solutions (Mathie and Cunningham, 2002). But this approach tends to undermine the very aim they are working for, which is the building of resilient communities.

A resilient community is one which has the confidence to solve its own problems. But the conventional needs-based approach by external agencies tends to encourage community leaders to play up the severity of the problems in order to attract institutional funding. 'People in the communities start to believe what their leaders are saying. They begin to see themselves as deficient and incapable of taking charge of their lives and of the community. Community members no longer act like citizens; instead they act like "clients" or consumers of services with no incentive to be producers' (Mathie and Cunningham, 2002).

An alternative approach is asset-based community development (ABCD), which recognizes that it is the capacities of local people and their associations that build resilient communities. The process of recognizing these capacities begins with the construction of a new lens through which communities can 'begin to assemble their strengths into new combinations, new structures of opportunity, new sources of income and control, and new possibilities for production' (Kretzmann and McKnight, 1993; Mathie and Cunningham, 2002).

> Such unrealized resources include not only personal attributes and skills, but also the relationships among people through social, kinship or associational networks. By mobilizing these informal networks, formal institutional resources can be activated – such as local government, formal community-based organisations, and private enterprise. In fact, the key to ABCD is the power of local associations to drive the community development process and to leverage additional support and entitlements. These associations are the vehicles through which all the community's assets can be identified and then connected to one another in ways that multiply their power and effectiveness ... ABCD pays particular attention to the assets inherent in social relationships.
>
> (Mathie and Cunningham, 2002)

An asset-based approach to community development is implied in the CRPD and the CBR Guidelines, and has been gradually adopted by those working in community disability programmes for some time. This is especially true of approaches to livelihoods. For example, Theresa Lorenzo, who teaches disability studies at Cape Town University, describes livelihood as 'the assets that people use to earn enough money to support themselves and their families through a variety of activities' (Lorenzo, Ned-Matiwane and Cois, 2013). These assets include five categories:

- Human assets (health and education)
- Social assets (social support systems)
- Financial assets (work and other sources of income)
- Physical assets (living situation, facilities and services)
- Natural assets (resource based activities).

All five assets are encapsulated in the CBR matrix. Even without labels like 'asset-based community development', there is increasing awareness that charity must be replaced by solidarity and partnership (Doane, 2013). The relationships implicit in the words *solidarity* and *partnership* are fundamentally different from those implied in the word *charity*. In *Representations of Global Poverty: Aid, Development and International NGOs* (Dogra, 2012), Dogra states that the view of poverty in poor countries transmitted by aid agencies is entirely divorced from the real root causes of poverty and actually exacerbates the problem. If we see poor people as separate from us and their problems as theirs alone, we fail to understand the interconnectedness of all our lives and that the root causes of poverty lie in unequal relationships. Such an understanding demands empathy, solidarity and partnership, not charity.

Since the 1990s, the social model and now the human rights-based approach have received increasing international attention. This is reflected in the language and content of the CRPD and also in the CBR Guidelines. The philosophy, practice and experience of CBR are firmly rooted in the social and rights models where empathy and solidarity are the defining attitudes, and partnership the defining relationship.

The present thinking on disability, exemplified by the CRPD, the *World Report* and the CBR Guidelines, has much to offer the general debate about creating a more equitable and asset-based approach to international development. These documents present an approach to disability which is based on equal, reciprocal relationships where both parties benefit. That is, they are relationships which strengthen for the common good (MacLachlan, Carr and McAuliffe, 2010). A discussion of livelihoods provides an ideal context in which to illustrate this approach.

The formal and informal economies

It is necessary first to clarify an important distinction in the world of work in the Global South: the difference between the formal and informal economies.

The *formal economy* comprises public and private sector jobs that are covered by employment legislation relating to job security, minimum wage, occupational safety and health. Workers have the option of joining trade unions to represent their interests. Employers may form representative associations which deal with policy issues such as corporate social responsibility, including employment opportunities for disabled persons. Formal sector jobs often offer benefits such as pensions, health insurance and holidays, dictated by employment law. But even without such laws, employers in the formal sector may see the commercial benefit of corporate responsibility, creating an environment where a contented labour force engaged in decent work is more productive than one where workers toil in drudgery.

Many people in poor countries aspire to formal sector jobs, but disabled persons frequently lose out in the competition for such jobs, against other highly qualified job applicants, particularly in developing countries (ILO, 2008).

The *informal economy* refers to the income-generating activities of people not engaged in the formal economy – small-scale enterprises, which are usually labour intensive, unregistered and unregulated; they operate in highly competitive markets which depress the price they can charge for their labour. They are unregulated in the sense that they have no work contracts and offer no social security such as pensions or health insurance (ILO, 2008).

The International Labour Organization (ILO) describes the informal economy thus:

> The informal economy thrives in a context of high unemployment, underemployment, poverty, gender inequality and precarious work. It plays a significant role in such circumstances, especially in income generation, because of the relative ease of entry and low requirements for education, skills, technology and capital. But most people enter the informal economy not by choice, but out of a need to survive and to have access to basic income-generating activities.
>
> (ILO, 2013)

Generally speaking, the formal sector, focused on clerical and office-based jobs, requires higher levels of education than the informal, which relies mainly on low-level manual skills.

The informal economy is the dominant arena for work and employment in developing countries. In many countries of Africa, 90 per cent of the labour force is in the informal economy; in Asia, between 47 per cent and over 90 per cent; and in Latin America, approximately 25 per cent. In India, despite an enormous government bureaucracy, the largest film industry in the world, a space programme and major industrial companies like Tata that are effectively multinationals, 94 per cent of the workforce still works in the informal sector. This means that despite impressive national growth figures, the vast majority of its population are still locked into poverty.

However, with globalization and the world financial crisis, the distinction between formal and informal sector operations has become increasingly blurred. The nature of production and employment in the global economy is leading to increased use of informal employment arrangements in formal enterprises, making use of outsourced workers under employment arrangements that are not governed by labour contracts. For example, the clothing industry relies not only on vast sweat shops employing hundreds of women, but also on piece work where families, including young children, complete orders at home in wretched conditions where they have no rights at all. Sometimes the informal economy supplies essential services which should be provided within the formal economy, such as garbage collection and recycling.

It is more accurate to speak of a continuum from informal to formal ends of the economy, rather than two distinct sectors (ILO, 2008). But the difference is nonetheless important, because of the legal and practical implications.

The complexity of the formal/informal split also makes it very difficult to produce employment figures which are useful. To say that Nepal, for example, has an unemployment rate of 45 per cent (Wikipedia, 2014) is meaningless. Is a woman selling vegetables in the market employed or not? Or a man supporting his family on half an acre of land? It depends on what is meant by employment. That is why global figures on the employment of disabled people are unreliable, because most of those who do work are in the informal sector.

As far as persons with disabilities are concerned, the main point to make about the informal economy is that in it employment law is very difficult or impossible to enforce. Because the majority of poor people in work in developing countries, including disabled people, are in the informal sector, whether the national laws include non-discrimination or not makes little difference to their employment prospects or job security. International and national legislation provides an ideal to be aimed at, but the reality for the vast majority of poor people, including disabled people, in low income countries is that 'the right to employment' means nothing, and they must depend on non-formal strategies to make a living.

We examine here ways in which the employment of disabled people can be enhanced in both the formal and informal economies, by seeing development as a process of creating networks of mutually supportive relationships within communities and between communities and the wider world (see case example, Box 12.1).

Box 12.1. An example of mutual support from Zimbabwe

Opha in Zimbabwe is a wheelchair user who sells fruit in the Bulawayo market (Coleridge, 2013). Two things strike a visitor to her stall: First, she has a radiant smile, and is very outgoing. Second, her bananas are more expensive than her neighbours'. How can this be? She says: 'I have my customers who always buy from me, even though my bananas are a bit more expensive'. On further enquiry it emerges that she belongs to four different community savings groups: one for meeting utility bills, one for funeral expenses, one for school expenses for her niece, and a disability mutual support group. She earns very little, about $50 a month. She is unmarried but supports her niece through school. She is part of a network of mutually supportive relationships that, despite a very low income, enable her not only to survive but to thrive.

The word used for such relationships in southern Africa is *ubuntu*. Archbishop Desmond Tutu describes it thus:

Ubuntu is the essence of being human. It speaks of the fact that my humanity is caught up and is inextricably bound up in yours. I am human because I belong. It speaks about wholeness, it speaks about compassion. A person with ubuntu is welcoming, hospitable, warm and generous, willing to share. Such people are open and available to others, willing to be vulnerable, affirming of others, do not feel threatened that others are able and good, for they have a proper self-assurance that comes from knowing that they belong in a greater whole. They know that they are diminished when others are humiliated, diminished when others are oppressed, diminished when others are treated as if they were less than who they are. The quality of ubuntu gives people resilience, enabling them to survive and emerge still human despite all efforts to dehumanise them.

(Tutu, 2004)

The concept is not unique to southern Africa, and has been voiced by poets, philosophers, politicians and spiritual leaders everywhere. Paulo Freire, the Brazilian educator who has probably had more influence on development thinking than any other single individual in the past 50 years, wrote:

To be human is to engage in relationships with others and with the world.

(Freire, 1996)

Opha sells her bananas at a higher price than her neighbour because the principle of *ubuntu* still operates in Zimbabwe. She is part of a network of mutual support; members of this network are happy to pay a few cents more for her bananas simply because it is a reciprocal arrangement.

Ubuntu also operates among the market traders. If Opha leaves her stall to go and collect fruit from the wholesaler, her neighbour looks after it – and sells her fruit at her price. The market traders all help each other in various ways. This gives a totally different view of 'market forces' than the one presented by modern economists, who see the market as fundamentally competitive. 'In fact, economic theory fails to recognize the concept of community at all' (Mathie and Cunningham, 2002).

Opha says: 'I fear God. I do not use money recklessly. I have an eye for detail. I make friends with my customers. If I am regarded as successful it is because of these things.'

But the real key to her success is that she does not sit at home 'demanding her rights'. She is proactive and approaches life with a positive and optimistic frame of mind. She reaches out to people; she makes friends; she gives, of herself, of her time, of her very limited money. She is part of a wide set of mutually supportive relationships. Opha earns $50 a month, which theoretically places her on the threshold of absolute poverty. But is she poor?

In industrialized countries, the unit supported by a wage earner is normally the nuclear family. But in non-industrialized countries the wages of one person may be the principal support for an extended family of up to 20 people. In this situation, any direct or indirect contribution from family members is welcome, including from disabled members. A 12-year-old girl who looks after younger siblings, for example, is making an indirect economic contribution because she enables the mother to work on the family plot or run a stall in the market. Nevertheless, if she forgoes her own education, her personal development will be held back. (The immensely important topic of carers and their rights is treated in Chapter 15.) So where a family has a disabled member, it is important for CBR workers, social workers and others relating to disability, to have a grasp of the whole family context and see where a disabled member can make a contribution even if it is not an activity which earns an income directly.

A different kind of example of this concept is the work of David Luyombo in Uganda, a disabled man who trained as a paravet in order to promote better family livelihoods in his home rural area. He breeds goats, cows, chickens and pigs, and gives an animal to a family with a disabled member. When the animal produces its first young, the kid, calf, chick or piglet is given to another family with a disabled member. This means that even if the disabled person is not actually capable of physical work (for example a child with severe cerebral palsy), he or she can still be an asset to the family because the child's presence means the family receives an animal (Coleridge, 2013).

Western economic theories emphasize individual achievement and sees market forces as a competitive system, but this obscures the fundamental importance of cooperation and collaboration. Networks of mutual support and partnerships which create trust are the basis of survival in the informal sector; their creation requires a view of development that is based on solidarity and an understanding of the interconnectedness of all development activities.

Access to capital for small businesses

To establish a small business in the informal economy requires capital. Micro-credit schemes are common in development programmes, but for people with disabilities two particular problems with these arise. The first is that people with disabilities tend to resist taking a loan from micro-credit lenders because they fear they will not be able to repay. Second, micro-credit organizations may be reluctant to lend to disabled people because they think they do not meet the criteria for being a reasonable risk.

A full treatment of micro-finance in relation to people with disabilities can be found elsewhere, especially Martinelli and Mersland (2010). Here we focus on alternative approaches using groups.

To overcome the reluctance of mainstream banks to lend to poor people, in the 1980s Muhammed Younis set up the Grameen Bank in Bangladesh to pioneer the concept of the group guaranteed loan. In this concept, a loan is given to individual members of a group of between five and ten people. The condition is that each member of the group guarantees the repayment of the other members of the group. This approach has become the backbone of most rural development efforts in Bangladesh. It has, in particular, enhanced the status and development prospects for women, who form 90 per cent of the loan groups.

However, the Grameen Bank was not set up with disabled people in mind. The loan groups are self-selecting, and it is rare for them to include a disabled person. Members join with others whom they perceive as being likely to succeed in their business and repay, and they tend to see disabled people as not falling into that category.

In addition, this loan system relies on money from outside the group, meaning that there is a degree of dependency on external funding. It is common for groups to take another loan from another agency to repay the first loan, and get trapped in a perpetual cycle of debt.

In India a different system has been established which does not rely on outside money and which is inherently more accessible to disabled people. Self-help groups of between 10 and 20 people form a savings group in which each member puts an agreed sum into a common pot each week or each month. At regular intervals, one member of the group will take the sum accumulated in the pot as a loan, to be used for a peak expenditure such as medical treatment, a school uniform, a new roof, or to set up a small business. She then repays that loan to the group at an interest rate agreed by the group, usually about 2 per cent a month. This means that the pot is continually growing.

There are millions of these savings groups all over India and in other countries. In India their collective savings amount to many millions of rupees. The system has become a central strategy for not only surviving but also thriving for people in poor communities all over the world. It is well illustrated by the case of Opha above.

But Opha is something of an exception. The inclusion of disabled people in such savings groups meets the same problem as the Grameen bank groups: they tend to be seen as a poor risk. But increasingly disabled people in India and elsewhere are setting up their own savings groups and demonstrating that they are just as capable of saving and building up their own financial resource base as anyone else.

Such savings groups are a major tool for empowerment. Based on trust, they build mutually reinforcing relationships. They break the mould of donor and recipient, and create a situation where, even though people may be materially poor, they can thrive. They also provide an excellent opportunity to develop skills which are transferable to formal sector jobs, such as running a meeting, keeping records, managing finance, communication in both speech and writing, cooperation and team work. They also build knowledge of the job market through contact with other groups, banks, officials, social workers and NGO staff.

Creating networks in the formal economy

The example of Opha illustrates the survival strategies used by millions of people in the informal economy in poor countries. Nevertheless, a job in the formal economy is a very attractive proposition and remains the goal of those who complete an education to secondary or tertiary level, including disabled people. Formal employment is seen to provide income, security and benefits that the informal economy cannot match. The same principles of creating networks of mutual support apply in the formal economy.

This point is understood very well by vocational training centres (VTCs) in India run by the Leprosy Mission. These are for young people who have leprosy or whose parents have leprosy. Nowadays leprosy can be cured with drugs, but the stigma remains very strong and is often a serious bar to employment.

The VTCs run by the Leprosy Mission train young people (both boys and girls) in motor mechanics, carpentry, electrical fitting, tailoring and the other vocational skills that VTCs teach all over the world. But many VTCs around the world have a rather poor record of employment for their graduates. In the case of the Leprosy Mission schools, 90 per cent of their graduates find employment within a year of graduating. Why? There are three reasons.

First, these VTCs focus not just on technical skills but on life skills. It is not enough to learn motor mechanics. To be successful in employment one also needs to have determination, aspirations, social responsibility, willingness to take risks, optimism, friendliness, persistence in the face of setbacks, creativity, openness to other views, critical thinking and high personal standards.

These qualities can be taught, for example by role models and by creating a culture in the training centre where these values are demonstrated and prized. The Leprosy Mission schools recognize that operating a successful car repair business, for example, requires more than a knowledge of motor mechanics: relations with customers and relationships within the workforce are equally important. A reputation for honest and transparent dealing in business will establish a secure and sustainable customer base. This reputation overrides all other considerations, including the fact that a car repair business employs people who have had leprosy, with all the stigma that it carries.

Second, these VTCs have placement officers whose job it is to develop relationships with potential employers in the formal sector. Once a company has seen that graduates from these VTCs have valuable personal qualities besides their technical skills, that they are conscientious, creative, positive, reliable and honest, they regard the VTCs as excellent sources of new recruits.

This reinforces the business case for hiring people with disabilities in the formal economy, which can be applied everywhere (Business and Disability, 2014). They make good, dependable employees; they have higher job retention rates; many employers report that teamwork and morale improves when disabled workers become part of the staff; consumers are likely to look favourably upon businesses that employ people with disabilities.

Third, the schools have vibrant alumni associations, where previous graduates, now in jobs, can support younger graduates in finding and keeping employment. This network of peer support has the following vital functions:

(a) For young graduates trying to find their way in the bewildering world of work, those who have already navigated it successfully are much better placed to give guidance and will be more effective than school staff.

(b) It spreads and localizes the task of giving support; it would be impossible for school staff to give such support to all their graduates.

(c) It solves a serious problem common to many VTCs around the world which lose touch with their graduates: they do not know how many of them enter and keep employment. This in turn means that they do not know how effective their courses are. But in the case of the Leprosy Mission VTCs, the alumni associations, which keep in touch with the parent school, enable the schools to evaluate the success of their courses because they have an ongoing view of how many graduates enter and keep employment.

These three factors – life skill training, placement officers and alumni associations – draw on the principle of creating networks of supportive relationships. They also demonstrate a recognition that creating a successful livelihood has to be approached holistically and cannot be seen as a matter simply of technical skills and income (Coleridge, 2007).

Sylvana Lakis is the founder and director of the Lebanese Physically Handicapped Union (LPHU), which sees employment as its chief responsibility on behalf of disabled people. Its approach has focused on three elements: doing research to find out where disabled people are employed and in what circumstances, building relationships with potential employers, and arranging training of disabled people to fit skills demanded by employers.

LPHU has established employment advice centres for disabled people in many parts of Lebanon. These centres function as reference points for both employers and disabled job seekers. Their task is to get in touch with employers in their area of operation, find out what skills they are looking for, and then set up ways in which disabled people can acquire the necessary skills. LPHU also has a website for disabled job seekers, which similarly aims to match job seekers with job opportunities. Sylvana herself and the other staff of the employment advice centres continually develop contacts with employers in a range of industries in order to help disabled people find jobs. The result is that LPHU has found jobs for disabled people in a wide variety of jobs in the formal economy in Lebanon, including banks, a telephone company, a film archive and restoration company, architectural model making, journalism and many others. These examples show that LPHU has moved right away from stereotyping disabled people into low-skilled, dull and repetitive jobs, and has succeeded in placing them in creative enterprises in which they are proud to work and find genuine fulfilment.

The examples of the Leprosy Mission VTCs and LPHU show how high-quality holistic training, researching the market and building networks of support are necessary for disabled people to enter the formal job market. But the biggest bar to disabled people getting jobs in the formal economy is lack of secondary and further education. In most low-income countries, primary education is free, but secondary education is not, and university is beyond the means of all but a small minority (see Chapter 9). And even where primary education is free, access is often difficult or impossible for children with disabilities. Furthermore, class size and poorly trained teachers mean that children with communication impairments, in particular, may learn very little.

Here too support mechanisms are vital. In the case of David Luyombo, the paravet in Uganda quoted above, his mother was determined that he should get an education, despite his polio. When he was small, she carried him to primary school (his father, a farmer, regarded his polio as a complete disaster and saw no hope for his son). His mother scrimped and saved and managed to pay for his secondary schooling. He then trained as an accountant, regarded as a suitable job for a person with limited mobility. But his real ambition was to work in development in rural Uganda, and so he trained as a paravet, with the fees paid by an NGO. This gave him the knowledge and background to launch his own development enterprise in his home area. This has blossomed into a rural development association which has provided training for hundreds of disabled people and their families from all over Uganda, not only in animal husbandry, but also in innovative ways to grow better crops.

David says he owes his success in getting an education to his mother. Unlike his father, who regarded his disability as an impossible impediment, his mother believed in him and saw from the first that his future lay in being educated to the highest level possible. The father is typical of many parents who see disability as an insuperable obstacle and who are not prepared to invest time, effort and money in enabling their disabled child to go through school. But as we have noted, jobs in the informal economy focus mainly on manual skills, whereas those in the formal economy depend on education. This is precisely why disabled people, for whom manual work may be a significant problem, should aim at the formal job market, and every effort must be made to enable them to achieve the highest educational standard of which they are capable.

The rapid advances in computer technology in particular have opened up whole fields of new possibilities for disabled people in the formal economy. For example, blind people can now be fully functional on a computer, which means they have access to written materials which before they could only access with the greatest difficulty, if at all (see Chapter 11).

The creation of networks of mutual support opens up opportunities for disabled people to get jobs in the formal sector which would not be there if they simply sat at home. Being part of a family and wider friendship circle which believes in them, and which supports their ambitions and aspirations, means that multiple antennae will be active looking for suitable openings. And if disabled people are more visible and active in community affairs, potential employers will be more aware of their potential.

Once in a formal sector job, a disabled person can be helped to gain self-confidence through being mentored by someone already familiar with the job. This could be a staff member, union member or volunteer, whose role is to ensure that necessary adjustments to the workplace are made, to help the employer and worker to solve any problems that might arise and to ensure the worker is performing adequately in the job.

Using corporate responsibility in the formal sector

Many large businesses, including multinationals, take the issue of corporate responsibility seriously. The use of child labour and exploitation of sweatshop workers make for damaging headlines and loss of customer loyalty. Employing disabled people is a positive step towards enhancing and making visible a profile of corporate social responsibility.

The ILO Global Business and Disability Network (Business and Disability, 2014) is open to multinational enterprises and employers' organizations or business networks who are interested in disability inclusion in the workplace and throughout their operation and sphere of influence. The membership includes, to a lesser extent, global and regional networks of NGOs and disabled people's organizations who can provide technical assistance and linkage to other organizations to help companies achieve disability inclusion.

The four objectives of the network are as follows:

1. Share knowledge and identify good practices among companies and employers' organizations.
2. Develop joint products and services for companies and employers to facilitate hiring and retention.
3. Strengthen the work of employers' organizations and business networks that have greater access to small and medium-size companies at the national level, and building their technical expertize on disability issues.
4. Link companies to ILO activities and partners at the national level, and work through local offices and supply chains.

Companies or employers' organizations in the Network agree to work towards providing equal treatment and equal opportunity for disabled persons at work and in seeking employment. Members are guided by the *ILO Code of Practice for Managing Disability in the Workplace* (ILO, 2002) and agree to participate in Network activities, respond to Network queries or surveys, and share information in accordance with the four goals of the Network.

Conclusions

This chapter has tried to show what an inclusive society looks like when development is seen as a way of creating and enhancing mutually supportive relationships. It has also shown what happens when disabled people themselves take the initiative to achieve their rights and work as positive, proactive and creative agents of change.

As we stated at the beginning, a paradigm of aid defined primarily by the presence of donor and recipient is inherently one of unequal relationships characterized by dominance and subservience. Such unequal relationships inevitably create a situation where justice is absent, and identities and self-image are damaged. The donor has an unreal sense of his or her own importance, and the recipient remains, whatever the language employed by the donor, an object of charity.

Development is not something that is done by one person to another, by one country to another or by one aid agency to poor people. Development is about eschewing dominance, creating a situation where justice is achievable, and promoting a positive identity (MacLachlan, Carr and McAuliffe, 2010).

Creating networks of mutual support, illustrated by the examples given above, is a model of development that is already a reality for large numbers of people, both in fully developed CBR programmes and in community initiatives like those of Opha and David. In this model, there is no difference between helper and helped, and everyone is empowered to fulfil his or her potential.

Perhaps this model could be the greatest contribution that CBR and work in disability can make to new thinking about aid and development. By joining the debate on these terms, it would show that 'disability and development' is not a marginal issue: creating networks of mutual support as illustrated by disabled people is central to the whole concept of aid and development.

The CRPD and the new CBR Guidelines mark a paradigm shift in our view of disability because they see disabled people as agents of their own change, *within a context of mutually supporting relationships*. It is not that disabled people are now expected to do everything on their own and by themselves. The point is enshrined in the idea of *ubuntu*: if another human being is diminished, I am diminished. We are all part of a common humanity in which it is entirely in our own interests to help each other. CBR is, at its best, a network of supporting relationships which provide purpose and value to the lives of all those concerned, not just of disabled people.

The creation of a just society is a joint responsibility between government and citizens. Within the human rights framework, governments are duty bearers, and citizens are rights holders. It is the responsibility of governments to enact legislation and to provide essential services, and it is the responsibility of citizens to hold governments to account for those primary functions. Legislation and essential services provide the baseline and framework for citizens to play their part, in which both disabled and non-disabled citizens work together to create the network of mutually supporting relationships that are the basis of an inclusive society.

Summary of key points

- Livelihoods are used in this chapter as a way of illustrating an approach to development which focuses on building communal networks of mutual support.
- This approach runs counter to conventional economic theories which emphasize competition and the individual, and which ignore the value and power of community-driven cooperation and collaboration.
- It also runs counter to much aid and development practice which tends to underline problems instead of the assets in a community.

- It illustrates how networks of mutual support can be used in both the informal and formal economies to enable disabled people to be part of a livelihood approach which is not based on competition but on enhanced social relationships that are beneficial to all.
- This approach is implied in key texts that have emerged in the past few years, notably the UN Convention on the Rights of Persons with Disabilities, and the CBR Guidelines.
- Micro-credit is presented through the mechanism of group savings and self-help groups, which open up opportunities for disabled people to learn skills which are transferable to jobs in both the formal and informal sectors.

STUDY QUESTIONS

1. Has this chapter changed the way you think about international development? If it has, explain how your view has changed. If it has not, what do you agree with most in this chapter, and what do you agree with least?

2. Read the component on 'Livelihood' in the CBR Guidelines (http://www.who.int/ disabilities/cbr/guidelines/en/), and write down examples of how it reflects the idea of building networks of mutual support.

3. What does your own experience tell you about the ideas presented in this chapter?

Further reading and resources

P. Coleridge. (1993). *Disability, Liberation and Development*. (Oxford: Oxfam).

P. Coleridge, C. Simonnot and D. Steverlynk. (2011). *Study of disability in EC development cooperation*, http://ec.europa.eu/europeaid/what/social-protection/documents/223185_disability_study_en.pdf.

P. Coleridge and B. Venkatesh. (2010). *Community Approaches to Livelihood Development: Self-help Groups in India*. In T. Barron and J. Ncube (Eds.), *Poverty and Disability* (London: Leonard Cheshire Disability).

P. Coleridge. (2007). *Economic Empowerment*. In T. Barron and P. Amerena, *Disability and Inclusive Development* (London: Leonard Cheshire Disability).

R. Heron and B. Murray. (2003). *Assisting disabled persons in finding employment. A practical guide* (Geneva: International Labour Organization).

International Labour Organization (ILO). (2008). *Skills Development through Community Based Rehabilitation (CBR). A good practice guide*, http://www.ilo.org/wcmsp5/groups/public/---ed_emp/---ifp_skills/documents/publication/wcms_132675.pdf.

E. Martinelli and R. Mersland. (2010). *Micro-credit for People with Disabilities*. In T. Barron and J. Ncube (Eds.), *Poverty and Disability* (London: Leonard Cheshire Disability).

D.A. Perry. (2003). *Moving forward: Toward decent work for people with disabilities. Examples of good practice in vocational training and employment from Asia and the Pacific* (Bangkok: International Labour Organization).

WHO. (2010). *Community-based Rehabilitation CBR Guidelines, Livelihood* (Geneva: WHO), http://www.who.int/disabilities/cbr/guidelines/en/.

Independent Living: Experiences from Japan and the Asia-Pacific Region

13

Kamal Lamichhane

> *States Parties to the present Convention recognize the equal right of all persons with disabilities to live in the community, with choices equal to others, and shall take effective and appropriate measures to facilitate full enjoyment by persons with disabilities of this right and their full inclusion and participation in the community, including by ensuring that: (a) persons with disabilities have the opportunity to choose their place of residence and where and with whom they live on an equal basis with others and are not obliged to live in a particular living arrangement.*

UN Convention on the Rights of Persons with Disabilities
Article 19: Living independently and being included in the community

Introduction

Independent living (IL) is a concept that demands a paradigm shift from an individual/medical understanding of disability to that of a human rights-based approach. It is 'a philosophy and a disabled people's movement who work for the self-determination, equality of opportunities and personal respect' (Ratzka, 2005). It postulates that people with disabilities are the best experts on their needs; they must therefore take the initiative – individually and collectively – in designing and promoting better solutions for their lives. Emerging from the political activism of people with disabilities in the United States of America (US), the core ideas of IL lie in the de-medicalization of disability and the de-institutionalization of people with disabilities (DeJong, 1979). The IL movement has spread from the US to other parts of the world over the years, and it has become one of the goals of the disability community across the globe. However, the implementation of IL is not without its caveats. In this context, this chapter discusses some of the challenges to implementing IL when the needs of persons with disabilities are different, depending on the type and nature of their impairments and their country's cultural and socio-economic development. The chapter is organized as follows. The first section discusses the concept, philosophy and history of the IL movement. The second section discusses some of the challenges of implementing the Japanese IL model in Asian contexts. Lastly, the chapter concludes with some of the recommendations for strengthening the IL movement in these countries.

Concept and history of independent living

Historically, people with disabilities were considered to be passive recipients of services delivered in the spirit of charity. The US civil rights movement of the 1960s was a critical point in history when it comes to changes to this approach to disability. Following this movement, disabled activists in the US started to demand disability rights, inclusion and anti-discrimination measures as part of the Disability Rights Movement (DRM) (see Chapter 4). The DRM shifted the paradigm from a charitable ethos to people with disabilities being the ones deciding on matters directly concerning their lives and being active players as consumers, as well as producers, of services. The concept of IL that emerged after the civil rights movement in the US and the social model of disability developed in Britain (see Chapter 2) can be seen as complementary. The IL movement advocates for placing people with disabilities in the driving seat for issues and policies concerning themselves. The social model of disability identifies society as the cause of disability. Disabled people, therefore, are leaders in demanding societal responses to disability. The IL movement advocates for freedom of choice, reflected in the slogan largely used worldwide 'Nothing about us without us' (Charlton, 1998). IL has grown and expanded over the years through the work of disability activists and is reflected in Article 19, 'Living independently and being included in the community', of the Convention on the Rights of Persons with Disabilities (CRPD) (UN, 2006) (see Chapter 3). This article makes provisions for persons with disabilities to live in the community, to choose where and with whom they live, without any discrimination on the basis of disability.

IL is based on a philosophy of equality and independence in decision making, but the concept tends to be wrongly understood on occasions. For example, when IL is incorrectly assumed to be against the concept of interdependency. In that case, IL denies cooperation, collaboration and support between people with and without disabilities (Williams, 1983). These conflicting understandings particularly exist where organizations 'for' persons with disabilities, that is where disabled people are not necessarily represented in the organization management, play a leading role in disability issues (see Chapter 4). However, in reality, IL does not mean people with disabilities doing everything by themselves, in isolation, or without the help of anyone else. Rather, the IL movement demands the same choices and control in everyday lives as non-disabled persons enjoy.

The history of the IL movement now spans more than five decades and has seen a broader social shift in policies from exclusion to inclusion in the community, and from charitable responses to the right to personal assistance services. The first centre for IL (CIL) was established in Berkeley – the birthplace of the IL movement – in 1972. It was run by people with disabilities to promote equal participation in the community. The Boston CIL was opened two years later, with an emphasis on transitional housing and attendant care services (DeJong, 1979). The IL movement was boosted after 1981, the International Year of Disabled Persons (IYDP), and several ILCs have since then been established in the US and elsewhere (Levy, 1988; Pelka, 1997; Shapiro, 1993).

The IL movement in Japan is directly influenced by the concepts and approaches of IL in the US. After the IYDP, Japanese people with disabilities went to the US to learn more about IL and its implementation; the first ILC in Asia was then established in Tokyo in 1986 (Hayashi and Okuhira, 2008). In 1991, the Japan Council on Independent Living (JIL) was established, and by 2000, there were 20 ILCs in the Tokyo metropolitan area and about 60 in other Japanese cities. After first establishing ILCs in Japan, their home country, Japanese IL advocates sought to further expand it to other Asian countries. With the establishment of a number of ILCs, the disability rights movement in Asia has gained momentum in recent decades. The next two case examples show the beginning of the IL movement in Japan (see Box 13.1) and how the model is slowly being implemented in Viet Nam (see Box 13.2).

Box 13.1.   Independent living in Japan

The Human Care Association was established in Japan in 1986 as a day centre for people with disabilities run by people with disabilities themselves. This association later developed into offering different services to address the needs of disabled people, including a personal assistance service for people with disabilities and an IL programme, the first established in Japan. The personal assistance service aimed at empowering people with disabilities to live independent lives, by providing support with activities of daily living such as dressing, cooking, showering and so on. These services were paid through registration fees by members of the ILC, that is, people using the personal assistance services. The IL programme was structured in three parts: (1) IL skills training, (2) peer counselling, and (3) an overseas training programme. The first two, along with the personal assistance services, are common components to ILC around the world.

IL skills training. This training is aimed at enabling persons with disabilities to live independent lives in the community as opposed to lives dependent on their families or at institutions. The training is delivered by a peer counsellor, a person with a disability, and consists of 12 sessions with an average of six to eight trainees. The areas covered in the programme include goal setting, identity establishment, health and medical care, communication with attendants, human relationships, management of money and time, shopping, meal planning and cooking, sexuality and the utilization

(continued)

Box 13.1. Continued

of social resources. Training methods include discussions and role playing, and are supported by a training manual.

Peer counselling. This counselling is provided on an individual basis by a disabled peer counsellor and aims to discuss challenges to leading an independent life in the community.

Overseas training programme. This programme consists of trips to other cities, such as Berkeley in the United States or Adelaide in Australia, to study accessibility in other societies (Nakanishi, 2007).

Box 13.2. Independent living in Viet Nam (Socialist Republic of Vietnam)

Viet Nam (Socialist Republic of Vietnam) has a population of 95 million people, out of which over 5 million live with disabilities. Although the Disability Law of Vietnam came into effect in 2011, its implementation is still in its early development in relation to guidelines for service providers. The development of disability services in the country is in general shaped by international tendencies towards disability in developing countries, such as the employment of community-based rehabilitation (CBR) professionals. The role of social work is also critical in disability service provision in Vietnam with the plan to employ 60,000 social workers to manage disability services from 2012.

In this context, the Hanoi IL centre captures an uncommon approach to disability in the country and offers a unique set of services, to which only a minimal fraction of the Vietnamese disabled population has access. According to the centre director, CBR has a stronger endorsement by the government, professionals and people with disabilities than the philosophy of IL. In 2012, only 57 people with disabilities availed of its services. The centre, based on the Japanese IL model, offers services for people with disabilities, including peer counselling, training on living and working skills (individual capacity building), advocacy skills and personal assistants. The centre receives funding from the government and international donors.

Hoang's story focuses on his experience of IL training at this centre. Hoang learned about IL through a workshop organized by the centre in the locality where he lived, Hai Phong, the third most populous city in Vietnam. He was the first person to avail of a personal assistant in his city of almost 2 million people. Before taking part in IL training, he did not participate in social activities or go out. The personal assistance support enabled him to be more proactive in going out or visiting his friends. The IL training helped him with basic daily tasks that he felt could not manage before and gave him a sense of being in charge of his own life. Hoang had to take a long journey to attend the training in Hanoi, where he joined a group of people with disabilities, some judged by Hoang to be in a worse condition than him, but yet remaining optimistic. The peer counselling session allowed Hoang to share experiences with other disabled people at the training and learn from them (Hanoi Independent Living Centre, 2014).

Challenges to enhancing independent living

Within Asia, the IL movement has been successfully implemented in Japan and South Korea. More recently, IL is being implemented using the Japanese model in other Asian countries (Hayashi and Okuhira, 2008). However, there is over- all relatively little knowledge of IL in this world region (Nakanishi, 2007). Cultural differences, a top-down approach, diversity and poverty, among other factors, pose challenges to the implementation of IL in a manner that is rele- vant to and sustainable in the local context. This section discusses the imple- mentation of IL in the Asian region within various economic, political, social and cultural circumstances.

Cultural differences

Despite the IL movement being effective in a number of developed coun- tries, the same is hardly happening in developing countries. One of the major reasons preventing its successful implementation is the lack of a cultural fit between the IL philosophy and the socio-economic context where IL is being implemented. Several studies, for example, have acknowledged that the con- cept of IL is not being appropriately applied to diverse populations (Fitzgerald, Williamson, Russell and Manor, 2005; Kliewer, Biklen and Kasa-Hendrickson, 2006; Teasley, Baffour and Tyson, 2005). The following case example high- lights some of the existing challenges in implementing IL (see Box 13.3).

However, Hayashi and Okuhira (2008) highlighted many problems in teaching these trainees the concept of IL, claiming that trainees kept strong ties with their families, were not flexible in understanding and adapting to dif- ferent cultural costumes (for example, eating Japanese food, being punctual), and they lacked humility.

Box 13.3.   Independent Living training in the Asia-Pacific region

IL training for young people with disabilities living in the Asia-Pacific region began in Japan in 1999, as part of the Asian and Pacific Decade of Persons with Disabilities (1993–2002) and under the support of the Duskin Ainowa Foundation. The Japanese Society for the Rehabilitation of Persons with Disabilities (JSRPD), which is under the auspices of the Duskin Ainowa Foundation, is the implementing organization of the Duskin Leadership Training Program in Japan (DLTJ, 2014). Since 1999, the JSRPD has invited seven to eight persons every year to attend a 10-month long programme on the evolution of the disability rights movement with a particular focus on the concept of IL (Hayashi and Okuhira, 2008). So far, more than 100 people from over 20 Asian nations have benefitted from this training programme. IL training is conducted in the Japanese language. Trainees are offered a three-month Japanese language course before training commences. Then trainees are provided with an individual training course that mainly includes IL in Japan, the Japanese welfare system and Digital Accessible Information System (DAISY). Following completion of the IL training programme, some people with disabilities have attempted to establish ILCs as an NGO in their home countries.

It may have a negative impact if we neglect the cultural differences of each nation and attempt to impose the so-called 'Japanese' or 'Western' concept of IL while disregarding the differences and diversity of cultures. With regard to family ties, Japanese IL implementers often encourage people from other Asian nations to leave their families and live separately as a first stage in applying IL. This may be considered IL in Japan but may not be applicable to other contexts where, regardless of disability status, people often live with their extended family.

Connected to the latter point, individuals with disabilities coming to Japan for leadership training were sending their allowances to their family back home, which Hayashi and Okuhira (2008) considered to be a hindrance to achieving IL for the disabled person. The mutual benefit between individuals with disabilities and their families cannot be allowed to be an obstacle for the IL of people with disabilities. This is particularly the case in the resource-poor situation of countries where state support is absent or poorly available; family support is much more crucial in the independence of people with disabilities (see Chapter 12, on livelihoods and Chapter 15, supporting family carers). Even developed countries with strong social welfare systems in place are facing challenges to provide disability pensions and universal health care, and this is certainly a major challenge in poor economies. A crucial issue is, of course, how strong the countries' economies are (see Chapter 6 on disability and poverty).

The question is who is responsible for the financial arrangements when the state is not in the position to support the living expenses? By encouraging people to live separately from their extended family, it is unclear how family support can be provided. Alternatively, IL implementation may involve empowering people with disabilities to enforce their rights and responsibilities, so they can work toward raising awareness on disability, starting from their families and moving onto the communities where they live, ensuring families understand people's impairments, avoiding any kind of disability-based discrimination and being included in all forms of household decision making. With the mutual family support, regardless of disability status, lives may become easier and interdependent.

I was also one of the JSRPD trainees. From my experience as a trainee in the past, one of the biggest barriers of the training programme was language. Hayashi and Okuhira (2008) have also acknowledged that language is a common issue for the trainees, which poses challenges to learn about IL in Japan. However, their argument goes on to indirectly claim that trainees have to follow a Japanese model, understand Japanese culture and even learn these all through the Japanese language if they are to successfully implement IL in their respective home countries.

Yet cultural differences within countries may add further challenges to its implementation. For example, Japan has a homogenous population and as a country can more effectively implement one policy throughout the nation. In contrast, Nepal, with more than 120 ethnic groups and languages, may not be able to implement the same policy to cover all groups. Hayashi and Okuhira (2008) state that trainees with disabilities from Asian developing countries coming to Japan were less flexible in adapting to the Japanese culture. However, it is equally important to acknowledge that Japan, being a country with a homogenous population, is likely to have less understanding of diversity.

One may regard cases like this as a globalized localism, an imposition of the concept of IL that fits within a particular culture into other cultural contexts. It is counterproductive if we attempt to impose culture-specific successful practices in other cultures while disregarding the fact that their cultures and customs have equally important values which cannot be overlooked. The export of the Western concept of IL that fails to consider the local context may result in failure.

Institutionalization

In countries with developed economies, such as the US or Japan, institutionalization of people with disabilities was a common social response to disability until well into the 20th century. Institutional lives were characterized by lack of control over the smallest decisions, medicalization, lack of freedom and privacy, and physical and psychological abuse. Despite the too often atrocious conditions of institutional living, people were able to share those days of confinement with others and, in exceptional cases, have access to education. Segregated living and special schooling even resulted in some groups of visually impaired people and Deaf people becoming united and demanding their right to participate in their communities.

The ongoing model of IL trains people with disabilities in developing countries to fight against institutionalization, which is an appropriate measure in line with the CRPD. In countries where traditionally disabled people have not been institutionalized, however, their confinement happens at home, with their family looking after them in the best of cases but lacking access to education, employment, training and all too often without hope for a better future. In these cases, access to basic services should be prioritized over efficiently managing their work and debating who should be in the driving seat of their lives. The lack of cultural and historical synergies between societies where the IL movement flourished and those where it is being adopted may explain some of the difficulties in successfully implementing the model. It is relevant to note that more than 80 per cent of people with disabilities live in low- and middle-income countries (ILO, 2007). However, most disability programmes and strategies are created by developed countries.

Poverty and resource-poor environments

According to World Health Organization and World Bank (2011), persons with disabilities make up nearly 15 per cent of the global population and represent one of the poorest and most marginalized segments of society (ILO, 2007; DFID, 2000). It is also estimated that disabled people make up 15 to 20 per cent of the poor in developing countries (Elwan, 1999). Although there are multiple factors contributing to poverty among people with disabilities, poor and unequal access to education or employment and the unequal distribution of other resources are likely to be among the major causes (Lamichhane, Paudel and Kartika, 2014) (see Chapter 6 for a discussion on disability and poverty).

The relationship between poverty and disability is complex, as both may correlate to each other (Lamichhane et al., 2014). On one hand, because of the poor financial conditions of some families, people with disabilities are likely to be deprived of basic facilities, for example access to education and health care, and might rely on their family for subsistence. On the other hand, there may be a possibility that, when families engage in caring for their disabled members, their income level may be reduced considerably, consequently making both people with disabilities and their families poor (see Chapter 15). The prevalence rate of disability is also higher in those countries with higher rates of poverty.

According to Hayashi and Okuhira (2008), the services offered by Japanese ILCs – mainly peer counselling and a personal attendant programme – are covered by charging fees. Is this model feasible in low-income countries where there is no welfare state and only a few disabled people may get small monthly allowances? Are individuals with disabilities in a position to pay for services through ILCs? And are the implementing agencies of IL effective enough to offer services to their fellow disabled citizens within these economic constraints?

Other barriers to the implementation of IL

In this section, I consider additional barriers to the implementation of IL: inaccessibility, intellectual disability and disability stigma.

Inaccessibility of infrastructures. Transportation systems and environments with high barriers of access make it difficult for disabled people to navigate their communities; this is even more accentuated in rural areas. This problem is made even more difficult with the lack of disability support systems, such as personal assistance schemes and assistive technologies. Even when such services are available, people with disabilities may not be able to afford paying for them. Under such circumstances, even though there is increasing awareness of the IL movement, there is still a long journey ahead for the development of ILCs in terms of their expansion in the rural areas of low-income countries.

Intellectual disability. Article 19, 'Living independently and being included in the community', of the CRPD emphasizes the independence and freedom of choice for living by people with disabilities. Despite the CRPD being an important landmark achievement towards promoting and protecting the human rights of people with disabilities, IL, particularly for those with intellectual disabilities in developing countries, fails to be a priority. Most of the activities of IL are focused on people with physical impairments. For instance, among the training programmes of JSRPD for Asian young people with disabilities, they have not yet designed programmes focusing on intellectual disability. Primarily, the care of these individuals lies with their family members.

In more affluent countries, although the majority of people with intellectual disabilities still live with their families or in group settings, there is an increasing number of people with intellectual disabilities living independently in what is called 'supported living'. This option offers people with intellectual disabilities the possibility to live in an accessible home while having access to 24-hour support on an individual needs basis. It is an intermediate option between 24-hour supported medical care and independent living. Some people have support workers helping them with activities of daily living such as cooking, paying bills, coordination of services, administration of medication and ensuring their health, safety and well-being, whereas others receive support to travel to and join different activities such as work, education courses or leisure programmes. The support intensity, that is the time supporters work with people with intellectual disabilities, also varies according to individual needs. The following case illustrates this concept (see Box 13.4).

Disability stigma. Yeo and Moore (2003) report that in some developing countries, the belief persists that disability is associated with evil, witchcraft, bad omens or infidelity (see Chapter 5). Such a biased belief is one of many other reasons to negatively affect the social inclusion and economic empowerment of disabled people. Additionally, the misunderstanding of disability encourages people to perceive that a functional bodily limitation or impairment is a problem of the individual. This negative understanding of impairment hinders the removal of disabling barriers, which is required to facilitate IL of individuals with disabilities. Discrimination resulting from stigma and negative attitudes towards disability is detrimental to the smooth expansion and implementation of the IL movement.

Conclusions and future directions

People with disabilities, scholars in disability studies and other stakeholders do not diverge much on their opinions of the importance of IL. However, the crucial issue is how to strengthen it through the effective utilization of limited resources. Although the concept of IL has been instrumental in shifting the focus of disability issues from the individual to society, as well as in

---

Box 13.4.   Independent Living and people with intellectual disability in Ireland

A 65-year-old Irish man with intellectual disability recently moved from a group home, where he had lived with other people, to his own apartment. He had previously lived in a total of four group homes and before that, in two institutions; in one he shared a dorm with 30 other men when he was 16 years old, and he shared the second with 35 other men. He notes he could not sleep properly and had no privacy in those places. In 2009, despite it not being his own choice, he moved to the house where he lives now. He expresses great satisfaction at being able to do whatever he wants and having the house to himself. He says that additional pleasure is gained by being his own boss and not having anyone tell him what to do. He receives support from staff to do his grocery shopping, pay his bills and meet his medical needs. Support staff also help him to go out for dinner and drive him into town at the weekends.

considering disability from a human rights-based perspective, some of the reasons why it continues to have a weaker presence in developing countries are the lack of cultural adaptations, coupled with a lack of resources and underlined by a persistent charity approach.

In countries like the US or Japan, IL has expanded, as these countries already have in place the foundations of equal opportunities for people with disabilities. However, the same is not the case in low- and middle-income countries in the Asian region. The marginalization experienced by people with disabilities in social, economic and political activities across countries in Africa, Asia and Latin America, where lack of education and employment is the norm for disabled people, is much more serious than in developed countries. They are not only facing challenges in access and quality of education but are also disproportionately unemployed, underemployed and underpaid. However, it is equally important for countries to develop policies and support provisions based on the CRPD so that people with disabilities can enjoy living independently and being included in the community.

Though some developed nations offer financial aid and material goods, and even send representatives to organize seminars on IL, these may be not enough to run ILCs in developing countries. Holding seminars can empower some people with disabilities but cannot reach many of them who live in rural areas. Because support from developed countries may not be sustainable, people with disabilities should encourage their governments to prepare a conducive environment for their community living, for example by supporting independent living through adjacent houses or annexes to the family home where people with disabilities can live next to their families, enabling people with disabilities to avail of support while keeping independence, and by supporting the contribution of people with disabilities to their household income, using strategies such as micro-credits (see Chapter 11).

Although the theoretical concept of IL has taken considerable shape, concrete strategies to promote the social inclusion and economic empowerment of people with disabilities still have to be implemented in many parts of the world. This process requires collaboration between the valuable insights of NGOs, the resources of policymakers and people with disabilities themselves. Empowering people with disabilities to achieve independence and improve their quality of life is a step towards IL. However, without first providing access and opportunities to critical services such as education, healthcare and the labour market, the empowerment of people with disabilities may not be possible. In the developed nations, education for children with disabilities was made compulsory more than 50 years ago. In these countries, almost 99 per cent of people, regardless of disability status, are literate or educated. However, the same is not the case for low- and middle-income countries. Given the limited resources of low-income countries, one can ask where resources should be primarily spent: should the focus be on education or on other programmes such as microfinance, or changing people's attitudes and building barrier-free infrastructures? We should not look for a single answer to these questions, as these factors are all interconnected towards achieving independence of people with disabilities. For example, without improved accessibility, people with severe impairments remain deprived of basic social services such as education and healthcare, and are deterred from enjoying living independently in the community.

In this sense, it is important to develop comprehensive policies toward bringing disability issues into the framework of sustainable and inclusive development as well as making people with disabilities dignified members of the society.

Summary of key points

- Independent living (IL) has grown and expanded over the years through the work of disability activists. It is endorsed by the CRPD in Article 19, 'Living independently and being included in the community'.
- Despite the growing attention to IL on a global level, its expansion within the Asian region is limited.
- The implementation of IL in cultural contexts different to the one where it was developed faces several challenges, including cultural differences, poverty and inequality, the stigma attached to disability, inaccessible infrastructures, and lack of attention to people with intellectual disabilities.
- Besides modifying the concept of IL to meet contextual differences, it is equally important that countries provide basic access to education and employment for people with disabilities in line with the CRPD; thus ultimately empowering them to take a leadership role in all processes, including decision making.

STUDY QUESTIONS

1. What living options are available to disabled people in your own country? If disabled people avail of independent living services, what cultural adaptations have been made to the services? If disabled people do not live independently, what are the major challenges for the implementation of IL?
2. How can IL be strengthened within the circumstances of limited resources?
3. What role can and should the international community play to support the effective implementation of IL in low- and middle-income countries?

Further reading and resources

Asia-Pacific Network for Independent Living Centres: http://apnil.org/
Duskin Leadership Training in Japan: http://www.normanet.ne.jp/~duskin/english/index.html
European Network on Independent Living: http://www.enil.eu/

Independent Living in Japan: http://homepage2.nifty.com/ADI/
Independent Living in Latin America: http://www.independentliving.org/docs6/berman
   -bieler.html
Independent Living Institute: http://www.independentliving.org/
Independent Living Institute Library: http://www.independentliving.org/library.html
The African view of Independent Living: http://www.independentliving.org/docs6/
   malinga2003.html
The Disability rights and independent living movement: http://bancroft.berkeley.edu/
   collections/drilm/
C. Willig Levy. (1998). A people's history of the independent living movement, http://
   www.independentliving.org/docs5/ILhistory.html

People with Disabilities Entering the Third Age

Philip McCallion
Mary McCarron

1. States Parties recognize the right of persons with disabilities to an adequate standard of living for themselves and their families, including adequate food, clothing and housing, and to the continuous improvement of living conditions, and shall take appropriate steps to safeguard and promote the realization of this right without discrimination on the basis of disability. ... 2 (b) To ensure access by persons with disabilities, in particular women and girls with disabilities and older persons with disabilities, to social protection programmes and poverty reduction programmes.

**UN Convention on the Rights of Persons with Disabilities
Article 28: Adequate standard of living and social protection**

State Parties shall (b) Provide those health services needed by persons with disabilities specifically because of their disabilities, including early identification and intervention as appropriate, and services designed to minimize and prevent further disabilities, including among children and older persons.

**UN Convention on the Rights of Persons with Disabilities
Article 25: Health**

Introduction

The United Nations Convention on the Rights of People with Disabilities sets out a series of principles important for all people with disabilities that apply regardless of age (see Chapter 3). An especially vulnerable group in older age are those with intellectual and developmental disabilities (I/DD). However national and international policy aspirations about the type of life possible for people with I/DD appear to be very similar across the adulthood years, rather than tied to specific age groups.

Regardless of levels of economic development, the maturity and extensiveness of service systems, countries around the world share a universal desire as people with I/DD age, for them to experience quality health care, social inclusion, meaningful occupation, choice, self-direction, family support and engagement, and avoidance of institutionalization (Bigby, McCallion and McCarron, 2014; Kwok, Cui and Li, 2011; Lecomte and Mercier, 2008; Njenga, 2009; Parmenter, 2008; Perkins and Moran, 2010; Temple and Stanish, 2008). Thus any review of ageing in people with I/DD must consider the extent to which these principles and goals are being addressed, the barriers to be overcome and the unique issues for people with I/DD that will make attainment difficult.

Among the unique issues they face as they age are (1) the different ageing profile of people with I/DD as compared to the general population, (2) balancing unique needs – particularly health and support needs – with continued access and participation in mainstream community life, (3) understanding the roles of families and (4) resources and readiness to support people with I/DD as they age, particularly in nations where people with I/DD did not survive into old age or where services and supports overall for people with I/DD are in the early stages of development.

A different ageing profile

People with mild I/DD in developed countries are now reported to have a life expectancy close to that of the general population, but differences still exist for those with more severe impairments or specific genetic syndromes. In Australia people with mild (74 years), moderate (67.6 years) and severe (58.9 years) levels of impairment are living/surviving much closer to the population median of 78.6 years (Bittles et al., 2002). Given similar increases in longevity in the United States, Factor, Heller and Janicki (2012) estimated that between 2010 and 2030, the number of people aged over 60 years with I/DD will almost double from 850,6000 to 1.4 million. In Ireland the National Intellectual Disability Database has documented a 60 per cent growth from 1996 to 2010 in those over age 55 years (Kelly and Kelly, 2011). Less is known about the ageing of people with I/DD in developing countries given low levels of services to which people may be connected and less systematic assessment approaches (Kwok, Cui and Li, 2011; Njenga, 2009). However, in their general populations increasing numbers of people are living to much older ages (Kaneda, 2006), which probably means that there is also a growing ageing population with I/DD (Janicki, 2009).

People ageing with I/DD are a diverse group with some experiencing age-related health conditions relatively early. For people with Down syndrome, there is higher prevalence and earlier onset of age-related sensory and musculoskeletal disorders and an exceptional risk of developing dementia, both of which may result in additional disabilities (Bittles, Bower, Hussain and Glasson, 2007; Holland, 2000; Torr, Strydom, Patti and Jokinen, 2010). Additional health needs for people with a range of I/DD also stem from the interaction of ageing and secondary conditions associated with their impairment, its progression or as the consequence of long-term poor-quality health care (Haveman et al., 2009). As they age, many people with cerebral palsy, for example, report reduced mobility, increased pain, and bowel and bladder problems, probably a result of the long-term effects of muscle tone abnormalities and overuse of some joints and immobility of others (Bigby, McCallion and McCarron, 2014). Immobility, small body size, poor diet and prolonged use of anti-convulsant drugs may also contribute to early and increased risk of osteoporosis, falls and fractures (Foran, McCarron and McCallion, 2013). Largely unexplored is the effect of polypharmacy – the taking of multiple medications – in older age, but this is likely to be an issue more for individuals in developed than in developing countries. In developing countries, further unresearched impacts on older age are poor nutrition and absent or inadequate health care (Adnams, 2010; Girimaji and Srinath, 2010; Parmenter, 2008).

Different patterns of ageing among people with different etiologies, differences across levels of intellectual impairment and differences from the general population have encouraged attention to both different patterns in multi-morbidity and its consequences for older age in people with I/DD (McCarron, McCallion, Reilly and Mulryan, 2014), as well as the consequences of poor access and inadequate healthcare (Bigby, McCallion and McCarron, 2014). Recent data from the United Kingdom on premature death among people with I/DD (Heslop et al., 2013) has highlighted the importance of this issue in all countries.

Premature ageing

A research focus on premature ageing among people with I/DD has proven to be a double-edged sword. On the one hand it has reflected unique patterns of ageing, particularly evident in people with Down syndrome, where features such as onset of dementia symptoms, appear earlier (McCarron et al., 2014). Such highlighting in developed countries challenges mainstream services to re-examine criteria such as age 60 and 65 years as eligibility cut-offs for ageing-focused services. However, it has also led to a tendency to obscure middle age for people with I/DD, and to simply regard people in their 40s or 50s as old (Bigby, McCallion and McCarron, 2014). This tendency is a disservice to the individuals themselves and one that may encourage developing countries to neglect the middle-age stage of life. Given an ever further extending old age in the general population there are efforts to postpone designation as 'aged' and to differentiate between young, middle and old-old (Zanjani, Schaie and Willis, 2006). Insistence on ageing beginning in the age 40's and 50's for people with I/DD means potentially an even longer old age for them and may support a lack of, rather than an increased attention, to this stage of life.

Evenhuis and her colleagues (2012) in the Netherlands challenge the notion of premature ageing. They argue that although people with I/DD have a pattern of age-related health vulnerabilities that differ from the general population, this is more about their frailty – that is high vulnerability to adverse health conditions – rather than to ageing itself. They found that people with

I/DD at age 50–64 had a prevalence of frailty (11 per cent) similar to that of the general population aged at 65 years and older (7–9 per cent). However, they argued that rather than irreversible premature ageing, high levels of frailty among people with I/DD were associated with potentially preventable and reversible factors including very low levels of physical activity, social relationships and community participation (Hilgenkamp, Reis, Wijck and Evenhuis, 2012; Schoufour, Echteld and Evenhuis, 2012). These are preventable and reversible factors that should be addressed as priorities in middle and older age. Such findings have important implications for nations and for the design of services, regardless of their level of economic development, and may indeed encourage developing nations to husband scarce resources and invest more in prevention and health promotion approaches rather than the more expensive treatment and care management approaches favoured by developed nations (Kaneda, 2006).

People with I/DD: Ageing with disadvantages

Data gathered in developed countries suggest that people with I/DD embark on the ageing process from a particularly disadvantaged position in terms of health and greater risk of adverse outcomes. During both child-and adulthood they are more likely to have lived in poverty, have poorer physical and mental health, and have lived unhealthy and sedentary lifestyles than the general population. Moreover they are less likely to have benefitted from preventative health screening or other health promotion measures (McCallion, Ferretti and Kim, 2013). Higher rates of obesity, nutritional problems and cholesterol, and lower rates of physical activity all potentially increase the chances in later life of diseases such as diabetes, hypertension, heart disease and arthritis (Bigby, McCallion and McCarron, 2014; McCallion et al., 2013a). These are diseases of both affluent and increasingly of less affluent countries. Although similar data are not yet collected in less developed nations, poorer health is likely to be similar, if not higher, for people with I/DD. Such chronic conditions also reduce quality of life as well as higher risk for mortality and increased morbidity.

The life experiences of adults with I/DD are also characterized by economic and social exclusion (see Chapter 6). Low rates of employment (Bigby, McCallion and McCarron, 2014) mean limited opportunities to accumulate wealth and a heavy reliance on government income support schemes that are close to or below poverty lines (see Chapter 12). In developed countries, this means an absence of funds to secure access to private health and social care systems and dependence on public health and welfare systems. Their social exclusion results in small and deficient informal networks to offer instrumental support, social participation, emotional well-being, individual advocacy and negotiation of formal services. They are also less likely to have married or had children, meaning they do not have the relatives that provide the bulk of care for older people, and unlike other single or childless groups do not have compensatory robust networks of close friends (McCallion, Ferretti and Kim, 2013a; McCallion, Swinburne, Burke, McGlinchey and McCarron, 2013b).

These challenges are even more onerous in developing countries where public systems of support are not well developed or accessible to the majority of the population (Lecomte and Mercier, 2008; Kaneda, 2006; Wong, Gerst, Michaels-Obregon and Pallino, 2011), and informal family and community supports are overwhelmed by other financial and social pressures.

Balancing unique needs with continued community access and participation

To better understand the challenges in ageing for people with I/DD, it is necessary to explore (1) their changing physical and mental health status, (2) their use of health services, (3) their social networks and supports including living arrangements and income available and (4) their experience of personally defined quality of life.

Changing physical and mental health status. Throughout the age range, individuals with I/DD have a greater variety of health care needs compared to those of the same age and gender in the general population (McCallion et al., 2013a), which may vary by level and type of disability (Moss, 1993). Van Schrojenstein Lantaman-De Valk, Metsemakers, Haveman and Crebolder (2000) compared 318 people with ID receiving health care within a general practice with others and found that people with learning (I/DD) disabilities had 2.5 times the health problems of those without such lifelong disabilities. These conditions were highly influenced by a lack of information, lack of exercise, poor mobility, poor eating habits, and medication use (for a review, see Haveman et al., 2009).

Among the population of adults with I/DD, there is also a reported high point prevalence rate (more than one-third) of mental health problems (Cooper, Smiley, Morrison, Williamson and Allan, 2007). Bhaumik, Tyrer, McGrother and Ganghadaran (2008) also highlighted higher psychiatric morbidity among elderly (compared with younger) adults with I/DD. Social, cultural, environmental and developmental factors (Hastings, Hatton, Taylor and Maddison, 2004; Day and Jancar, 1994), and the consequences of polypharmacy and inadequate review of prescribed medications (Mikkelsen, 2007) are reported to have significant impact on the expression of both psychiatric and behavioural disorders in older people with I/DD. In developing countries, there is less concern about polypharmacy, with more critical issues around lack of diagnosis, use of inappropriate rather than too many medications and a greater likelihood that mental health concerns are considered simply part of the experience of having an I/DD, with even greater adverse consequences for quality of life.

Health service needs. There has been controversial evidence in various countries that the experience of poor health and early mortality among people with I/DD may be related to the location and to the types and quality of health care services that people with I/DD receive (see for example Strauss, Kastner and Shavelle, 1998, Heslop et al., 2013; McCallion and McCarron, 2013b). The following have also been reported (see McCallion et al., 2013a, for a review):

- People with I/DD are more likely (compared to the general population) to lead unhealthy lifestyles and not to access health promotion and health screening services, contributing to physical ailments in later life.
- Health problems of persons with I/DD are not recognized, and reliance on their health management by proxy (family members and care staff) increases access barriers and the likelihood that health needs identified at screening are not subsequently met.
- People with I/DD, as compared to peers without identified disability, have higher levels of obesity, have a more sedentary lifestyle, participate less in physical activity and are more likely to consume high-fat diets prepared by poorly trained staff and family members.
- Health promotion programmes are seldom targeted at people with ID, yet they have been shown to increase disease prevention and case finding. There is a lack of specialist knowledge and training amongst multidisciplinary team members such as therapists, social workers and psychologists.

In less developed countries, disease screenings and health promotion are less available, presenting challenges for population health overall (Wong et al., 2011). As nations, developed and developing, seek to reorient themselves toward more of a chronic disease prevention approach in response to growing ageing populations (Kaneda, 2006), additional efforts to include ageing persons with I/DD must be recognized and planned for (see Chapter 10 on inclusive health).

Social networks and supports. Community living and integration for people with I/DD is a relatively new phenomenon given the institutional approaches that have dominated in more developed, usually Western countries. Contemporary service policy and provision under the continuing influence of normalization (Nirje, 1969) and later, Social Role Valorization (Wolfensberger, 1985), continues to ensure the movement of people from institutional, congregated settings into the community and is committed to the community maintenance of those living in family care (Janicki, Dalton, McCallion, Baxley and Zendell, 2005). Yet, there are also reports of people with I/DD moving to institutional settings as they age (Bigby, McCallion and McCarron, 2014) despite findings for those living in community settings of increased adaptive behaviour, better health, and improved quality of life (McCallion et al., 2013a).

If ageing presents increased health needs, the challenge is to ensure that counterbalancing services assure opportunities for community living and quality lives as these promote better health (see Chapter 13 on independent living). Independent, successful ageing and retirement for the general population is usually supported by pensions, other financial resources, good health and health care, social networks and family supports (McCallion et al., 2013b). Such resources are not as available to people with ID. The absence of children and spouses and accrued retirement income, which is the reality for almost all persons with I/DD, means that community maintenance and participation in older age will be more difficult. In addition, as the family carers of adults with I/DD themselves age beyond their caring capacity, additional formal supervised living arrangements need to be developed, but there are questions about their affordability (Bigby, McCallion and McCarron, 2014). Even in countries with well-developed residential networks such as the United States and the United Kingdom, increased longevity among those already living there means that fewer places are becoming free over time. How then will ageing lives be supported?

The issue is further complicated by more recent questioning of the absolute value of community living. It is argued that the data actually highlight that community presence is easier to achieve than community integration, and although movement of people with I/DD into the community has successfully occurred, achieving actual integration has not (Verdonschot, de Witte, Reichrath, Buntinx and Curfs, 2009). But such questions, rather than permitting a return to institutions, instead challenge whether the community-based system of care developed in mainly Western countries for adults with I/DD is fit for purpose when it comes to ageing and whether it is an appropriate model to emulate in developing countries.

The concept of continuing community integration of adults with I/DD is poorly understood and deserves to be considered in a manner similar to that of ageing the general population. Placing value on relationships with families, and peers, and further exploring of the 'sense of community' for people with I/DD as they age is warranted (see case example, Box 14.1).

In addition, the prevalent negative perceptions in many countries of the ageing services for the general population held by disability providers and advocates, and outright ageism, are actually producing protective attitudes among I/DD staff towards their ageing consumers, thereby supporting a self-serving

---

Box 14.1.   Daily life in a developing country: The case of Bao

Bao is a 54-year-old man with I/DD, living in a rural community with his widowed mother. Their hut and its small piece of land where they grow some vegetables are on a corner of a small family farm that now belongs to his oldest brother.

Mother: Bao is a good boy and my oldest son is also a good man, one who understands his obligations to his mother. His wife thinks that they should not have obligations to Bao ... it is enough that they will take care of me in my old age ... she doesn't understand why he is still here ... She is not bad person ... it's just that most families would not have kept a son like Bao ... he might not have lived in another family ... or he would have gone to an orphanage ... one more mouth to feed and for why? ... he would not be able to contribute to the farm they would think ... We had some good seasons, good crops those first few years ... there was enough food ... and then while he never was as good on the farm as our other sons ... he grew strong ... he didn't complain ... he does not speak much ... and he listened ... sometimes other boys teased him and he would get angry ... he could break things when he was angry but he's quieter now. ... Neither of us is much help on the farm now, but Bao carries water for me and he will help his brother. ... There aren't many people on the farms anymore ... young people are all going to the city ... the old ways are being forgotten ... I'm glad I'm so old; maybe I will die before I'm forgotten ... maybe Bao will too.

desire to continue to maintain these individuals within the I/DD services. Rather, an openness to new types of supports, engagement with service provision for other older adults and a more shared view of the attributes of successful ageing (see for example, Rowe and Kahn, 1998) are needed. These have the potential to support improved cross-system responses, more affordable supports and approaches that may be implemented more readily in multiple countries.

Understanding and supporting the role of families

The role of family in the lives of people with I/DD is complex. Even in societies with well-developed out-of-home care, there have always been a large number of people with I/DD living with their family (McCallion and Kolomer, 2003). There are also some individuals who are living with spouses/partners and living independently with informal or formal supporters. In countries without extensive residential systems, almost everyone is living with family, with some living independently. There is also a great likelihood that where there are cultural expectations of family care and concerns for the welfare/safety of the person with I/DD, such family caring is well established. However, changing family demographics, including declines in birth rates and family sizes, economic concerns and rural to urban transitions, are all straining family caring (Jackson, Howe and Nakashima, 2011; McCallion, 2006). Another concern in developed countries is that existing services systems – for example those in the United States, United Kingdom, Netherlands and Australia – reflect the values and experiences of the traditional population. Growing minority populations often reflect more familial rather than the individualistic values underlying advocacy and service delivery perspectives (McCallion and Grant-Griffin, 2000). To the extent that there will be greater diversity in populations of older adults with I/DD in developed countries, there is likely to be demand for different types of services.

Popular conceptions are that caregiving families are likely to include younger persons, persons with less severe levels of I/DD and persons who do not present significant health and care issues. Yet there are findings, for example regarding dementia care, where families are coping with care needs at least as pressing and demanding as those in group home facilities (McCallion, Nickle and McCarron, 2005). Although there are reported trends for increased placement of people with I/DD later in life (see for example Kelly and Kelly, 2013), this seems driven more by life transitions, including death or infirmity among older family caregivers, than by needs of the person with I/DD (Lightfoot and McCallion, 2015).

When parents die, siblings or more distant relatives, such as nephews, nieces and cousins, are their closest family members. There have been suggestions that despite such relatives having close relationships and an interest in advocacy and service coordination, they are less ready to replace the 'caring for' primary care role played by parents (Bigby, 1997). However, more recent longitudinal follow-up and secondary data analyses have confirmed that siblings are stepping in and assuming such care in very large numbers (Fujiura, 2012; Zendell, 2011). The long-term ability of siblings to continue such roles in the face of declining birth rates, geographic mobility and multiple caregiving demands remains to be established (McCallion and Kolomer, 2003). There are also new challenges for carers given the increased ageing of people with I/DD.

Siblings have always played a role in the care of their family members with intellectual disability (McCallion and Toseland, 1993). Burke, Taylor, Urbano and Hodapp (2012) report data that female siblings in close relationships with or living close to their brother or sister are more likely to assume higher levels of caregiving when parents are no longer able. However Zendell (2011), in a national survey sample, found a much fuller range of caregiving roles for siblings, regardless of gender. In addition, there are changing gender roles among parents. Traditionally, women were the primary caregivers while fathers worked. These gender patterns are now changing. An important concern, therefore, is not to stereotype families and fathers as there is evidence that fathers feel isolated and judged by assumptions that caregiving is a mother's role (McCallion and Kolomer, 2003; Fujiura, 2012). Unexplored is the extent to which there are changing gender roles in less developed countries.

As nations consider how they will afford expanding formal systems of old age supports, an important policy concern will be the support of family carers, where such supports will be located in service systems and how they will be calibrated to account for the reality that available family members will decline in number (Kaneda, 2006; Lightfoot and McCallion, 2015). In developed countries, the care of ageing persons with I/DD and supports for their caregivers have remained largely within the purview of disabilities service providers. This is now changing. For example, in the United States, National Family Caregiver programmes funded by the Administration on Ageing/Administration on Community Living have included such family caregivers of people with I/DD as a targeted population for agencies that traditionally serve older adults (see also Chapter 15, supporting family carers).

Transition Challenges. When persons with I/DD were not expected to live into old age, there was a reasonable expectation that parents would outlive their offspring and offer a lifetime of care. Instead, ageing parents now increasingly cope with their own health problems and eventual death (Heller and Factor, 1991). Parents are often averse to creating detailed future care plans for their adult children with intellectual/developmental disabilities (Bigby, McCallion and McCarron, 2014), including speaking of future living arrangements with other family members (McCallion and Kolomer, 2003).

There are five types of long-term plans:

- *Explicit succession plans* formally transferring the responsibilities of overseeing care of the adult with I/DD to an appointed person;
- *Implicit succession plans*, where it is largely unstated but expected or hoped for that there will be someone willing to assume transfer of the responsibilities of overseeing care of the adult with I/DD;
- *Financial plans* where, independent of who will manage care, there will be financial arrangements to cover some of the costs;

- *Residential plans* for where the person will live in the future; and
- *Guardianship plans* that address decision making and consent on behalf of the person with I/DD. This is an area where legal requirements vary across nations; families may have different beliefs and expectations than legal authorities; and where there may be conflicts with rights of the individual to be treated as a self-determining adult.

A new issue in developed countries will be in helping families to understand that the future may not be about movement to an out-of-home setting for their relative (see Box 14.2). Instead, they will need help to explore continued maintenance in their existing home; accessing of services for both the individual with I/DD and for themselves; involvement of other family members,

---

Box 14.2. Family in a developed country – Sadie

Sadie, a 60-year-old woman with Down syndrome, has always lived in the family home, originally with both parents and two sisters, but then only with her father during the last eight years of his life. Now she lives alone in the family home and attends a day programme three days per week for four hours each day.

Sadie: It has always been my house ... When Mam was alive, she wanted my sisters to take care of me and live with me. Dad always said this would be my home. Then Mam died and my sisters got married. Dad retired and we just lived here. We'd go for car rides and do the shopping together. I liked that. Dad wanted me to go to a workshop. I didn't like that. I stopped going. He said okay. Then he died. My sister Penny said she'd help. She said I could live with her, but this is my house ... Dad promised ... left me money ... Penny helps ... Fills out forms ... takes me shopping ... It's not the same, but it's okay... She checks on me .... There's a woman, Kate, that comes in sometimes and cleans and makes me dinner ... I think the government pays her ... but it's my house ...

Penny: Yes, I'm her sister, and we all know it's Sadie's house. Dad asked me to help. Services said she could move into a group home – the visiting nurse thought it would be better for her ... but it's not what Sadie wants, and I don't think Dad would have been happy about it ... She can do a lot for herself, but my husband and I take turns to stop by on the way home from work, and I take care of the bills, although most of the expenses are paid out of her disability allowances ... I take her shopping ... The woman next door used to take her to church every Sunday, but she hasn't been well ... We were concerned about her being in the house all day herself with nothing to do ... She never liked going to the workshop, but a new day programme opened, and she goes now a few days a week and has made some friends ... A bus picks her up and takes her back ... Still, it's a lonely life ... My other sister takes her for a week's holidays every year, and we have her over for all the holidays and any family celebrations like her birthday ... but I can't really say she has much contact with people outside of the day programme ... Still, she seems happy with her independence ... She had a fall a few weeks ago ... says she got dizzy ... broke her arm ... We're all very worried ... I talked with services, but there's not much they can do ... They have someone stopping in most days to check on her and make her dinner to be sure she's eating properly ... But it's a worry ...

(continued)

Box 14.2.   Continued

Could this be the start of more concerns? ... I've read about dementia for people with Down syndrome ... They told me there's no waiting list for a place in a group home, but it would probably take two years to happen (sounds like a waiting list to me) ... but I don't know I'd want it anyway ... My husband's always been very good, but he will say he wasn't expecting that Sadie would be part of our retirement ... He's 66 ... Still, who knew she'd live this long and would still be the boss in her own house ... I always knew there'd be responsibilities, and so far we are managing ... It can be lonely at times for Sadie and actually lonely for us too ...

---

neighbours and friends through 'circles of support' (O'Brien and O'Brien, 1998); and the purchasing of services from a range of providers (Hewitt et al., 2010; Bigby, McCallion and McCarron, 2014).

Resources and readiness to support people with I/DD as they age

As people age, changes may be needed to the intensity and nature of the support they require or their daily pattern of activity. These can result, for example, on retirement from a vocational programme. This has resource implications in terms of both cost and skills of staff and must also be sensitive to the needs of co-residents whose needs may be changing at a different rate (Janicki et al., 2005). In developed countries, people who are already living in some form of shared supported accommodation – such as group homes or larger residential facilities – are often faced with inflexible staffing and funding arrangements. They are particularly susceptible to having to move home as they age, when their support needs diverge too far from the original model of services or those of co-residents (Janicki et al., 2005). The degree of change increases vulnerability to moving; those whose support needs were fairly low earlier in life are particularly at risk.

Alternatively, for those who have lived with parents for most of their lives and or who have remained outside the I/DD service system, gaining entry to the system in later life is likely to be difficult both in terms of proving eligibility and because of a high level of unmet demand for community-based support or supported accommodation. More challenging is the risk that services provided are neither appropriate nor consistent with maintaining choice and community living. There is evidence from Australia, for example, that when parents are no longer able to provide primary care, people are being diverted away from the disability service system and may be inappropriately referred to residential aged-care facilities in the absence of other alternatives (Bigby, McCallion and McCarron, 2014). In many developing countries, service systems are underdeveloped, and any such developments are more likely targeted at children and young adults (Kwok, Cui and Li, 2011; Lecomte and Mercier, 2008; Njenga, 2009; Temple and Stanish, 2008). These are also countries where old-age services systems are also in early stages of development (Kaneda, 2006). Here too there may simply not be services to be referred to and/or that referrals will be to resources that are not appropriate.

However, 'services', regardless of country, should not be seen only in terms of out-of-home placement and day programmes. Greater progress on quality health care, physical activity and social connections earlier in the life course may positively influence both the nature and severity of issues that otherwise would impair later life. Similarly, if person-centred, flexible, individualized support were available during adulthood, the challenge of adapting support to meet changed needs as people age may not be as great. Finally, if the focus of remaining in the community was less on building group homes and I/DD-specific formal programmes, and more on supporting people where they have always lived, a greater range of alternatives and greater integration with other ageing-related resources may be possible. In developing countries in particular, these may also be more easily afforded.

Conclusions

Preparation for ageing is a lifelong task. The disadvantageous position from which people with I/DD embark on the ageing process highlights the importance of a life-course perspective to understanding issues associated with ageing and thinking about support needs. Opportunities earlier in the life course for things such as personal development, quality health care and lifestyles, social networks and employment/meaningful activities all impact on the issues likely to confront people as they age. The historic time through which a person has lived, economic constraints and the caring cultures of the nations in which people with I/DD live – all have shaped individual life experiences alongside competing social concerns, thereby producing unique challenges for existing and emerging service systems. These all influence provision and opportunities for people with I/DD as they age and must be addressed or counter-balanced in public policy and practice if the principles in the United Nations Convention on the Rights of People with Disabilities (UN, 2006) are to continue to be addressed.

The unique needs of cohorts of persons who have spent extended periods in out-of-home care are an important concern for public policy in developed countries. Equally, given that a majority of people with I/DD in most developed countries live independently or with family (Braddock et al., 2013; Kelly and Kelly, 2013), policy approaches must also support people with I/DD who live and want to live in genuine community settings where they may have family and neighbourhood networks.

In developing countries, there must be hesitancy to adopt Western 'brick and mortar' residential and day programme options that will exhaust limited resources and emulate a cultural view of I/DD that may not be congruent with their own mores. That said, developing countries must also respond to the challenges of the increasing ageing of their own populations with the likely erosion of prior family structures able to support people with I/DD because of globalization, urbanization and growing economic challenges.

Regardless of level of development, a more sustainable approach is likely to be one that builds towards a healthy and fulfilling older age that is genuinely supported in the community, rather than one that seeks to create or emulate the community and/or only responds to morbidity associated with ageing. If person-centred, flexible, individualized supports become more available during adulthood, the challenge of adapting support to meet changed needs as people age may not be as daunting, because a greater range of supports and alternatives will be available and greater integration with other ageing-related resources may be possible. United Nations principles will then be realized.

Summary of key points

- Increased ageing among people with intellectual disabilities is occurring in both developed and developing countries.
- Realization of the principles of the United Nations Convention on the Rights of People with Disabilities will require new service structures to better support advancing age.
- Developing countries should not feel bound to replicate the services systems in developed countries; neither can afford these service systems going forward, and the individualistic values underpinning them may not be consistent with other countries' values and mores.
- Greater attention is needed to helping people with disabilities, particularly intellectual and developmental disabilities, to age in place and to have the family supports, pensions and other resources to live the lives they desire with prolonged good health.

STUDY QUESTIONS

1. What are the additional health challenges faced by people with intellectual and developmental disabilities as they age, and what is needed to assure better health?

2. What are the respective roles of out of home living arrangements, and of families in supporting people with intellectual and developmental disabilities as they age, and what are the differences in their roles in developing and developed countries?

3. What is different about dementia and its impact for people with intellectual and developmental disabilities as compared to the general population?

Further reading and resources

C. Bigby, P. McCallion and M. McCarron. (2014). 'Serving an elderly population'. In M. Agran, F. Brown, C. Hughes, C. Quirk and D. Ryndak (Eds.), *Equality and Full Participation for Individuals with Severe Disabilities: A Vision for the Future* (Baltimore: Paul H. Brookes), pp. 319–348.

E. Heikkinen. (2003). *What are the main risk factors for disability in old age and how can disability be prevented?* Copenhagen, WHO Regional Office for Europe, Health Evidence Network report; http://www.euro.who.int/document/E82970.pdf.

P. McCallion, J. Swinburne, E. Burke, E. McGlinchey and M. McCarron. (2013). 'Understanding the similarities and differences in ageing with an intellectual disability: Linking Irish general population and intellectual disability datasets.' In R. Urbano (Ed.), *Using Secondary Datasets to Understand Persons with Developmental Disabilities and their Families (IRRDD-45)* (NY: Academic Press).

M. McCarron, P. McCallion, E. Reilly and N. Mulryan. (2014). 'A prospective 14 year longitudinal follow-up of dementia in persons with down syndrome', *Journal of Intellectual Disability Research*, 58(1), 61–70.

Supporting Family Caregivers

Roy McConkey

The family is the natural and fundamental group unit of society and is entitled to protection by society and the State, and that persons with disabilities and their family members should receive the necessary protection and assistance to enable families to contribute towards the full and equal enjoyment of the rights of persons with disabilities.

**UN Convention on the Rights of Persons with Disabilities
Preamble (x)**

Introduction

Internationally, people with disabilities are dependent on family carers. This is especially so in childhood but in most countries their caregiving extends well into adulthood and often for a lifetime. The UN Convention of the Rights of Persons with Disabilities (CRPD) recognizes this in its preamble, but too often the enormous contribution of families to the well-being of persons with disabilities is overlooked and indeed taken for granted. Rather it behoves the world community to proactively support carers so that they are sustained in the common goal of achieving a better life for their relatives and the wider community of persons with disabilities (Kyzar, Turnbull, Summers and Gómez, 2012).

This chapter primarily focuses on carers of people with intellectual and developmental disabilities, although much of the content is applicable with other disabling conditions, whether present from birth or acquired through injury or disease. It starts by outlining some of the challenges facing caregivers internationally. We then examine three strategies of proven worth in creating better lives for caregivers: namely the provision of home-based support, the promotion of parental advocacy and the nurturing of community engagement. Within each of these strategies, we emphasize the importance to family carers of receiving *informational support* that enables them to be better informed about disabilities and the services and supports available. They need to be given *practical supports* that can make the caring role easier. This can range from assistive devices to financial assistance, to breaks from caring. Carers also require *emotional support*, especially when the strains and stresses of caring threaten the health and well-being of mothers particularly.

The concluding section assesses the prospects for giving family carers a fairer deal in the coming decades wherever in the world they live.

The challenges of caregiving

Family carers the world over face multiple disadvantages, but three in particular are worth highlighting. First, many personally experience the stigma of disability that persists in nearly all societies in both overt and covert forms (Ali, Hassiotis, Strydom and King, 2012). Mothers particularly have often borne the blame of giving birth to a defective baby: the consequence of some unidentified sin (see Chapter 5). The resulting guilt can be lifelong, yet remarkably this spurs most parents to devote their lives to caring for a much-loved child often in the face of societal pressures to 'put the child away'. In extreme forms this resulted in infanticide – a dark chapter in even recent human history – but this attitude was expressed also in the era of institutionalization of children that was instigated and perpetuated by the learned doctors of the day.

Globally parents have been to the fore in forcing societies to reappraise their beliefs about disability. Significantly, this was done initially within local communities, which then became a national, and later an international endeavour throughout the decades of the last century. Parental advocacy for social justice resulted in the first ever UN Declaration on the Rights of Persons with Disabilities – that of persons with mental retardation in 1971. Parents can justifiably claim to have pioneered the rights approach to disability, although globally many families still remain trapped in cultural responses that at best perpetuate a charitable ethos (see Chapter 2).

A second challenge facing many family carers is the social exclusion they experience. Faced with antagonistic reactions from both the wider family circle and an unwelcoming community, the withdrawal of parents from social interactions might be viewed as an adaptive response that enables them to forge harmonious relationships within their close family. This protective response is also seen in the continuing desire of some parents around the world to the keep the 'disabled child' hidden and house-bound; a strategy, incidentally, deployed by the British Royal Family in the last century http://en.wikipedia.org/wiki/Prince_John_of_the_United_Kingdom.

A more modern reason for a family's social exclusion arises from the efforts the parents devote to caregiving tasks, which results in little time for other pursuits – including paid employment. The self-sacrificing care provided by family members extends far beyond what professional carers would be expected or could be paid to do, but the consequences can be deleterious for the caregivers and the person for whom they care (Wang, 2012). The lack of social supports acerbates the stresses of caring, resulting in poorer maternal health, which leads to a vicious circle that deepens social isolation

(McConkey, Truesdale-Kennedy, Chang, Jarrah and Shukri, 2008). In these circumstances, parents need the support of others to break out of these potentially malign caregiving practices, but sadly this is often in short supply internationally.

The third handicap that families face is poverty. Internationally, families with a disabled relative feature among the most impoverished, whether the countries are among the richest or the poorest (UNICEF, 2013). Remarkably the reasons are similar across the economic gradient: such as low educational attainment, poorer health, low income and substandard housing. Some solutions have already been noted – reducing stigma and social exclusion. But the prospect of escaping from a life of poverty is dependent on the successful implementation of poverty alleviation strategies aimed at the whole community and from which families and people with disabilities can also benefit. To date there is little evidence that strategies targeted solely at the disabled family are sustainable and effective, no matter how attractive they initially appear (Palmer, 2011) (see Chapter 6 for a discussion on disability and social exclusion and Chapter 12 on Livelihoods).

Despite the disadvantages of stigma, social isolation and poverty, the unsung success of family care is the extent to which many parents rise above these challenges to provide a reasonable life for their relatives. Their self-reliance, determination and sheer hard work make this possible, but more could be done to inculcate and support these caregiving attributes while helping to ensure a better quality of life for carers in the world community (Lunsky, Tint, Robinson, Gordeyko and Oullette-Kuntz, 2014).

Admittedly not all carers can sustain their caring role, and a small minority may neglect or abuse the disabled person (Hughes et al., 2012). There is clear evidence internationally that children with disabilities are at much greater risk of being taken into care than their non-disabled peers, with the added jeopardy of being placed in institutions, a form of provision that still dominates in certain countries across most continents (see Chapter 8). Yet the best alternative to natural families is undoubtedly another family. Hence the rediscovery in the West of fostering and adoption as preferred alternatives to children's homes and residential schools, no matter how well the latter are staffed and resourced. Thus the recruitment and support of alternative family carers is a necessity in modern support services, and not alone for children (Dowling, Kelly and Winter, 2012). Successful schemes based around host families have been used with teenagers and adult persons (McConkey, McConaghie, Roberts and King, 2004). Hence this chapter embraces the contribution of alternative families as well as that of natural parenting.

Various models have evolved to define and explain the caregiving experience (Raina et al., 2004). One of the most pertinent when it comes to reducing the negative impacts experienced by family carers is the support model promoted by Dunst and colleagues (Dunst, Trivette and Deal, 1988). Three inter-linked support strategies for family carers are now considered that have international applicability: home-based support, promoting parental solidarity and community engagement.

Home-based support

In Western countries, one of the success stories of modern disability services has been the advent of home visiting schemes in which a trained worker regularly visits the family to advise and guide the family on coping with the daily challenges of disability. This is particularly so with babies and young children, as parents are best placed to offer early intervention to promote the child's physical, social and cognitive development (Korfmacher et al., 2008). It is well recognized now that parents' continuing contribution to the child's growth and development can outpace that of teachers and therapists (Roberts and Kaiser, 2011).

Initially the focus of home visitors was on the assessment and treatment of the child, but with experience their role has widen considerably, with a shift of emphasis to family-centred supports, including emotional support to mothers and giving advice on other family matters, as well as acting as an advocate for the family (Dunst, Johanson, Trivette and Hamby, 1991). In Northern Ireland for example, families with a preschooler diagnosed as having autism were visited at home for 15 sessions over a nine-month period by a speech and language therapist who guided mothers on activities they could use at home to promote the child's communication and social development. Those children who received the service showed marked gains over a contrast group who received usual services. Moreover, mothers' emotional well-being also showed significant gains from the home visits (McConkey et al., 2010).

Around the same time as the shift to family-centred care was taking place in affluent countries, the World Health Organization started to promote the concept of community-based rehabilitation (CBR) as a means of helping people with disabilities in the developing world (Helander, 1993). Here, too, a trained worker, who may be paid or unpaid, visits the person with a disability at home to show the person and his or her family members what they can do to help their disabled member and to offer the family support and encouragement (see Chapter 16).

In Northern Malawi, for example, community home visitors were recruited from local villages to provide guidance to parents whose children have or are at risk of having an intellectual disability. They were trained and supported by professional staff over 17 days to assess the child's development, identify learning goals and help parents with physiotherapy, and occupational and sensory exercises. All workers were provided with a bicycle, and they travelled from between 1.5 and 5 km to support their families once a week, for around one hour. The number of families each visited varied from between 7 and 12 (average 10). As payment, the home visitors received food supplies rather than cash. In an independent evaluation, parents reported satisfaction with the support received and increased involvement by fathers and siblings in the care of the child. Mothers held positive views of the home visits but noted varied progress in their child's development (Kelly, Ghalaieny and Devitt, 2012).

Although the evidence remains equivocal as to the impact such CBR programmes have on the development of the person with disabilities, there is widespread agreement that they are valued highly by families (Robertson, Emerson, Hatton and Yasamy, 2012). Gallagher (1992) attributed this to 'a new spirit of optimism and encouragement within the family', replacing the despair and feelings of hopeless that usually flow from disability.

In truth, home visitors are not a new concept. The extended family or 'tribe' has often provided an advisor or confidante to new mothers with whom they can discuss their concerns. The home visiting concept builds on this tradition by introducing the family to a person who has particular expertize or interest in the disability. However, cultures vary in their tolerance of an 'outsider' becoming involved in family issues, and services must be sensitive to this when recruiting staff to act as home visitors. Nonetheless, a shared culture is an important prerequisite, especially with immigrant families (Lindsay, King, Klassen, Esses and Stachel, 2012).

The approach of providing personal home-based care is now also widely accepted in developed countries as a means of giving carers extra help at home or short breaks from caring. Formal procedures, underpinned by legislation or policies, have been devised to assess the needs of carers and ensure their needs are met through a family support plan. A range of support services has evolved in richer countries in response to the demands of carers. These schemes recognize the carer as a beneficiary of services, as well as the person with a disability (Ward, 2001). In different parts of the United Kingdom, families caring for children with life-limiting illnesses or disabilities receive a weekly visit of up to three hours, when trained staff look after the child in the home while parents go out, or else the staff lend a hand with housework so parents have time to spend with other children (Social Care Institute for Excellence [SCIE], 2008).

Nevertheless many carers still feel they have to fight for even a modicum of support from statutory services. A national survey of Ireland of carers of people with intellectual disabilities summarized the necessary improvements needed to better meet their needs (Chadwick et al., 2013):

> Families ... provided with flexible and timely support at critical times; being offered services, support, entitlements and information without having to fight for them; knowing that their family member with intellectual disabilities is well cared for, listened to and provided with opportunities to develop and be part of the community; and carers being shown respect, listened to and involved in decisions.
>
> (p. 119)

Supporting family carers

Experience has shown that it is the personal qualities that home visitors bring to the job, rather than the professional background from which they come, that ultimately appear to contribute more to their effectiveness as family supporters. In particular, it is important that home visitors

- **empathize with the culture of the family.** Families are then more accepting and trusting of them when they are recruited from and are respected in their local community;

- **create trusted relationships with the carers.** They provide much needed emotional support to mothers in particular;
- **respond practically to the family's needs.** Parents should experience some immediate benefits from having a home visitor;
- **involve all family members.** Grandparents, siblings and cousins can all be recruited to assist with caring for the relative with disabilities;
- **empower families to be decision makers.** They should share information and expertize freely with families so that families are empowered to make decisions and find solutions to their specific problems;
- **create opportunities for social inclusion.** Home visitors will be able to mobilize local supports for families through their knowledge and contacts in the community.

The role of home supporter can be taken by a range of paid professionals but also by volunteer or unqualified workers following training. Hence the options for finding effective family supporters are available in most communities around the world, although extra efforts may be needed to recruit suitable persons to voluntary or low-paid positions, all of which is compounded by the inevitable turnover which occurs with them. Home support services often cost a fraction of the monies expended in specialist, centre-based services; hence they are particularly attractive in low-income countries. Nevertheless, this approach still struggles for adequate resources against the demands of professionalized services based in hospitals or community health centres.

However, family support services alone are unlikely to meet the needs of all family carers and obviously cannot do so if they do not exist. Thus we turn now to a second strategy: that of building parental advocacy and solidarity.

Parental advocacy and solidarity

When families mobilize together, they can change their communities and maybe even their nation. Certainly the history of disability is replete with the success that parent associations have had in advocating for social justice for their relatives and, in extreme instances, using judicial processes to uphold the rights of their children. Yet international and national success in promoting the rights of children and/or disabled persons does not guarantee their implementation at a local level. Parental advocacy continues to be needed especially with respect to children, although theirs cannot be the sole voice and does not replace the advocacy of persons with disability (see Chapter 4 on advocacy and lobbying). Indeed the potential for conflict between the views of carers and those of their relatives with disabilities need to be recognized and addressed, a point we will come back to later.

By definition, pioneering parents were exceptional people. They tended to be better-educated, articulate, affluent and well-connected in society. And although motivated to get the best for their child, they argued for a better deal for similarly affected families. Invariably they came together with others to share experiences and to join forces in making their views known. The parent association was born. A word of caution though: rarely have parent associations been systematically researched in developed countries – still less in the developing world. Hence the dangers of relying on the vagaries of subjective opinion need to be borne in mind plus the risk of presuming that experiences in one culture are applicable to all. Indeed, in more authoritarian systems community associations may be viewed with suspicion, if not actively discouraged.

Nurturing parent associations

In many countries around the world, the primary form of support for families has come mainly from associations formed and organized by parents. These can function quite informally, for example, parents meet weekly for a social gathering while their children play in community halls, leisure centres or local parks. Others have noted the potential offered by social media in facilitating social contact among carers, which in future years could become more common worldwide (Perkins and LaMartin, 2012).

> Online groups offer several advantages over traditional support groups: the opportunity of participation irrespective of transport issues or geographical location; having a larger group of participants (which would be more restricted in a physical group); greater availability for interaction that is not restricted to specific dates or times; and participants having control over their contributions, privacy, and extent to which they engage with others.
>
> (p. 56)

For the present, though, greater impact arguably can be gained when the parents are encouraged to join an existing association of parents. They now exist to a greater or lesser extent in most countries of the world. If there are none locally, professionals may stimulate parents to come together to form a legally recognized association – see the Case Study from Zanzibar (Box 15.1).

Box 15.1.   Case study: Zanzibar Association for People with Developmental Disability (ZAPDD)

Zanzibar is an archipelago on the coast of Tanzania, consisting of two main islands – Unguja and Pemba. Around 60 per cent of the population of 1 million live in poverty with an average life expectancy of 56 years. In 1997, the Zanzibar Association for People with Developmental Disability (ZAPDD) was established as a non-governmental organisation with 23 members, but today it has nearly 1,200 members of whom 200 are youth with developmental disabilities.

When there are more than 20 families in an area who have a child or young person with disabilities, a meeting is called to tell them about ZAPDD, its mission and objectives. The group is encouraged to form a local branch, electing a chairperson, secretary and treasurer. The local branch activities include recruiting more members

(continued)

Box 15.1. Continued

and dissemination of information about disability, rights and inclusion. A major function is to create awareness at a local level on the needs of people with disabilities and their inclusion in society. Meetings are held with local chiefs and government leaders. There are now over 50 branches throughout the two islands.

The branches elect their representatives at a regional level, which in turn elect the members of the National Executive Committee. It is responsible for making the rules and regulations of the Association according to the Constitution. They meet regularly with government departments and other partner organizations.

A major concern for parents was the lack of education for their sons and daughters. They obtained the support of the Ministry of Education to develop an inclusive education programme. With donor funding from Norway, they instigated three programmes of work.

First, they strengthened their branch network by appointing two full-time co-ordinators to support the committees and members in their activities. Second, ZAPDD branches were actively involved in lobbying and supporting the local schools chosen to take part in the pilot inclusive education programme (McConkey and Mariga, 2010). They elected parental representatives to the school committees whose role was to sensitize the community at large and to encourage parents to send their children to school. They assisted in producing an environment conducive for inclusive learning and also raised funds for materials and equipment. Fathers helped to make classrooms more accessible and they built toilets and new classrooms.

Third they launched a youth development programme aimed at students with disabilities who had dropped out of secondary schools. A fulltime co-ordinator used the ZAPDD local branch network to develop a programme of activities that included income generation, education around teenage issues such as HIV/AIDS and team sports such as basketball. Able-bodied students were easily recruited to play on the same team alongside their peers with disabilities and to take part in after-school training and informal competitions. The Association is a model of how parents can be supported to create a better future for their sons and daughters.

These groupings need not be confined solely to parents, as they usually welcome other family members or people who are 'friends'. The latter can include professional or community personnel involved with the client group. The mix is valuable especially as it brings a wider range of experience and expertize to the group, but care must be taken to avoid a 'takeover' by professionals with an agenda that can be different from those of the parents for whom the association was created. One safeguard is for parents to be in the majority on the management committee of the associations.

The functions of parent associations

These associations commonly fulfil four main functions: providing parents with solidarity, information, advocacy and practical supports.

Solidarity. The heartache that comes from feeling alone with a problem can be assuaged by meeting others who have been through or who are going through similar experiences. Equally it is easier to join others to challenge prevailing attitudes and practices in society rather than to take action single-handedly. Membership can also boost self-confidence and help to create a sense of pride in having a child with disability. This appears to be best fostered at a local level; hence national associations need to develop a network of branches.

Solidarity can also be nurtured internationally through Regional groupings of national associations, as has happened in the Asia-Pacific region, the Caribbean and in English speaking Africa as well as through worldwide organizations such as Inclusion International, which claims links with 20,000 associations of families and self-advocates (http://inclusion-international.org/).

Information. Parents bemoan the lack of information that is available to them even when they have access to a range of professionals. Often the need is for information that is tailored to their present needs and concerns and presented to parents in readily accessible ways. For example in Iran, 43 parents of children with autism were recruited from schools and clinics in Tehran and interviewed individually about the information they required (Samadi, McConkey and Kelly, 2012.) Their major concern was a lack of parental understanding about autism and its causes, along with reactions to the diagnostic process and the dearth of information provided to them. The majority of parents were dissatisfied with the professional assistance provided for their children, and many lacked informal support from their families. A six-session training course was then provided for them that covered the main themes requested by parents. After the course, parents rated their emotional well-being, stress and family functioning as much improved. These gains were maintained up to one year later (McConkey and Samadi, 2013).

Parent associations internationally often produce newsletters for their members; most organize meetings, conferences and training events with invited speakers. Some have telephone help lines, and others employ 'parent advisers' or development workers to provide information and training for their members.

Advocacy. National associations have a vital role to play in speaking up for the rights of people with disabilities. Parent associations often organize events to profile issues of concern and gain the interest of media such as radio and newspapers. Delegations from the association may also meet government officials to press their case. Likewise, the national association may support individual members as they confront local issues, such as school enrolment or police refusing to prosecute the rapist of a lady with intellectual disabilities.

Parents can become involved in the training of other parents and also of professionals (McConkey, Mariga, Braadland and Mphole, 2000). In Lesotho, Southern Africa, a five-day workshop was designed specifically to prepare 21 parents from the nine branches of Lesotho Society for Mentally Handicapped Persons (LSMHP) to act as trainers for other parents with a child who has a disability. The training also aimed to build their confidence and competence in training community groups as well as professional workers such as teachers. Evaluation data gathered at the end of the workshop confirmed that these aims were broadly met. Twelve months later, the participants had organized 19 training events throughout Lesotho for families and community groups, and they were able to report a variety of tangible outcomes resulting from their training, including a doubling in the membership of national society LSMHP and an increase in the number of children enrolled in mainstream schools. Income-generating projects had started for teenagers with disabilities, and a village playground was made accessible to people with disabilities.

The advocacy role of carers is likely to be more effective if alliances are made with other organizations who share a common interest, most notably organizations of people with disabilities. In many countries, there is now some form of national disability council that brings together all the disability organizations, although the inclusion of parent associations has proved controversial in some countries, as disabled activists are wary of parents taking control of their lives (see Chapter 3).

Support services to families

In many countries, associations have gone on to organize services for their members and for other families who have a child with disabilities; these include food distribution and clothing, the provision of medicines or aids such as wheelchairs, and the development of income-generation schemes for members or family carers such as mothers. More ambitiously, day centres and schools for children have been started as well as sheltered workshops for adult persons. Other associations have launched preschool home visiting services and supported employment schemes and residential facilities. In more developed countries, leisure schemes and holiday breaks for disabled people are common, as these forms of services are unlikely to receive government funding or require professional involvement.

Often these new services were developed as 'model schemes' with the hope that they would be taken over or emulated by government, which has indeed happened in many instances. But two risks are also present. The services are more likely to be available to the more affluent, better educated, urban-based families and people with disabilities, especially if charges are levied for using the service. Secondly, government agencies are given the perfect excuse for not developing services or making mainstream services available to those with disabilities, namely that the special services set up by parent associations are already doing the job! In reality, most associations invariably end up providing some services to their members, and it can hardly be otherwise when the needs in some countries are so great.

Challenges facing parent associations

Three common challenges face parent associations globally, although in varying degrees depending on their history and leadership.

Involving fathers. Invariably women have been to the fore in instigating and managing parent associations. A common complaint is the lack of support received from fathers. In part this may be because professional services have tended to relate more directly with mothers, although it is likely also to be reflective of wider cultural ethos in which child care is predominantly women's work. This has undoubtedly weakened the impact of parent associations, especially in their dealing with male-dominated politics and governmental systems. Few solutions have been found, although there are notable exceptions from around the world; so it is perhaps too soon to give up on the male of the species!

Redefining families. Modern families conform less and less to the stereotypical two-parent family, with grandparents playing an essential role in countries with high incidence of HIV/AIDS along with child-headed households. Likewise, as the incidence of divorce rises, so too does the number of single-parent families. Also, the number of people with disabilities living in reformed families is rising when their natural parents remarry. Moreover, with the breakdown of the extended family, parents come to depend on support from their friends, who may become more a part of the nuclear family than the child's blood relatives (Carpenter, 1998). The impact of these worldwide social changes on parent associations has not been studied, but a pragmatic response would be to ensure that membership of such groups is welcomed from all those who are playing a 'parenting' role, including foster and adoptive carers.

Ageing associations. Many associations were started by parents when their children were young. As their sons and daughters grow older, the needs and interests of the membership change. In time, it can mean that the association is no longer seen as relevant to younger parents, and so the association or branch 'dies out'. Equally, ageing parents may no longer be able to play an active part in associations. This may mean that pertinent issues for this group are not addressed. One solution is to try to enlist adult siblings to the membership of associations, although to date this does not appear to be happening to any great extent.

For the foreseeable future, associations of parents and friends will have a continuing role to play in supporting carers, albeit that in the electronic era that is dawning, more use will be made of social media such as Facebook or dedicated chat rooms and online advice services (see Chapter 11, assistive technology). However they evolve, associations do form a bridge between the family and the wider community. It is to the latter that we also need to look for further support to family carers.

Community engagement

Although we come to this last, encouraging family engagement with the local community is arguably the most important facet of their support. This not only addresses their social isolation but is essential for advocacy and offers the hope of alleviating poverty and maximizing the range of supports available to families and their disabled relatives.

A focus on community engagement can also resolve the tension that may arise between carers and the aspirations of people with a disability. Arguably, the greatest service families can provide for their disabled relatives is to nurture their independence by encouraging them to become self-reliant in their personal care, household tasks, participation in community activities and income generation. This is a formidable undertaking and one that cannot be accomplished by carers alone. Families need to actively engage with the community and its resources for this to happen. Nonetheless, the person's ongoing support from his or her family is essential, as this nurtures self-confidence while providing tangible encouragement and assistance.

First, we examine schemes centred on the person with disability, and then secondly, access the services available to the wider community. We end by exploring the need for a radical re-appraisal of how supports for family carers and people with disabilities are conceived and planned.

Co-operative action

In recent years. the concept of circles of support has gained credence as a means for giving people with disabilities the opportunity of widening their social networks and increased opportunities for leisure pursuits and productive work (see http://www.learningdisabilities.org.uk/our-work/family-friends-community/circles-of-support/). The circle is a means of supporting family carers and giving the person opportunities that the family is no longer able or willing to provide. The circle can be instigated by parents or by disability services that may recruit relatives, neighbours and friends to become members alongside any support workers involved with the person. The members of a circle can suggest ideas and help to plan new opportunities, particularly at a time of change such as moving on from school or further education and making plans for the future. Circles can meet as often as they like – sometimes twice a year – but when something major is planned, they meet more regularly. Circles have now been set up in workplaces and in schools to help people get included in mainstream settings. The emphasis is on fun and friendships among all members of circle.

Two features seem crucial to success. The circle is sufficiently large so that undue demands are not placed on any one member, and the recruitment of members reflects the interests and aspirations of the person with a disability around whom the circle functions. Invariably such schemes have to be locally devised and operated. They cannot be mandated nationally, although they do deserve to feature in modern policies and funding arrangements.

A variant of circles of support is the concept of micro-boards designed to manage funding received from government to provide personalized support services to the person with disabilities, who may or may not be living with family carers (see http://www.communityworks.info/articles/microboard.htm). In Canberra, Australia, Jan Kruger has set up a board for her son Jack, and invited his cousin; a neighbour; a person heavily involved in Scouts (as she is looking at reintroducing Jack into Scouts); staff from the local swimming pool; and his former soccer coach, who could assist in finding clubs which might include Jack in the game in a valued way.

In low-income countries, the recent re-iteration of community-based rehabilitation (CBR) schemes has placed increased emphasis on building community ownership of local schemes (WHO, 2010). In villages and townships, local

CBR management committees are proposed, consisting of disabled persons, family members, community leaders and interested community staff such as teachers and health workers. This group takes responsibility for different aspects of the CBR programme such as the support and training of families, provision of resource centres, community education initiatives and the development of community facilities that promote the well-being of everyone in the community. This community approach also brings together families and people with different disabilities, unlike traditional associations and services that tend to concentrate on a specific disability. Moreover relationships are forged among the various stakeholders based on an equality of esteem and mutual respect. However these schemes are invariably localized – often based in rural areas – as it is difficult to replicate this model at a national level. Instead, a national federation of local CBR schemes that retain their autonomy holds promise as a means of attaining a national voice and profile.

Community development and income generation

It's a truism that disabled people are more frequent among poorer families. However in more affluent countries, State pensions and social welfare payments help to offset some of the consequences, but this is not so in low-income countries. Foremost is the need to instigate and sustain income-generation initiatives for families and persons with disabilities because any member of the family who is not productive is then a drain on family resources. At a minimum, children with disabilities need to become self-reliant in their personal care and be able to undertake jobs around the home such as water fetching so that the family workload is shared and others are freed to earn an income (Palmer, 2011).

Co-operatives have been established for disabled people, or for their mothers, in which they generate the goods and services that will find a ready market in local communities, for example the production of school uniforms, leather goods, basketry and chicken rearing. Revolving loan and micro-credit schemes have been used to provide the necessary capital to individuals and communities. The repayments on the loans are used to help fund others to start similar schemes. In the Philippines, mothers of children with disabilities were given loans to enable them to rear pigs which were sold at festival time. Likewise in Malawi, a CBR project donated sewing machines to a mother's co-operative to make school uniforms while their children took part in educational activities in an adjoining room (see Chapter 12).

To date, schemes such as these are not widely established, and they may not be sustained when initial funding dries up. A more radical solution is gaining favour, namely integrating initiatives to assist people with disabilities, with those aimed at developing the wealth of the whole community. However these approaches will only become fully successful when society's attitude to disability is transformed from primarily a medical problem to a social issue, from a specialist concern to a community focus and from a charitable ethos to an issue of human rights (Hiranandani, Kumar and Sonpal, 2014). This is starting to happen through governmental policies stimulated by the United Nations Convention of Rights but the transformation has to be grown also at the grass roots, and that is the big challenge and a conundrum. Are impoverished communities able to help themselves and willing to devote scarce resources to their weaker members?

Conclusions

This review of family caregiving is incomplete in many respects, not least that much of our current knowledge and identification of priority concerns derive from high-income countries (McKenzie, McConkey and Adnams, 2013). We have much still to learn about how families cope in less studied cultures and countries. Much remains to be done to ensure the voices and experiences of family carers are documented and shared globally, as this provides a basis for their advocacy locally, nationally and internationally.

Perhaps the greatest unknown though is how the demographic and economic changes which are taking place in all countries – such as a greater preponderance of working mothers, increased migration and smaller nuclear families – will affect family caregiving in the future (Hoff, 2009). Will families have the time and resources to care for a disabled relative? Might there be greater pressure for people with disabilities to leave the family home, and what alternatives options will be available to them? One certainty can be stated: families of the future will require more rather than less support if they are to sustain their caregiving role.

For the present though, it is evident that much greater attention needs to be given in the training of professionals to family-centred approaches and partnership, working across sectors and support agencies. This investment is long overdue, especially within more affluent countries, but low-income countries need to ensure that this ethos permeates the training courses they develop in the future (Lorenzo, 2012). Professional support is a proven means of sustaining families in their caregiving while improving their quality of life.

Finally, the dilemma remains of how best to balance the needs of carers with the aspirations of the person with disability. The fear of self-advocates is that professionals such as social workers often privilege the wishes of carers over their own aspirations for a life of their choosing, rather than remaining dependent on their families. Both parties need to find, through dialogue, shared objectives that enable the person with a disability to remain part of the family even when living apart from the family. The wise words of the Dalai Lama seem especially apposite: 'Give the ones you love wings to fly, roots to come back, and reasons to stay'.

Summary of key points

- Internationally, families provide the bulk of care for persons with disabilities, often well beyond childhood. The CRPD recognizes this in its preamble, but too often the enormous contribution of families to the well-being of persons with disabilities is overlooked and indeed taken for granted.

- Family carers experience many disadvantages and often receive little support, with consequences both for themselves and their disabled relative.
- Home-based support for carers has proven especially effective, and a variety of models suited to both low-income and more affluent countries have emerged.
- Parental advocacy is a powerful force for change and is stronger when parents come together in associations.
- Community engagement is essential to creating a better quality of life for families and people with disabilities.
- Many challenges remain in meeting the needs of carers while respecting the aspirations of people with disabilities to live away from their families.

STUDY QUESTIONS

1. What changes to professional practice are required if a family-centred approach to their work is to be fully implemented?

2. How would you manage the suspected maltreatment of a person with a disability by their family carers – such as neglect or financial exploitation – when there are few, if any, alternative living arrangements available?

3. How could neighbours be mobilized within a local township or village to offer more support to families who have a child with a disability?

Further reading and resources

Families Special Interest Research Group of IASSIDD. (2013). 'Families supporting a child with intellectual or developmental disabilities: The current state of knowledge', *Journal of Applied Research in Intellectual Disabilities*. DOI: 10.1111/jar.12078.

HM Government. (2011). *Carers at the Heart of 21st-Century Families and Communities* (London: Department of Health).

Inclusion International. (2006). *Hear Our Voices: A Global Report: People with an Intellectual Disability and Their Families Speak Out on Poverty and Exclusion* (London: Inclusion International).

K.B. Kyza, A.P. Turnbull, J.A. Summers and V.A. Gómez. (2012). 'The relationship of family support to family outcomes: A synthesis of key findings from research on severe disability', *Research and Practice for Persons with Severe Disabilities*, 37(1), 31–44.

UNICEF. (2011). *The State of the World's Children 2013: Children with Disabilities* (New York: UNICEF).

Equipping Professionals with Competencies to Better Support Persons with Disabilities

16

Huib Cornielje
Daniel Tsengu

State Parties undertake (i) To promote the training of professionals and staff working with persons with disabilities in the rights recognized in the present Convention so as to better provide the assistance and services guaranteed by those rights.

**UN Convention on the Rights of Persons with Disabilities
Article 4(1): General obligations**

States Parties shall promote the development of initial and continuing training for professionals and staff working in habilitation and rehabilitation services.

**UN Convention on the Rights of Persons with Disabilities
Article 26(2): Habilitation and Rehabilitation**

Introduction

This chapter is about capacity building, or in plain English, it concerns education and is about training of rehabilitation professionals to enable them to better support persons with disabilities. It begins with an exploration of two key concepts related to education and training: competencies and support.

Over the years educational reforms have taken place in many parts of the world. Broadly speaking, education in Western society may be said to have moved from teacher-centred approaches to student-centred approaches, and from attention on acquiring knowledge to a focus on acquiring competencies. The latter meant also that new didactical methods are being used in education, and a paradigm shift can be seen whereby the focus nowadays is more on the integration of knowledge, skills and attitudes, rather than on acquiring knowledge only. During the past decade, both vocational training as well as higher education programmes adopted competency-based curricula development. In summary, it can be concluded that an educational change (student centred) has taken place as well as a curriculum change (work-field centred). The concept of competencies has become very popular in higher education, both at the policy-making level and at the level of educational practice. Competency-based education is currently the leading paradigm for innovation, both at the system level and the level of learning environments. An important reason for the popularity of the concept of competence is the expectation held by many stakeholders in the work field that the gap between the labour market and education can and will be reduced through competency-based education. What is a competence? A competence is the whole of knowledge, insights, skills and attitudes which a professional uses in different professional situations. Competency is about professional ability, and someone who is competent has enough skills and knowledge to be able to do something to a high or satisfactory standard.

In current educational programmes in Western society, it is the learning of the student that is the focal issue. In order to apply this didactical method, use is being made of problem-based learning approaches, with attention to reflective reasoning skills, analytical skills and the personal responsibility of the student for his or her own learning process. Students are increasingly expected to choose their own learning objectives and activities. Learning takes place within the context of the future application field. As such, there is also a new role for the teacher, who is becoming more and more a coach and facilitator instead of being the omnipotent lecturer who supposedly knows more than his or her students.

The term *support* needs also some explanation, as it is a term which for some people may have many negative connotations, for example 'giving assistance to' or 'to bear weight'. However, it can be viewed also from a more positive perspective, for instance 'to argue in favour of' or 'to advocate'. In our view, the provision of support can be seen in different ways: the teacher being a support to his or her students; rehabilitation professional or rehabilitation provider being more of a resource for the person with a disability; the professional being a facilitator of a rehabilitation process rather than someone who determines the rehabilitation objectives and decides about interventions. That means a shift in thinking, where the rehabilitation provider becomes an active partner and supporter of the person with a disability. This also implies a change in the position of persons with disability. Instead of accepting the usually dominant role of professionals, they will become active partners in their own rehabilitation process.

Education and training of rehabilitation professionals in a global perspective

Conventional training of rehabilitation professionals is the (assumed) responsibility of different faculties of universities or polytechnics, schools of health technologies and so on. Such conventional training equips professionals to effectively – and where possible on the basis of evidence – deal with an individual's disability. Depending on the specialization, this training focuses on impairment, activity limitation and/or participation restriction. For some professional training, there is also a more or less stronger focus on the influence of environmental factors on disability (for example, occupational therapists) and some may pay more attention to the personal factors that contribute to disability (such as clinical psychologists, educators). The availability and quality of such training is the responsibility of governments, and compared to 30 years ago, positive developments in Africa and Asia are taking place. New educational programmes have been introduced in a large number of African countries. However, often what is available is not sufficient and appropriate: it is often limited to training of physiotherapists, and training opportunities for many other – indispensable – rehabilitation professionals is non-existent.

Professional supremacy

Haig and colleagues (2009), writing about the status of rehabilitation in Africa, state:

> With no physiatrist role models …, medical school deans, department chairs, practicing physicians and hospital administrators have no idea of what is missing. They look to orthopedic surgeons (typically very busy in the operating room and with little formal training in rehabilitation) and others to perform the services. They often view physical medicine as equivalent to physical therapy, perhaps with a nod to orthotics and prosthetics. Yet the literature on rehabilitation is clear – disability is multifactorial. A multidisciplinary team led by a physician expert always outperforms individual therapists.
>
> (Haig et al., 2009)

Haig and colleagues clearly place the physiatrist (rehabilitation physician) in the driving seat, and it is true that in continents other than Africa the physiatrist has a key role in the management of the rehabilitation process and programme. Leadership in the field of rehabilitation is certainly needed, but in their analysis Haig and colleagues unfortunately are too strongly committed to the medical model of disability (see Chapter 2). When reviewing efforts of poverty-stricken countries to respond to the needs of persons with disability, the medical needs of persons with disability are not always the ones that matter most. What may be most important is the interaction of the person (with a disability) and society. In that interaction is expressed the exclusion or lack of participation or unequal opportunities to school and work that are of more importance than, for instance, the functioning of a leg. Perhaps the inability to earn an income because of stigma and prejudice plays a more crucial role in the life of a person with disability than merely a claw hand or a foot drop.

We do not deny the importance of good-quality training of rehabilitation professionals. We also see, however, the need to ensure that such training equips professionals to be able to address the multidimensional needs of persons with disabilities. Arguably, within medical training, including the training of physiatrists, and in training of allied health professionals such as speech therapists and physiotherapist, too little attention is given to the interaction of the person with a disability and the environment. Has it not become high time to expose such students fully to the contextual factors of disability?

During a monitoring visit to a community-based rehabilitation (CBR) project in Nigeria, a physiotherapy student was taken to the field to work with children with physical disabilities in the community. On arrival, a 15-year-old boy with severe contractures due to poliomyelitis was identified. The boy was crawling on the ground, and he looked extremely dirty. The student said that he couldn't assess the child unless he was brought to the hospital. The family members, however, said that the child could not be brought to the hospital because his parents believed that someone in the community was responsible for their child's condition, and as such, medical intervention would not help. The parents also said that they couldn't afford to pay the medical bill at the hospital because of poverty. The student felt that the parents were being unreasonable, and insisted that he could not attend to the child unless he was brought to the hospital. It is clear that this child was denied rehabilitation due to lack of understanding of the physiotherapy student on how social and environmental barriers such as negative beliefs, superstition and poverty play a clear and crucial role in the disability of this boy. What is worse is that even if this student had been informed about the existence of these barriers – which in fact he was by the relatives – he obviously could not handle it properly because his training did not inform him how such contextual factors could be dealt with in order to provide effective rehabilitation services in the community.

Educational programmes of rehabilitation professionals can be characterized as being highly specialized. Curricula of such programmes are subject to pressures for change, as on the one hand higher educational institutes are constantly confronted with needs for educational reform, and on the other hand scientific insights change rapidly as well. At the same time, it is also true that the influence of the disability rights movement in many higher education institutes is often minimal, although there are some exceptions. One might hope to see the disability rights agenda influencing curricula of many faculties that educate students in rehabilitation-related sciences. However, the authors' personal experiences in a number of educational programmes at various universities in Europe, as well as in Africa and Asia, indicate the opposite. Curricula of rehabilitation courses at a number of universities in West Africa (for example in Nigeria and Ghana) are often copies of Western curricula, still strongly focusing on knowledge and technical skills and largely ignoring the need to address attitudes, behaviours and practices in the field of disability and rehabilitation as well. Both authors are involved in developments in the field of CBR training at the Department of Special Education and Rehabilitation Sciences of the University of Jos in Nigeria and know from their own experience that it is hard to facilitate a change of mindset. It is even harder to create a learning environment for students and lecturers where it is understood that sufficient attention should be given to disability rights issues. It is also challenging to secure attention to the field of disability studies and even more difficult to involve persons with disability as external or guest lecturers in the classroom situation. During 2013, one of the authors was lecturing to a diverse group of staff members from NGOs who are active in the field of disability at one of the universities in Timor Leste. Some of the participants were making use of assistive devices such as wheelchairs, and so the Board of the university was asked to make the lecture room and nearby toilets accessible. This was done, and the training went very well. Less than a week after the training was finished, however, we were approached by the Board of the university and kindly asked to remove the ramps.

The above example clearly shows how challenging it is to equip rehabilitation professionals to support rehabilitation services where the leadership of institutions, directly responsible for education and policy making, does not have sufficient understanding about disability and its effects on persons with disability. Realizing the importance of raising awareness among leadership of training institutions on disability issues in order to achieve the much needed change in curricula as discussed above, the authors organized a Training of Trainers Workshop at the University of Jos in Nigeria, with the leadership of the university, including the vice chancellor, in attendance. On a field trip, some of the professors confessed: 'We thought we knew about disability, but our experience on this field trip has exposed our ignorance of the subject; we regret we were teaching our students the wrong thing'. Certainly, exposure of university leadership and lecturing staff to the realities of disability and its effects can have a big impact on the dynamics of training programmes in terms of better equipping (future) rehabilitation professionals.

Disability models and professional education

As Wallner observes, a critical issue is retaining rehabilitation and disability professionals trained in low- and middle-income countries

> With one notable exception, all universities in South Africa are at present training physiotherapy students in high-technology academic hospitals, and their graduates are most competent to practice their profession in these areas both in South Africa and abroad.
>
> (Wallner, 1992)

The brain drain of rehabilitation professionals to mainly Western and Arabic countries continues, and it can thus be concluded that all these professionals are trained in such a way that they become perfectly capable of working in affluent societies where rehabilitation is highly specialized. One wonders, however, whether rehabilitation professionals educated in the Asian, African and Southern American continents are equipped to effectively work in situations of poverty, which mainly will be found in rural, semi-urban and slum areas. How much of professional education is directed at the specific eco-social contexts in these parts of the world? How well does the education of rehabilitation professionals in Africa, for example, pay specific and explicit attention to African norms and values? Should specific attention be given to the specific characteristics of Africa such as the role of traditional health remedies (see Chapter 5); the importance of the extended family in the rehabilitation of persons with disability (see Chapter 15); attention to hierarchy (for example the professional who is on top); religious ideas and influences – both barriers and facilitators – in acceptance of disability? Conventional education of specialized rehabilitation professionals is largely dominated by medical or individual model thought, both in Western as well as in other Southern contexts. However, it is bizarre that the religious and moral interpretations of disability – the cultural model (Devlieger, 2005) – highly relevant in, for instance, Africa, often does not receive attention in African professional education.

The situation in other continents is, however, most likely similar. Yet the cultural model is on most continents probably the most prevalent model used by general society to view disability! This is even the case in North America and Europe, where people also try to get answers to the question of why they have a disability. It is, in essence, the existential question of 'Why (me)?' that Kushner (1983) describes in his best-selling book *When Bad Things Happen to Good People*.

If educational institutions start acknowledging that religious interpretations of disability are influential, and not just an ancient and alien way of explaining disability, it should have consequences for the education of the rehabilitation professional.

New trends ask for new developments in education too!

With an increasingly ageing population in many parts of the world – and a consequent rise in chronic diseases – there may be a rise in (more severe) disabilities. The increase in disability will place a greater financial responsibility on society. This development calls for new strategies in view of – often decreasing – available budgets for traditional sectors such as health and welfare. Instead of a strong conventional focus on medical and/or therapeutic and individually oriented interventions, professionals should become far more knowledgeable and competent to develop strategies that are rooted in the human rights-based approach (see Chapter 1). This would mean, for instance, a re-orientation of course curricula; it would mean a strong focus on shifting 'conventional and/or traditional' attitudes, but at the same time it would mean that teaching and training approaches need to reflect empowering and enabling strategies that are directed at interventions at the interface of individuals – with and without disability – and society. In other words, professionals need to be trained to seek creative solutions that move far beyond the medical or welfare sector only; this requires serious attention to the development of enabling environments. The disability process in such a more eco-social paradigm is not seen as simply an individual problem, and rehabilitation professionals need to be able to respond accordingly.

Critical to an expansion or a re-orientation of the role of the rehabilitation professions are the following:

- A shift from a conventional, rather medical rehabilitation approach towards a more social and human rights-based approach in rehabilitation (in which the ultimate goal is inclusion in society and equalization of opportunities).
- A change from the professional being the *manager* of the 'patient' to that of being a *resource* for the person with a disability and the chronically ill person, and as such enabling the person with a disability to achieve his or her personal goals in life to the greatest extent possible.
- A strong referral, managerial and capacity-building role in CBR programmes. Rehabilitation professionals should become much more involved in the development of essential rehabilitation services for those who are marginalized. They have an essential role to play to ensure that rehabilitation becomes accessible and available to all. CBR is not necessarily the only or best response to the needs of persons with disability. It is a complementary strategy alongside more specialized services provided by rehabilitation professionals. These rehabilitation professionals can play a vital role in improving the quality of such CBR services.
- An involvement of a much larger number of persons with disability in the education of rehabilitation professionals. The sooner students are confronted with, and challenged by, persons with disability, the better. Such exposure helps students to appreciate the realities of the lives of persons with disability; it helps them to understand more in-depth the lived experience and at an early stage confronts them with their own ignorance, biases and attitudes towards persons with disability. When the theory is made tangible in the life stories of persons with disability, there is hope that students become professionals with a deeper grasp of key theory and a more positive attitude overall.
- A stronger political representation of the rehabilitation professions via lobby groups and disability movements. Joint provider-consumer bodies could form powerful instruments in the development of an inclusive society for all. Professional associations have been bystanders for far too long in the debate about disability rights, and although self-advocacy by persons with disability is key to emancipation and empowerment, joint advocacy of persons with disability and their organizations with professionals and their organizations/associations will increase the chances that our societies really become more inclusive. It is joint action from the side of provider-consumer organizations that could have a strong influence on the required changes that need to take place at educational institutions.

If one agrees with the need for a reorientation of rehabilitation professionals as described above, this certainly has consequences for their education and training. Probably the most challenging issue is the importance of changing mindsets of the leadership and lecturing staff of educational institutions. As noted earlier, changing mindsets is a daunting task and probably will best take place when professionals and the public are literally confronted with the realities of life for people with disabilities.

Article 4(1.i) of the CRPD states that training in the rights covered in the Convention is to be provided to improve the assistance and service of professionals working with persons with disabilities. The CRPD presents challenges about how to develop a well-trained body of workers able to deliver CBR in a way that honours and promotes the principles of the CRPD. The disability and rehabilitation workforce has a larger remit than CBR, even if CBR is of great importance as the actual or potential front-line workforce in developing countries. CRPD also lays down a challenge to remodel the training of *all* professionals who may work with people with disabilities at any time, whether in developing or developed countries. There are many professionals who are likely to encounter and hopefully serve the needs of people with disabilities in different ways: medical doctors, nurses, teachers, therapists, social workers and so on. In all cases, it is essential that their training and continuing professional development opportunities be rigorously renewed so as to reflect authentically the values and ethos manifested in the CRPD. This represents quite a challenge to influence not only the practices of these professionals but also the mindsets of those who train them and who determine and deliver the content of training programmes in every country across the world. Whereas training for each discipline has to be adjusted in turn, it is also clear that there is a great need to begin to break free of overly 'siloed' thinking and practices in training. The CRPD provides a wonderful opportunity to escape silos of narrow disciplinary traditions and practices and instead to find common ground and a shared language about disability issues.

Shortages of rehabilitation professionals

The World Health Organization (WHO) formally initiated CBR in the late 1970s. Other United Nations agencies, such as the International Labour Organization, followed later. Originally, CBR was largely based on the principles of primary health care to address the (medical) rehabilitation needs of persons with disability in the South. It aimed to address the shortage of rehabilitation services for the majority of persons with a disability in the South by providing services in, and with, the community, using predominantly local resources. Community fieldworkers, with minimal training, offered basic, mainly medical rehabilitation interventions. The focus was on strategies, which could be understood and carried out by these workers, local volunteers or family members. The primary focus of CBR was to maximize individual functioning.

Although CBR was initially much dominated by the medical disability model, it nowadays has evolved into a community development-informed strategy that is aimed at participation of persons with disability in society, equal opportunities and inclusion. CBR is in fact a disability inclusive development strategy. CBR is increasingly recognized as an important instrument in implementing the United Nations Convention on the Rights of Persons with

Disability and in achieving the recently developed Sustainable Development Goals (United Nations, 2012).

Yet, CBR is still viewed with lots of suspicion by the global disability movement. Many rehabilitation professionals are also sceptical, as evidenced in the following quote:

> CBR is a politically expedient way to allocate the least amount of funds possible to the problem. After all, uneducated villagers do try to take control over their lives. They are cheaper than doctors, and they do not have the depth of medical knowledge to know what they are missing. With no experts who understand the medical aspects of rehabilitation to advise or to advocate, and with WHO blessings, governments often give complete responsibility for rehabilitation to ministries of social welfare, education, employment or agriculture. CBR is insufficient. The WHO and other policy makers need to recognize that, in every country with reasonable rehabilitation services, the medical programs are led by physicians who dedicate their careers to this cause.
>
> (Haig et al., 2009)

Although there is some merit in the points made, these comments arguably fail to appreciate the positive potential of CBR and over-state the centrality of traditional medical personnel. Should rehabilitation professionals not have a more humble attitude in order to play an even more significant role in the lives and rehabilitation pathways of persons with disability?

Training for CBR – past, present and future

Contrary to conventional training of highly specialized professionals, which takes place in higher-income countries, but also increasingly in middle- and lower-income countries, is the training of generalist rehabilitation workers who work more at the grass roots or community level. Because of lack of funds or because of lack of sufficient attention to the lived realities of people with disability, some countries, mainly in the African, Asian and South American continents, do not have (an adequate number of) educational facilities that offer training at specialized levels. The World Health Organization responded to such a scenario by introducing in the mid-1970s of the last century the so-called community-based rehabilitation. During the first two decades of its existence, CBR was mainly taking place within a bio-medical paradigm and was much influenced by the medical model paradigm. CBR, to a large extent, was aimed in those early years on improving coverage and ensuring that basic rehabilitation could be provided at the doorstep. CBR was made possible by training a new cadre of lay people in basic rehabilitation skills. Capacity building and the training of fieldworkers, volunteers and supervisors were fundamental to community-based rehabilitation. Indeed, the approach to CBR was based on a training manual (Helander, Padmani and Nelson, 1983), and in the early years there was a substantial emphasis on training and manuals (Loveday, 1990), which continued for many years.

The focus in more recent CBR training programmes is increasingly on the eco-social aspects and consequences of disability. Much attention should, therefore, now be paid to understanding disability and the necessary rehabilitation in the specific socio-economic and political context of the countries where training takes place. CBR training in such contexts is guided by development of programmes that lead to empowerment and inclusion of persons with disability in society. The primary focus of training is consequently on the enhancement of competencies in community development oriented CBR, with the aim of influencing resources, attitudes and participation relevant to the lives of people with disabilities. The need to recognize one's own negative attitudes towards people with disabilities is a particular feature that hopefully results in a change of the CBR trainee's behaviour towards persons with disability. With rehabilitation recognized as an integral part of a broader community development approach CBR training should be in sharp contrast with the conventional training of specialist rehabilitation professionals.

Training in clinical therapeutic and thus individual interventions remains an important aspect of rehabilitation and should not be ignored. However, in the context of the current CBR philosophy it is seen as of partial value in terms of moving towards full emancipation and participation of persons with disability in society. There is as such a distinct difference of models between past training curricula and current ones.

In recent decades, the focus in documents produced by key stakeholders in CBR has changed substantially. This has been partially in response to the perceived limitations of manuals and constraints of formulaic training, and partially in response to a growing awareness of the extent of CBR and the importance of rights and a human rights-based approach. The nature of CBR documents has shifted away from staff training manuals. The current CBR Guidelines (WHO, 2010) are not intended as fieldworker training materials, but rather as conceptual guidelines for CBR managers and planners. The Guidelines provide a conceptual framework for addressing important challenges such as empowerment and the rights of people with disabilities. These are also subjects that are highlighted in the *World Report on Disability* (WHO and World Bank, 2011) and certainly associated with and derived from the United Nations Convention on the Rights of Persons with Disabilities (UN, 2006). This is a very important emphasis and shift in thinking. However, it does not directly build the capacity or promote the capabilities of CBR fieldworkers. It also does not mean that automatically training programmes for CBR cadres adopt rights-based approaches. In recent years, there has arguably been an alarming lack of emphasis on the resources and strategies for building the capabilities of CBR workers. Likewise, there has been insufficient attention to questions of how to promote the learning and reasoning capabilities of CBR fieldworkers (Kuipers and Cornielje, 2013), how best to provide such training and how to develop appropriate materials to support such learning and capacity building.

Scaling up CBR: Continuing education and career structures

During the past four decades, CBR has increasingly become accepted as an alternative and appropriate strategy to meet the needs of persons with disabilities and their families; work towards inclusion of persons with disability into mainstream society; and improve the quality of life of persons with disability, largely in the Global South. Yet, CBR to quite some extent has remained within the domain of (international) non-governmental organisations and only in relatively few instances have programmes been scaled up to national levels. It is desirable that governments become responsible for setting up community-based rehabilitation systems. Governments should thus set the necessary frameworks under which CBR can develop in a contextualized way. At the same time, governments and other stakeholders, notably non-governmental organisations, training centres, universities and colleges involved in the training of CBR personnel, should develop strategic human resource development plans. Such plans should comprise agreed-upon policy documents on the required quantity and funding of personnel, the required competencies the employees need to demonstrate, and necessary support systems and the routes to acquisition and demonstration of the required competencies. Having a thoroughly thought-out human resource development plan helps in attracting the needed personnel and keeps them motivated in pursuing excellence in performance. Besides, human resource development plans should make specific provision for continuing education and career opportunities for CBR personnel. Given that training of CBR personnel at most will be a two-year training, it is apparent that this category of professionals needs continuing training opportunities as part of lifelong learning.

Learning for middle- and higher-income countries

The continued strain on health and welfare budgets, together with the – at times – dramatic increase of the ageing populations in Western, middle- and higher-income countries, pose real challenges for policy makers. In some cases, the public may place too much responsibility or expectation on governments, and instead of citizens becoming empowered and independent, there is a risk of new forms of dependency evolving. It appears that governments are slowly realizing the implications of this situation, which in part they may have created themselves. The Dutch government, for instance, recently decided to dismantle the system that they believe they can no longer sustain. The Dutch King Willem-Alexander told his country in April 2013 that the 'classic welfare state of the second half of the 20th century' was over. It would be replaced by a 'participation society' because the 'arrangements' the nation was operating under 'are not sustainable in their current form'. The suggested and required reforms will also require an overhaul of the highly specialized and institutionalized (rehabilitation) services. The Dutch public – notably elderly and persons with disability and their families – are gradually realizing the – at times – very painful consequences of these changes. Institutions are to be less used. There are limited independent and supported living options; people in need of long-term care and rehabilitation are forced to stay longer within their families; and the pressure on families to take on a caretaker role is rapidly increasing (see Chapter 15).

As reforms take place in many middle- and higher-income countries, there is something to learn from the way CBR cadres have been trained and deployed in the Global South. Experiences in the Global South show that there is a dire need to train a cadre of generically trained workers who very well know the resources within their communities; who are able to help people with disabilities in solving their problems; and who often act as liaison and resource persons for the person with disability, as well as for the highly specialized rehabilitation professional. It certainly does not mean the removal of the highly specialized rehabilitation professional, but it requires a reorientation of this professional: for example, it means that this professional should be trained to be part of a rehabilitation team that involves also community-based workers. That shift is to a large extent a matter of changing mindsets of the entire set of rehabilitation professions, probably a much harder task than training them with rehabilitation skills.

Conclusions

Governments, policy makers, planners and training institutes need to realize that disability is not an obstacle to success. They have a moral obligation to ensure that rehabilitation professionals are trained and employed in such a way that they join persons with disability in ensuring that barriers to participation will be removed instead of just 'treating', in an isolated way, impairments. They have an obligation to ensure that people with disabilities play a meaningful role in society. Rehabilitation professionals alone cannot guarantee even with excellent care that the subsequent quality of life of people with disability as a result of that high quality of service is equally excellent.

Summary of key points

- Educational reform of rehabilitation curricula is of utmost importance, as the main thrust of most of such training is still dominated by professionals who think and act within a medical model of disability only.
- Article 4(1.i) of the CRPD states that training in the rights covered in the Convention is to be provided to improve the assistance and service of professionals working with persons with disabilities.
- Education and training of rehabilitation professionals as well as fieldworkers in CBR should explicitly and adequately confront students/trainees with their attitudes and behaviour towards persons with disability and should closely work together with persons with disability in changing mindsets of students and trainees.

- Education and training of rehabilitation professionals and fieldworkers should be context specific, and there is an urgent need for contextualized curricula taking into account the local eco-social factors.
- CBR as an indispensable complementary strategy that leads to inclusion of persons with disability in society should receive the much-needed attention from academic faculties involved in the education of rehabilitation professionals.

STUDY QUESTIONS

1. What will change in education and training of rehabilitation professionals if the human rights-based approach of viewing disability becomes the dominant paradigm?

2. The person with disability may see you as the expert and may expect all answers to his or her problems from you, whereas you want to help the person to solve his or her own problems. Do you recognize that paradox, and how will you deal with it?

3. How can Western education of rehabilitation professionals learn from the concepts inherent in community-based rehabilitation as it has evolved in developing countries?

Further reading and resources

T. Lorenzo. (1994). 'The identification of continuing education needs for CBR workers in rural South Africa', *International Journal of Rehabilitation and Research*, 17, 241–251.

H. Mannan and M. MacLachlan. (2010). 'Human resources for health: Focusing on people with disabilities', *Lancet*, 375(9712), 375.

World Health Organization – Community-based Rehabilitation website: http://www. who.int/disabilities/cbr/en/.

Research Training and the Organizational Politics of Knowledge: Some Lessons from Training Disabled Researchers in Southern Africa

17

Leslie Swartz

> *States Parties undertake to collect appropriate information, including statistical and research data, to enable them to formulate and implement policies to give effect to the present Convention.*
>
> **UN Convention on the Rights of Persons with Disabilities Article 31(1): Statistics and data collection**

Introduction

This chapter presents a case study of the research training provided as part of the Southern African Federation for the Disabled (SAFOD) Research Programme. This apparently straightforward task has to be contextualized within the broader politics of knowledge in the African context and how knowledge is used – or not used – by disabled people's organisations (DPOs), donors, governments and service providers. Moreover, any research trainings need to be linked to the local realities regarding knowledge use. An outline is provided of the content and methodologies, but these are detailed elsewhere (see Swartz, 2009, 2013). Rather, the focus is on issues around knowledge and expertize that arose during the course of the training. In reflecting on this training, I suggest that the emphasis on context in the social model of disability is helpful in understanding both the success and the failures of the training. Finally, I outline some challenges and opportunities for the future.

Knowledge and danger

I begin with two stories that illustrate how knowledge can be perceived as dangerous in an African context. In April 2014, the Congregation of the People of Tradition for Proselytism and Jihad, better known as Boko Haram ('Western education is sinful/prohibited'), abducted 220 girls from their school in Nigeria (Globe and Mail, 2014). Part of the rationale behind this abduction, and others, was that secular education is sinful. The Nigerian Government, at the time of the writing of this chapter (2014), had undertaken to do all in its power to rescue these girls from this group, and a global groundswell of activism around the rights of these girls had developed. Nigeria is now the largest economy in Africa, has women ministers, and a growing technology infrastructure.

The second largest economy in Africa is that of South Africa. A few weeks after the abduction in Nigeria, and on the eve of his country's general election marking 20 years of democracy, the president of the Republic of South Africa and leader of the Africa National Congress (ANC) political party, the Hon Jacob Zuma, said the following in relation to widespread criticism of his having benefited from substantial expenditure of state funds on his personal residence at the village of Nkandla: 'The people are not worried about it ... As a result, people don't think the Nkandla issue is a problem to affect ANC voters. Not at all ... It's an issue with the bright people, (with) very clever people it's a big issue' (IOL, 2014). The political scientist, Xolela Mangcu claims of Zuma that he 'derides intellectuals as "clever blacks" or those who carry briefcases' (Mangcu, 2013, p. 112). In 2012, the following was reported about Zuma, speaking to a group of traditional leaders: 'Zuma also slammed black people "who become too clever", saying "they become the most eloquent in criticising themselves about their own traditions and everything"' (City Press, 2012).

These two examples may seem to constitute a strange place in which to begin a chapter on disability research capacity development, but I intend to show that this is not an irrelevant starting point. In both examples – that of Boko Haram and that of electioneering by South Africa's president – there is an assertion that knowledge can be dangerous. This is explicit in the Boko Haram position of the danger of secular education, and implicit in President Zuma's making a distinction between '*the* people' (emphasis added) and what he terms 'bright' or 'clever' people. A number of unflattering implications can be taken from this distinction between 'people' and 'clever people', but for purposes of this chapter the key implication is that the authentic people, the masses of voters in this case, can be distinguished from clever people (that is people who will question use of state resources for a lavish private residence for a state president or people who will question 'their own traditions'). Knowledge, or cleverness in this context, may be dangerous politically in that it could lead to criticism of the ruling party, but it may be dangerous in another way – by alienating people from their authenticity as part of what is constructed as 'the people' or their traditions – the mass of people who have legitimate claims on citizenship. These two contemporary African examples showing a mistrust of knowledge have many parallels in other contexts – in religions in which it is regarded as sinful to question things, in the attacks on and killings of intellectuals in repressive regimes throughout the world and in the anti-intellectualism of some liberation movements and postcolonial authorities (Gumede and Dikeni, 2009; Mangcu, 2013).

The issues of who knows things and who does not, of who may claim to know things and who may not legitimately make these claims to knowledge, are key questions which need to be considered in any attempt to develop a human rights approach to disability (see Chapter 2). Indeed, an important feature of the development of the politics of self-representation in disability struggles has been the critique of certain forms of knowledge. Disabled people have for centuries been objects of the 'knowledges' of professional groups (chiefly, but not only, medical groups), and part of the history of the social model of disability is not only a questioning of the authority and knowledge of professional 'experts' but also a recognition that parts of this professional knowledge may be hurtful or harmful.

Disabled people's lives have been limited and curtailed – and even damaged – by the application of knowledge to them and to decisions about their lives. This knowledge, however, has often carried the weight of being the knowledge held by professionals, knowledge based on science and research. Other oppressed groups, including women, black people, colonized people and homosexual people, have similarly been on the receiving end of what may be presented as scientific knowledge, but what is in fact knowledge with an aim and consequence to extend oppression and exclusion. Given that the majority of disabled people in the world live in low-income countries, it is true to say that most disabled people, through the inter-sectionality of their identities, live in contexts which have a history of double oppression in terms of the politics of knowledge – the history of the subjection of disabled people to the knowledge of non-disabled people, and the history of the subjection of inhabitants of the majority world to the knowledge of former colonial and current global powers. It stands to reason, given this history, that knowledge is not just a neutral thing in the context of contemporary global disability politics – knowledge carries the weight of complex histories. And all research, including disability-related research, raises questions about what people know and do not know, and about what 'knowledges' of various kinds may mean for people.

Training African disability activists in research skills and the question of knowledge

These issues came sharply into focus for me, a white South African non-disabled man, recruited by the SAFOD to train disability activists from ten Southern African countries in basic research skills as part of the SAFOD Research Programme. The programme was set up according to principles embodied within Articles 31 and 33 of the Convention on the Rights of Persons with Disabilities (CRPD), as noted at the outset of the chapter (see Chapter 3 for a discussion on the CRPD). An outline of the overall Programme is provided in Box 17.1.

Box 17.1. The Southern Africa Federation for the Disabled Research Programme (SRP)

SRP Purpose

'Disabled people's organisations enabled to undertake self-directed research and use its findings to influence policy and practice that is responsive to the needs of disabled people.'

SRP Vision

'SRP is a vehicle for promoting collective learning and capacity building through a process of planning, disseminating, applying new knowledge in decision making resulting in evidence-based actions and systems in order to promote a sense of ownership and sustainability. There is a core group of 20 trained young disabled researchers that are encouraged to carry out small practical research projects within their DPO settings in between regular formal training.'

SRP Approach

'Participatory Learning and Action Research (PLAR) approach to build SAFOD institutional capacity which will enable SAFOD to design, drive and deliver their own research programme, focusing on key disability issues, relating to poverty emancipation, social exclusion and human rights.'

SRP Trainees

- Twenty trainees, two from each SAFOD country (Angola, Botswana, Lesotho, Malawi, Mozambique, Namibia, South Africa, Swaziland, Zambia, Zimbabwe).
- Gender parity: Each country team consists of one woman and one man.

SRP Training

Four face-to-face workshops per year, with research work and homework in between. The training became a short course accredited by Stellenbosch University. (adapted in part from http://www.safod.org/SRP%20Web%20site/index.htm).

In order to teach the trainees something about the nature of data, and issues of reliability and validity, I set an initial task for all of them to collect data about their own national disabled people's organisations (DPOs) (see Chapter 4 for a description of DPOs). Some of the data were very straightforward, such as the name and address of the organization. Some were more complex – trainees were asked, for example, to try to ascertain the nature of the relationships between the DPOs, other civil society groupings and government. We workshopped the questions together, and once the trainees had agreed on a standard set of questions to ask of their own organizations, they went back to their home DPOs and asked the questions of DPO representatives, then prepared presentations on their findings for our next face-to face workshop.

When the trainees presented their findings, some interesting features emerged. In one of the countries, even the address of the head office of the organization (something I would have thought to be incontrovertible) was open to debate – there was a conflict going on between various factions in the DPO sector at that time.

For purposes of this chapter, I should like to discuss two of the responses to questions asked by trainees for their organizations:

1. In none of the countries could the organizations give an estimate of the number of people served by the organization. Answers to this seemingly simple question varied widely from 'We don't know' to 'We serve all the disabled people of our country, however many they may be'.
2. In all of the country responses, relationships with civil society and government were reported to be 'good'.

I shall deal with each of these findings in turn.

Record-keeping by DPOs

The first finding – either that organizations do not know the number of people they serve or that they serve 'all the people' – can be read in various ways. What was clear from this finding was that none of the national DPOs in any of the countries had a system of record-keeping whereby a fairly simple audit-type question could be answered. In principle, a national disability rights organization should serve all disabled people in a country, and in this sense there was no problem with this response. It was noteworthy (and surprising) to me, though, that none of the DPOs, all of which said elsewhere in their responses that they were inadequately funded and that they would wish to serve more people but were unable to do so through lack of capacity. When we explored other questions, including that of the constituent organizations of the DPOs, furthermore, it rapidly became clear that there were large constituency gaps in the organizations. One of the ten countries, for example, reported that they had membership of organizations for people with psychosocial disabilities, but still there seemed to be the bias, as is often common, to membership of people with mobility impairments, followed by people with visual impairments and then organizations for Deaf people (Swartz, 2009).

None of the trainees, nor, apparently, any of the DPOs themselves, raised any questions about the potentially multiple meanings of the question 'How many people does your organization serve?' This is clearly a question which can be answered in many ways, and distinctions can be drawn between direct participants in the programmes of a DPO, as against the potential ripple effects of such participation and as against the potential national impact of a broad disability rights campaign, for example. The trainees confirmed that none of their organizations kept records of numbers of people they believed they had reached or hoped to reach, except in the context of specific monitoring and evaluation exercises required by some external funders of specific projects.

Valid responses

This finding leads to the second one: that all the participants reported that their national DPOs had 'good' relationships with a range of stakeholders and interest groups. I had suggested to the trainees that they ask this question, partly because I thought the answers they received might be interesting and useful but also in order to introduce to them some of the challenges all researchers face in assessing validity of responses to research questions. I was able to use the opportunity of the responses received to help the trainees start to think more critically (to think as I believe researchers should) about what people say to them, and to demonstrate to them the importance of probing information received as part of interviews. We were able usefully to discuss the range of reasons why research participants may wish to respond positively to questions put to them in research contexts. In this way I could teach the trainees something about response sets (patterns of response determined by the questions), halo effects (one response influences all others), and problems of faking good and faking bad (intentional invalid responses scoring on the positive or negative). I felt very gratified when one of the participants said, 'I look now at the list of responses to a lot of questions, and I just see the answers "Good ... Good ... Good ..." and now I know I must be suspicious because this may not tell me much. Without having asked more, I don't know how to interpret what all the "Goods" mean.' To me, this response showed an important development in this trainee's ability to look critically both at how researchers formulate questions and how respondents respond to questions.

Based on this finding, I asked trainees in their country groups to sort responses to their questions into two groups, the first group being responses on the validity of which they felt comfortable with, and the second group being responses which they found difficult to interpret or the validity of which they questioned. Each country group had to report back to the plenary about how they had categorized the responses. Most participants could do the task well, and they felt they learned something about the concept of validity through this process. Predictably, in almost all cases, trainees were concerned about the validity of questions which in one way or another concerned the quality of performance of the DPO in question and its impact on disability rights in that country. Participants were also able to articulate the fact that some questions which may look very simple to answer are, in fact, very difficult indeed to address adequately, and they could say why questions which had looked to be very good ones in theory were not as well formulated as they could have been. In this way they learned practically about the difference between open (generating long responses) and closed-ended questions (generating short responses). They appreciated the importance in interviews of follow-up questions (allowing the interviewer to explore an issue more in depth) and clarifying questions. They came to understand the necessity to frame questions appropriately and of the difference between a question which a researcher wishes to explore (aim of the study) and the actual questions which are put to research participants as part of an interview or questionnaire. As one trainee put it, 'Now I know that if we want to know how well a DPO is doing, there is not much point in asking the DPO how they are doing. We have to have much more specific questions which give more information'.

Good research and good DPOs

Most participants did very well in this exercise, but one of the last country groups to present said that they knew that all their questions were good because they knew their national DPO was doing a good job, and the DPO also knew it. As tactfully as I could (and with some rather less tactful support from some other participants), I pointed out to this country group that the object of the exercise had not, in fact, been to evaluate how good the DPOs were, but rather to learn something about data quality. I asked them to put aside the question of whether in fact the DPO was doing well or not, and to look at the kinds of questions that we as researchers ask – what were better questions, and what were worse questions? I was not able to get this distinction across to this country group, though the distinction seemed well understood by other participants. The more we debated this point, furthermore, the more difficult the discussion became.

It seemed to me that two issues were at stake here. First, the country group in question felt increasingly pressed to defend what they claimed was the excellent functioning of their country level DPO. Second, they personally began to feel ever more threatened by the incredulity of the rest of the group, all of whom were trying to convince them of the distinction between learning about better and worse ways of formulating research questions, on the one hand, and discussing the strengths and weaknesses of a DPO on the other. By the end of the discussion (which was not resolved, but ended by a lunch break), I thought that these participants' own honour (and sense of humiliation) was conflated with their need to defend their home DPO and its honour. Over lunch, I heard one of these participants referring disparagingly to the fact that I was white and not disabled, and attributing what had happened in the conflict to my not understanding due to my outsider status and to my inappropriate use of authority. I have my own theories as to why this happened with this particular group, but I cannot mention these for reasons of confidentiality. However, it is important to note that the issue was not resolved and that it took some time and considerable effort on the part of both sides for this country group to have a restored sense of trust in me as a trainer and facilitator.

Gathering knowledge

These two issues relating to a simple data collection exercise as part of a basic disability research training, laid bare for me some core issues which for me underpin capacity development in disability-related research in the Global South. At the most banal level, such trainings may take place (as did ours) in the context of organizations which have no embedded tradition of collecting data to garner knowledge. The organizations may have no, or little, experience of how collecting data may help shape the life and activities of an organization.

They may, in fact, have no sense of routinely collected knowledge as a potential powerful instrument for change, development and advocacy. This was a group of people very eager to learn about research (and for the most part, in my view, at least as competent as my privileged graduate students at understanding research concepts, if not more so – see Swartz, 2009, 2013). But they were working in organizations where audits seemed to be conducted only when asked for by funders. They had little experience of how data and numbers could work for them. Furthermore, struggling with issues of knowledge and the quality of data, as we experienced in our training, can be experienced as deeply emotional and humiliating. These realizations forced me to think more deeply about what research is and what it is seen to be in contexts such as this research training.

The purpose of research

Almost any text one reads on disability, and especially on disability in low- and middle-income countries, calls for 'more research' – we need to know more. It is, of course, true that it is in the interests of any researcher to call for 'more research' – this is what keeps us in business – but I do not believe that calls for 'more research' are made purely cynically or from self-interest from researchers. I am one of those who call for more research, and though I am not necessarily the best person to judge my motives on this issue, I do not believe that my own motives are purely selfish. But I have come to see that when I call for 'more research', I may be calling for something slightly different from what is called for by some people in DPOs in the Global South. Until I conducted the SAFOD training, I had not sufficiently considered the fact that though research is there to answer substantive questions, it also has a performative aspect.

This was brought home to me forcefully in the context of a research dissemination workshop in South Africa. We had partnered with a DPO to conduct research into disability and HIV issues, and in the dissemination workshop I presented results showing that reported rates of violence (including sexual violence) against disabled women were lower than we had expected. Our DPO partner spoke after me, and to the audience of influential policy makers she said that she was pleased that research had now shown that rates of violence against disabled women were high. In this activist context, I did not correct her (which was arguably an ethical failure on my part), and I realized that a substantial part of the DPO's investment in this research on disability and HIV had less to do with what would be found, in terms of data, than with the performative aspects of the research. My research group and I were associated with a high-status research university and our implicit role was less to find out new things but rather that to add the weight of our authority to the existing claims the DPO was making in terms of the needs they perceived to be important in the disability/HIV field. To me as a researcher, it is axiomatic that the data I collect may not give me the results I expect (otherwise, there is no point to collecting data), but the idea that research may give us answers we do not expect or do not like may be quite threatening to an activist organization dependent for its existence on donor funding. An activist organization has as its raison d'être the need for activism and more work around the issues that concern it.

I thus came to see that though the trainees and I were in the main making what I thought to be good progress in terms of understanding some fundamental issues underpinning any research enterprise, these issues might not be shared by the organizations on whose behalf they were being trained to be able to participate in research projects. In meetings with leaders of these organizations, my sense that we were out of step to a degree, was confirmed. The DPO leaders were exceptionally hospitable and grateful for the work we were doing and very keen to offer support in any way they could. But the clear expectation was that research would inevitably lend support to views they already held. There was also no sense that a research or knowledge-centred approach would change the functioning of their organizations in any way. Research would be a welcomed add-on but would not change the organization in any way.

These views should not have been surprising, for at least two reasons. First, it is not reasonable to expect people untrained in research to know what research involves. For example, many members of the public would consider researchers who change their minds when new evidence is found to be poor researchers who do not know their field properly. Indeed, debates about empirical verification versus narrative fidelity to the agendas of particular interest groups have formed part of discussions on the role of research in the policy arena in wealthier countries recently (Shanahan, Jones and McBeth, 2011; Shanahan, Jones, McBeth and Lane, 2013). Second, in many contexts, research is constructed as an activity requiring high levels of skill, and people unused to participating in research processes would not necessarily have a way of thinking about how to engage with a research approach. In the SAFOD programme specifically, furthermore, nowhere was it stated that the research would have any role in changing the functioning of the DPOs themselves.

Outcomes from the training

At the end of the training, therefore, I was confident that many of the trainees had learned some valuable skills and, probably more importantly, had learned of the importance of critical and questioning thinking not only in research contexts but more broadly. Here are some comments made by trainees in this regard:

> Being a researcher is an interesting thing because, since the SRP trainings, I do not just make conclusions about what I see and hear, but gather more information about the claims.
>
> (Emmie Chiumia, Malawi)

> (Before the training) I was not able to debate or be involved in dialogues with convincing reason, but now even in validation workshops I have ability to point out the gaps of the report and suggest what can be done to make the report be acceptable.
>
> (Pascalina Letsau, Lesotho)

The most interesting stage of research to me is data analysis because it really makes me reason, work out solutions to a prevailing situation and become analytical about any information and even issues I am faced with. It makes me suspicious and unsatisfied until one works out the true position about a certain issue. This is the most outstanding skill I have learned since 2009 from the SRP and which I think must be an attribute of every advocate.

(Simate Simate, Zambia)

In all these cases, trainees identified the scepticism and inquiry associated with research as a key lesson learned – and they also showed how they have been able to apply this attitude in contexts not labelled as 'research' contexts. To me, this feedback was gratifying, and I believe that these trainees and others gained not only in some technical skills but also in an approach to knowledge which I view as fundamental to being able to be a reflective and competent researcher – and a reflective and competent contributor to any organization. But I was not convinced that the organizations to which these participants belonged had changed, and it is to this issue that I turn in the next section.

Back to the social model: the context of knowledge and learning

The purpose of the SAFOD Research Programme training was, as stated on the SRP website: 'Disabled people's organisations enabled to undertake self-directed research and use its findings to influence policy and practice that is responsive to the needs of disabled people' (http://www.safod.org/SRP%20 Web%20site/index.htm). The ideology of the Programme, therefore, fitted well into the paradigm of emancipatory research: a research designed to increase emancipation of participants as it adds to knowledge (Jones, Marshall, Lawthom and Read, 2013; McColl, Adair, Davey and Kates, 2013; Petersen, 2011). The aim was not simply to train the trainees with whom I worked but also to empower their organizations, but I am not convinced that this aim was achieved. In retrospect, it is possible to see that the design of the research programme had flaws from the start in that the links between the training and the functioning of the national DPOs had not been adequately thought about. This I am able to say with hindsight, and I do not believe that this shows a design flaw on the part of those who set up the programme. I think it is an important lesson for the future which could be arrived at only through experience. But I also believe that there are more fundamental issues at stake.

There has been sterling work done in the Global North about building the capacity of disabled people, including people with intellectual disability, to play key roles in formulating questions and collecting, analysing and reporting data (see Box 17.2). This research has taken place within an enabling research environment – for example people with intellectual disability have been well supported by experienced and sophisticated researchers (Bigby, Frawley and Ramcharan, 2014a, 2014b).

Inclusive research, as it is known, can be seen as a form of emancipatory research, but with a particular focus – the aim is to include all participants

> ## Box 17.2.   Involving people with intellectual disabilities in research in Ireland
>
> The slogan 'Nothing about us without us' applies equally to people with intellectual disabilities, although this truism is often forgotten because of their cognitive limitations. Although they have been the subjects of research, few opportunities have been given to them to become involved in undertaking a research study. In Ireland, no national study had been conducted to discover what life was like for people with intellectual disabilities. To do this, staff at the National Institute for Intellectual Disability at Trinity College Dublin adopted a community of practice approach that involved a core group of five people with intellectual disabilities, four university researchers and three service support staff. An additional cadre of 15 co-researchers was recruited and trained, who undertook data gathering and analysis with 23 focus groups involving 168 participants from across the island of Ireland.
>
> The research experience was documented through oral feedback, reports, minutes of meetings and an end-of-project review. Valuable insights were gained into how the various steps of the research process could be adapted to ensure co-researchers with intellectual disabilities were fully involved. This included identifying the research questions; recruiting co-researchers; training co-researchers; gathering data through focus groups; analysing the data and presenting of the findings through audio-visual means as well as accessible text.
>
> Further details of the findings are provided in:
>
> P. O'Brien, R. McConkey, and E. García-Iriarte. (2014). 'Co-researching with people who have intellectual disabilities: Insights from a national survey', *Journal of Applied Research in Intellectual Disabilities, 27*(1), 65–75.
>
> The findings from the study are reported in:
>
> E.G. García Iriarte, P. O'Brien, R. McConkey, M. Wolfe and S. O'Doherty. (2014). 'Identifying the key concerns of Irish persons with intellectual disabilities', *Journal of Applied Research in Intellectual Disabilities, 27*(6), 564–575.

in the research in all aspects for the research process, from conceptualizing research questions to analysing and disseminating the findings of the research. There can be no question that this work has increased the possibilities for meaningful participation in research by disabled people, including people once considered cognitively incapable of contributing to research except as objects of the 'knowledges' of others. Inclusive research has shown very clearly how great the contribution can be of the thinking, expertize and insider knowledge of disabled people to how research is done and to the difference research can make to people's lives.

In the context of disability-related research in Southern Africa, by contrast, this highly enabling environment is not present. As I have suggested at the outset of this chapter, some of the reasons for the lack of this enabling environment lie in the realm of the politics of knowledge far beyond the relatively narrow realm of the DPO. Partly because of the global relationships between knowledge and power, furthermore, there has at times been posited a false binary between the value of indigenous 'knowledges' and the value of global research and science, a binary which was exploited in the context of AIDS denialism in Southern Africa, and which led to the unnecessary deaths of hundreds of thousands of people (Nattrass, 2010). There has been the false assertion that in order to be an authentic African, one must disavow outsider knowledge (Mangcu, 2013). This kind of discursive positioning cannot but have particular resonance for disabled African people, who in their own context share with disabled people worldwide a history of disavowal and exclusion. This may make them especially susceptible to wishing to be seen as part of the 'authentic' mainstream. This is not an optimal environment in which to become a disability researcher.

At a more mundane but no less important level, the SAFOD trainees were operating in organizations which did not have the skills to support them optimally – in fact, part of their role as very novice researchers was constructed as to develop their own organizations. This would be very difficult to achieve as a novice researcher.

In retrospect, it is clear that what we should have designed was a more active iterative process of engagement both with the trainees and with the organizations as a whole. It was not enough to have, as we did, meetings with leadership representatives from the organizations before the training started and towards the end of the process as part of feedback. But the kind of intensive engagement we would have needed would have been very expensive and ideally would have included multiple visits by the trainers to work with the DPOs on issues of knowledge within their own organizations.

It is clear, when we contrast the experiences of well-supported disabled people in research processes in well-resourced contexts, compared with those of the SAFOD trainees, that, as the social model of disability and all that has followed it emphasizes, context matters. To assume that we could embed our achievements more fully than we were able to was an incorrect assumption, and an assumption which failed to take adequate account of the enablers and barriers in the social environment.

This failure to understand context fully was, I think, understandable for a number of reasons. I did not understand, nor would I have imagined, the extent of challenge around knowledge issues in Southern African DPOs had I not first had the engagement that I did have with the trainees and their organizations. Nor would it have been reasonable for others to have anticipated the challenges. It is also the case that in many ways the SAFOD Research Programme was driven by an idealistic wish to make a radical change to how knowledge would be used by DPOs in Southern Africa. Without this big vision, the project would probably not have happened at all, and there is no question in my mind that now that the project has been completed, many of us have learned a great deal. The social model of disability is also about the creation of enabling environments and the progressive realization of these, and I like to think of the SAFOD programme as part of a bigger enabling process for people with disabilities to urge States in conducting research on disability issues (Article 31) and for people with disabilities to participate in the monitoring of the CRPD (Article 33).

Conclusions

It is reasonably easy to train groups of people in some of the technical skills associated with research, and these skills are important. The more fundamental challenge for the achievement of disability rights, in low-resource contexts in particular, is to create an environment in which knowledge can be usefully generated and used. This is not a question limited to research issues, but more fundamentally about how DPOs in specific sociopolitical contexts can develop their capacity to become more flexible as thinking organizations. Research capacity cannot and should not be seen as a separate add-on. At best, research thinking should play a role that all good research plays – to unsettle, to provide better questions (rather than simply more answers) and to challenge organizations to develop their reflexive thinking skills. This cannot be achieved simply by training researchers – a much more fundamental engagement with organizational processes is needed.

Summary of key points

- Developing research capacity for members of DPOs in low- and middle-income countries is important so as to enable them to inform policy making (Article 31) and monitor the implementation of the CRPD (Article 33).
- Trainees commonly work in contexts within which there are major challenges regarding the use of research and knowledge to inform practice and policy.
- It is crucial to understand research capacity within a much broader context of how knowledge is used or not used by DPOs, donors, governments and service providers, and to link any research trainings to the local realities regarding knowledge use.
- Empowerment practices are commonly directed at organizations or groups rather than individuals. Unless careful attention is given to the relationship between trainees and their organizations, and to how they will feed their learning into their organizations, dissemination of new knowledge and skills will be compromised.

STUDY QUESTIONS

1. If you were to plan a similar research training for persons with disabilities, how would you ascertain their perceptions of the uses to which new knowledge derived from research would be put?

2. In the context of large divides in terms of access to education and resources, how is it possible to conduct research in the most emancipatory way possible?

3. How possible is it to empower organizations as opposed to just individuals? What can we do to optimize the chances of transfer from small-scale trainings to large-scale organizations?

Further reading and resources

C. Barnes and G. Mercer. (1997). 'Breaking the mould? An introduction to doing disability research'. In C. Barnes and G. Mercer (Eds.), *Doing Disability Research* (Leeds: The Disability Press), pp. 1–14.

C. Barnes. (2003). 'What a difference a decade makes: Reflections on doing "emancipatory" disability research', *Disability and Society*, 18(1), 3–17.

Disability Knowledge and Resources project, http://r4d.dfid.gov.uk/.

SAFOD training is available from https://www.youtube.com/watch?v=r8U9QjyRAcI.

E. Stone and M. Priestley. (1996). 'Parasites, pawns and partners: Disability research and the role of non-disabled researchers', *British Journal of Sociology*, 47(4), 699–716.

L. Swartz. (2013). 'Between faith and doubt: Training members of disabled people's organisations in Southern Africa in basic research skills'. In J. Claassens, L. Swartz and L. D. Hansen (Eds.), *Searching for Dignity: Conversations on Human Dignity, Theology and Disability* (Stellenbosch: SUNMedia), pp. 81–90.

L. Swartz. (2009). 'Building disability research capacity in low-income contexts: Possibilities and challenges'. In M. MacLachlan and L. Swartz (Eds.), *Disability and International Development: Towards Inclusive Global Health* (New York: Springer), pp. 91–103.

J. Walmsley and K. Johnson. (2003). *Inclusive Research with People with Learning Disabilities: Past, Present and Futures* (London: Jessica Kingsley Publishers).

G. Zarb. (1992). 'On the road to Damascus: First steps towards changing the relations of disability research production', *Disability, Handicap and Society*, 7(2), 125–138.

References

Abbott, C. (2007). *Report 15, E-Inclusion: Learning Difficulties and Digital Technologies* (Bristol, UK: Futurelab).

Abbott, C., Brown, D., Evett, L., Standen, P. and Wright, J. (2011). *Learning Difference and Digital Technologies: A Literature Review of Research Involving Children and Young People Using Assistive Technologies 2007–2010*, accessed 1 April 2014 from http://clahrc-ndl.nihr.ac.uk/research/groups/longtermconditions/documents/at20072010abbottetal.pdf.

Abidi, J. (2014). www.dpi.org and personal communication.

Adnams, C.M. (2010). 'Perspectives of intellectual disability in South Africa: Epidemiology, policy, services for children and adults', *Current Opinion in Psychiatry*, 23, 436–440.

Aguilar Tamayo, M.F. (2004). 'El concepto de desarrollo en Vygotski como marco de reflexión para el uso de tecnologías en la enseñanza y aprendizaje en personas con discapacidad', *Plasticidad y Restauración Neurológica*, 3(1–2), 45–58.

G.L. Albrecht, K.D. Seelman and M. Bury (Eds.). (2001). *Handbook of Disability Studies* (Thousand Oaks, CA: Sage).

Alcantud Marín, F. and Soto, F.J. (2003). *Tecnologías de ayuda en personas con trastornos de comunicación*, accessed 15 May 2014 from http://dialnet.unirioja.es/servlet/autor?codigo=888650#ArticulosRevistas.

Aldersey, H.M. (2013). 'Disability advocacy in Kinshasa, Democratic Republic of the Congo', *Disability & Society*, 28(6), 784–797.

Ali, A., Hassiotis, A., Strydom, A. and King, M. (2012). 'Self stigma in people with intellectual disabilities and courtesy stigma in family carers: A systematic review', *Research in Developmental Disabilities*, 33(6), 2122–2140.

Al Thani, S.H.K. (2006). 'Disability in the Arab region: Current situation and prospects', *Journal for Disability and International Development*, 3, 4–9.

Altman, B.M. (2001). 'Disability definitions, models, classification schemes, and applications'. In G.L. Albrecht, K.D. Seelman and M. Bury (Eds.), *Handbook of Disability Studies* (Thousand Oaks, CA: Sage).

Alves, T. and Lopez, L. (2008). 'Asociación Obra Social Irma Dulce, Premio Reina Sofía 2007 de Rehabilitación y de Integración', *Boletín del Real Patronato sobre Discapacidad*, 63, 14–23.

American Association on Intellectual and Developmental Disabilities (AAIDD). (2012). *User's Guide for Intellectual Disability: Definition, Classification, and Systems of Supports*, Eleventh Edition. (Washington, DC: AAIDD).

American Community Survey. (2012). Accessed 16 May 2014 from http://www.census.gov/acs/www/data_documentation/2012_release/.

American Community Survey. (2011). Accessed 16 May 2014 from http://www.census.gov/pro d/2012pubs/acsbr11-01.pdf.

American Community Survey. (2008). Accessed 16 May 2014 from http://www.census.gov/acs/www/data_documentation/2008_release/.

Amin, M., MacLachlan, M., Mannan, H., El Tayeb, S., El Khatim, A., Swartz, L., Munthali, A., Van Rooy, G., McVeigh, J., Eide, A. and Schneider, M. (2011). 'EquiFrame: A framework for analysis of the inclusion of human rights and vulnerable groups in health policies', *Health & Human Rights: An International Journal*, (13)2, 1–20.

Ansello, E.F. and Coogle, C.L. (2000). 'Building intersystem cooperation: Partners III integrated model'. In M.P. Janicki and E.F. Ansello (Eds.), *Community Supports for Aging Adults with Lifelong Disabilities* (Baltimore, MD: Paul H. Brookes).

Anthony, A. (2011). 'Conceptualising disability in Ghana: Implications for EFA and inclusive Education', *International Journal of Inclusive Education*, 15(10), 1073–1086.

Area Moreira, M. (2010). 'Reflexiones sobre la alfabetización tecnológica'. In P.P. Hall (Ed.), *Nuevas Tecnologías y Educación* (Madrid: <insert publisher>), pp. 85–88.

Asian Development Bank. (2000). *Technical Assistance for Identifying Disability Issues Related to Poverty Reduction* (Manila, Philippines: Asian Development Bank).

Assistive Technology Industry Association (ATiA). (2014). 'What is Assistive Technology?', accessed 21 April 2014 from http://www.atia.org/i4a/pages/index.cfm?pageid=1.

The Associated Press. (2012). 'The shocking cost of war: Afghanistan and Iraq veterans are 'the most damaged generation ever' with almost HALF seeking disability benefits', *Mail Online*, 28 May, [Online]. accessed 24 February from http://www.dailymail.co.uk/news/article-2150933/The-shocking-cost-war-Afghanistan-Iraq-veterans-damaged-generation-HALF-seeking-disability-benefits.html

Atilola, O., Omigbodun, O., Bella-Awusah, T., Lagunju, I. and Igbeneghu, P. (2014). 'Neurological and intellectual disabilities among adolescents within a custodial institution in South-West Nigeria', *Journal of Psychiatric and Mental Health Nursing*, 21, 31–38.

Atkin, K. and Hussain, Y. (2003). 'Disability and ethnicity: How young Asian disabled people make sense of their lives'. In S. Riddell and N. Watson (Eds.), *Disability, Culture and Identity* (New York: Routledge).

A.B. Atkinson and J. Hills (Eds.). (1998). *CASE Paper 4: Exclusion, Employment and Opportunity* (London: London School of Economics, Centre for Analysis of Social Exclusion), accessed 8 March 2014 from http://eprints.lse.ac.uk/5489/1/exclusion,_employment_and_opportunity.PDF.

Australian Institute of Health and Welfare. (2004). *Disability and Its Relationship to Health Conditions and other Factors*, accessed 24 February 2014 from http://www.aihw.gov.au/WorkArea/DownloadAsset.aspx?id=6442455793.

Azmi, S., Hatton, C., Emerson, E. and Caine, A. (1997). 'Listening to adolescents and adults with intellectual disabilities from South Asian communities', *Journal of Applied Research in Intellectual Disabilities*, 10(3), 250–263.

Aznar, A.S., González Castañón, D. and Olate, G. (2012). 'The ITINERIS scale on the rights of persons with intellectual disabilities: Development, pilot studies and application at a country level in South America', *Journal of Intellectual Disability Research*, 56(11), 1046–1057.

Bakiman, B.K. (2012). *RIGHTS-DR CONGO: Disabled Left to Fend for Themselves* (Kikwit, DRC: Inter Press Service News Agency), accessed 25 February 2014 from http://www.ipsnews.net/2012/03/rights-dr-congo-disabled-left-to-fend-for-themselves/.

Baladerian, N.J., Coleman, T.F. and Stream, J. (2013). *Abuse of People with Disabilities: Victims and Their Families Speak Out: A Report of the 2012 National Survey of Abuse of People with Disabilities* (Los Angeles, CA: Spectrum Institute).

Ball, S.J., Maguire, M., Braun, A. and Hoskins, K. (2011a). 'Policy subjects and policy actors in schools: Some necessary but insufficient analyses', *Discourse: Studies in the Cultural Politics of Education*, 33(4), 611–624.

Ball, S.J., Maguire, M., Braun, A. and Hoskins, K. (2011b). 'Policy actors: Doing policy work in schools', *Discourse: Studies in the Cultural Politics of Education*, 33(4), 625–639.

Ballestero, F. (2004). *Informe anual sobre el desarrollo de la Sociedad de la Información en España*, accessed 15 May 2014 from http://fundacionorange.es/areas/25_publicaciones/publi_251_4_2.asp.

Banos Smith, H. (2014). 'Children's reintegration: Longitudinal study of children's reintegration in Moldova', *Moldova Partnerships for Every Child*, accessed 10 June 2014 from http://www.familyforeverychild.org/wp-content/uploads/2014/02/Children-s_Reintegration_in_Moldova.pdf.

Barnes, C. (2010). 'A brief history of discrimination and disabled people'. In L. Davis (Ed.), *The Disability Studies Reader* (New York: Routledge).

Barnes, C. (2006). 'What a difference a decade makes: Reflections on doing "emancipatory" disability research'. In L. Barton (Ed.), *Overcoming Disabling Barriers: 18 Years of Disability and Society* (New York: Routledge).

Barnes, C. (2001). *Rethinking Care from the Perspective of Disabled People: Conference Report and Recommendations*, World Health Organization Disability and Rehabilitation Team, accessed 12 April 2012 from www.leeds.ac.uk/disability-studies/archiveuk/WHO/whoreport.pdf.

Barnes, C. and Mercer, G. (2010). *Exploring Disability*, 2nd edn (Cambridge: Polity Press).

Barnes, M. (2005). *Social Exclusion in Great Britain. An Empirical Investigation and Comparison with the EU* (Aldershot, UK: Ashgate).

Barr, O., Gilgunn, J., Kane, T. and Moore, G. (1999). 'Health screening for people with learning disabilities by a community learning disability nursing service in Northern Ireland', *Journal of Advanced Nursing*, 29, 1482–1491.

Barron, T. and Ncube, J.M. (2010). *Poverty and Disability* (London: Leonard Cheshire Disability), accessed 27 February 2014 from http://www.dpiap.org/resources/pdf/Poverty_Disability_Summary_Booklet_LCD_11_11_09.pdf.

Bayat, M. (2014). 'Understanding views of disability in Côte d'Ivoire', *Disability and Society*, 29, 30–43.

Beange, J., McElduff, H. and Baker, A. (1992). 'People with mental retardation have an increased prevalence of Osteoporosis: A population study', *American Journal on Mental Retardation*, 103, 19–28.

Benda, P., Havlíček, Z., Lohr, V. and Havránek, M. (2011). 'ICT helps to overcome disabilities', *Economics and Informatics*, 3(4), 63–69.

Bennet, M. (2011). 'Children's social identities', *Infant and Child Development*, 20(4), 353–363.

Bhaumik, S., Tyrer, F.C., McGrother, C. and Ganghadaran, S.K. (2008). 'Psychiatric service use and psychiatric disorders in adults with intellectual disability', *Journal of Intellectual Disability Research*, 52(11), 986–995.

Bickenbach, J.E. (2009). 'Disability, culture and the UN convention', *Disability & Rehabilitation*, 31(14), 1111–1124.

Bickenbach, J.E., Chatterji, S., Badley, E.M. and Üstün, T.B. (1999). 'Models of disablement, universalism and the international classification of impairments, disabilities and handicaps', *Social Science & Medicine*, 48(9), 1173–1187.

Bigby, C. (2010). 'A five-country comparative review of accommodation support policies for older people with intellectual disabilities', *Journal of Policy and Practice in Intellectual Disabilities*, 7, 3–15.

Bigby, C. (2002). 'Ageing people with a lifelong disability: Challenges for the aged care and disability sectors', *Journal of Intellectual and Developmental Disability*, 27, 231–241.

Bigby, C. (1997). 'When parents relinquish care: The informal support networks of older people with intellectual disability', *Journal of Applied Intellectual Disability Research*, 10(4), 333–344

Bigby, C., Frawley, P. and Ramcharan, P. (2014a). 'A collaborative group method of inclusive research', *Journal of Applied Research in Intellectual Disabilities*, 27(1), 54–64.

Bigby, C., Frawley, P. and Ramcharan, P. (2014b). 'Conceptualizing inclusive research with people with intellectual disability', *Journal of Applied Research in Intellectual Disabilities*, 27(1), 3–12.

Bigby, C., McCallion, P. and McCarron, M. (2014). 'Serving an Elderly Population'. In M. Agran, F. Brown, C. Hughes, C. Quirk and D. Ryndak (Eds.), *Equality & Full Participation for Individuals with Severe Disabilities: A Vision for the Future* (Baltimore: Paul H. Brookes).

Bines, H. and Lei, P. (2011). 'Disability and education: The longest road to inclusion', *International Journal of Educational Development*, 31(5), 419–424.

Biswas, P. and Robinson, P. (2013). 'Evaluating interface layout for visually impaired and mobility-impaired users through simulation', *Universal Access in the Information Society*, 12, 55–72, doi 10.1007/s10209-011-0265-5

Bittles, A.H., Bower, C., Hussain, R. and Glasson, E.J. (2007). 'The four ages of Down syndrome', *European Journal of Public Health*, 17(2), 221–225.

Bittles, A.H., Petterson, B., Sullivan, S., Hussain, R., Glasson, E. and Montgomery, P. (2002). 'The influence of intellectual disability on life expectancy', *Journal of Gerontology: Medical Sciences*, 57(7), 470–472.

Borg, J., Lindstrøm, A. and Larsson, S. (2009). 'Assistive technology in developing countries: National and international responsibilities to implement the Convention on the Rights of Persons with Disabilities', *Lancet*, 374(9704), 1863–1865.

Bothma, M., Gravett, S. and Swart, E. (2000). 'The attitudes of primary school teachers towards inclusive education', *South African Journal of Education*, 20, 200–204.

Bøttcher, L. and Dammeyer, J. (2012). 'Disability as a dialectical concept: Building on Vygotsky's defectology', *European Journal of Special Needs Education*, 27(4), 433–446.

Boushey, H., Brocht, C., Gundersen, B. and Bernstein, J. (2001). *Hardships in America: The Real Story of Working Families* (Washington, DC: Economic Policy Institute).

Boylan, E. (1991). *Women and Disability* (London: Zed Books).

Braddock, D.L., Hemp, R., Rizzolo, M.C., Tanis, E.S., Haffer, L., Lulinski, A. and Wu, J. (2013). *State of the States in Developmental Disabilities, 2013* (Washington, DC: American Association on Intellectual and Developmental Disabilities).

Braddock, D.L., and Parish, S.L. (2001). 'An institutional history of disability'. In G.L. Albrecht, K.D. Seelman and M. Bury (Eds.), *Handbook of Disability Studies* (Thousand Oaks, CA: Sage).

Braithwaite, J. and Mont, D. (2009). 'Disability and poverty: A survey of World Bank poverty assessments and implications', *ALTER-European Journal of Disability Research*, 3(3), 219–232.

Brehmer-Rinderer, B., Zigrovic, L., Naue, U. and Weber, G. (2013). 'Promoting health of persons with intellectual disabilities using the UN convention on the rights of persons with disabilities: Early implementation assessment in Spain and Hungary', *Journal of Policy and Practice in Intellectual Disability*, 10(1), 25–36.

Brehmer-Rinderer, B., Zigrovic, L. and Weber, G. (2014). Evaluating a health behaviour model for persons with and without an intellectual disability, *Journal of Intellectual Disability Research*, 58(6), 495–507.

Brooks-Gunn, J. and Duncan, G.J. (1997). 'The effects of poverty on children', *The Future of Children*, 7(2), 55–71.

R. Brown and R. Faragher (Eds.). (2014). *Quality of Life and Intellectual Disability: Knowledge Application to Other Social and Educational Challenges* (New York: Nova Science Publishers).

Buchan, J. and Dal Poz, M.R. (2003). 'Role definition, skill mix, multi-skilling and "New Workers"'. In P. Ferrinho and M. Dal Poz (Eds.), *Towards a Global Health Workforce Strategy* (Belgium: ITG Press), pp. 275–300, accessed 12 April 2012 from www.itg.be/itg/GeneralSite/infservices/downloads/shsop21.pdf.

Bullock, C.C. and Mahon, J.M. (2000). *Introduction to Recreation Services for People with Disabilities: A Person Centred Approach*, 2nd edn (Illinois: Sagamore Publishing Campaign).

Burchardt, T. (2003). *Being and Becoming: Social Exclusion and the Onset of Disability* (London: ESRC Centre for Analysis of Social Exclusion, London School of Economics), accessed 10 March 2014 from http://eprints.lse.ac.uk/28310/1/CASEreport21.pdf.

Burg, S.L. and Shoup, P.S. (1999). *The War in Bosnia Herzegovina: Ethnic Conflict and International Intervention* (New York: M.E. Sharpe Inc.).

Burke, M.A. and Eichler, M. (2006). *The BIAS FREE Framework: A Practical Tool for Identifying and Eliminating Social Biases in Health Research*, accessed 11 April 2012 from http://whqlibdoc.who.int/hq/2006/GFHR_The_BIAS_FREE_eng.pdf.

Burke, M.M., Taylor, J.L., Urbano, R., Hodapp, R.M. (2012). 'Predictors of future caregiving by adult siblings of individuals with intellectual and developmental disabilities', *American Journal of Intellectual and Developmental Disabilities*, 117(1), 33–47.

Business & Disability. (2014). Accessed 30 July 2014 from http://www.businessand disability.org (home page).

Byrnes, A. (2014). 'The role of national human rights institutions'. In M. Sabatello and M. Schulze (Eds.), *Human Rights and Disability Advocacy* (Philadelphia: University of Pennsylvania Press), pp. 223–238.

Calderisi, R. (2007). *The Trouble with Africa: Why Foreign Aid Is Not Working* (New York: Palgrave Macmillan).

Campbell, F.K. (2009). *Contours of Ableism: The Production of Disability and Abledness* (Basingstoke: Palgrave Macmillan).

Carin, B. and Bates-Earner, N. (2012). *Post 2015 Goals, Targets and Indicators.* Conference report. (Paris: Centre for International Governance Innovations and Korean Development Institute).

Caro, D.A., Murray, S.F. and Putney, P. (2004). *Evaluation of the Averting Maternal Death and Disability Program; A Grant from the Bill and Melinda Gates Foundation to the Columbia University Mailman School of Public Health*, accessed 15 May 2012 from www.amddprogram.org/v1/resources/2004%20AMDD%20 EVALUATION%20REPORT.pdf.

Carpenter, B. (1998). 'Defining the family: Towards a critical framework for families of children with disabilities', *European Journal of Special Needs Education*, 13(2), 180–188.

Carpenter, J. and McConkey, R. (2012). 'Disabled children's voices: The nature and role of future empirical enquiry', *Children & Society*, 26: 251–261.

Census of India. (2012). *Overview of Statistical Evidences on Disability* (New Delhi: Census of India), accessed 22 April 2014 from http://mospi.nic.in/Mospi_New/upload/ disablity_india_statistical_date_11mar2011/Chapter%202%20-Overview.pdf.

Centers for Disease Control and Prevention. (2011). 'Health disparities and inequalities report', *Mortality and Morbidity Report Weekly*, 60, accessed 22 April 2014 from http://www.cdc.gov/mmwr/pdf/other/su6001.pdf.

Centro Nacional de Memoria Histórica. (2013). *BASTA YA! Colombia: Memorias de guerra y dignidad, Informe General Grupo de Memoria Histórica* (Colombia: National Center of Historic Memory).

Chadwick, D., Mannan, H., Garcia Iriarte, E., McConkey, R., O'Brien, P., Finlay, F., Lawlor, A. and Harrington, G. (2013). 'Family voices: Life for family carers of people with intellectual disabilities in Ireland', *Journal of Applied Research in Intellectual Disabilities*, 26(2), 119–132.

Chalken, S., Seutloadi, K. and Sadek, S. (2009). *Literature Review: SAFOD-Southern African Federation of the Disabled* (Bulawayo: SAFOD).

Charlton, I.J. (1998). *Nothing about US without US: Disability Oppression and Empowerment* (Berkeley and Los Angeles: University of California Press).

Chataika,T., McKenzie, J., Swart, E. and Lyner-Cleophas, M. (2012). 'Access to education in Africa: Responding to the United Nations Convention on the Rights of Persons with Disabilities', *Disability and Society*, 27(3), 385–398.

Chen, A.Y. and Newacheck, P. (2006). 'Insurance coverage and financial burden for families of children with special health care needs', *Ambulatory Pediatrics*, 6, 204–209.

Cheng, Y. and Chen, S. (2010). 'Improving social understanding of individuals of intellectual and developmental disabilities through a 3D-facial expression intervention program', *Research In Developmental Disabilities*, 31(6), 1434–1442.

China Disabled Persons' Federation. http://www.cdpf.org.cn/english/home.htmhttp://www.ilo.org/wcmsp5/groups/public/---asia/---ro-bangkok/---ilo-beijing/documents/publication/wcms_142315.pdf.

City Press. (2012). 'Zuma scolds clever blacks', accessed 30 July 2014 from http://www.citypress.co.za/news/zuma-scolds-clever-blacks-20121103/.

Cleaver, S., Hunter, D. and Ouellette-Kuntz, H. (2009). 'Physical mobility limitations in adults with intellectual disabilities: A systematic review', *Journal of Intellectual Disability Research*, 53(2), 93–10.

Cobigo, V., Ouellette-Kuntz, H., Lysaght, R. and Martin, L. (2012). 'Shifting our conceptualization of social inclusion', *Stigma Research & Action*, 2(2), 75–84.

Cobley, D.S. (2013). 'Towards economic participation: Examining the impact of the Convention on the Rights of Persons with Disabilities in India', *Disability & Society*, 28(4), 441–455.

Coghlan, B., Ngoy, P., Mulumba, F., Hardy, C., Bemo, V.N., Stewart, T., Lewis, J. and Brennan, R. (2007). 'Mortality in the Democratic Republic of Congo: An Ongoing Crisis,' accessed 24 February 2014 from http://www.rescue.org/sites/default/files/resource-file/2006-7_congoMortalitySurvey.pdf.

Cohen, D. (2006). 'Disabled Veterans'. In G.A. Albrecht, J. Bickenbach, D.T. Mitchell, W.O. Schalick and S. Synder (Eds.), *Encyclopedia of Disability* (Thousand Oaks, CA: Sage Publications).

Coleridge, P. (2013). *Community Approaches to Livelihood: Creating Networks of Mutually Supporting Relationships* (Behinderung und der Dritte Welt, Autumn 2013).

Coleridge, P. (2007). *The Leprosy Mission India. Evaluation of the Vocational Training for Earning Power Project*. March 2007. Unpublished report.

Coleridge, P. (1993). *Disability, Liberation and Development* (Oxford: Oxfam).

Coleridge, P., Simonnot, C. and Steverlynk, D. (2011). 'Study of Disability in EC Development Cooperation', accessed 30 July 2014 from http://ec.europa.eu/europeaid/what/social-protection/documents/223185_disability_study_en.pdf.

Commission on Social Determinants of Health. (2008). *Closing the Gap in a Generation: Health Equity through Action on the Social Determinants of Health*, Final Report of the Commission on Social Determinants of Health (Geneva: World Health Organization), accessed 12 April 2012 from http://www.searo.who.int/LinkFiles/SDH_SDH_FinalReport.pdf.

Commonwealth of Australia. (2011). *National Disability Strategy 2010–2020* (Canberra, Australia).

Contreras, D.G., Ruiz-Tagle, J., Garcés, P. and Azócar, I. (2006). *Socio-Economic Impact of Disability in Latin America: Chile and Uruguay* (Santiago, Chile: Universidad de Chile, Departamento de Economía).

Cook, A.M. and Polgar, J.M. (2008). *Cook and Hussey's Assistive Technologies: Principles and Practice* (St. Louis, Missouri: MOSBY, Elsevier).

Cooper, S.A., Smiley, E., Morrison, J., Williamson, A. and Allan, L. (2007). 'Mental ill-health in persons with ID: Prevalence and associated factors', *British Journal of Psychiatry*, 190, 27–35.

Cortiella, C. (2013). *Diplomas at Risk: A Critical Look at the Graduation Rate of Students with Learning Disabilities* (New York, NY: National Center on Learning Disabilities).

Council of Europe. (2006). *Disability Action Plan 2006–2015*, http://www.coe.int/t/e/social_cohesion/soc-sp/integration/02_Council_of_Europe_Disability_Action_Plan/.

Cousins, J.B. and Earl, L.M. (1992). 'The case for participatory evaluation', *Educational Evaluation and Policy Analysis*, 14(4), 397–418.

Croft, A. (2010). 'Including disabled children in learning: Challenges in developing countries. CREATE pathways to access', *Research Monograph*, 36, accessed 12 December 2013, http://files.eric.ed.gov/fulltext.

Cuervo Echeverri, C.L., Pérez Acevedo, L. and Trujillo Rojas, A. (2008). *Modelo conceptual colombiano de discapacidad e inclusión social*. (Bogotá: Universidad Nacional de Colombia). ISBN: 9789587191035.

Cullen, K., McAnaney, D., Dolphin, C., Delaney, S. and Stapleton, P. (2012). *Research on the Provision of Assistive Technology in Ireland and Other Countries to Support Independent Living Across the Life Cycle* (Dublin: Work Research Centre).

D'amant, A. (2012). 'Within and between the old and the new: Teachers becoming inclusive practitioners', *Perspectives in Education*, 30(1), 53–56.

Darke, P. (1998). 'Understanding cinematic representations of disability.' In T. Shakespeare (Ed.), *The disability reader: Social science perspectives* (London, New York: Cassell).

Davies, D.K., Stock, S.E. and Wehmeyer, M.L. (2002). 'Enhancing independent task performance for individuals with mental retardation through use of a handheld self-directed visual and audio prompting system', *Education and Training in Mental Retardation and Developmental Disabilities*, 37(2), 209–218.

Davies, D.K., Stock, S.E. and Wehmeyer, M.L. (2001). 'Enhancing independent Internet access for individuals with mental retardation through use of a specialized web browser: A pilot study', *Education and Training in Autism and Developmental Disabilities*, 36(1), 107–113.

Davies, G.A. (2009). 'Wounded Veteran Kortney Clemons takes on Oscar Pistorius at the Paralympic World Cup', *The Telegraph*, 23 May, accessed 24 February 2014 from http://www.telegraph.co.uk/sport/olympics/paralympic-sport/5373861/Wounded-veteran-Kortney-Clemons-takes-on-Oscar-Pistorius-at-the-Paralympic-World-Cup.html.

Davis, L.J. (2013). *The End of Normal: Identity in a Biocultural Era* (Ann Arbor: The University of Michigan Press).

Davis, L.J. (2010). 'Constructing normalcy'. In L.J. Davis (Ed.), *The Disability Studies Reader* (New York: Routledge).

Day, K. and Jancar, J. (1994). 'Mental and physical health and ageing in mental handicap: A review', *Journal of Intellectual Disability Research*, 38(3), 241–256.

Deegan, M.J. and Brooks, N.A. (1985). *Women and Disability: The Double Handicap* (New Brunswick, USA: Transaction Books).

DeJong, G. (1979). 'Independent living: From social movement to analytic paradigm', *Archives of Physical Medicine and Rehabilitation*, 60, 435–446.

Department for International Development (DFID). (2010). 'Rations and child screening make for healthier picture in Eritrea', accessed 15 May 2012 from www.dfid. gov.uk/Stories/Case-Studies/2010/Rations-and-child-screening-make-for-healthier-picture-in-Eritrea/.

Department for International Development (DFID). (2000). *Disability, Poverty and Development* (London: DFID), accessed 12 June 2013 from http://www.dfid.gov. uk/pubs/?les/disability.pdf.

Department for Work and Pensions. (2013). *Fulfilling Potential: Building a Deeper Understanding of Disability in the UK today* (UK: Crown Copyright).

De Silva de Alwis, R. (2010). *The Intersections of the CEDAW and CRPD: Putting Women's Rights and Disability Rights Into Action In Four Asian Countries* (Wellesley, MA: Wellesley Centers for Women, Wellesley College).

De Sousa Santos, B. (2002). 'Hacia una concepción multicultural de los derechos humanos', *El Otro Derecho*, 28, 59–83.

Devlieger, P.J. (2005). 'Generating a cultural model of disability'. Paper presented at the 19th Congress of the European Federation of Associations of Teachers of the Deaf (FEAPDA), University of Leuven and University of Illinois, Chicago (USA).

Devlieger, P.J. (1995). 'Why disabled? The cultural understanding of physical disability in an African society'. In B. Ingstad and S.R. Whyte (Eds.), *Disability and culture* (Berkeley: University of California Press), pp. 94–106

Dhungana, B.M. (2006). 'The lives of disabled women in Nepal: Vulnerability without support', *Disability and Society*, 21(2), 133–146.

Disability Information Forum (DINF). (2012). *Incheon Strategy to 'Make the Right Real' for Persons with Disabilities in Asia and the Pacific* (Bangkok: UNESCAP), accessed 18 March 2014 from http://www.dinf.ne.jp/doc/english/twg/incheon_strategy121123_e. html#KEY.

Disability Rights Promotion International. (2011). *A Guide to Disability Rights Monitoring: Participant Version Regional Training* (Toronto: York University), http://www.yorku.ca/drpi.

Disabled Persons South Africa (DPSA). (1993). *Advocacy Training Manual* (South Africa: Disabled Persons South Africa).

Dixon, L., Green-Paden, L., Delahanty, J., Lucksted, A., Postrado, L. and Hall, J. (2001). 'Variables associated with disparities in treatment of patients with schizophrenia and Comorbid Mood and Anxiety Disorders', *Psychiatric Services*, 52(9), 1216–1222.

Doane, D. (2013). 'From charity to solidarity', *Resurgence*, 280.

Dogra, N. (2012). *Representations of Global Poverty: Aid, Development and International NGOs* (Nandita Dogra, IB Tauris).

Dowling, S., Kelly, B. and Winter, K. (2012). *Disabled Children and Young People Who Are Looked After: A Literature Review* (Belfast: Queen's University Belfast).

Doyle, S. and Flynn, E. (2013). 'Ireland's ratification of the UN Convention on the Rights of Persons with Disabilities: Challenges and opportunities', *British Journal of Learning Disabilities*, 41, 171–180.

Driedger, D. (1989). *The Last Civil Rights Movement; Disabled People's International* (London: Hurst & Co.).

Driscoll, B. (2013). 'Debenhams diversity campaign uses plus size model, paralympian and a 69 year old', *The Huffington Post United Kingdom*, 15 April 2013, accessed 30 July 2014, http://www.huffingtonpost.co.uk/ (home page).

Dunst, C.J., Johanson, C., Trivette, C.M. and Hamby, D. (1991). 'Family-oriented early intervention policies and practices: Family-centered or not?', *Exceptional Children*, 58(2), 115–126.

Dunst, C.J., Trivette, C.M. and Deal, A.G. (1988). *Enabling and Empowering Families: Principles and Guidelines for Practice* (Cambridge MA: Brookline Books).

Durham University. (2014). *Definitions of Accessibility and Usability*, https://www.dur.ac.uk/ (home page).

Durkin, M.S. and Gottlieb, C. (2009). 'Prevention versus protection: Reconciling global public health and human rights perspectives on childhood disability', *Disability & Health Journal*, 2(1), 7–8.

Duskin Leadership Training Program in Japan (DLTJ). (2014). Accessed 19 March 2014 from http://www.normanet.ne.jp/~duskin/english/index.html (home page).

Dye, T.R. (1981). *Understanding Public Policy*, 4th edn (Englewood Cliffs, NJ: Prentice-Hall).

Echeverría, J. (2004). *Los señores del aire: Telépolis y el tercer entorno*, 2nd edn (Barcelona: Destino).

Economic and Social Commission for Asia and the Pacific (ESCAP). (2010). *Disability at a Glance 2010: A Profile of 36 Countries and Areas in Asia and the Pacific* (Bangkok: United Nations Social Development Division), http://www.unescap.org.

Economic and Social Commission for Asia and the Pacific (ESCAP). (1995). *Hidden Sisters: Women and Girls with Disabilities in the Asian and Pacific Region.* (ST/ESCAP/1548) (New York: United Nations).

Economic and Social Commission for Western Asia (ESCWA). (2012). *Managing change: Mainstreaming disability into the mainstream process.* E/ESCWA/SDD/2012/Brochure.1, http://www.escwa.un.org.

Economic Commission for Latin America and the Caribbean (ECLAC). (2011). *An Analysis of the Status of Implementation of the Convention on the Rights of Persons with Disabilities in the Caribbean* (Port of Spain, Trinidad: United Nations. ECLAC).

Economic Commission for Latin America and the Caribbean (ECLAC) and UNICEF. (2013). 'Rights of children and adolescents with disabilities', *Challenge Newsletter*, 15. Santiago. http://www.eclac.org.

Eide, A.H. and Loeb, M.E. (2006). *Living Conditions Among People with Activity Limitations In Zambia: A National Representative Study* (Oslo, Norway: SINTEF Health Research), accessed 20 July 2014 from http://www.sintef.no/upload/Helse/Levek%C3%A5r%20og%20tjenester/ZambiaLCweb.pdf.

Eide, A.H. and Øderud, T. (2009). 'Disability and assistive technology in low-income countries'. In M. MacLachlan and L. Swartz (Eds.), *Disability & International Development: Towards Inclusive Global Health* (New York: Springer).

Einfeld, S.L., Stancliffe, R.J., Gray, K.M., Sofronoff, K., Rice, L., Emerson, E. and Yasamy, M.T. (2012). 'Interventions provided by parents for children with intellectual disabilities in low and middle income Countries', *Journal of Applied Research in Intellectual Disabilities*, 25(2), 135–142.

Eloff, F.I. and Kqwete, L.K. (2007). 'South African teachers' voices on support in inclusive education', *Childhood Education, International Focus*, 351–355.

Eloff, F.I., Swart, E. and Engelbrecht, P. (2002). 'Including a learner with physical disabilities: Stressful for teachers?', *KOERS*, 67(1), 77–100.

Elwan, A. (1999). *Poverty and Disability: A Survey of Literature*, Social Protection Discussion Paper, No. 9932 (Washington, DC: World Bank).

Emerson, E. (2007). 'Poverty and people with intellectual disabilities', *Mental Retardation and Developmental Disabilities Research Reviews*, 13, 107–113.

Emerson, E. and Hatton, C. (2009). 'Socioeconomic position, poverty and family research', *International Review of Research in Mental Retardation*, 37, 97–129.

Equalities and Human Rights Commission. (2010). *The United Nations Convention on the Rights of People with Disabilities: What Does it Mean for You?* (London: EHRC), http://www.equalityhumanrights.com.

European Commission. (2002). 'Definitions of disability in Europe: A comparative analysis'. *Directorate-General for Employment and Social Affairs*, accessed 9 September 2013 from http://ec.europa.eu (home page).

European Commission. (2003). 'Equal Opportunities for People with Disabilities: A European Action Plan' (2004–2010) [COM(2003) 650 final].

European Council of Ministers. (1985). 'Council decision 85/8/EEC of 19 December 1984 on specific community action to combat poverty', *Official Journal of the European Community* (OJEC), 1 2, Brussels.

Evans, E., Howlett, S., Kremser, T., Simpson, J., Kayess, R. and Trollor, J. (2012). 'Service development for intellectual disability mental health: A human rights approach', *Journal of Intellectual Disability Research*, 56(11), 1098–1109.

Evans, G.W. (2004). 'The environment of childhood disability', *American Psychologist*, 59(2), 77–92.

Evenhuis, H., Hermans, H., Hilgenkamp, M., Bastiaanse, L. and Echteld, M. (2012). 'Frailty and disability in older adults with intellectual disabilities: Results from the healthy ageing and intellectual disability study', *Journal of American Geriatric Society*, 60, 934–938.

Factor, A., Heller, T. and Janicki, M. (2012). 'Bridging the aging and developmental disabilities services networks: Challenges and best practices'. In RRTC State of Science Conference (Ed.), *Lifespan Health and Function of Adults with Intellectual and Developmental Disabilities: Translating Research into Practice* (Chicago, IL: University of Illinois at Chicago Department on Disability and Human Development), 107–121.

Farmer, P.E. (2011). 'Editor's note', *Health and Human Rights, An International Journal*, accessed 11 April 2012 from www.hhrjournal.org/index.php/hhr/article/view/440/702.

Feika, S. (2013). 'In our own words: Disabled journalists recount the stories of blind', *New Internationalist*, 467, accessed 24 February 2014 from http://newint.org/issues/2013/11/01/.

Felce, D. (2010). Editorial foreword, *Journal of Applied Research in Intellectual Disability*, 23, 97–99.

Fetterman, D. and Wandersman, A. (2005). *Empowerment Evaluation: Principles in Practice* (New York: The Guilford Press).

Filmer, D. (2008). 'Disability, poverty, and schooling in developing countries: Results from 14 household surveys', *World Bank Economic Review*, 22(1), 141–163.

Finkelstein, V. (1980). *Attitudes and Disabled People: Issues for Discussion* (New York: World Rehabilitation Fund).

Fischer, H. (2014). *A Guide to U.S. Military Casualty Statistics: Operation New Dawn, Operation Iraqi Freedom and Operation Enduring Freedom, Congressional Research Service*, 7-5700, accessed 30 July 2014 from http://www.fas.org/sgp/crs/natsec/RS22452.pdf.

Fitzgerald, M.H., Williamson, P., Russell, C. and Manor, D. (2005). 'Doubling the cloak of (in)competence in client/therapist interactions', *Medical Anthropology Quarterly*, 19(3), 331–347.

Flaskerud, J.H. and Winslow, B.J. (1998). 'Conceptualizing vulnerable populations health-related research', *Nursing Research*, 47(2), 69–78.

Foran, S., McCarron, M. and McCallion, P. (2013). 'Expanding assessment of fear of falling among older adults with an intellectual disability: A pilot study to assess the value of proxy responses', *ISRN Geriatrics*, 2013.

Freire, P. (1968, 1996). *Pedagogy of the Oppressed* (London: Continuum).

French, S. and Swain, J. (2007). 'The perspective of the disabled people's movement'. In M. Davies (Ed.), *The Blackwell Companion to Social Work*, 3rd edn (Oxford: Blackwell Publishing).

Fujiura, G.T. (2012). 'Structure of I/DD households in the US: The Family in 2010'. Paper presented at the American Association on Intellectual and Developmental Disabilities, Charlotte, North Carolina.

Fujiura, G. T. and Rutkowski-Kmitta, V. (2001). 'Counting disability'. In G.L. Albrecht, K.D. Seelman and M. Bury (Eds.), *Handbook of Disability Studies* (Thousand Oaks, CA: Sage).

Fujiura, G.T. and Yamaki, K. (2000). 'Trends in demography of childhood poverty and disability', *Exceptional Children*, 66(2), 187–199.

Fyson, R. and Crombie, J. (2013). 'Human rights and intellectual disabilities in an era of "choice"', *Journal of Intellectual Disability Research*, 57(12), 1164–1172.

Gallagher, J.J. (1992). 'Longitudinal interventions: Virtues and limitations'. In T. Thompson and S.C. Hupp (Eds.), *Saving Children at Risk: Poverty and Disabilities* (Newbury Park, CA: Sage Publications).

D. Gallie and S. Paugam (Eds.). (2000). *Welfare Regimes and the Experience of Unemployment in Europe* (Oxford, UK: Oxford University).

García, A. (2011). *Redes Sociales Para Personas Con Discapacidad*, accessed 23 April 2014 from http://www.consumer.es/web/es/solidaridad/proyectos_y_campanas /2011/03/25/199594.php.

García Iriarte, E., Kramer, J.C., Kramer, J.M. and Hammel, J. (2009). '"Who did what?": A participatory action research project to increase group capacity for advocacy', *Journal of Applied Research in Intellectual Disabilities*, 22(1), 10–22.

García Iriarte, E., O'Brien, P., McConkey, R., Wolfe, M. and O'Doherty, S. (2014). 'Identifying the key concerns of Irish persons with intellectual disabilities', *Journal of Applied Research in Intellectual Disabilities*, 27(6), 564–575.

Gauger, A. (2006). *EU Lobbying Handbook: A Guide to Modern Participation* (Brussels: Heilos Media).

Gerber, D.A. (2006). 'War'. In G.A. Albrecht, J. Bickenbach, D.T. Mitchell, W.O. Schalick and S. Snyder (Eds.), *Encyclopedia of Disability* (Thousand Oaks, CA: Sage Publications).

Ghana Education Service. (2005). *Special Educational Needs policy framework: Special Education Division* (Republic of Ghana: Accra).

Ghosh, S. and Magaña, S. (2009). 'A rich mosaic: Emerging research on Asian families of persons with intellectual and developmental disabilities', *International Review of Research in Mental Retardation*, 37, 179–212.

Ghosh, S. and Parish, S. (2013). 'Prevalence and economic well-being of families raising multiple children with disabilities', *Children and Youth Services Review*, 35(9), 1431–1439.

Giddens, A. and Sutton, P.W. (2013). *Sociology*, 7th edn (Malden, MA: Polity Press).

Girimaji, S.C. and Srinath, S. (2010). 'Perspectives of intellectual disability in India: Epidemiology, policy, services for children and adults', *Current Opinion in Psychiatry*, 23, 440–446.

Gladstone, M., Lancaster, G.A., Umar, E., Nyirenda, M., Kayira, E., van der Broek, N.R. and Smyth, R.L. (2010). 'The Malawi developmental assessment tool (MDAT): The creation, validation, and reliability of a tool to assess child development in rural African settings', *PloS Medicine*, 7(5).

Global Health Workforce Alliance and World Health Organization. (2008). *Scaling Up, Saving Lives*, http://www.who.int/workforcealliance/knowledge/resources/scalingup/en/.

Globe and Mail. (2014). '"I abducted your girls", Boko Haram leader declares in new video', accessed 30 July 2014 from http://www.theglobeandmail.com/ (home page).

Goffman, E. (1963). *Stigma: Notes on the Management of Spoiled Identity* (New York: Simon and Schuster).

Gobrial, E. (2012). 'Mind the gap: The human rights of children with intellectual disabilities in Egypt', *Journal of Intellectual Disability Research*, 56(11), 1058–1064.

Goggin, G. and Newell, C. (2005). *Disability in Australia: Exposing a Social Apartheid* (Sydney: UNSW Press).

Gómez Pérez, J.R. (2004). 'Las TIC en Educación', accessed 21 April 2014 from http://boj.pntic.mec.es/jgomez46/ticedu.htm.

Goodley, D. (2011). *Disability Studies: An Interdisciplinary Introduction* (London: Sage).

D. Goodley, B. Hughes and L. Davis (Eds.). (2012). *Disability and Social Theory: New Developments and Directions* (London: Palgrave Macmillan).

Goodwin, M. and Armstrong-Esther, D. (2004). 'Children, social capital and health: Increasing the well-being of young people in rural Wales', *Children's Geographies*, 2(1), 49–64.

C. Gore and J.B. Figueiredo (Eds.). (1997). *Social Exclusion and Anti-Poverty Policy: A Debate* (Geneva, Switzerland: International Labour Organization).

Gottlieb, C., Maenner, M., Cappa, C. and Durkin, M. (2009). 'Child disability screening, nutrition, and early learning in 18 countries with low and middle incomes: Data from the third round of UNICEF's multiple indicator cluster survey (2005–06)', *Lancet*, 374, 1831–1839.

Government of Ecuador. (2011). *Country Report Submitted to the United Nations Convention on the Rights of Persons with Disabilities Monitoring Committee*, accessed 29 January 2014 from www.internationaldisabilityalliance.org/.

Government of India. (1995). *The Persons with Disabilities* (Equal Opportunities, Protection of Rights and Full Participation) *Act of 1995*, accessed 11 August 2013 from http://www.svayam.com/pdf/Persons_With_Disabilities_Act_1995%5B1%5D.

Government of India, Planning Commission. (2012). *Twelfth Five-Year Plan (2012–2017)*. (New Delhi: Planning Commission).

Government of India, Planning Commission. (2007). *Eleventh Five-Year Plan (2007–2012)*. *Inclusive Growth* (New Delhi: Planning Commission).

Government of India, Planning Commission. (2002). *Tenth Five-Year Plan (2002–2007)*. (New Delhi: Planning Commission).

Government of South Africa. (1997). *White Paper on an Integrated National Disability Strategy*, Office of the Deputy President T.M Mbeki (Western Cape, South Africa: Rustica Press).

Government of South Africa. (2002). *Advocacy Training Manual Disabled Persons South Africa* (Cape Town, South Africa).

Grammenos, S. (2003). *Illness, Disability and Social Inclusion* (Dublin, Ireland: European Foundation for the Improvement of Living and Working Conditions), accessed 23 February 2014 from http://www.eurofound.europa.eu/pubdocs/2003/35/en/1/ef0335en.pdf.

Grech, S. (2012). 'Disability and the majority world: A neocolonial approach'. In D. Goodley, B. Hughes and L.J. Davis (Eds.), *Disability and Social Theory: New Developments and Directions* (Basingstoke: Palgrave Macmillan), pp. 52–69.

Grech, S. (2011). 'Recolonizing debates or perpetuated coloniality? Decentring the spaces of disability, development and community in the Global South', *International Journal of Inclusive Education*, 15(1), 87–100.

Grech, S. (2008). 'Living with disability in Rural Guatemala: Exploring connections and impacts on poverty', *International Journal of Disability, Community and Rehabilitation*, 7(2), accessed 22 April 2014 from http://www.ijdcr.ca/VOL07_02_CAN/articles/grech.shtml.

Green, S.E. (2003). 'What do you mean "What's wrong with her?" Stigma and the lives of families of children with disabilities', *Social Science & Medicine*, 57(8), 1361–1374.

Grimes, P., Sayarath, K. and Outhaithany, S. (2011). 'The Lao PDR Inclusive education project 1993–2009: Reflections on the impact of a national project aiming to support the inclusion of disabled students', *International Journal of Inclusive Education*, 15(10), 1135–1152.

Groce, N.E. (2014). 'Disability and the League of Nations: The crippled child's bill of rights and a call for an International Bureau of Information, 1931', *Disability & Society*, 29(4), 503–515.

Groce, N.E. (1997). 'Women with disabilities in the developing world arenas for policy revision and programmatic change', *Journal of Disability Policy Studies*, 8(1–2), 177–193.

Groce, N.E., London, J. and Stein, M.A. (2013). *Intergenerational Poverty and Disability.* (London, UK: Leonard Cheshire Center), accessed 15 May 2014 from http://www.ucl.ac.uk/lcccr/centrepublications/workingpapers/WP17_Disability_and_Inheritance.pdf.

M.W. Gumede and L. Dikeni (Eds.). (2009). *The Poverty of Ideas: South African Democracy and the Retreat of Intellectuals* (Johannesburg: Jacana Media).

Gutiérrez, P. and Martorell, A. (2011). 'Las personas con discapacidad intelectual ante las TIC', *Comunicar: Revista Científica de Educomunicación*, 36(28), 173–180.

Guzmán, A. and Balcázar, F. (2010). 'Disability service's standards and the worldviews guiding their implementation', *Journal of Postsecondary Education and Disability*, Special Issue: Disability Studies, 23(1), 65–72.

Haig, A.J., Im, J., Adewole, D., Nelson, V. and Krabak, B. (2009). 'The practice of physical medicine and rehabilitation in sub-Saharan Africa and Antarctica: A white paper or a black mark?', *Disability and Rehabilitation*, 31(13), 1031–1037.

Handicap International. (2014). *New Study Shows Legacy of Disability from Explosive Weapon use in Syria*, accessed 22 February 2014 <http://www.handicap-international.org.uk/where_we_work/middle_east/syria/stories/20140122-study-shows-legacy-disability-explosive-weapon-use-Syria>.

Handicap International. (2013). *The Bravest Three-Year-Old you will Ever Meet*, accessed 22 February 2014 from http://www.handicap-international.us/the_bravest_three_year_old_you_ll_ever_meet.

Hanoi Independent Living Centre. (2014). *Hoang's Story*, accessed 15 January 2014 from http://eng.ttsongdoclaphn.vn/index.php?option=com_content&view=frontpage&Itemid=11 (home page).

Hansen, D.L. and Morgan, R.L. (2008). 'Teaching grocery store purchasing skills to students with intellectual disabilities using a computer-based instruction program', *Education and Training in Autism and Developmental Disabilities*, 43(4), 431–442.

Hansen, R., Phute, T., Dembe, K., Chikanza, S., Rigby, J. and Bloom, E. (2005). *Strengthen and Measuring Advocacy-Capacity of Civil Society Organisations: Best Practice Series* (Harare, Zimbabwe: Pact Inc.).

Harpur, P. (2012). 'Embracing the new disability rights paradigm: The importance of the Convention on the Rights of Persons with Disabilities', *Disability & Society*, 27(1), 1–14.

Harris, J. and Roulstone, A. (2011). *Disability, Policy and Professional Practice* (London: Sage).

Hastings, R.P., Hatton, C., Taylor, J.L. and Maddison, C. (2004). 'Life events and psychiatric symptoms in adults with intellectual disabilities', *Journal of Intellectual Disability Research*, 48, 42–46.

Hatton, C., Azmi, S., Caine, A. and Emerson, E. (1998). 'Informal carers of adolescents and adults with learning difficulties from the south Asian communities: Family circumstances, service support and carer stress', *British Journal of Social Work*, 28(6), 821–837.

Hatton, C. and Emerson, E. (2009). 'Does socioeconomic position moderate the impact of child behaviour problems on maternal health in South Asian families with a child with intellectual disabilities', *Journal of Intellectual & Developmental Disability*, 34(1), 10–16.

Haveman, M., Heller, T., Maaskant, M., Lee, L., Shooshtari, S. and Strydom, A. (2009). 'Health risks in older adults with intellectual disabilities: A review of studies', (IASSID report), accessed 1 August 2011 from http://www.IASSID.org (home page).

Hayashi, R. and Okuhira, M. (2008). 'The independent living movement in Asia: Solidarity from Japan', *Disability & Society*, 23(5), 417–429.

Hayden, M. (2013). *Primary School Teachers' Perceptions of Enablement for Inclusive Classrooms: An Empirical Study of Inclusive Education in Bangladesh*, accessed 12 January 2014 from http://sussexciejournal.files.wordpress.com/2013/12/cie_bangladesh-inclusive-education_dissertation.pdf.

Heer, K., Larkin, M., Burchess, I. and Rose, J. (2012). 'The cultural context of care-giving: Qualitative accounts from South Asian parents who care for a child with intellectual disabilities in the UK', *Advances in Mental Health and Intellectual Disabilities*, 6(4), 179–191.

Helander, E. (1993). *Prejudice and Dignity: An Introduction to Community-based Rehabilitation* (New York: UNDP).

Helander, E., Padmani, M. and Nelson, G. (1983). *Training Disabled People in the Community: A Manual on Community-Based Rehabilitation for Developing Countries* (Geneva: WHO).

Heller, T. and Factor, A. (1991). 'Permanency planning for adults with mental retardation living with family caregivers', *American Journal of Mental Retardation*, 96(2), 163–176.

Hendricks, A. (2007). 'UN Convention on the Rights of Persons with Disabilities', *European*, 14, 273–298.

Heslop, P., Blair, P.S., Fleming, P., Hoghton, M., Marriott, A. and Russ, L. (2013). 'The confidential inquiry into premature deaths of people with intellectual disabilities in the UK', *Lancet*, 383(9920), 889–895.

Hewitt, A., Lightfoot, E., Bogenschutz, M., McCormack, K., Sedlezky, L. and Doljanic, R. (2010). 'Parental caregivers' desires for lifetime assistance planning for future supports for their children with intellectual and developmental disabilities', *Journal of Family Social Work*, 13(5).

Hilgenkamp, M., Reis, D., Wijck, R. and Evenhuis, H. (2012). 'Physical activity levels in older adults with intellectual disabilities are extremely low', *Research in Developmental Disabilities*, 33, 477–483.

Hiranandani, V., Kumar, A. and Sonpal, D. (2014). 'Making community inclusion work for persons with disabilities: Drawing lessons from the field', *Community Development*, 45(2), 150–164.

Hoff, A. (2009). *Families, Care and Work: Changes and Challenges* (Oxford: The Oxford Institute of Ageing, University of Oxford).

Holland, A. (2000). 'Incidence and course of dementia in people with down's syndrome: Findings from a population based study', *Journal of Intellectual Disability Research*, 44(2), 138–146.

Hon, C., Sun, P., Suto, M. and Forwell, S.J. (2011). 'Moving from China to Canada: Occupational transitions of immigrant mothers of children with special needs', *Journal of Occupational Science*, 18(3), 223–236

Houtenville, A.J. (2013). *2013 Annual Disability Statics Compendium* (Durham, NH: University of New Hampshire: Institute on Disability), accessed February 24, 2013 from http://disabilitycompendium.org/docs/default-source/2013-compendium/download-the-2013-compendium.pdf?sfvrsn=0.

Howell, C. (2006). *Equity, Difference and the Nature of the Academic Environment: An Investigation into the Responses of South African Universities to the Admission and Participation of Disabled Students*, unpublished PhD thesis, Department of Sociology, Graduate School of Humanities (Cape Town: University of Cape Town).

Huddart, J., Picazo, O.F. and Duale, S. (2003). *The Health Sector Human Resource Crisis in Africa: An Issues Paper* (Washington, DC: United States Agency for International Development, Bureau for Africa, Office of Sustainable Development), accessed 29 July 2014 from http://pdf.usaid.gov/pdf_docs/PNACS527.pdf.

Hughes, K., Bellis, M.A., Jones, L., Wood, S., Bates, G., Eckley, L., McCoy, E., Mikton, C. and Shakespeare, T. (2012). 'Prevalence and risk of violence against children with disabilities: A systematic review and meta-analysis of observational studies', *The Lancet*, 380(9845), 8–14.

Human Rights Watch. (2011). *Colombia is 100th Country to Ratify Disability Rights Treaty*, accessed 22 February 2014 from http://www.hrw.org/news/2011/05/16/colombia-100th-country-ratify-disability-rights-treaty.

Hunt, P. (1966). *Stigma: The Experience of Disability* (London: Geoffrey Chapman).

Hussain, K. (2012). *Fostering Inclusive Education in Pakistan: Access and Quality in Primary Education through Community School Networks Global Scholars Program Working Paper Series*, Working Paper No. 6 (Washington, DC: Brookings).

Hussain, Y. (2005). 'South Asian disabled women: Negotiating identities', *The Sociological Review*, 53(3), 522–538.

Hwang, S.K. and Charnley, H. (2010a). 'Honourable sacrifice: A visual ethnography of the family lives of Korean children with autistic siblings', *Children & Society*, 24(6), 437–448.

Hwang, S.K. and Charnley, H. (2010b). 'Making the familiar strange and making the strange familiar: Understanding Korean children's experiences of living with an autistic sibling', *Disability & Society*, 25(5), 579–592.

Inclusion Europe. (2010). *European Disability Strategy 2010–2020*, Easy-Read Version (Brussels: Inclusion Europe), http://www.inclusion-europe.org.

Inclusion International. (2014). *Independent But Not Alone: A Global Report on the Right to Decide* (London: Inclusion International), http://www.inclusion-international .org (home page), (also in Spanish).

Inclusion International. (2008). *Priorities for people with intellectual disabilities in implementing the United Nations Convention on the Rights of Persons with Disabilities: The Way Ahead* (London: Inclusion International), http://www.inclusion-international.org (home page).

B. Ingstad and S. Reynolds Whyte (Eds.). (2007). *Disability in Local and Global Worlds* (Berkeley and Los Angeles: University of California Press).

B. Ingstad and S. Reynolds Whyte (Eds.). (1995). *Disability and culture* (Berkeley and Los Angeles: University of California Press).

Integrated Regional Information Networks (IRIN). (2010). *Senegal: Children with Disability – When Stigma Means Abandonment*, accessed 12 April 2012 from www.irinnews.org/Report/90139/SENEGAL-Children-with-disability-when-stigma-means-abandonment.

International Communication Union (ITU). (2006). *World Summit on the Information Society-WSIS, Tunise Agenda for the Information Society*, accessed 15 April 2014 from https://www.itu.int/wsis/index.html.

International Criminal Court (ICC). (2013). '*Our Voices Matter: Congolese Women Demand Justice and Accountability*' Women's Initiatives for Gender Justice, accessed 24 February 2014 from http://www.iccwomen.org/videos/index.php.

International Disability Alliance (IDA). (2013). *The Arab Spring and the rise of Tunisians with Disabilities: Interview with Imed Ouretani* (IDA Human Rights Publication Series), accessed 29 January 2014 from http://www.international disabilityalliance.org/M (home page).

International Disability Alliance (IDA). (2010). *Effective Use of International Human Rights Monitoring Mechanisms to Protect the Rights of Persons with Disabilities*, accessed 10 May 2014 from http://www.internationaldisabilityalliance.org.

International Labour Organization (ILO). (2014). *Zuma justifies Nkandla*, accessed 30 July 2014 from http://www.iol.co.za/news/politics/zuma-justifies-nkandla-1.1683938.

International Labour Organization (ILO). (2013). *Study on Work and Employment of Persons with Disabilities, Human Rights Council in March 2013, ILO Contribution*, accessed 30 July 2014 from http://www.ilo.org/global/publications/lang--en/index.htm (home page).

International Labour Organization (ILO). (2008). *Skills Development through Community Based Rehabilitation (CBR). A good practice guide*, http://www.ilo.org/wcmsp5/groups/public/---ed_emp/---ifp_skills/documents/publication/wcms_132675.pdf.

International Labour Organization (ILO). (2007). *Facts on Disability in the World of Work. Public Fact Sheet*, accessed 27 January 2014 from http://www.ilo.org/asia/info/public/background/WCMS_098454/lang--en/index.htm.

International Labour Organization (ILO). (2002). *Managing Disability in the Workplace, A Code of Practice* (Geneva: ILO), http://www.businessanddisability.org/images/pdf/code_practice.pdf.

Invalidnost. (2010). *CDF (Communication Development Fund)*, accessed 30 July 2014 from http://www.cdf.org.rs/en/projects/invalidnost.

Jackson, R., Howe, N. and Nakashima, K. (2011). *Global Aging Preparedness Index* (Washington, DC: Center for Strategic and International Studies).

Jameel, S.S. (2011). 'Disability in the context of higher education: Issues and concerns in India', *Journal for Inclusive Education*, 2(7), accessed 12 November 2013 from http://corescholar.libraries.wright.edu (home page).

Janicki, M.P. (2009). 'The aging dilemma: Is increasing longevity among people with intellectual disabilities creating a new population challenge in the Asia-Pacific Region', *Journal of Policy & Practice*, 6(2), 73–76.

Janicki, M.P., Dalton, A.J., Henderson, C.M. and Davidson, P.W. (1999). 'Mortality and morbidity among older adults with intellectual disability: Health services considerations', *Disability and Rehabilitation*, 21, 284–294.

Janicki, M.P., Dalton, A.J., McCallion, P., Baxley, D.D. and Zendell, A. (2005). 'Group home care for adults with intellectual disabilities and Alzheimer's disease', *Dementia*, 4(3), 361–385.

Jegatheesan, B. (2009). 'Cross-cultural issues in parent professional interactions: A qualitative study of perceptions of Asian American mothers of children with developmental disabilities', *Research & Practice for Persons with Severe Disabilities*, 34(3–4), 123–136.

Jenkins, S.P. and Rigg, J.A. (2003). *Disability and Disadvantage: Selection, Onset, and Duration Effects* (London, UK: Centre for Analysis of Social Exclusion, London School of Economics), accessed 10 March 2014 from http://eprints.lse.ac.uk/6323/1/Disability_and_Disadvantage_Selection_onset_and_duration_effects.pdf.

Johnson, K. (2013). 'The UN Convention on the Rights of Persons with Disabilities: A framework for ethical and inclusive practice?', *Ethics and Social Welfare*, 7(3), 218–231, DOI: 10.1080/17496535.2013.815791.

Johnstone, B., Glass, B.A. and Oliver, R.E. (2007). 'Religion and disability: Clinical, research and training considerations for rehabilitation professionals', *Disability & Rehabilitation*, 29(15), 1153–1163.

Joint Learning Initiative Strategy Report. (2004). *Human Resources for Health: Overcoming the Crisis* (Cambridge: Harvard University Press), accessed 12 April 2012 from www.who.int/hrh/documents/JLi_hrh_report.pdf.

Jones, I., Marshall, J., Lawthom, R. and Read, J. (2013). 'Involving people with communication disability in research in Uganda: A response to the World Report on Disability', *International Journal of Speech-Language Pathology*, 15(1), 75–78.

Kabbara, N. (2013). 'CRPD Ratification and Implementation: The Arab World as an Example'. Paper presented at the International Conference 2008–2013: *Five Years Enforcement of the International Convention on the Rights of Persons with Disabilities* (CERMI and University Carlos III), accessed 14 November 2013 from http://www.cermi.es (home page).

Kalinnikova, L. and Trygged, S. (2014). 'A retrospective on care and denial of children with disabilities in Russia', *Scandinavian Journal of Disability Research*, DOI: 10.1080/15017419.2013.861865.

Kallonga, E. (2001). *Lobbying and Advocacy*, accessed 30 July 2014 from http://www.hakikazi.org/tcdd/newpage14.htm.

Kalyanpur, M. (2011). 'Paradigm and paradox: Education for all and the inclusion of children with disabilities in Cambodia', *International Journal of Inclusive Education*, 15(10), 1053–1071.

Kaneda, T. (2006). *Health Care Challenges for Developing Countries with Aging Populations* (Washington, DC: Population Reference Bureau).

Kassar, A. (2013). *Rapid Assessment of the Needs of War Victims with Disabilities*, Global Arab Network, accessed 21 February 2014 from http://www.english.globalarabnetwork.com/2013020212810/Culture/rapid-assessments-of-the-needs-of-war-victims-with-disabilities-in-syria.html.

Kassar, A. (2012). *The War Victims and Persons with Disabilities in Syria*, Global Arab Network, accessed 21 February 2014 from http://www.english.globalarabnetwork.com/2012111212768/Syria-Politics/the-war-victims-and-persons-with-disabilities-in-syria.html.

Kelly, A., Ghalaieny, T. and Devitt, C. (2012). 'A pilot study of early intervention for families with children with or at risk of an intellectual disability in Northern Malawi', *Journal of Policy and Practice in Intellectual Disabilities*, 9(3), 195–205.

Kelly, F. and Kelly, C. (2013). *Annual Report of the National Intellectual Disability Database Committee* (Dublin: Health Research Board).

Kelly, F. and Kelly, C. (2011). *Annual Report of the National Intellectual Disability Database Committee* (Dublin: Health Research Board).

Khan, N.Z., Muslima, H., Begum, D., Shilpi, A.B., Akhter, S., Bilkis, K., Begum, N., Parveen, M., Ferdous, S., Morshed, R., Batra, M. and Darmstadt, G.L., (2010). 'Validation of rapid neurodevelopmental assessment instrument for under-two-year-old children in Bangladesh', *Pediatrics*, 125(4), 755–762.

Kilkelly, U. (1996). 'UN committee on the rights of the child – an evaluation in the light of recent UK experience', *Child and Family Law Quarterly*, 8(2), 105–120.

Kliewer, C., Biklen, D. and Kasa-Hendrickson, C. (2006). 'Who may be literate? Disability and resistance to the cultural denial of competence', *American Education Research Journal*, 43(2), 163–192.

Korfmacher, J., Green, B., Staerkel, F., Peterson, C., Cook, G., Roggman, L., Fladowski, R.A. and Schiffman, R. (2008). 'Parent involvement in early childhood home visiting', *Child & Youth Care Forum*, 37(4), 171–196.

Kozleski, E.B., Artiles, A.J., Fletcher, T. and Engelbrecht, P. (2009). 'Understanding the dialectics of the local and the global in education for all: A comparative case study', *International Critical Childhood Policy Studies Journal*, 2(1), 15–29.

Kramer, J.M., Kramer, J.C., García Iriarte, E. and Hammel, J. (2011). 'Following through to the end: The use of inclusive strategies to analyze and interpret data in participatory action research with individuals with intellectual disabilities, *Journal of Applied Research in Intellectual Disabilities*, 24, 263–273.

Kretzmann, J. and McKnight, J. (1993). *Building Communities from the Inside Out* (Chicago, IL: ACTA publications).

Kuhn, J. (1970). *The Structure of Scientific Revolutions*, 2nd edn (Chicago: University of Chicago Press).

Kuipers, P. and Cornielje, H. (2013). 'Alternative responses to the Human Resource Challenge for CBR', *Disability, CBR and Inclusive Development*, 23(4), 17–23.

Kuppers, P. (2003). *Disability and Contemporary Performance: Bodies on Edge* (New York and London: Routledge).

Kushner, H.S. (1983). *When Bad things Happen to Good People* (London: Pan).

Kwok, H.W.M., Cui, Y. and Li, J., (2011). 'Perspectives of intellectual disability in the People's Republic of China: Epidemiology, policy, services for children and adults', *Current Opinion in Psychiatry*, 23, 408–412.

Kyzar, K.B., Turnbull, A.P., Summers, J.A. and Gómez, V.A. (2012). 'The relationship of family support to family outcomes: A synthesis of key findings from research on severe disability', *Research and Practice for Persons with Severe Disabilities*, 37(1), 31–44.

Lagomasino, I.T., Dwight-Johnson, M., Miranda, J., Zhang, L., Liao, D., Duan, N. et al. (2005). 'Disparities in depression treatment for Latinos and site of care', *Psychiatric Services*, 56, 1517–1523.

Lamichhane, K., Paudel, D.B. and Kartika, D. (2014). 'Analysis of poverty between people with and without disabilities in Nepal', JICA-RI Working Paper No. 77, JICA Research Institute, Japan, March 2014.

Lancet Editorial. (2008). 'The bamako call to action: Research for health', *Lancet*, 372(9653), 1855.

L.L. Langness and H.G. Levine (Eds.). (1986). *Culture and retardation: Life histories of mildly mentally retarded persons in American society* (Boston: Dordrecht).

Lányi, C.S., Brown, D.J., Standen, P.J., Lewis, J. and Butkute, V. (2012). 'Results of user interface evaluation of serious games for students with intellectual disabilities', *Acta Polytechnica Hungarica*, 9(1).

Lawson, A. (2006). *The EU Rights based Approach to Disability: Some Strategies for Shaping an Inclusive Society* (Cornell University ILR School, Gladnet Collections), accessed 31 January 2014 from http://digitalcommons.ilr.cornell.edu (home page).

Lechtig, A., Cornale, G., Ugaz, M.E. and Arias, L. (2009). 'Decreasing stunting, anemia, and vitamin A deficiency in Peru: Results of the Good Start in Life program', *Food and Nutrition Bulletin*, 30(1), 37–48; and UNICEF Peru Country Office, 'Annual Report 2000' (internal document).

Lecomte, J. and Mercier, C. (2008). 'The WHO atlas on global resources for persons with intellectual disabilities: A right to health perspective', *Salud Publica de Mexico*, 50(2), 160–166.

Le Fanu, G. (2013). 'Reconceptualising inclusive education in international development'. In L. Tikly and A. Barrett (Eds.), *Education, quality and social justice in the global South* (London: Routledge).

Lei, P. and Myers, J. (2011). 'Making the grade? A review of donor commitment and action on inclusive education for disabled children', *International Journal of Inclusive Education*, 15(10), 1169–1185.

Leonard Cheshire International. (2013). *Research Toolkit for Disabled People's Organisations: How to Undertake and Use Applied Research* (London, UK: University of London Leonard Cheshire Inclusive Development Centre), http://www.ucl.ac.uk/lc-ccr.

Levitas, R., Pantazis, C., Fahmy, E., Gordon, D., Lloyd, E. and Patsios, D. (2007). *The Multi-Dimensional Analysis of Social Exclusion: A Research Report for the Social Exclusion Task Force* (Bristol, UK: Department of Sociology and School for Social Policy, Townsend Centre for the International Study of Poverty and Bristol Institute for Public Affairs, University of Bristol), accessed 12 March 2014 from http://roar.uel.ac.uk/1781/1/multidimensional.pdf.

Levy, C.W. (1988). *A People's History of the Independent Living Movement* (Lawrence, KS: University of Kansas).

Liesa Orús, M. and Vived Conte, E. (2010). 'Discapacidad, edad adulta y vida independiente. Un estudio de casos', *Educación y diversidad*, 4(1), 101–124.

Lightfoot, E. and McCallion, P. (2015). 'Older adults and developmental disabilities'. In B. Berkman and D. Kaplan (Eds.), *Handbook of Social Work in Health & Aging*, 2nd edn (New York: Oxford University Press).

Lindsay, S., King, G., Klassen, A.F., Esses, V. and Stachel, M. (2012). 'Working with immigrant families raising a child with a disability: Challenges and recommendations for healthcare and community service providers', *Disability and Rehabilitation*, 34(23), 2007–2017.

Link, B.G. and Phelan, J.C. (2001). 'Conceptualizing stigma', *Annual Review of Sociology*, 27, 363–385.

Lipsey, M. and Cordray, D. (2000). 'Evaluation methods for social intervention', *Annual Review Psychology*, 51, 345.

Lipton, M. (1997). *Defining and Measuring Poverty: Conceptual Issues* (New York: UNDP/Hynab Development Papers).

Llewellyn, G., Emerson, E., Madden, R. and Honey, A. (2012). *The well-being of Children with Disabilities in the Asia-Pacific Region: An Analysis of UNICEF MICS 3 Survey Data from Bangladesh, Lao PDR, Mongolia and Thailand* (University of Sydney: Centre for Disability Research and Policy).

Lollar, D.J. and Crews, J.E. (2003). 'Redefining the role of public health in disability', *Annual Review of Public Health*, 24, 195–208.

T. Lorenzo (Ed.). (2012). *Marrying Community Development and Rehabilitation: Reality or Aspiration for Disabled people?* (Cape Town: Disability Innovations Africa).

Lorenzo, T., Ned-Matiwane, L. and Cois, A. et al. (2013). *Youth, Disability and Rural Communities: Facing the Challenges of Change* (Cape Town University DCA Series 3: Youth, Disability and Rural Communities).

Loveday, M. (1990). *The HELP Guide For Community Based Rehabilitation Workers: A Training Manual* (Cape Town: SACLA Health Project).

Luckasson, R. and Schalock, R.L. (2013). 'Defining and applying a functionality approach to intellectual disability', *Journal of Intellectual Disability Research*, 57(7), 657–668.

Lunsky, Y., Tint, A., Robinson, S., Gordeyko, M. and Oullette-Kuntz, H. (2014). 'System-Wide information about family carers of adults with intellectual/developmental disabilities – A scoping review of the literature', *Journal of Policy and Practice in Intellectual Disabilities*, 11(4), 8–18.

Lynch, P., McCall, S., Douglas, G., McLinden, M. and Bayo, A. (2011). 'Inclusive educational practices in Uganda: Evidencing practice of itinerant teachers who work with children with visual impairment in local mainstream schools', *International Journal of Inclusive Education*, 15(1), 1119–11134.

MacDonald, C. (2012). 'Understanding participatory action research: A qualitative research methodology approach', *Canadian Journal of Action Research*, 13(2), 34–50.

Mackay, D. (2014). Foreword in M. Sabatello and M. Schulze (Eds.), *Human Rights and Disability Advocacy* (Philadephia, PA: University of Pennsylvania Press).

MacLachlan, M. (2012a). 'Community based rehabilitation and inclusive health: A way forward', *Statement to the United Nations Commission for Social Development*, New York, 2 February 2012.

MacLachlan, M. (2012b). 'Rehabilitation psychology and global health'. In P. Kennedy (Ed.), *Oxford Handbook of Rehabilitation Psychology*, (Oxford, UK: Oxford University Press), Ch. 30.

MacLachlan, M. (2006). *Culture & Health: A Critical Perspective Towards Global Health* (Chichester, UK: John Wiley & Sons Ltd).

MacLachlan, M., Amin, M., Mannan, H., El Tayeb, S., Bedri, N., Swartz, L., Munthali, A., Van Rooy, G. and McVeigh, J. (2012). 'Inclusion and human rights in health policies: Comparative and benchmarking analysis of 51 policies from Malawi, Sudan, South Africa and Namibia', *PLoS One*, 7(5).

MacLachlan, M., Carr, S., and McAuliffe, E. (2010). *The Aid Triangle: Recognizing the Human Dynamics of Dominance, Justice and Identity* (London: Zed Books).

MacLachlan, M., Khasnabis, C. and Mannan, H. (2012). 'Inclusive health', *Tropical Medicine & International Health*, 17(1), 139–141.

MacLachlan, M., Mannan, H. and McAuliffe, E. (2011a). 'Access to health care of persons with disabilities as an indicator of equity in health systems', *Open Medicine*, 5(1), 10–12.

MacLachlan, M., Mannan, H. and McAuliffe, E. (2011b). 'Staff skills not staff types for community based rehabilitation', *Lancet*, 377(9782), 1988–1989.

MacQuarrie, A. and Laurin-Bowie, C. (2014). 'Our lives: People with intellectual disabilities and their families'. In M. Sabatello and M. Schulze (Eds.), *Human Rights and Disability Advocacy* (Philadephia, PA: University of Pennsylvania Press).

Madans, J.H., Loeb, M.E. and Altman, B.M. (2011). 'Measuring disability and monitoring the UN convention on the rights of persons with disabilities: The work of the Washington group on disability statistics', *BMC Public Health*, 11(4).

Maeda, Y., Tsjimura, E., Sigita, K., Oka, T. and Yokota, M. (2009). 'An adaptive user interface for Universal Multimedia Access'. Paper presented at the International Conference on Complex, Intelligent and Software Intensive Systems, 2009, Fukuoka.

Magaña, S. and Ghosh, S. (2013). 'Older adults of color with developmental disabilities and serious mental illness: Experiences and service patterns'. In K. Whitfield and T. Baker (Eds.), *Handbook of Minority Aging* (New York: Springer).

Magaña, S., Parish, S.L. and Cassiman, S.A. (2008). 'Policy lessons from low-income mothers with disabilities: A primer on inadequate incomes, work disincentives, and bureaucratic insensitivity', *Journal of Women, Politics and Policy*, 29, 181–206.

Magee, A. (2012). 'In the field: Life on the frontline in West Africa', *Plan Ireland Annual Newsletter*. Accessed 26 June 2014 from http://issuu.com/planireland/docs/plan_ireland_annual_newsletter_2011_12.

Mandell, D.S. and Novak, M. (2005). 'The role of culture in families' treatment decisions for children with autism spectrum disorders', *Mental Retardation and Developmental Disabilities Research Reviews*, 11, 110–115.

Mangcu, X. (2013). 'Retracing Nelson Mandela through the lineage of black political thought: From Walter Rubusana to Steve Biko', *Transition*, 112(1), 101–116.

Mannan, H., Amin, M., MacLachlan, M. and the EquitAble Consortium. (2012). 'Noncommunicable disease priority actions and social inclusion', *Lancet*, 379(9812), 17–18.

Mannan, H., Boostrom, C., MacLachlan, M., McAuliffe, E., Khasnabis, C. and Gupta, N. (2012). 'A systematic review of the effectiveness of alternative cadres in community based rehabilitation', *Human Resources for Health*, 10(20).

Mannan, H., MacLachlan, M., McVeigh, J. and the EquitAble Consortium. (2012). 'Core concepts of Human Rights and Inclusion of Vulnerable Groups in the United Nations Convention on the Rights of Persons with Disabilities', *Alter – European Journal of Disability Research*, 6(3), 159–177.

Mannan, H., McVeigh, J., Amin, M., MacLachlan, M., Swartz, L., Munthali, A. and Van Rooy, G. (2012). 'Core concepts of human rights and inclusion of vulnerable groups in the disability and rehabilitation policies of Malawi, Namibia, Sudan, and South Africa', *Journal of Disability Policy Studies*.

Mannan, H., Amin, M., MacLachlan, M. and the EquitAble Consortium. (2011). *The EquiFrame Manual: A Tool for Evaluating and Promoting the Inclusion of Vulnerable Groups and Core Concepts of Human Rights in Health Policy Documents* (Dublin: The Global Health Press).

Mannan, H. and MacLachlan, M. (2010). 'Human resources for health: Focusing on people with disabilities', *Lancet*, 375(9712), 375.

Maren, M. (1997). *The Road to Hell: The Ravaging Effects of Foreign aid and International Charity* (Simon and Schuster).

Marrero Expósito, C. (2006). *Interfaz Gráfica de Usuario: Aproximación Semiótica y Cognitiva* (Tenerife, Spain: Universidad de la Laguna).

Martinelli, E. and Mersland, R. (2010). 'Micro-credit for people with disabilities'. In T. Barron and J. Ncube (Eds.), *Poverty and Disability* (London: Leonard Cheshire Disability).

Mathie, A. and Cunningham, G. (2002). *From Clients to Citizens: Asset-Based Community Development as a Strategy for Community-Driven Development* (Canada: Coady International Institute. St. Francis Xavier University).

Mathieson, J., Popay, J., Enoch, E., Escorel, S., Hernandez, M., Johnston, H. and Rispel, L. (2008). *Social Exclusion Meaning, Measurement and Experience and Links To Health Inequalities: A Review of Literature* (WHO Social Exclusion Knowledge Network Background Paper), accessed 18 March 2014 from http://www.who.int/social_determinants/media/sekn_meaning_measurement_experience_2008.pdf.

Matonya, M. (2012). 'Individuals – needs support in Tanzanian higher education: Experience of women with disabilities', *EDULEARN 12 Proceedings*, 2329–2336.

Matshedisho, K.R. (2007). 'Access to higher education for disabled students in South Africa: A contradictory conjuncture of benevolence, rights and the social model of disability', *Disability & Society*, 22(7), 685–699.

Maudslay, L. (2014). 'Inclusive education in Nepal: Assumptions and reality. A research note', *Childhood*, 21(3).

Maulik, P.K. and Darmstadt, G.L. (2007). 'Childhood disability in low- and middle-income Countries: Overview of screening, prevention, services, legislation, and epidemiology', *Pediatrics*, 120(1), S1–S55.

Mbewe, M. and Lee, P. (1991). 'The SAFOD Development activists Handbook' (Bulawayo: Zimbabwe).

McCallion, P. (2006). 'Older adults as caregivers to persons with developmental disabilities'. In B. Berkman and D'Ambruoso (Eds.), *Handbook of Social Work in Health & Aging* (New York: Oxford University Press), pp. 363–370.

McCallion, P., Ferretti, L. and Kim, J. (2013a). 'Challenges in translating an evidence-based health self-management intervention for grandparent caregivers'. In B. Hayslip, Jr. and G.C. Smith (Eds.), *Resilient Grandparent Caregivers: A Strengths-Based Perspective* (New York: Routledge), pp. 195–208.

McCallion, P. and Grant-Griffin, L. (2000). 'Redesigning services to meet the needs of multi-cultural families'. In M.P. Janicki and E. Ansello (Eds.), *Aging and Developmental Disabilities* (Baltimore, MD: Paul Brookes Publishing Company), pp. 97–108.

McCallion, P. and Kolomer, S.R. (2003). 'Aging persons with developmental disabilities and their aging caregivers'. In B. Berkman and L. Harootyan (Eds.), *Social Work and Health Care in an Aging World* (New York: Springer).

McCallion, P. and McCarron, M. (2013b). 'Death of people with intellectual disabilities in the UK', *Lancet*, 383(9920), 853–855.

McCallion, P., Nickle, T. and McCarron, M. (2005). 'A comparison of reports of caregiver burden between foster family care providers and staff caregivers of persons in other settings', *Dementia*, 4(3), 401–412.

McCallion, P., Swinburne, J., Burke, E., McGlinchey, E. and McCarron, M. (2013c). 'Understanding the similarities and differences in aging with an intellectual disability: Linking Irish general population and intellectual disability datasets'. In R. Urbano (Ed.), *Using Secondary Datasets to Understand Persons with Developmental Disabilities and their Families* (New York: Academic Press).

McCallion, P. and Toseland, R.W. (1993). 'An empowered model for social work services to families of adolescents and adults with developmental disabilities', *Families in Society*, 74, 579–589.

McCarron, M., McCallion, P., Reilly, E. and Mulryan, N. (2014). 'A prospective 14 Year longitudinal follow-up of Dementia in persons with Down syndrome', *Journal of Intellectual Disability Research*, 58(1), 61–70.

McCaw-Binns, A., Ashley, D., Samms-Vaughan, M., Wilks, R., Ferguson, T., Younger, N., Reece, J.A., Tulloch-Reid, M. and Foster-Williams, K. (2010). 'Cohort profile: The Jamaican 1986 birth cohort study', *International Journal of Epidemiology*, 40(6), 1469–1476.

McColl, M.A., Adair, W., Davey, S. and Kates, N. (2013). 'The learning collaborative: An approach to emancipatory research in disability studies', *Canadian Journal of Disability Studies*, 2(1), 71–93.

McConkey, R., Kelly, F. and Craig, S. (2012). 'A national comparative study over one decade of children with intellectual disabilities living away from their natural parents', *British Journal of Social Work*, doi: 10.1093/bjsw/bcs170.

McConkey, R. and Mariga, L. (2010). 'Building social capital for inclusive education: Insights from Zanzibar', *Journal of Research in Special Educational Needs*, 11(1), 12–19.

McConkey, R., Mariga, L., Braadland, N. and Mphole, P. (2000). 'Parents as trainers about disability in low income countries', *International Journal of Disability, Development and Education*, 47, 309–317.

McConkey, R., McConaghie, J., Roberts, P. and King, D. (2004). 'Family placement schemes for adult persons with intellectual disabilities living with elderly carers', *Journal of Learning Disabilities*, 8, 267–282.

McConkey, R. and Samadi, S.A. (2013). 'The impact of mutual support on Iranian parents of children with an autism spectrum disorder: A longitudinal study', *Disability and Rehabilitation*, 35(9), 775–784.

McConkey, R., Truesdale-Kennedy, M., Chang, M.Y., Jarrah, S. and Shukri, R. (2008). 'The impact on mothers of bringing up a child with intellectual disabilities: A cross-cultural study', *International Journal of Nursing Studies*, 45, 65–74.

McConkey, R., Truesdale-Kennedy, M., Crawford, H., McGreevy, E., Reavey, M. and Cassidy, A. (2010). 'Preschoolers with autism spectrum conditions: The impact of a home-based intervention to promote their communication', *Early Child Development and Care*, 180(3), 299–315.

McKenzie, J.A., McConkey, R. and Adnams, C. (2013). 'Intellectual disability in Africa: Implications for research and service development', *Disability and Rehabilitation*, 35(20), 1750–1755.

McKenzie, K. (2007). 'Digital divide: The implications for social inclusion', *Practice & Research: Learning Disability Practice*, 10(6), 16–21.

Mechling, L.C. and O'Brien, E. (2010). 'Computer-based video instruction to teach students with intellectual disabilities to use public bus transport', *Education and Training in Autism and Developmental Disabilities*, 45(2), 230–241.

Melamed, C. and Sammans, E. (2013). *Equity, inequality and human development in a post 2015 Framework* (New York: United Nations Development Programme).

Mikkelsen, E.J. (2007). *The Rational use of Psychotropic Medication for Individuals with Intellectual Disabilities* (New York: NADD: Kingston).

Miles, M. (2002). 'Some influences of religions on attitudes towards disabilities and people with disabilities', *Journal of Religion, Disability & Health*, 6(2–3), 117–129.

Miles, S., Merumeru, L. and Lene, D. (2014). 'Making sense of inclusive education in the Pacific region: Networking as a way forward', *Childhood*, 21(3).

Miles, S. and Singal, N. (2008). 'The Education for all and inclusive education debate: Conflict, contradiction or opportunity?', *International Journal of Inclusive Education*, accessed 22 April 2012, from http://www.leeds.ac.uk/disabilitystudies/archiveuk/miles/IJIE_MilesandSingal_resubmission.pdf.

Millennium Development Goals Indicators. (2010). *Workshop on Millennium Development Goals Monitoring, Geneva, Switzerland, 8–11 November 2010*, accessed 12 April 2012 from http://unstats.un.org/unsd/mdg/Host.aspx?Content=Capacity/Geneva.htm.

Ministry of Health, Government of Jamaica. (2010). *Child Health & Development Passport to Revolutionize Jamaica's Approach to Managing Children's Health & Development*, accessed 15 May 2012 from www.moh.gov.jm (home page).

Mitchell, D. and Snyder, S. (2001). *Narrative Prosthesis: Disability and the Dependencies of Discourse* (Ann Arbor: University of Michigan Press).

Mittler, P. (2012). 'It's our convention: Use it or lose it?', *Development, CBR and Inclusive Development*, 23(2), 7–21.

Mo3aq-news.com. (2011), accessed 20 January 2014 from http://www.mo3aq-news.com/index.php (home page).

Moriarty, L. and Dew, K. (2011). 'The United Nations convention on the rights of persons with disabilities and participation in Aotearoa New Zealand', *Disability & Society*, 26(6), 683–697.

Morley, L. and Croft, A. (2011). 'Agency and advocacy: Disabled students in higher education in Ghana and Tanzania', *Research in Comparative and International Education*, 6(4), 383–399.

Moss, S. (1993). *Aging and Developmental Disabilities: Perspectives from Nine Countries* (Durham, NC: IEEIR).

Moyi, P. (2012). 'Access to education for children with disabilities in Uganda: Implications for education for all', *Journal of International Education and Leadership*, 2(2), 1–13.

Muthukrishna, A. and Ebrahim, H. (2014). 'Motherhood and the disabled child in contexts of early education and care', *Childhood*, 21(3).

Muthukrishna, A. and Morojele, P. (2014). 'South Africa Case study'. In MiET Africa (Ed.), *South Africa Case Study. A North–South Partner-Driven Co-Operation Project: Teaching for Inclusion and Democracy* (Durban: MiET Africa).

Nagata, K.K. (2003). 'Gender and disability in the Arab region: The challenges in the New Millennium', *Asia Pacific Disability Rehabilitation Journal*, 14, 10–17.

Nakanishi, S. (2007). *Independent Living Movement In Developing Countries. Disabled People International (DPI) Japan*, accessed 25 March 2014 from http://tinyurl.com/2eeldt.

Nasser, K.R. (2011). 'Social inclusion of children with physical disability in Palestine', *Research Thesis Submitted in Partial Fulfillment of the Masters in Global Health*, (Trinity College Dublin, Ireland).

Nasser, K.R. and MacLachlan, M. (2012). 'Community based rehabilitation, social inclusion and mental health in Palestine', Centre for Global Health Working Paper.

National Assistive Technology Research Institute, NATRI. (2006). *What is Assistive Technology?*, accessed 27 April 2014 from http://natri.uky.edu/resources/fundamentals /defined.html.

Nattrass, N. (2010). 'Still crazy after all these years: The challenge of AIDS denialism for science', *AIDS and Behavior*, 14(2), 248–251.

Nel, N., Müller, H., Hugo, A., Helldin, R., Bäckmann, O., Dwyer, H. and Skarlind, A. (2011). 'A comparative perspective on teacher attitude-constructs that impact on inclusive education in South Africa and Sweden', *South African Journal of Education*, 31, 74–90.

Newacheck, P.W. and Kim, E.S. (2005). 'A National profile of health care utilization and expenditures for children with special health care needs', *Archives of Pediatrics and Adolescent Medicine*, 159, 10–18.

Nirje, B. (1994). 'The normalisation principle and its human management implications, SRV-VRS', *The International Social Role Valorization Journal*, 1(2), 19–23.

Nirje, B. (1969). 'The normalisation principle and human management implications'. In R. Kugel and W. Wolfensberger (Eds.), *Changing Patterns in Residential Services for the Mentally Retarded* (Washington, DC: Presidents Committee on Mental Retardation), pp. 179–195.

Njenga, F. (2009). 'Perspectives of intellectual disability in Africa: Epidemiology, policy, services for children and adults', *Current Opinion in Psychiatry*, 22, 457–461.

O'Brien, J. and O'Brien, C.L. (1998). *A Little Book About Person Centered Planning* (Toronto, Canada: Inclusion Press).

O'Brien, P., McConkey, R. and García Iriarte, E. (2014). 'Co-researching with people who have intellectual disabilities: Insights from a national survey', *Journal of Applied Research in Intellectual Disabilities*, 27:1, 65–75.

Obiozor, W.E., Onu, V.C. and Ugwoegbu, I. (2010). 'Academic and social challenges facing students with developmental and learning disabilities in higher institutions: Implications for African colleges and universities', *African Journal of Teacher Education*, 1(1), 126–40.

O'Connell, M. (2007). *The Advocacy Sourcebook* (London: WaterAid), p. 30.

Office of the High Commissioner for Human Rights (OHCHR). (2013). 'Persons with disabilities "forgotten victims" of Syria's conflict', accessed 22 February 2014 from http://www.ohchr.org/en/NewsEvents/Pages/DisplayNews.aspx?NewsID=13736& LangID=E.

Office of the High Commission on Human Rights (OHCHR). (2012a). *Biennial Report of the CRPD Committee to the Secretary General* (New York: United Nations).

Office of the High Commission on Human Rights (OHCHR). (2012b). *The Convention on the Rights of Persons with Disabilities Training Guide*, Professional Training Series No. 19, www.ohchr.org/Documents/Issues/Disability/OHCHR_ TrainingGuideCRPDandOP.doc.

Office of the High Commission on Human Rights (OHCHR). (2012c) *Human Rights Indicators: A Guide to Measurement and Implementation* (Geneva: OHCHR).

Office of the High Commission on Human Rights (OHCHR). (2010). *Monitoring the Convention on the Rights of Persons with Disabilities: Guidance for Human Rights Monitors*, Professional Training Series 17 (Geneva: OHCHR).

Office of the High Commission on Human Rights (OHCHR). (2009). *Guidelines on Treaty-Specific Documents txo be Submitted by States Parties Under Article 35, Paragraph 1, of the Convention on the Rights of Persons with Disabilities,* CRPD/C/2/3, (Geneva: OHCHR), http://www.ohchr.org.

Oliven, A.C. (2012). 'Inclusion policies in the Brazilian system of higher education: The public and the private sectors', *Journal of US-China Public Administration,* 9(11), 1302–1310.

Oliver, M. (2013). 'The social model of disability 30 years on', *Disability & Society,* 28(7), 1024–1026.

Oliver, M. (1990). *The Politics of Disablement* (New York: Palgrave Macmillan).

Ollerton, J. and Horsfall, D. (2013). 'Rights to research: Utilising the convention on the rights of persons with disabilities as an inclusive participatory action research tool', *Disability & Society,* 28(5), 616–630.

Orange Foundation. (2012). *eEspaña 2012: Informe anual 2012 sobre el desarrollo de la sociedad de la Información en España* (Madrid: Fundación Orange).

Organisation for Economic Co-operation and Development (OECD). (2013). *Contribution on Education to the Post 2015 Framework: PISA for Development* (Paris: OECD).

Organisation for Economic Co-operation and Development (OECD). (2012). *Beyond MDGs: Towards an OECD Contribution to the Post 2015 Agenda* (Paris: OECD).

Organisation for Economic Co-operation and Development (OECD). (2001). *Understanding the Digital Divide,* accessed 21 April 2014 from http://www.oecd.org/sti/1888451.pdf.

Ortoleva, S. and Lewis, H. (2012). *Forgotten Sisters – A Report on Violence Against Women with Disabilities: An Overview of its Nature, Scope, Causes and Consequences* (Boston, MA: Northeastern University School of Law), accessed 30 July 2014 from http://ssrn.com/abstract=2133332.

O'Sullivan, C. and MacLachlan, M. (2009). 'Childhood disability in Burkina Faso and Sierra Leone: An exploratory study'. In M. MacLachlan and L. Swartz (Eds.), *Disability & International Development: Towards Inclusive Global Health* (New York: Springer).

O'Sullivan, C. and MacLachlan, M. (2008). 'A snapshot of childhood disability in sub-saharan Africa', *Report to Irish Aid & Health Research Board.*

Osamu, N. (2013). 'Challenges of the harmonisation and ratification of the Convention on the Rights of Persons with Disabilities by Japan,' *Journal of Policy and Practice in Intellectual Disabilities,* 10(2), 93–95.

Oxford English Dictionary (Online). (2014), accessed 30 July 2014 from http://www.oed.com.ezproxy1.library.usyd.edu.au/.

A. Pacey and P.R. Payne (Eds.). (1985). *Agricultural Development and Nutrition* (New Delhi: Concept Publishing Company).

Pacific Islands Forum Secretariat. (2014). *Disability in the Pacific,* accessed 30 July 2014 from http://www.forumsec.org.fj/pages.fm/strategic-partnerships-coordination/disability/disability-in-pacific.html.

Palmer, M. (2011). 'Disability and Poverty: A Conceptual Review', *Journal of Disability Policy Studies,* 21(4), 210–218.

Palmer, S.B., Wehmeyer, M.L., Davies, D.K. and Stock, S.E. (2012). 'Family members' reports of the technology use of family members with intellectual and developmental disabilities', *Journal of Intellectual Disability Research,* 56(4), 402–414.

Pan American Health Organization. (2008). *Human Rights & Health: Persons with Disabilities,* accessed 11 April 2012 from www.paho.org/english/dd/pub/10069_Disabilities.pdf.

Parish, S.L. and Cloud, J.M. (2006). 'Financial well-being of young children with disabilities and their families', *Social Work*, 51, 223–232.

Parish, S.L., Rose, R.A. and Andrews, M.E. (2009). 'Income poverty and material hardship among US women with disabilities', *The Social Service Review*, 83, 33–52.

Parish, S.L., Rose, R.A., Andrews, M.E., Grinstein-Weiss, M. and Richman, E.L. (2008). 'Material hardship in U.S. families raising children with disabilities', *Exceptional Children*, 75, 71–92.

Parish, S.L., Rose, R.A. and Swaine, J.G. (2010). 'Financial well-being of US parents caring for co-resident children and adults with developmental disabilities: An age-cohort analysis', *Journal of Intellectual and Developmental Disabilities*, 35, 235–243.

Parish, S.L., Seltzer, M.M., Greenberg, J.S. and Floyd, F.J. (2004). 'Economic implications of caregiving at midlife: Comparing parents with and without children who have developmental disabilities', *Mental Retardation*, 42(6), 413–426.

Parish, S.L., Shattuck, P.T. and Rose, R.A. (2009). 'A multi-level analysis of state Medicaid and financial burden of raising children with special health care needs', *Pediatrics*, 435–442.

Parmenter, T.R. (2008). 'The present, past and future of the study of intellectual disability, Challenges in developing countries', *Salud Publica de Mexico*, 50(2), 124–131.

Parnes, P., Cameron, D., Christie, N., Cockburn, L., Hashemi, G. and Yoshida, K. (2009). 'Disability in low-income countries: Issues and implications', *Disability and Rehabilitation*, 31, 1170–1180.

Parsons, A. (2009). *The Global Health Debate* (Washington, DC: Foreign Policy in Focus), accessed 15 May 2012 from www.fpif.org/articles/the_global_health_debate.

Patel, V. (2014). On *'The Life Scientific'*, BBC Radio 4, 5 March 2014.

Pather, S. (2011). 'Evidence on inclusion and support for learners with disabilities in mainstream schools in South Africa: Off the policy radar?', *International Journal of Inclusive Education*, 15(10), 1103–1117.

Peace Direct. (2014). 'Insight direct: Colombia: Guide to the conflict and peace-building in Colombia,' *Insight on Conflict*, accessed 24 February 2014 from http://www. insightonconflict.org/conflicts/colombia/.

Pelka, F. (1997). *The Disability Rights Movement* (Santa Barbara, CA: ABC-CLIO).

Penhaul, K. (2001). 'Land Mines: Deadly tradition in Colombia war-torn country – the only one in this hemisphere where devices are still being sown', *San Francisco Chronicle. Common Dreams: Building Progressive Community*, 12 August, accessed 24 February 2014 from http://www.commondreams.org/headlines.shtml?/ headlines01/0812-02.htm.

People's Health Movement. (2009). *The People's Charter for Health*, accessed 15 May 2012 from www.phmovement.org/en/resources/charters/peopleshealth.

L.O. Pérez Acevedo. (2012). 'Modelo conceptual colombiano de discapacidad e inclusión social'. In M.E. Almeida and M.A. Angelino (Eds.), *Debates y perspectivas en torno a la discapacidad en América Latina*, E-book ISBN 978-950-698-303-1.

Perkins, E.A. and LaMartin, K.M. (2012). 'The internet as social support for older carers of adults with intellectual disabilities', *Journal of Policy and Practice in Intellectual Disabilities*, 9(1), 53–62.

Perkins, E.A. and Moran, J.A. (2010). 'Aging adults with intellectual disabilities', *Journal of the American Medical Association*, 304(1), 91–92.

Perlin, M. (2013). 'Human rights law for persons with disabilities in Asia and the Pacific: The need for a Disability Rights Tribunal', *Journal of Policy and Practice in Intellectual Disabilities*, 10(2), 96–98.

Perrin, J.M. (2002). 'Health services research for children with disabilities', *The Milbank Quarterly*, 80(2), 303–324.

Perumal, J. (2005). *Inclusive Education Policy and Practice a Secondary School in KZN: An Ethnographic Study Exploring Tensions and Possibilities*, unpublished PhD thesis (Durban: University of KwaZulu-Natal).

Peters, S.J. (2009). 'Review of marginalisation of people with disabilities in Lebanon, Syria and Jordan'. Background Paper prepared for the *Education for All Global Monitoring Report* (2010), accessed 15 March, 2014, from http://addc.byte2.com/documents/resources/unesco-review-of-marginalisation-of-people-with-disabilities-in-lebanon-syria-and-jordan_956.pdf.

Peters, S.J. (2004). *Inclusive Education: An EFA Strategy for all Children* (Washington, DC: World Bank), accessed 12 November 2012 from http://siteresources.worldbank.org/EDUCATION/Resources/278200-1099079877269/547664-1099079993288/InclusiveEdu_efa_strategy_for_children.pdf.

Petersen, A.J. (2011). 'Research with individuals labelled "other": Reflections on the research process', *Disability & Society*, 26(3), 293–305.

Phillips, S.D. (2012). 'Implications of EU accession for disability rights legislation and housing in Bulgaria, Romania, Croatia, and the Former Yugoslav Republic of Macedonia', *Journal of Disability Policy Studies*, 23(1), 26–38.

Popay, J., Escorel, S., Hernández, M., Johnston, H., Mathieson, J. and Rispel, L. (2008). *Understanding and Tackling Social Exclusion: Final Report To the Who Commission On Social Determinants of Health* (Geneva, Switzerland: World Health Organization), accessed 17 March 2014 from http://www.who.Int/Social_Determinants/Knowledge_Networks/Final_Reports/Sekn_Final%20report_042008.Pdf?Ua=1.

Porterfield, S.L. (2002). 'Work choices of mothers in families with children with disabilities', *Journal of Marriage and the Family*, 64, 972–981.

Poston, D.J. and Turnbull, A.P. (2004). 'Role of spirituality and religion in family quality of life for families of children with disabilities', *Education and Training in Developmental Disabilities*, 95–108.

Priestley, M. (2001). *Disability and the Life Course: Global Perspectives* (Cambridge: Cambridge University Press).

Pruchno, R.A. and McMullen, W.F. (2004). 'Patterns of Service Utilization by adults with a developmental disability: Type of service makes a difference', *American Journal of Mental Retardation*, 109, 362–378.

Quinn, G. (2009). 'Bringing the UN Convention on rights for persons with disabilities to life in Ireland', *British Journal of Learning Disabilities*, 37, 245–249.

Radio Netherlands Worldwide Africa. (2014). *Congo's Beach Port Is Haven for Disabled Traders*, accessed 11 August 2014 from http://www.rnw.nl/africa/bulletin/congos-beach-port-haven-disabled-traders.

Raina, P., O'Donnell, M., Schwellnus, H., Rosenbaum, P., King, G., Brehaut, J. et al. (2004). 'Caregiving process and caregiver burden: Conceptual models to guide research and practice', *BMC Pediatrics*, 4(1), 1–13.

Rao, I. (2004). *Equity to Women with Disabilities* (India, Bangalore: CBR Network), accessed 18 March 2014, http://v1.dpi.org/lang-en/resources/details.php?page=90.

Ratzka, A. (2005). *ILI Promotes the Self-determination of People with Disabilities*, Independent Living Institute, accessed 14 February 2014 from http://www.independentliving.org.

Redley, M., Maina, E., Keeling, A., and Pattni, P. (2012). 'The voting rights of adults with intellectual disabilities: Reflections on the arguments, and situation in Kenya and England and Wales', *Journal of Intellectual Disability Research*, 56(11), 1026–1035.

Republic of South Africa. (1997a). *South African Higher Education Act 101* (Pretoria: Government Printer).

Republic of South Africa. (1997b). *White Paper: The Integrated National Disability Strategy* (Pretoria: Government Printer).

Republic of South Africa. (1996). *South African Schools Act 84 of 1996* (Pretoria: Government Printer).

Republic of South Africa, Department of Education. (2008). *Guidelines for Inclusive Teaching and Learning* (Pretoria: Government Printer).

Republic of South Africa, Department of Education. (2011). *Guidelines for Responding to Learner Diversity in the Classroom through Curriculum and Assessment Policy Statements* (Pretoria: Government Printer).

Republic of South Africa, Department of Education. (2008). *National Strategy on Screening, Identification, Assessment and Support (SIAS) – Operational Guidelines* (Pretoria: Department of Education).

Republic of South Africa, Department of Education. (2007). *Conceptual and Operational Guidelines for the Implementation of Inclusive Education: District Support Teams (DST)* (Pretoria: Department of Education).

Republic of South Africa, Department of Education. (2001a). *White Paper 6: Special Needs Education: Building an Inclusive Education and Training System* (Pretoria: Government Printer).

Republic of South Africa, Department of Education. (2001b). *National Plan for Higher Education* (Pretoria: Government Printer).

Republic of South Africa, Department of Education. (1997). *White Paper 3: A Programme for the Transformation of Higher Education* (Pretoria: Government Printer).

Republic of Uganda. (1995). *Constitution of the Republic of Uganda*, accessed 19 July 2013 from http://www.parliament.go.ug/index (home page).

Rice, J. and Robb, A. (2004). 'Learning to listen', *Nursing Older People*, 15(10), 10–13.

Richard, B. (2014). 'Families, well-being and inclusion: Rethinking priorities for children with cognitive disabilities in Ladakh, India', *Childhood*, 21(3).

Rioux, M. and Carbert, A. (2003). 'Human rights and disability: The international context', *Journal on Developmental Disabilities*, 10, 2.

Roberts, A., Townsend, S., Morris, J., Rushbrooke, E., Greenhill, B., Whitehead, R., Matthews, T. and Golding, L. (2013). 'Treat me right, treat me equal: Using national policy and legislation to create positive changes in local health services for people with intellectual disabilities', *Journal of Applied Research in Intellectual Disabilities*, 26, 14–25.

Roberts, L., Roalfe, A., Wilson, S. and Lester, H. (2007). 'Physical health care of patients with schizophrenia in primary care: A comparative study', *Family Practice*, 24(1), 34–40.

Roberts, M.P. and Kaiser, A.P. (2011). 'The effectiveness of parent-implemented language interventions: A meta-analysis', *American Journal of Speech-Language Pathology*, 20, 180–199.

Robertson, J., Emerson, E., Hatton, C. and Yasamy, M.T. (2012). 'Efficacy of community-based rehabilitation for children with or at significant risk of intellectual disabilities in low- and middle-income countries: A review', *Journal of Applied Research in Intellectual Disabilities*, 25(2), 143–154.

Roca-Dorda, J., Roca-González, J. and Del Campo, M.E. (2004). 'De las ayudas técnicas a la tecnología asistiva'. Paper presented at the Tecnoneet 2004: Retos y realidades de la Inclusión Digital, 23–25 September 2004, Murcia (Spain), accessed 30 July 2014 from http://sid.usal.es/libros/discapacidad/22197/8-4-2/de-las-ayudas-tecnicas-a-la-tecnologia-asistiva-conferencia.aspx.

Rodríguez de las Heras, A. (2006). 'Principios de una Sociedad del Conocimiento'. Paper presented at the Las tecnologías en la escuela inclusiva. Nuevos escenarios, nuevas oportunidades'. Paper presented at the IV Congreso Nacional de Tecnología Educativa y Atención a la Diversidad (Tecnoneet) and VI Congreso Iberoamericano de Informática Educativa Especial (CIIEE), Murcia (España).

Roebeling, G. and de Vries, J. (2011). *Advocacy and Policy Influencing for Social Change* (Bosnia and Herzegovina: Technical Assistance for Civil Society Organisations), p. 20–28.

Room, G. (1995). *Beyond the Threshold: The Measurement and Analysis of Social Exclusion* (Bristol, UK: The Policy Press).

Rossi, P.H., Lipsey, M.W. and Freeman, H. (2004). *Evaluation: A Systematic Approach* (Thousand Oaks, CA: Sage).

A. Roulstone and C. Barnes. (Eds.). (2005). *Working Futures? Disabled People, Policy and Social Inclusion* (Bristol, UK: The Policy Press, University of Bristol).

Rowe, J. and Kahn, R. (1998). *Successful Aging* (New York: Random House).

Rutter, M. (1990). 'Psychosocial resilience and protective mechanism'. In J. Rolf, A.S. Masten, D. Cicchetti, K.H. Neuchterlein and S. Weintraub (Eds.), *Risk and Protective Factors in the Development of Psychopathology* (Cambridge: Cambridge University Press).

M. Sabatello and M. Schulze (Eds.). (2014). *Human Rights and Disability Advocacy* (Philadelphia: University of Pennsylvania Press).

Saith, R. (2001). 'Social exclusion: The concept and application to developing countries. Queen Elizabeth house', *Working Paper Series*, 72.

Salcedo, V. (2013). 'Memories of war and dignity: Report on victims of Colombia's conflict, *Just the Facts*, accessed 24 February 2014 from http://justf.org/blog/2013/07/25/memories-war-and-dignity-report-victims-colombias-conflict.

Samadi, S.A., McConkey, R. and Kelly, G. (2012). 'The information and support needs of Iranian parents of children with autism spectrum disorders', *Early Childhood Development and Care*, 182(11), 1439–1454.

Samuels, C.A. (2014). 'Graduation disparities loom large for students with special needs', *Ed Week*, 33(19), 1–8.

Satre, D.D., Campbell, C.I., Gordon, N.S. and Weisner, C. (2010). 'Ethnic disparities in accessing treatment for depression and substance use disorders in an integrated health plan,' *International Journal of Psychiatry in Medicine*, 40(1), 57–76.

Savidis, A., Grammenos, D. and Stephanidis, C. (2007). 'Developing inclusive e-learning and e-entertainment to effectively accommodate learning difficulties', *Universal Accesss Information Society*, 5, 401–419, doi: 10.1007/s10209-006-0059-3.

Schalock, R.L. (2009). 'La nueva definición de discapacidad intelectual, apoyos individuales y resultados personales', *Siglo Cero, Revista Española sobre Discapacidad Intelectual*, 40(1), 22–39.

Scheer, J. and Groce, N. (1988). 'Impairment as a human constant: Cross-cultural and historical perspectives on variation', *Journal of Social Issues*, 44(1), 23–37.

Schoufour, J., Echteld, M. and Evenhuis, H. (2012). 'Frailty in eldery with intellectual disabilities', *Journal of Intellectual Disabilty Research*, 56, 661.

Schoufour, J. D., Mitnitski, A., Rockwood, K., Evenhuis, H.M. and Echteld, M. A. (2013). 'Development of a frailty index for older people with intellectual disabilities: Results from the HA-ID study'. *Research in Developmental Disabilities*, 34, 1541–1555.

Schulze, M. (2010). 'Understanding the UN convention on the rights of persons with disabilities: A handbook on human rights and persons with disabilities', Handicap International, accessed 20 January 2015 from http://www.internationaldisabil

ityalliance.org/sites/disalliance.e-presentaciones.net/files/public/files/HI_CRPD_Manual_sept2009_final%5B1%5D.pdf.

Schur, L., Kruse, D. and Blanck, P. (2013). *People with Disabilities: Sidelined or Mainstreamed?* (Cambridge: Cambridge University Press).

Selwyn, N. and Facer, K. (2007). 'Beyond the digital divide. Rethinking digital inclusion for the 21st century'. In FutureLab (Ed.), *Opening Education*, 5, 1–40.

Sen, A. (2009). *The Idea of Justice* (Cambridge, MA: Harvard University Press).

Sen, A. (2008). 'Why and how is health a human right?', *Lancet*, 372(9655), 2010.

Sen, A. (2000). *Social Exclusion: Concept, Application, and Scrutiny* (Manila, Philippines: Office of Environment and Social Development, Asian Development Bank).

Sen, A. (1999). *Development as Freedom* (New York: Knopf).

Sentenac, M., Gavin, A., Gabhainn, S.N., Molcho, M., Due, P., Ravens-Sieberer, U., De Matos, M., Malkowska-Szkutnik, A., Gobina, I., Vollebergh, W., Arnaud, C. and Godeau, E. (2013). 'Peer victimization and subjective health among students reporting disability or chronic illness in 11 Western countries', *The European Journal of Public Health*, 23(3), 421–426.

Sevillano García, M.L. (2010). 'Sociedad de la Información-sociedad del conocimiento: Relaciones y convergencia'. In (Ed.), *Nuevas Tecnologías en Educación Social* (Madrid: McGraw-Hill Interamericana de España).

Shakespeare, T. (2014). *Disability Rights and Wrongs Revisited* (London & New York: Routledge).

Shakespeare, T. (2010). 'The social model of disability'. In L.J. Davis (Ed.), *The Disability Studies Reader* (New York: Routledge).

Sham, S. (1996). 'Reaching Chinese children with learning disabilities in greater Manchester', *British Journal of Learning Disabilities*, 24(3), 104–109.

Shanahan, E.A., Jones, M.D. and McBeth, M.K. (2011). 'Policy narratives and policy processes', *Policy Studies Journal*, 39(3), 535–561.

Shanahan, E.A., Jones, M.D., McBeth, M.K. and Lane, R.R. (2013). 'An angel on the wind: How heroic policy narratives shape policy realities', *Policy Studies Journal*, 41(3), 453–483.

Shapiro, J.P. (1993). *No Pity: People with Disabilities Forging a New Civil Rights Movement* (New York: Times Books).

Sharma, R. (2001). *An Introduction to Advocacy: Training Guide* (Washington, DC: SARA Project, Academy for Educational Development).

Sherlaw, W., Lucas, B., Jourdain, A. and Monaghan, N. (2014). 'Disabled people, inclusion and policy: Better outcomes through a public health approach?', *Disability & Society*, 29(3), 444–459.

Shildrick, M. (2012). 'Critical disability studies: Rethinking the conventions for the age of postmodernity'. In N. Watson, A. Roulstone and C. Thomas (Eds.), *Routledge Handbook of Disability Studies* (London: Routledge).

'The shocking cost of war: Afghanistan and Iraq veterans are "the most damaged generation ever" with almost HALF seeking disability benefits'. (2012). *Mail Online*, 28 May, accessed 24 February 2014 from http://www.dailymail.co.uk/news/article-2150933/The-shocking-cost-war-Afghanistan-Iraq-veterans-damaged-generation-HALF-seeking-disability-benefits.html.

Shogren, K.A. and Turnbull, H.R. (2014). 'Core concepts of disability policy, the convention on the rights of persons with disabilities, and public policy research with respect to developmental disabilities', *Journal of Policy and Practice in Intellectual Disabilities*, 11(1), 19–26.

Silver, H. (1994). 'Social Exclusion and Social Solidarity: The Three Paradigms', *International Labour Review*, 133, 531–578.

Singal, N. (2011). 'Disability, poverty and education: Implications for policies and practices', *International Journal of Inclusive Education*, 15(10), 1047–1052.

Singal, N. (2009). *Education of Children with Disabilities in India*. Background Paper Prepared for the Education for All Global Monitoring Report 2010 (Paris: UNESCO).

N.J. Smelser and P.B. Baltes (Eds.). (2001). *International Encyclopaedia of the Social and Behavioural Sciences* (Oxford, UK: Elsevier).

Social Care Institute for Excellence. (2008). *Having a Break: Good Practice in Short Breaks for Families with Children Who have Complex Health Needs and Disabilities* (London: SCIE).

Srivastava, M., De Boer, A. and Pijl, S.J. (2015). 'Inclusive education in developing countries: A closer look at its implementation in the last 10 years', *Educational Review*, 67(2), 1–17.

Stainton, T. and Claire, I. (2012). 'Human rights and intellectual disabilities: An emergent theoretical paradigm.' *Journal of Intellectual Disability Research*, 56(2), 1011–1013.

Stainton, T., Hole, R., Charles, G., Yodanis, C., Powell, S. and Crawford, C. (2006). *Services for Seniors with A Developmental Disability: Literature and Initial Program Review* (Province of British Columbia, Canada: Ministry of Children and Family Development).

Stang Alva, M.F. (2011). *Las personas con discapacidad en América Latina: Del reconocimiento jurídico a la desigualdad real* (Santiago de chile: Centro Latinoamericano y Caribeño de Demografía, División de Población de la CEPAL, United Nations).

Stein, M.A. (2007). Disability human rights, *California Law Review*, 95, 75–121.

Stevens, C.S. (2010). 'Disability, caregiving and interpellation: Migrant and non-migrant families of children with disabilities in Australia', *Disability & Society*, 25(7), 783–796.

Strauss, D., Kastner, T.A. and Shavelle, R. (1998). 'Mortality of adults with developmental disabilities living in California Institution and community care, 1985–1994', *Mental Retardation*, 36(5), 360–371.

Streeten, P. (1984). 'Basic needs: Some unsettled questions', *World Development*, 12(9).

Stubbs, D. and Tawake, S. (2009). *Pacific Sisters with Disabilities: An Intersection of Discrimination* (Suva, Fiji: UNDP Pacific Centre).

Sutherland, A. (2008). 'Choices, rights and cabaret: Arts and collective identity'. In J. Swain and S. French (Eds.), *Disability on Equal Terms* (London: Sage).

Swain, J. and French, S. (2008). 'Affirming identity'. In J. Swain and S. French (Eds.), *Disability on Equal Terms* (London: Sage).

Swart, E., Engelbrecht, P., Eloff, I., Pettipher, R. and Oswald, M. (2005). 'Developing inclusive school communities: Voices of parents of children with disabilities', *Education as Change*, 8(1), 80–108.

Swartz, L. (2013). 'Between faith and doubt: Training members of disabled people's organisations in southern Africa in basic research skills'. In J. Claassens, L. Swartz and L.D. Hansen (Eds.), *Searching for Dignity: Conversations on Human Dignity, Theology and Disability* (Stellenbosch: SUNMedia).

Swartz, L. (2009). 'Building disability research capacity in low-income contexts: Possibilities and challenges'. In M. MacLachlan and L. Swartz (Eds.), *Disability and International Development: Towards Inclusive Global Health* (New York: Springer).

H. Tajfel (Ed.). (1978). *Differentiation between Social Groups: Studies in the Social Psychology of Intergroup Relations* (London: Academic Press).

Tarakeshwar, N. and Pargament, K.I. (2001). 'Religious coping in families of children with autism', *Focus on Autism and Other Developmental Disabilities*, 16(4), 247–260.

Teasley, M., Baffour, T.D. and Tyson, E.H. (2005). 'Perceptions of cultural competence among urban school social workers: Does experience make a difference?', *Children & Schools*, 27(4), 227–236.

Temple, V.A. and Stanish, H.I. (2008). 'Physical activity and persons with intellectual disability: Some considerations for Latin America', *Salud Publica de Mexico*, 50(2), 185–193.

Thomas, C. (2002). 'Disability theory: Key ideas, issues, and thinkers'. In C. Barnes, M. Oliver and L. Barton (Eds.), *Disability Studies Today* (Cambridge: Polity).

Thompson, J.R., Bradley, V.J., Buntinx, W.H.E., Schalock, R.L., Shogren, K.A., Snell, M.E. and Yeager, M.H. (2010). 'Conceptualizando los apoyos y las necesidades de apoyo de personas con discapacidad intelectual', *Siglo Cero, Revista Española sobre Discapacidad Intelectual*, 41(1), 7–22.

Thomson, R.G. (1996). *Extraordinary Bodies: Figuring Physical Disability in American Culture and Literature* (New York: Columbia University Press).

Torr, J., Strydom, A., Patti, P. and Jokinen, N. (2010). 'Ageing in Down syndrome: Morbidity and mortality', *Journal of Policy and Practice in Intellectual Disabilities*, 7(1), 70–81.

Torrente, J., Del Blanco, A., Serrano-Laguna, A., Vallejo-Pinto, J.A., Moerno-Ger, P. and Fernández-Manjón, B. (2010). 'Towards a low cost adaptation of educational games for people with disabilities', *Computer Science and Information Systems*, 11(1), 369–391, doi: 10.2298/CSIS121209013T.

J. Tøsseboro (2004). 'Understanding disability: Introduction to the special issue of SJDR', *Scandinavian Journal of Disability Research, Special Issue: Understanding Disability*, 6(1), 3–7. doi: 10.1080/15017410409512635.

Townsend, P. (1993). *The International Analysis of Poverty* (London: Harvester Wheatsheaf).

Trani, J.F., Bakhshi, P., Noor, A.A., Lopez, D. and Mashkoor, A. (2010). 'Poverty, Vulnerability, and Provision of Healthcare in Afghanistan', *Social Science and Medicine*, 70, 1745–1755.

R. Traustadóttir (July 2004). *Disability Studies: A Nordic Perspective. British Disability Studies Association Conference*, Lancaster.

Trollope-Kumar, K. and Last, J.M. (2002). 'Cultural factors'. In L. Breslow (Ed.), *Encyclopedia of Public Health* (New York: Macmillan Reference).

Tutu, D. (2004). *God has a Dream* (New York: Doubleday).

Tutu, D. (1999). *No Future without Forgiveness* (New York: Random House).

Underhill, J.W. (2012). *Ethnolinguistics and Cultural Concepts: Truth, Love, Hate and War* (Cambridge & New York: Cambridge University Press).

UNESCO. (2010). *Reaching the Marginalized EFA Global Monitoring Report* (Oxford: Oxford University Press).

UNESCO. (2004). *The Right to Education for Persons with Disabilities*, an EFA Flagship Paper (Paris: UNESCO).

UNESCO. (2000). *Dakar Framework for Action: Education for all – Meeting our Collective Commitments*. World Education Forum, April 26–28, in Dakar, Senegal.

UNESCO. (1994). *The Salamanca Statement and Framework for Action on Special Needs Education*, World Conference on Special Needs Education: Access and Quality, 7–10 June, Salamanca (Spain).

UNESCO Institute of Statistics and UNICEF. (2012). *World-Inequalities Data Base on Education (WIDE)* (Paris: UNESCO), http://www.education-inequalities.org.

UNESCO, UNDP, UNICEF and World Bank. (1990). *Final Report: World Declaration on Education for all – Meeting Basic Learning Needs*, 5–9 March, in Jomtien, Thailand.

UNICEF. (2013). *Education equity now! A Regional Analysis of the Situation of Out of School Children in Central and Eastern Europe and the Commonwealth of Independent States – Summary Brochure*, (Geneva: UNICEF Regional Office for

Central and Eastern Europe and the Commonwealth of Independent States), accessed 30 July 2014 from http://www.unicef.org/ceecis/UNI154796.pdf.

UNICEF. (2013). *The State of the World's Children: Children with Disabilities* (New York: UNICEF).

UNICEF. (2012). *The Right of Children with Disabilities to Education: A Rights-based Approach to Inclusive Education*, accessed 1 February 2014 from http://www. unicef.org/ceecis/UNICEF_Right_Children_Disabilities_En_Web.pdf.

UNICEF. (2009). *Tracking Progress on Child and Maternal Nutrition: A Survival and Development Priority*, accessed 11 April 2012 from www.unicef.pt/docs/Progress_ on_Child_and_Maternal_Nutrition_EN_110309.pdf.

UNICEF. (2008). *Monitoring Child Disability in Developing Countries: Results from the Multiple Indicator Cluster Surveys* (New York: UNICEF).

UNICEF. (2005). *Children and Disability in Transition in CEE/CIS and Baltic States*, accessed 12 April 2012 from www.unicef-irc.org/publications/pdf/ii12_dr_eng.pdf.

UNICEF. (2003). *Lobbying: An Advocacy Tool*, http:/www.advocate-for-children.org/ advocacy/lobbying/start.

UNICEF. (1990). *Strategy for Improved Nutrition of Children and Women in Developing Countries*, accessed 11 April 2012 from http://repository.forcedmigration.org/show_ metadata.jsp?pid=fmo:3066.

UNICEF and University of Wisconsin. (2008). 'Monitoring child disability in developing countries: Results from the multiple indicator cluster surveys', accessed 11 April 2012 from www.childinfo.org/files/Monitoring_Child_Disability_in_Developing_Countries.pdf.

United Nations. (2014a). *Incorporating the provisions of the Convention on the Rights of Persons with Disabilities in the post-2015 development agenda*, Conference of State Parties to the Convention on the Rights of People with Disabilities, Seventh session, CRPD/CSP/2014/2 (New York: United Nations).

United Nations. (2014b). *Millennium Development Goals Indicators: State of Palestine*, http://mdgs.un.org/unsd/mdg/Date.aspx.

United Nations. (2012). *Realising the Future We Want for All: Report to the Secretary General by the UN Task Team on the Post-2015 UN Development Agenda* (New York: United Nations).

United Nations. (2011a). *Disability and the Millennium Development Goals: A Review of the MDG Process and Strategies for Inclusion of Disability Issues in Millennium Development Goal Efforts*, http://www.un.org/disabilities/documents/review_of_ disability_and_the_mdgs.pdf.

United Nations. (2011b). *World Programme of Action Concerning Disabled Persons*, http://www.un.org/esa/socdev/enable/diswpa04.htm.

United Nations. (2010a). *Analysing and Measuring Social Inclusion in a Global Context* (New York: Department of Economic and Social Affairs), accessed 10 March 2014 from http://www.un.org/esa/socdev/publications/measuring-social-inclusion.pdf.

United Nations. (2010b). *Keeping the Promise: Realizing the Millennium Development Goals for Persons with Disabilities towards 2015 and Beyond* (New York: United Nations), http://www.un.org/disabilities/documents/events/idpd10_philippines.pdf.

United Nations. (2010c). *The Millennium Development Goals* (New York: United Nations).

United Nations. (2007). *Handbook for Parliamentarians on the Convention on the Rights of Persons with Disabilities and its Optional Protocol – From Exclusion to Equality: Realizing the Rights of Persons with Disabilities* (Geneva: United Nations).

United Nations. (2006). *Convention on the Rights of Persons with Disabilities and Optional Protocol*, adopted on 13 December 2006 (New York: United Nations General Assembly). http://www.un.org/disabilities/convention/conventionfull.shtml.

United Nations. (1993). *Standard Rules on Equalization of Opportunities for Persons with Disabilities* (New York: United Nations Department of Public Information).

United Nations. (1990). *Convention on the Rights of the Child*, www2.ohchr.org/english/law/crc.htm.

United Nations. (1982). World programme of action concerning disabled persons, http://www.un.org/disabilities/default.asp?id=23.

United Nations. (1948). *The Universal Declaration of Human Rights*, http://www.un.org/en/documents/udhr/.

United Nations Development Group. (2011). *Including the Rights of Persons with Disabilities in United Nations Programming at Country Level: A Guidance Note for UN Country Teams and Implementing Partners* (New York: United Nations).

United Nations Development Programme. (2006). *Poverty, Unemployment and Social Exclusion*, accessed 15 February 2014 from http://www.undp.hr/upload/file/104/52080/FILENAME/Poverty,%20Unemployment%20and%20Social%20Exclusion.pdf.

United Nations Economic Council. (2012). *Report of the Washington Group on Disability Statistics*, E/CN.3/2012/21 (New York: UN Statistical Commission).

United Nations High Commissioner for Refugees. (2013). *Lebanon Response Plan*, accessed 22 February 2014 from http://unhcr.org/51b0a6059.pdf.

United Nations Secretary-General. (2013). *Report of the High Level Meeting on Disability and Development in the Realisation of the Millennium Development Goals for Persons with Disabilities*, General Assembly Resolution A/68/L.1 (New York: United Nations).

US Central Intelligence Agency. (2012). The World Factbook: West Bank, https://www.cia.gov/library/publications/the-world-factbook/geos/we.html.

USER Behavioristics. (2014). 'Game usability, playtesting, usability evaluation', accessed 10 April 2014 from http://userbehavioristics.com/index.htm (home page).

Ustun, T.B., Kostanjsek, N., Chatterji, S., and Rehm, J. (Eds.) (2012). World Health Organization, 'Measuring Health and Disability: Manual for WHO Disability Assessment Schedule (WHODAS 2.0)', accessed 15 May 2012 from http://apps.who.int/bookorders/anglais/detart1.jsp?sesslan=1&codlan=1&codcol=15&codcch=748#

Vaillant, D. (2011). 'Preparing teachers for inclusive education in Latin America', *Prospects Quarterly*, accessed 15 January 2014 from http://denisevaillant.com/articulos/2011/Prospects2011.pdf.

Van Dijk, J.A.G.M. (2006). 'Digital divide research, achievements and shortcomings', *Poetics*, 34, 221–235.

van Schrojenstein Lantman-De Valk, H.M., Metsemakers, J.F., Haveman, M.J. and Crebolder, H.F. (2000). 'Health problems in people with intellectual disability in general practice: A comparative study', *Family Practice*, 17(5), 405–407.

Väyrynen, S. (2005). *Schools of Thought: Understanding Inclusion and Exclusion in Education in Finland and South Africa*, unpublished PhD thesis (Canterbury: Canterbury Christchurch University College, University of Kent).

Verdonschot, M.M.L., de Witte, L.P., Reichrath, E., Buntinx, W.H. and Curfs, L.M. (2009). 'Community participation of people with an intellectual disability: A review of empirical findings', *Journal of Intellectual Disability Research*, 53(4), 303–318.

Verdugo, M., Navas, P., Gómez, E. and Schalock, R. (2012). 'The concept of quality of life and its role in enhancing human rights in the field of intellectual disability', *Journal of Intellectual Disability Research*, 56(6), 1036–1045.

Veterans Health Care. (2013). *VA Disability Compensation Rates*, accessed 24 February 2014 from http://www.military.com/benefits/veterans-health-care/va-disability-compensation-rates.html.

Vishwanath, T. and Serajuddin, U. (2012). *Poverty in MENA: Advances and Challenges* (Washington, DC: World Bank).

Vygotsky, L. (1993). 'The fundamental problems of Defectology'. In *Collected Works of L.S. Vygotsky* (Ed.), *The Fundamentals of Defectology*, vol. 2 (New York: Plenum Press).

Wahlbin, K. and Hunter Utt, M. (2012). *Usability Testing for People with Disabilities*, accessed 17 April 2014 from https://wiki.state.ma.us/confluence/display/assistivetechnologygroup/Usability+Testing+for+People+with+Disabilities.

Wallner, P. (1992). 'Physiotherapy in transition: A personal view', *Physio Forum*, 1, 2–3.

Walmsley, J. (2001). 'Normalisation, emancipatory research and inclusive research in learning disability', *Disability & Society*, 16(2), 187–205.

Walmsley, J. and Johnson, K. (2003). *Inclusive Research with People with Learning Disabilities: Past, Present and Futures* (London: Jessica Kingsley Publishers).

Wang, K.Y. (2012). 'The care burden of families with members having intellectual and developmental disorder: A review of the recent literature', *Current Opinion in Psychiatry*, 25(5), 348–352.

Ward, C. (2001). *Family Matters: Counting Families In* (London: Department of Health).

Waters, H.E. and Boon, R.T. (2011). 'Teaching money computation skill to high school students with mild intellectual disabilities via the TouchMath© program: A multi-sensory approach', *Education and Training in Autism and Developmental Disabilities*, 46(4), 544–555.

Welch, P. (September, 2002). 'Applying the capabilities approach in examining disability, poverty and gender'. In *Proceedings of the Conference Promoting Women's Capabilities: Examining Nussbaum's Capabilities Approach* (Cambridge, UK: St. Edmunds' College).

Whitehouse, P. and George, D.R. (2014). 'Prevention: How the paradigm is shifting', *The Journal of Prevention of Alzheimer's Disease*, 1(1), 1–5.

World Health Organization, UNICEF. (2012). *Early Childhood Development & Disability: A Discussion Paper* (Geneva: WHO Press).

Why Won't America Ratify the UN Convention on Children's Rights? (2013). The Economist Explains Blog, 6 October, accessed 21 June 2014 from http://www.economist.com/blogs/economist-explains (home page).

Wikipedia. (2014). 'List of countries by unemployment rate', accessed 30 July 2014 from http://en.wikipedia.org/wiki/List_of_countries_by_unemployment_rate.

Wildeman, R.A. and Nomdo, C. (2007). *Implementation of Inclusive Education: How Far Are We? Occasional Papers* (Cape Town: Institute for Democracy in Africa [IDASA]).

Williams, G.H. (2001). 'Theorizing disability'. In G.L. Albrecht, K.D. Seelman and M. Bury (Eds.), *Handbook of Disability Studies* (Thousand Oaks, CA: Sage).

Williams, G.H. (1983). 'The Movement for Independent Living: An Evaluation and Critique', *Social Science & Medicine*, 17(5), 1003–1010.

Wiman, R. (1997). *The Disability Dimension in Development Action: Manual on Inclusive Planning* (Helsinki, Finland: United Nations), accessed 30 July 2014 from http://www.un.org/disabilities/documents/toolaction/FF-DisalibilityDim0103_b1.pdf.

Wolfensberger, W. (1985). 'An overview of social role valorisation and some reflections on elderly mentally retarded persons'. In M. Janicki and H. Wisniewski (Eds.), *Aging and Developmental Disabilities: Issues and Approaches* (Baltimore: Paul Brookes Publishing).

Wong, R., Gerst, K., Michaels-Obregon, A. and Pallino, A. (2011). *Burden of Aging in Developing Countries: Disability Transitions in Mexico Compared to the United States: A Working Paper* (Galveston, TX: University of Texas).

World Bank. (2000). *Implementation Completion Report on an International Development Association Credit in the Amount of $10 Million to Bosnia and Herzegovina for a War Victim's Rehabilitation Project. Report No: 20578-BIH*, accessed 22 February 2014 from http://www.worldbank.org/projects/P044424/war-victims-rehabilitation-project?lang=en&tab=overview.

World Health Organization (WHO). (2014). *Vahid's Story* (Regional Office for Europe Mental Health), accessed 24 February 2014 from http://www.euro.who.int/en/health-topics/noncommunicable-diseases/mental-health/personal-stories/vahids-story.

World Health Organization (WHO). (2013). *International Perspectives on Spinal Cord Injury* (Geneva: WHO).

World Health Organization (WHO). (2011). *Mental Health Atlas* (Geneva: WHO).

World Health Organization (WHO). (2010). *Community-based Rehabilitation: CBR Guidelines* (Geneva: WHO), www.who.int/disabilities/cbr/guidelines/en/index.html.

World Health Organization (WHO). (2009). 'Maximizing positive synergies collaborative group: An assessment of interactions between global health initiatives and country health systems', *Lancet*, 373(20), 2137–2169.

World Health Organization (WHO). (2007). *International Classification of Functioning, Disability and Health – Children and Youth Version ICF-CY* (Geneva: WHO).

World Health Organization (WHO). (2001). *International Classification of Functioning, Disability and Health (ICF)* (Geneva: WHO), http://www.sustainable-design.ie/arch/ICIDH-2Final.pdf.

World Health Organization (WHO). (1978). *Declaration of Alma-Ata, International Conference on Primary Health Care, Alma-Ata, USSR, 6–12 September 1978*, accessed 15 May 2012 from www.who.int/hpr/NPH/docs/declaration_almaata.pdf.

World Health Organization (WHO) and World Bank. (2011). *World Report on Disability* (Geneva: WHO, World Bank).

World Programme of Action Concerning Persons with Disabilities. (1982).

World Vision UK. (2007). *Education's Missing Millions: Including Disabled Children in Education through EFA FTI Processes and National Sector Plans* (Milton, UK: World Vision).

Wright, S. (1998). 'The politicization of "culture"', *Anthropology Today*, 14(1), 7–15.

Yeo, R. (2001). *Chronic Poverty and Disability*. Background Paper No. 4 (Chronic Poverty Research Center), accessed 14 March 2014 from http://www.chronicpoverty.org/uploads/publication_files/WP04_Yeo.pdf.

Yeo, R. and Moore, K. (2003). 'Including disabled people in poverty reduction work: "Nothing about us, without us"', *World Development*, 31, 571–590.

Zanjani, F.A.K, Schaie, F.W. and Willis, S.L. (2006). 'Age group and health status effects on health behavior change', *Behavioral Medicine*, 32, 36–46.

Zarb, G. (1992). 'On the road to Damascus: First steps towards changing the relations of disability research production', *Disability and Society*, 7, 125–138.

Zendell, A. (2011). *Decision-making Processes among Siblings Caring for Adults with Intellectual or Developmental Disabilities*, unpublished PhD thesis (University at Albany).

Zola, I.K. (1989). 'Toward the necessary universalising of a disability policy', *The Milbank Quarterly*, 67(2), 401–428.

Index